The Greatest Cult Television Shows of All Time

The Greatest Cult Television Shows of All Time

Christopher J. Olson
CarrieLynn D. Reinhard

ROWMAN & LITTLEFIELD
Lanham • Boulder • New York • London

Published by Rowman & Littlefield
An imprint of The Rowman & Littlefield Publishing Group, Inc.
4501 Forbes Boulevard, Suite 200, Lanham, Maryland 20706
www.rowman.com

6 Tinworth Street, London, SE11 5AL, United Kingdom

British Library Cataloguing in Publication Information Available

Library of Congress Cataloging-in-Publication Data Available

ISBN 9781538122556 (cloth)
ISBN 9781538122563 (ebook)

♾™ The paper used in this publication meets the minimum requirements of American National Standard for Information Sciences—Permanence of Paper for Printed Library Materials, ANSI/NISO Z39.48-1992.

To all the innovative television creators
who tell stories that change our world.

Contents

Acknowledgments   xi

Introduction   xiii

Absolutely Fabulous (1992–2012)   1

Adventure Time (2010–2018)   3

The Adventures of Pete & Pete (1992–1996)   6

Aqua Teen Hunger Force (2000–2015)   8

Are You Afraid of the Dark? (1990–2000)   10

Arrested Development (2003–2019)   12

Arrow (2012–2020)   14

Avatar: The Last Airbender (2005–2008)   16

The Avengers (1961–1969)   18

Babylon 5 (1994–1998)   21

Battlestar Galactica (1978–1979)   23

Baywatch (1989–2001)   26

Beauty and the Beast (1987–1990)   28

The Black Adder (1982–1983)   29

Buffy the Vampire Slayer (1997–2003)   31

Charmed (1998–2006)   34

Community (2009–2015)   36

Cowboy Bebop (1998–1999)   39

Crazy Ex-Girlfriend (2015–2019)   41

The Critic (1994–2001)   43

Daria (1997–2001)   46

Dark Shadows (1966–1971)   48

Darkwing Duck (1991–1992)   50

Deadwood (2004–2006)   52

Degrassi Junior High (1987–1989)   54

A Different World (1987–1993)   56

Doctor Who (1963–Present)   59

Dragon Ball Z (1996–2003)   61

Family Guy (1999–Present)   64

Farscape (1999–2003)   66

Fawlty Towers (1975–1979)   68

Fraggle Rock (1983–1987)   70

Freaks and Geeks (1999–2000)   73

Frisky Dingo (2006–2008)   75

Futurama (1999–2013)   77

Gargoyles (1994–1996)   80

Gilligan's Island (1964–1967)   83

Gilmore Girls (2000–2007)   85

The Golden Girls (1985–1992)   88

Hannibal (2013–2015)   91

He-Man and the Masters of the Universe (1983–1985)   93

Home Movies (1999–2004)   96

H.R. Pufnstuf (1969–1970)   98

Iron Chef (1993–1999)   101

It's Always Sunny in Philadelphia (2005–Present)   104

The Joy of Painting (1983–1994)   107

Key & Peele (2012–2015)   110

The Kids in the Hall (1988–1994)   112

Kolchak: The Night Stalker (1974–1975)   115

The League (2009–2015)   117

Lost (2004–2010)   119

Lost in Space (1965–1968)   121

Lucha Underground (2014–Present)   124

Max Headroom (1987–1988)   126

Monty Python's Flying Circus (1969–1974)   129

Mr. Show with Bob and David (1995–1998)   131

My Little Pony: Friendship is Magic (2010–2019)   133

My So-Called Life (1994–1995)   135

Mystery Science Theater 3000 (1988–2018)   138

The Office (2001–2003)   141

Outlander (2014–Present)   143

Oz (1997–2003)   145

Parks and Recreation (2009–2015)   148

Pee-wee's Playhouse (1986–1991)   150

Pinky and the Brain (1995–1998)   153

Police Squad! (1982)   155

The Prisoner (1967–1968)   157

Quantum Leap (1989–1993)   160

Queer as Folk (1999–2000)   162

Red Dwarf (1988–2017)   165

The Ren & Stimpy Show (1991–1996)   167

Rocko's Modern Life (1993–1996)   169

Roswell (1999–2002)   171

Sailor Moon (1992–1997)   174

Saved by the Bell (1989–1992)   176

Scrubs (2001–2010)   178

SCTV (1976–1984)   180

Sense8 (2015–2018)   182

Smallville (2001–2011)   184

South Park (1997–Present)   187

Space Ghost Coast to Coast (1994–2008)   189

Spaced (1999–2001)   191

Sports Night (1998–2000)   193

Star Trek (1966–1969)   195

The State (1993–1995)   198

Steven Universe (2013–Present)   200

Strangers with Candy (1999–2000)   201

Supernatural (2005–2020)   203

Tenacious D (1997–2000)   206

The Tick (1994–1997)   208

True Blood (2008–2014)   210

The Twilight Zone (1959–1964)   212

Twin Peaks (1990–1991)   215

Upright Citizens Brigade (1998–2000)   218

Veronica Mars (2004–Present)   220

The Walking Dead (2010–Present)   223

The Wire (2002–2008)   225

The X-Files (1993–2018)   228

Xena: Warrior Princess (1995–2001)   231

The Young Ones (1982–1984)   234

Notes   237

Index   299

About the Authors   305

Acknowledgments

The authors would like to thank the following people for their insight and their help in completing these entries: Sabrica Barnett, Sam Belfeuil, Jeremy Butler, Bertha Chin, Salvatore diSalvatore, Wendy Guelig-Gmiterek, Chris LaFrombois, Julia Largent, Earl Kellner, Ellen Wetherbee Rosewall, Jerry Salisbury, Joe Serio, Dave Stanley, Shane Tilton, Rebecca van Doren, Sean Weitner, and Chelsea Zhao. We would also like to thank our families for all the love and support they have given us over the years. In addition, we wish to thank Stephen Ryan of Rowman & Littlefield for his assistance in getting this project off the ground as well as his guidance during the writing process. Finally, we want to thank our editorial team of John Cerullo, Michael Tan, Deni Remsberg, Elizabeth Swayze, and Dina Gulak for helping us bring this project over the finish line.

Introduction:
Defining the Greatest Cult Television Shows of All Time

Since the dawn of television, thousands of series from around the world have been forgotten, consigned to the dustbins of human memory or lost to the ravages of time. Meanwhile, some shows have attained classic status, being thought to in some way represent the pinnacle of drama or comedy, reality or fantasy. Canonical shows like *M*A*S*H* or *Cheers*, *The Tonight Show with Johnny Carson* or *The Honeymooners* are taught in schools and preserved in museums so that future generations can learn what makes a good television show.

Some shows, however, are fondly remembered by just a small few. These shows are preserved and shared from generation to generation or community to community by fans who spread tapes or share streams. Such shows may not be great examples of what television can offer but rather programs that people have loved and continue to love. These are the cult television shows.

Any television show can attract such a cult audience. Indeed, these days, some seem premade to do just that. Since the rise of cable networks and streaming sites, mainstream audiences have become increasingly fractured and fragmented as they have access to more options for their television viewing. In such a media landscape, TV producers try to reach smaller but more loyal audiences, and niche or cult content can better facilitate a show's success.[1] The lines between mainstream and cult have been blurred, often intentionally.[2] Additionally, while in the past a cult TV show often conformed to one specific genre, most often science fiction or fantasy, these programs now encompass all genres and frequently even blend genres.[3] Finally, while past cult shows tended to attract a specific audience—usually "socially awkward teenage boys"[4]—cult TV shows now appeal to all audiences.

A show's following and fanbase determines its status as cult—at least from an academic perspective.[5] Though small, often numbering in just millions around the globe, this fanbase keeps a cult TV show alive. As film and television scholar Stacey Abbott writes, "Cult television persists because the creators and the fans keep fighting for their little, original, often challenging shows, never forgetting to 'Never Give Up—Never Surrender!'"[6] Some cult TV shows encourage audience participation, inspiring devoted fans to engage in multiple viewings to understand complicated meanings and relationships.[7] Cult TV fans also revel in discussing the show with other fans and take great joy in producing fan fiction, fan art, and even essays analyzing or critiquing the show.[8] Not all cult TV shows inspire fans the same way, and not all fans engage in the same activities around their cult TV show, but each cult TV show inspires its fans, who keep watching even when others tune out.

Cult TV shows typically exist on a culture's margins, generating low ratings but attracting loyal fans who tune in every week to watch or who binge-watch an entire season in one day.[9] Some shows initially draw a sizeable audience only to lose all but their core fans by the time the first run ends and the series stumbles to cancellation. Other shows may grow their cult audience over time as they gain more acceptance among the majority, mainstream audience. Thus some cult TV shows actually managed at some point during their initial run to pull in decent ratings, especially before the current era of the fragmented audience.[10] Yet those numbers often dwindled toward the end of the show's run or soon after its departure from the airwaves.

Regardless of how mainstream audiences respond to a cult TV show when it first aired, these shows manage to maintain a devoted fanbase. Even if they sought a large audience—which, given the commercial nature of most television, is necessary for basically every show—cult TV shows also cultivated an avid fanbase who would regularly return to the series and anything related to it.[11] Mainstream status comes and goes, but cult lasts forever. Ardent fans keep the show circulating long after its original run ends. Fans and fandoms increase as the show expands into other channels via syndication and streaming or to other technologies via discs and downloading.[12] The cult propagates itself.

With this basic definition of cult television in place, literally hundreds of shows since the beginning of television and from around the world could qualify for that status. What makes any of those shows one of the greatest of all time? In looking across various definitions of cult TV, Sara Gwenllian-Jones and Roberta E. Pearson found that

> in the media, in common usage, and sometimes even in academia, "cult" is often loosely applied to any television program that is considered offbeat or edgy, that draws a niche audience, that has a nostalgic appeal, that is considered emblematic of a particular subculture, or that is considered hip.[13]

We used similar criteria to help us narrow down and create our admittedly highly subjective list.

The first consideration came from the fact that we looked for shows that aired in the United States via over-the-air or cable broadcasting and subsequently developed a cult audience there. Hollywood productions have long set the global standard for film and television entertainment, providing templates for other national and cultural media production. Of course, more than just Hollywood television aired in the United States. Some shows, like British comedy or Japanese anime, were imported into the United States through narrowly targeted channels such as PBS or Cartoon Network to reach specific audiences who would appreciate the content's uniqueness in comparison to mainstream American programming.[14] Focusing on these shows allowed us to narrow down the list while also considering shows from other countries that were not just U.S. productions or co-productions. We recognize that this perspective perhaps reinforces colonialist and cultural imperialist issues, but hopefully our work here inspires others to create their own lists from different cultural and national perspectives.

The second consideration took into account how cult TV shows can seem transgressive when they first air. According to Sergio Angelini and Miles Booy,

> when cults first emerged around television shows, the appeal was to a minority audience who took content and form seriously and who came to believe that within a select number of broadcasts material was being effectively smuggled in, providing viewers with something new, different, and perhaps even subversively dangerous.[15]

Maybe the series challenged the Hollywood industry traditions by doing something no one else was doing such as experimenting with genre or storytelling.[16] Maybe it represented a counterculture that challenged mainstream tastes or sensibilities and therefore seemed strange to viewers who just did not "get it."[17] Maybe these shows spoke to people viewed as "abnormal" at the time, audiences that other shows ignored. Maybe they spoke to marginalized people in a way few others at the time did. Because they are often aimed at viewers outside or at the margins of the middle-of-the-road, mainstream audience, cult TV shows frequently do new, different, odd, or even radical things. The shows presented here were unlike other television shows when they first aired.

A third consideration involved whether a cult TV show developed a legacy not just through its fandom but also through its influence on society, culture, or even the industry. These were shows that made some sort of lasting impact on viewers or on the television business itself.[18] Maybe the creative people behind the show went on to produce more transgressive or even mainstream work. Maybe they changed how mainstream audiences viewed the transgressive content or marginalized people portrayed onscreen. Maybe the fans' activism, either as individuals or as a community, helped change the industry, society, or culture in some way. The shows included in this book left their mark and changed the world through their presence.

Our greatest cult TV shows did not need to conform to all these criteria at the same time (for instance, a show can leave a legacy without being transgressive, or vice versa), but all the shows discussed here still boast devoted cult fanbases that keep the flame alive. More and more cult TV shows premiere every year as the number of TV channels and streaming services expands, fragmenting the audience into smaller and smaller niches. However, we deliberately cut off our list with shows that had premiered by 2015 because we believe that it takes at least five years for a TV show to attain cult status. We also opted to forgo numbering the list and instead present it in alphabetical order as we believe that trying to quantify art (especially art that encompasses different styles, genres, and production practices) is a reductive process. Instead, we believe that the series gathered in this volume all deserve to be included in any conversation about the greatest cult TV shows ever made.

One last note: While discussing the shows included here, we tried to avoid spoilers but occasionally found them unavoidable. So when reading entries about shows you have yet to watch, please proceed with caution. Ultimately, we hope you will enjoy reading about some of the greatest cult TV shows of all time.

A

ABSOLUTELY FABULOUS (1992–2012)

Creator: Jennifer Saunders
Cast: Jennifer Saunders (Edina Monsoon), Joanna Lumley (Patsy Stone), Julia Sawalha (Saffron Monsoon), June Whitfield (June Monsoon), Jane Horrocks (Bubble)
Genre: Comedy

Synopsis

Aging party girls Edina and Patsy engage in madcap misadventures while Edina's straight-laced daughter Saffron struggles to maintain order in their dysfunctional household.

Production History

In 1978, Dawn French and Jennifer Saunders met while attending the Royal Central School of Speech and Drama in London.[1] Nearly ten years later, they launched their own self-titled sketch show on BBC2,[2] with Saunders often playing the straight woman to French's more exaggerated characters.[3] In 1992, when French took time off to raise her newly adopted daughter,[4] Saunders created the sitcom *Absolutely Fabulous* (also known as *Ab Fab*). Based on the *French and Saunders* skit "The Modern Mother and Daughter"[5] and partly inspired by PR consultant Lynne Franks,[6] the show focused on the relationship between an irresponsible mother and her more sensible daughter. In the show, Saunders played aging fashionista Edina Monsoon while producers cast veteran actress Joanna Lumley as Patsy Stone based on a suggestion from *The Full Wax* star Ruby Wax, who later served as *Ab Fab*'s script editor.[7] The rest of the cast fell into place soon after, and the show debuted on November 12, 1992.

Ab Fab initially aired on BBC2 because network executives expected the series to appeal to a small audience.[8] However, the show earned high ratings, prompting a move to the more mainstream BBC1.[9] The lead characters proved so popular with audiences that Saunders tried to make them more loathsome to prevent people from viewing them as role models.[10] In 1993, *Ab Fab* won the first of many British Academy of Film and Television Arts (BAFTA) awards, and the following year Comedy Central started airing the series in the United States.[11] Not long after,

Aging party girls Edina (Jennifer Saunders, left) and Patsy (Joanna Lumley) hatch their next wacky scheme. *BBC Enterprises/Photofest*

American networks tried (unsuccessfully) to produce their own adaptations of *Ab Fab*, including one developed for ABC by Roseanne Barr and starring Carrie Fisher and Barbara Carrera.[12] Meanwhile, Fox tried to launch their own version with Kathryn Hahn and Kristen Johnson in the lead roles.[13] Saunders decided to end the show after the third series in 1996 with the ninety-minute episode "The Last Shout,"[14] but *Ab Fab* returned in August 2001 with six new episodes. Two Christmas specials followed in 2002 and 2004,[15] bookending the final series that aired in 2003. *Ab Fab* spawned a film adaptation that hit theaters in 2016,[16] but currently no further productions are planned.[17]

Commentary

Throughout its various incarnations, *Absolutely Fabulous* uses its fame-hungry, style-obsessed, developmentally stunted central characters to critique media culture and privileged lifestyles. Patsy and Edina regularly stumble into wacky situations that would leave them feeling humiliated and defeated if they had any sense of shame or self-awareness. In that regard, as Paul Flynn noted in 2011, the show predicted the twenty-first-century pop cultural landscape[18] with its vapid celebrities who go to great lengths to remain relevant in a media ecology marked by short memories and fickle attention spans. *Ab Fab* first emerged in the 1990s during the infancy of both reality TV and the Internet, but if the show debuted today Patsy and Edina would no doubt occupy the roles of catty reality TV stars or past-their-prime social media influencers. As it stands, *Ab Fab* holds up quite well thanks to its prescient outlook and sidesplitting humor.

The show introduced many American viewers to British comedy thanks to its near-constant presence on Comedy Central during the mid- to late 1990s. *Ab Fab* delighted viewers with its uproarious dialogue ("Oh, she's so cold, sweetie! I'll just bet she has her period in cubes!"), riotous physical comedy (a drunken Patsy slowly topples into an open grave), and delightfully silly characters (including Jane Horrocks's charmingly addle-brained Bubble). At the same time, *Ab Fab* portrayed middle-aged women as funny, sexy, and neurotic—that is, complex—and therefore struck a chord with women and gay men. According to critic Guy Lodge, *Ab Fab* was "anarchically feminine,"[19] which might explain why Patsy and Edina reached iconic status for certain viewers, most notably drag queens. In fact, the characters became so popular in drag circles that Saunders and Lumley were invited to judge an Edina and Patsy lookalike competition at a New York City gay bar during Pride Week in 2002, and the duo even received the Lesbian, Gay, Bisexual and Transgender Pride Award.[20] *Ab Fab* appealed to viewers of all persuasions, but queer fans turned the show into a true cult phenomenon.

With its clever satirical humor, over-the-top situations, and multifaceted female characters, *Ab Fab* is now justly recognized as a pioneering comedy that remains beloved long after the party ended.

See also *The Golden Girls* (1985–1992), *The Young Ones* (1982–1984)

SPOTLIGHT: DAWN FRENCH AND JENNIFER SAUNDERS

Dawn French and Jennifer Saunders met at the Royal Central School of Speech and Drama in London in 1977, and soon after the duo performed comedy sketches together at the Comic Strip Club.[21] From there, they made the leap to television, first in *The Comic Strip Presents* and then in their own show *French and Saunders*, which ran from 1987 to 2007. During that time, French also starred in *The Vicar of Dibley* while Saunders appeared as a guest on various comedy shows. Saunders then created *Ab Fab* while French was busy with family obligations.[22] Throughout their work together, French and Saunders earned great success and critical praise for their written sketches and improvisational skills.[23]

ADVENTURE TIME (2010–2018)

Creator: Pendleton Ward
Cast: Jeremy Shada (Finn), John DiMaggio (Jake), Tom Kenny (Ice King), Hynden Walch (Princess Bubblegum), Niki Yang (BMO/Princess Rainicorn), Pendleton Ward (Lumpy Space Princess), Olivia Olson (Marceline)
Genre: Action, Adventure, Comedy, Fantasy, Science Fiction

Synopsis

Finn the Human and his adoptive brother Jake the Dog embark on adventures in the Land of Ooo, a surreal, post-apocalyptic kingdom populated by numerous weird and wacky characters.

Production History

In 2006, shortly after graduating from CalArts, animator Pendleton Ward made *Adventure Time*,[24] a seven-minute-long animated short that followed a young boy and a magical dog as they tried to save Princess Bubblegum from the clutches of the wicked Ice King. Ward took the short to Nickelodeon to pitch a series but network executives rejected the idea.[25] Ward moved on and accepted a gig as a writer and storyboard artist on the Cartoon Network series *The Marvelous Misadventures of Flapjack*, where he learned the animation process.[26] During this time, Nickelodeon aired the *Adventure Time* short on January 11, 2011, as part of their *Random! Cartoons* show.[27] The short landed on the Web soon after and became a viral sensation.[28] The resulting buzz prompted Cartoon Network to greenlight an *Adventure Time* series that debuted in April 2011.[29]

Adventure Time became a surprise hit, shocking both Ward and executives at Cartoon Network, who had no idea how to handle the show's newfound success.[30] Though aimed primarily at kids, the show's audience soon expanded to include adults who responded to the surreal weirdness and touching stories.[31] Given this, Cartoon Network executives struggled with how to market the show because they thought adults would have little interest in *Adventure Time* video

Jake the Dog (left) and Finn the Human defend the denizens of Ooo from all sorts of evil. *Cartoon Network/Photofest*

games, comic books, costumes, and other products aimed at kids.[32] At the same time, the production schedule was starting to take a toll on Ward, who quietly quit his position as showrunner during the series' fifth season (fans only learned about this stunning shakeup after a *Rolling Stone* article broke the news a few years later).[33] At that point, co-executive producer Adam Muto assumed the position of showrunner though Ward remained on staff as a writer and storyboard artist,[34] meaning the show retained his quirky sense of humor.

Despite the shortsightedness of Cartoon Network executives, *Adventure Time* spawned numerous popular ancillary products including a video game, an ongoing comic book series, and action figures. It also changed the landscape of animation as animators who worked on the show—such as Rebecca Sugar (*Steven Universe*), Kyle Carrozza (*Mighty Magiswords*), and Matt Burnett and Ben Levin (*Craig of the Creek*)—have produced new shows that keep *Adventure Time*'s adventurous spirit alive. Sadly, Cartoon Network canceled *Adventure Time* in February 2017 after nine seasons though new episodes continued to run until 2018.[35]

Commentary

Adventure Time appealed to both kids and adults because it boasted a heady mix of surreal weirdness, nonsensical humor, and heartbreaking tenderness. Series creator Pendleton Ward crafted a series in which anything could (and usually did) happen, and those things are often either laugh-out-loud hilarious or just downright bizarre. This sort of off-kilter silliness appeals to kids, whose own imagination and sense of humor tend to work in a similar way. At the same time, the show frequently tugs at viewers' heart strings, as when it reveals the connection between Marceline and the Ice King (S4E25, "I Remember You"), or when Flame Princess leaves a besotted Finn heartbroken (S5E30, "Frost & Fire"). Amid all the ridiculousness, the show's creative team developed fully formed characters and placed them in some genuinely touching and heartrending stories, making the whole series far more involving and emotionally resonant than the average kids' show. *Adventure Time* appeals to a broad audience thanks to its ability to balance both humor and heart.

The show also plays around with gender in several interesting ways and therefore resonates with viewers who identify as masculine, feminine, or anything in between. Finn emerges as a complex character who navigates complicated feelings as he grows from boy to man. More importantly, unlike most stoic male heroes, he expresses his feelings rather than repressing them, making him a powerful role model for both boys and girls growing up in a world marked by changing ideas about gender. Meanwhile, the show portrays the various princesses as smart, competent, and tough, demonstrating that heroes come in all shapes, sizes, and sexes. Furthermore, the princesses often prove more than capable of saving themselves and standing up to the various villains who threaten the Land of Ooo (such as the Ice King, the Lich King, and Uncle Gumbald), and they often do so with words and brainpower rather than violence. Overall, *Adventure Time* challenges long-standing narratives about what it means to be a hero (or even just a boy or a girl), and as such it stands as an important show that imparts many significant life lessons to younger viewers.

In addition to its outrageous humor, well-developed characters, and willingness to take risks, *Adventure Time* also features gorgeous animation that looks and feels like nothing else, and the animators frequently experimented with different styles and designs that took the series into some truly strange directions. In the end, *Adventure Time* remains a fun and funny series that has a lot of smart things to say about the human condition, all of which add to its cultish appeal.

THE ADVENTURES OF PETE & PETE (1992–1996)

Creators: Will McRobb, Chris Viscardi
Cast: Michael C. Maronna (Big Pete Wrigley), Danny Tamberelli (Little Pete Wrigley), Judy Grafe (Joyce Wrigley), Hardy Rawls (Don Wrigley), Alison Fanelli (Ellen Hickle), Toby Huss (Artie), Michelle Trachtenberg (Nona Mecklenberg)
Genre: Comedy

Synopsis

This quirky series follows two red-headed brothers as they navigate small-town life in the fictional suburb of Wellsville.

Production History

In the late 1980s, Will McRobb and Chris Viscardi made promos for the various syndicated shows that aired on the cable channel Nickelodeon.[36] However, the duo harbored higher aspirations, and in 1989 they developed *The Adventures of Pete & Pete*, a series of sixty-second shorts about two brothers (both named Pete) that aired between Nickelodeon's full-length programming.[37] McRobb and Viscardi received substantial assistance from former-journalist (and McRobb's high school classmate) Katherine Dieckmann, who in 1989 directed the music video for REM's "Stand."[38] The shorts became so popular that in 1991 Nickelodeon aired five episode-length *Pete & Pete* specials.[39] Two years later, the network greenlit a full series,[40] with Dieckmann serving as one of the principal directors.[41] The show ran for two additional thirteen-episode seasons before ending its run in December 1996.[42]

During its brief run, *Pete & Pete* struck a chord with tweens and college students thanks to its surreal humor, heartfelt stories, and punkish sensibilities. Each episode opened with the anthemic (if somewhat incomprehensible) theme song "Hey Sandy" composed and performed by Polaris (consisting of Mark Mulcahy, Dave McCaffrey, and Scott Boutier of the New Haven college rock band Miracle Legion).[43] *Pete & Pete* also boasted cameo appearances from several popular comedians, musicians, and character actors including Steve Buscemi, Ellen Cleghorne,

Janeane Garofalo, Debbie Harry, David Johansen, Bebe Neuwirth, Kate Pierson, Iggy Pop, Michael Stipe, and Adam West.[44]

These days, *Pete & Pete* enjoys a reputation as one of the best series to emerge from Nickelodeon's golden age (the 1990s).[45] In 2012, fans of the show organized a reunion of the original cast that took place at the Bowery Ballroom in New York City and featured a performance by The Blowholes, the fictional band formed by Little Pete in the season 1 finale, "Hard Day's Pete."[46] The show's idiosyncratic spirit lives on in the podcast *The Adventures of Danny and Mike*, which follows *Pete & Pete* stars Danny Tamberelli and Mike Maronna as they embark on various adventures together.

Commentary

Pete & Pete captured the zeitgeist of the 1990s and distilled it into a kid-friendly package that also resonated with college-age adults, particularly those into the burgeoning alternative scene of the time. The show brought a quirky, punk-rock attitude to children's television thanks in large part to the influence of Katherine Dieckmann, who infused the show with a daring attitude and a flair for experimentation. *Pete & Pete* struck the perfect balance between the surreal and the mundane in a way that recalled adult-oriented shows like *Twin Peaks* and *Get a Life* but remained wholly accessible to impressionable suburban kids thanks to its relatable story lines and heartwarming attitudes. Overall, *Pete & Pete* offered viewers extreme weirdness and life-affirming messages in equal measure, which might explain its longevity among people of a certain age.

Pete & Pete's humor emerges as its primary draw because the show consistently avoids the clichés of the American sitcom in favor of some truly surreal comedy. On the surface, *Pete & Pete* looks like a standard situation comedy, complete with schlubby dad, attractive mom, and wisecracking kids, yet it feels unlike anything else on television thanks to a sly wit and an idiosyncratic sense of humor that often veers into the utterly bizarre. From Little Pete's friendship with local superhero Artie (aka the Strongest Man in the World) to Big Pete wearing a bear costume while driving a golf cart that sucks up golf balls to punk rock icon Iggy Pop playing a square suburban dad, *Pete & Pete* inundates viewers with things they've never seen before and takes them to some genuinely weird places. At the same time, however, the stories remain eminently relatable; whether it's a story about Little Pete and his friends rebelling against their bedtime (S1E3, "The Nightcrawlers") or Big Pete and his best friend, Ellen, trying to make sense of their complicated feelings for one another (S2E5, "Time Tunnel"; S3E6, "Crisis in the Love Zone"), *Pete & Pete* remains totally identifiable despite all the strangeness.

In addition to the humor and the heart, *Pete & Pete* features an abundance of great music by the trio Polaris (including the fantastic theme song "Hey Sandy" and the toe-tapping tune "Summerbaby" from S1E8, "Hard Day's Pete") and a parade of game guest stars, all of whom mesh perfectly with the show's unusual sensibilities. Furthermore, as the titular characters, Mike Maronna and Danny Tamberelli deliver earnest performances and display some seriously funny comedic chops throughout.

Though it only ran for a few years, *Pete & Pete* nevertheless left an indelible mark on popular culture due to its peculiar outlook, idiosyncratic humor, and willingness to push the boundaries of children's television programming.

See also *Rocko's Modern Life* (1993–1996)

AQUA TEEN HUNGER FORCE (2000–2015)

Creators: Dave Willis, Matt Maiellaro
Cast: Dave Willis (Meatwad/Carl Brutananadilewski), Dana Snyder (Master Shake),
   Carey Means (Frylock), Schooly-D (Narrator)
Genre: Comedy

Synopsis

Three anthropomorphic food items—a meatball, a shake, and a box of french fries—share absurd adventures with their retired and thoroughly exasperated next-door neighbor.

Production History

After a brief career as a production assistant and assistant director on films like *Basket Case 3: The Progeny* and *Hellraiser III: Hell on Earth*,[47] Matt Maiellaro landed a gig with Cartoon Network in 1994 writing for the recently launched surrealist animated talk show *Space Ghost: Coast to Coast*.[48] The following year Dave Willis accepted a job as a production assistant for Andy Merril, who voiced breakout character Brak, and soon after joined the show's writing staff.[49] After writing fifty episodes of *Space Ghost*, Maiellaro and Willis developed an idea for a new series that would use characters featured in the episode "Baffler Meal" (S8E1).[50] Around that time, Cartoon Network launched Adult Swim, a late-night block of programming aimed at adults.[51] Mike Lazzo, head of programming and development for Cartoon Network (and later Adult Swim's senior executive vice president) enjoyed *Space Ghost*, and he greenlit Maiellaro and Willis's new show, which premiered on September 9, 2001 (one week after Adult Swim's debut) under the title *Aqua Teen Hunger Force* (*ATHF*).[52]

Originally framed as an adventure series starring a trio of crime-fighting foodstuffs, *ATHF* instead eschewed ongoing plotlines.[53] The show's absurdist humor and shocking situations perplexed Cartoon Network executives, so Maiellaro and Willis turned the characters into private investigators in the second episode but dropped that conceit two episodes later.[54] Audiences, meanwhile, turned *ATHF* into Adult Swim's most popular show.[55] The series ran for thirteen seasons,[56] with Maiellaro and Willis writing all 138 eleven-minute episodes (though they often made changes based on suggestions from the voice actors).[57] In 2007, *ATHF* spawned a theatrical film adaptation, *Aqua Teen Hunger Force Colon Movie Film for*

Theaters,[58] which launched a guerilla marketing publicity stunt that caused a bomb scare in Boston, Massachusetts.[59] Midway through production of season 11,[60] Cartoon Network decided to end the long-running series[61] even though it still generated revenue and ratings.[62] The final episode of *ATHF* aired on August 30, 2015.

Commentary

During its impressive fifteen-year run, *ATHF* served up hundreds of bizarre characters and surreal situations. The show, which appealed mainly to stoners and oddballs, helped kick off a new wave of animation aimed at adults. As noted in an article posted on the AV Club, the show often felt like an absurdist *Seinfeld*—a hangout series about nothing.[63] Cultural critic Alex Wilgus similarly notes that "*ATHF* is a show without any central meaning, and the brilliance of its satirical vision is to reflect a world that has, literally, lost its plot."[64] *ATHF* featured outlandish circumstances (the gang encounters a robot ghost that tries to teach them the meaning of Christmas) and uproarious dialogue (after applying flame decals to his above-ground pool, Carl exclaims, "It's like my pool is tearin' ass around the backyard, but it's stayin' still"). The cheap and delightfully stiff animation only adds to the show's quirky charms.

Frylock (left), Master Shake (center), and Meatwad just want to hang out but instead wind up embroiled in various zany situations. *First Look Intl/Photofest*

In many ways, *ATHF* prefigured the sort of nonsensical, short-form comedy that littered the Internet during the early years of the twenty-first century. In an interview with *Vice*, co-creator Dave Willis explained that he saw the absurdist humor that defined the burgeoning World Wide Web as the future of comedy.[65] *ATHF* helped expose that sort of surreal hilarity to a wider (though still niche) audience. The show poked meanspirited fun at everything and everyone, presenting the world as a cruel place filled with curious weirdos, pathetic losers, and creepy perverts. *ATHF* presented the central trio as lazy anarchists who want nothing more than to lounge around watching TV but instead wind up causing chaos due to their thoughtlessness. The show thereby offered up a slight critique of the slacker lifestyle lived by much of its core audience, but the series was ultimately more interested in zany sight gags and outrageous toilet humor. While *ATHF* alienated many viewers with its strange sensibilities and shocking humor, it nevertheless attracted a devoted cult of misfits and outsiders.

See also *Frisky Dingo* (2006–2008), *Space Ghost Coast to Coast* (1994–2008)

SPOTLIGHT: ADULT SWIM

Ted Turner launched Cartoon Network to rerun MGM and Hanna-Barbera cartoons, but that changed when Mike Lazzo, head of original programming, oversaw the production of the network's first original show *Space Ghost Coast to Coast*.[66] The Adult Swim block (which ran from 8:00 p.m. to 6:00 a.m.)[67] launched in 2001 and included *Space Ghost Coast to Coast*, *Harvey Birdman Attorney at Law*, *The Brak Show*, and *Aqua Teen Hunger Force* as well as *Home Movies*, recently canceled by UPN.[68] Adult Swim also brought more mature anime to the United States such as *Cowboy Bebop*, which "aired uncensored with a few Japanese references changed."[69] Adult Swim continues to win its targeted young adult audience with original shows like *Robot Chicken* and *Rick and Morty* as well as reruns of *Family Guy* and *Bob's Burgers*.[70]

ARE YOU AFRAID OF THE DARK? (1990–2000)

Creators: D. J. MacHale, Ned Kandel
Cast: Ross Hull (Gary), Daniel DeSanto (Tucker), Raine Pare-Coull (Betty Ann), Jodie Resther (Kiki), Jason Alisharan (Frank), JoAnna Garcia Swisher (Sam)
Genre: Drama, Fantasy, Horror, Mystery, Science Fiction, Thriller

---

Synopsis

In this terrifying anthology series, a group of friends gather around a campfire to tell scary stories.

Production History

Co-produced by Cinar Films and Nickelodeon Productions, the anthology horror series *Are You Afraid of the Dark?* debuted on the Canadian television channel YTV on October 31, 1990.[71] Developed by D. J. MacHale and Ned Kandel, the show failed to appear on American screens until 1992 because executives at Nickelodeon initially rejected it as too terrifying for kids.[72] Yet recently hired executive Jay Mulvaney, who later served as a producer on other Nickelodeon shows like *The Adventures of Pete & Pete* and *The Tomorrow People*, greenlit the show based on the three-page treatment.[73] *Are You Afraid of the Dark?* drew inspiration from classic short stories and morality plays for its tales of terror aimed at kids and teens,[74] bookending them with a framing device that featured a group of kids called the Midnight Society telling scary stories around a campfire. Filmed mainly in Quebec,[75] the series featured young Canadian actors like Ryan Gosling, Neve Campbell, Jewel Staite, Jay Baruchel, Elisa Cuthbert, and Hayden Christensen, all of whom achieved stardom in the years after.[76]

Are You Afraid of the Dark? aired as part of Nickelodeon's SNICK block of programming, which broadcast at 9:30 p.m. on Saturday nights.[77] According to MacHale, the network wanted to reach viewers "too young to be on a date and too old to be in bed."[78] Throughout the show, producers shot an entire season's worth of campfire segments in one week[79] but avoided showing the members of the Midnight Society lighting the fire because they worried about teaching kids to play with matches.[80] *Are You Afraid of the Dark?* received some pushback from Nickelodeon's Standards and Practices Department but never from network executives as they received no complaints about the show.[81] *Are You Afraid of the Dark?* earned high ratings[82] as well as a nomination for an NAACP Award thanks to its diverse cast.[83] As of this writing, the show remains unavailable on either DVD or Blu-Ray, but it streams on Amazon Prime.[84] In 2018, Nickelodeon announced plans to produce both a new three-part limited series, which premiered in October 2019,[85] and a theatrical film adaptation.[86]

Commentary

Throughout its run, *Are You Afraid of the Dark?* produced terrifying content aimed at pre-teens and teens, creating effective scares that avoided crossing into truly horrific stories. Yet the show refused to shy away from the truly disturbing aspects of teenage life. Much like Rod Serling in *The Twilight Zone*, the Midnight Society told supernatural morality tales designed to frighten and entertain viewers. *Are You Afraid of the Dark?* understands that children enjoy feeling scared because they face numerous fears in their own lives. Kids are small creatures in a big world filled with potential dangers, but they are expected to explore that world and master it as they grow older. Following in the footsteps of authors like Roald Dahl, Shel Silverstein, and R. L. Stine, *Are You Afraid of the Dark?* took the approach that fear is good for kids if it teaches rather than traumatizes them.[87] The series used unsettling stories as metaphors for real-life issues, including self-doubt ("The Tale of Many Faces," S7E12), guilt ("The Tale of the Shiny Red Bicycle," S2E10), and even death ("The Tale of Station 109.1," S5E3).[88]

Are You Afraid of the Dark? set out to scare children but also understood that they could handle such frights. Young viewers loved the show because it served up chilling tales about creepy clowns, ghastly ghosts, spooky vampires, and other things that leave kids squirming with both fear and delight. Yet *Are You Afraid of the Dark?* truly resonated with young viewers because it taught them how to cope with their own anxieties. Rather than try to protect children from the horrors of everyday life, the show embraced the terror and introduced kids to recognizable characters also dealing with traumatic situations, thus empowering young viewers to face their own fears. Learning to face uncertainty is an important part of growing up, and *Are You Afraid of the Dark?* strove to help its viewers feel brave enough to do just that, which explains why kids who grew up with the show now consider it a cult classic.

ARRESTED DEVELOPMENT (2003–2019)

Creator: Mitchell Hurwitz
Cast: Jason Bateman (Michael Bluth), Portia de Rossi (Lindsey Bluth Fünke), Will Arnett (Gob Bluth), Michael Cera (George-Michael Bluth), Alia Shawkat (Maeby Fünke), Tony Hale (Buster Bluth), David Cross (Tobias Fünke), Jeffrey Tambor (George Bluth Sr.), Jessica Walter (Lucille Bluth)
Genre: Comedy

Synopsis

This acclaimed, unconventional sitcom follows the travails of the wealthy, dysfunctional, possibly criminal Bluth family.

Production History

In 2002, Hollywood mainstay Ron Howard conceived an idea for a sitcom about a dysfunctional family.[89] He hired former *Golden Girls* scribe Mitchell Hurwitz to write the pilot episode of *Arrested Development*, which Hurwitz completed in January 2003.[90] The pilot shot that March,[91] and just two months later the show landed on Fox's fall 2003 schedule[92] with Howard serving as executive producer and an uncredited narrator.[93] Despite airing after *American Idol* during its first season and *The Simpsons* in its second,[94] *Arrested Development* struggled to find viewers.[95] The show also suffered from rocky relationships on set, most notably between Jeffrey Tambor and Jessica Walter, who accused Tambor of sexual harassment and bullying.[96] In addition, Hurwitz clashed with 20th Century Fox over budget costs, including his own compensation.[97] *Arrested Development* ran from 2003 to 2006,[98] and its failure to capture a wide audience led to its cancelation after fifty-three episodes.

During its brief time on the air, the show earned critical praise and won numerous awards.[99] In July 2004, *Arrested Development* netted five Emmy Awards while series star Jason Bateman received a Golden Globe for Best Actor the following year. However, none of this prevented Fox from reducing the second season from twenty-two to eighteen episodes.[100] In 2005, the network moved *Arrested Development* to Monday nights, airing the last four episodes of the abbreviated thirteen-episode third season against the 2006 Winter Olympics, and Fox Entertainment president Peter Liguori announced the show's end soon after.[101] The network distributed the series via DVD,[102] thus helping *Arrested Development* find a wider audience, and in 2006 Fox negotiated digital streaming deals with MSN, HD Net, and G4.[103] Seven years after *Arrested Development* wrapped its initial run, Netflix produced a two-part season of the show, which earned mixed reviews from critics and fans.[104] The streaming giant has yet to announce any further seasons.[105]

Commentary

With its wacky characters, zany situations, and memorable dialogue, *Arrested Development* seems tailor-made for a cult audience. The show revolves around the madcap misadventures of the affluent Bluth family, a dysfunctional clan of sociopaths, narcissists, and buffoons who engage in all manner of unsavory or illegal activities, including embezzlement, incest, and fraud. Michael, the exasperated heart of both the show and the family, struggles to keep his family together while also providing a positive model for his son, the shy and awkward George Michael. At the same time, Michael endeavors to clean up the messes left behind by his corrupt father, George Sr., who landed in prison after brokering an illegal land development deal with Saddam Hussein and the Iraqi state. Michael finds his efforts thwarted by his equally crooked mother, Lucille, and shady siblings Lindsay, Gob, and Buster. Other members of the daffy dynasty include Lindsay's incompetent husband, Tobias Fünke, their perpetually annoyed daughter Maeby, Lucille's adopted South Korean son Annyong (Justin Lee), and Gob's illegitimate offspring Steve Holt (Justin Grant Wade). These outrageous characters and their foibles provide most of the laughs in *Arrested Development*, and fans love to watch them fall flat on their faces again and again.

The show also featured endlessly quotable dialogue written by the likes of Troy Miller, Joe Russo, Anthony Russo, Paul Feig, Jay Chandrasekhar, and series creator Mitchell Hurwitz. Lines like "If I wanted something your thumb touched, I'd eat the inside of your ear!" (S1E5, "Charity Drive") and "Are you forgetting that I was a professional twice over? An analyst and therapist? The world's first analrapist?" (S3E3, "Forget Me Now") leave fans in stitches to this day. In addition, *Arrested Development* serves up plenty of uproarious situations, including the police naming Gob's African American ventriloquist dummy Franklin Delano Bluth an accessory in the kidnapping of family patriarch George (S2E18, "Righteous Brothers"); Buster and Lucille entering a creepy mother-son pageant together (S2E13, "Motherboy XXX"); and Michael's multi-episode romance with a developmentally disabled woman he mistakes for a British spy. The show also contributed to the rise of several future Hollywood stars such as Michael Cera and Alia Shawkat. *Arrested Development* even parodied current social and cultural issues, most notably the Iraq War,[106] though such political messaging had vanished by the time the fifth season rolled around.[107] While the most recent seasons that appeared on Netflix offer diminishing returns, *Arrested Development* remains one of the most beloved and admired sitcoms of all time.

See also *Community* (2009–2015), *It's Always Sunny in Philadelphia* (2005–Present), *The Office* (2001–2003), *Parks and Recreation* (2009–2015)

ARROW (2012–2020)

Creators: Greg Berlanti, Marc Guggenheim, Andrew Kreisberg
Cast: Stephen Amell (Oliver Queen), David Ramsey (John Diggle), Emily Brett Rickards (Felicity Smoak), Katie Cassidy (Laurel Lance), Paul Blackthorne (Quentin Lance), Willa Holland (Thea Queen)
Genre: Action, Drama, Mystery, Science Fiction

Synopsis

Five years after a boating accident leaves him stranded alone on a deserted island, billionaire playboy Oliver Queen returns to Starling City to fight crime as the masked superhero Green Arrow.

Production History

In 2011, producer Greg Berlanti approached CW Network's development head Thom Sherman with an idea for a live-action televisions series based on DC Comics character Green Arrow, pitching it as a sophisticated and edgy thriller in the style of *The Bourne Identity*.[108] Sherman greenlit the show under the title *Arrow*, and casting commenced soon after. CW casting director David Rapport remembered working with a talented young actor named Stephen Amell on an episode of *Beverly Hills 90210*; he showed Amell's picture to showrunners Berlanti, Andrew Kreisberg, and Marc Guggenheim, who all wanted the hunky performer brought in to audition.[109] Amell quickly rose to the top of the pack due to his acting ability and physicality, although upon landing the role he increased his training by attending the Tempest Freerunning Academy and learning archery.[110] Patricia Gonsalves served as the show's on-set archery technician and consultant and spent two months training Amell.[111]

Director David Nutter, who had worked on genre series like *Smallville* and *Supernatural*, helmed the pilot episode of *Arrow*, which shot entirely in Vancouver.[112] The series relied on practical effects and stunts,[113] with Amell performing most of his own stunts.[114] *Arrow* debuted on the CW Network on October 10, 2012.[115] During its first two seasons, the show averaged 3.5 million viewers—largely in the coveted eighteen-to-thirty-four-year-old demographic—but the ratings dropped to under 2 million viewers per episode starting in season five.[116] In early 2019, Amell suggested he wanted to move on to other projects, and not long after producers announced that *Arrow* would end following its eighth season.[117]

Commentary

Superhero shows have a long history on television, but they were often considered frivolous, silly, campy, or childish. Live-action superhero shows have consistently suffered from small budgets that prevented their superheroes from engaging in the spectacular actions that make them so popular, leaving them tackling low-level villains (like muggers and bank robbers) or engaging in cheesy, unbelievable action sequences. When special effects finally caught up with television budgets, the industry still wanted to keep superheroes grounded (for instance, in *Smallville*, Clark Kent only becomes Superman in the show's final shot). *Arrow* changed all that. The show built on realistic action sequences performed by Stephen Amell to create a series that allowed for both real-world and high-fantasy storylines. *Arrow* provided the foundation for an entire shared DC television universe that echoes the vaunted Marvel Cinematic Universe. This so-called Arrowverse helped bring other DC characters to life in different series that could then participate in a yearly DC crossover event.[118] While struggling to compete in movie theaters, DC came to dominate television with *Arrow*, currently the longest running live-action superhero TV show.

The series helped the CW Network attract a male audience, thus broadening its "appeal beyond female viewers who had been flocking to series like *Gossip Girls*."[119] Despite the low profile of the Green Arrow character, the common perception of superheroes as appealing mainly to boys helped secure the network's investment in *Arrow* and later the entire Arrowverse. Indeed, fans and comics creators alike considered Green Arrow comical, so the series' more realistic take helped attract a male audience interested in the "grim and gritty" DC movies. Yet *Arrow* also demonstrated that a female audience would watch a superhero series. The show focused on developing characters and character relationships, television tropes commonly thought to draw a female audience who care about romantic subplots. At the same time, many female fans enjoyed watching the lithe, athletic Amell—so much so that he appeared shirtless twenty-three times in the first season alone.[120] In some ways, this female or queer gaze defines the thriving superhero genre, with Marvel movies also using their male characters to appeal to women and gay viewers. Producing a show that attracts a wide audience without cheapening its canonic material makes *Arrow* an important cult television series.

See also *Smallville* (2001–2011)

AVATAR: THE LAST AIRBENDER (2005–2008)

Creators: Michael Dante DiMartino, Bryan Konietzko
Cast: Zach Tyler (Aang), Mae Whitman (Katara), Jack De Sena (Sokka), Dante Basco
    (Prince Zuko), Jessie Flower (Toph), Mako (Uncle Iroh)
Genre: Action, Adventure, Fantasy, Mystery

Synopsis

After a century of hibernation, the last of the elemental warriors known as airbenders returns to end the Fire Nation's tyrannical rule.

Production History

When creating *Avatar: The Last Airbender*, co-creators Bryan Konietzko and Michael DiMartino drew on American fantasy epics, Japanese anime, Hong Kong action films, Eastern philosophies, and various mythologies.[121] The duo developed the show's mythos in the two weeks between conceiving the idea and pitching it to executives at Nickelodeon.[122] *Avatar* premiered on the network in 2005 and ran for three seasons of sixty-one episodes.[123] For the martial arts movements and philosophies, Konietzko and DiMartino looked to various Asian cultures but avoided perpetuating stereotypes by hiring Media Action Network for Asian Americans vice president Edwin Zane as a consultant.[124] The showrunners based each bending style on a different Chinese martial art and drew inspiration for the show's various societies from real-world cultures; for example, the Water Tribe's society recalls Inuit and Sireniki cultures while waterbending resembles Tai Chi.[125]

The show's first season earned huge ratings and appealed to viewers of all ages.[126] Each season of *Avatar* detailed how lead character Aang learned the different bending styles: Water in season 1, Earth in season 2, and Fire in season 3.[127] Critics praised the show for its captivating universe, complex characters, delightful humor, touching emotions, and sophisticated themes that included critiques of imperialism and war.[128] A whopping 5.6 million viewers watched the four-part series finale,[129] which involved story beats developed long before the show debuted.[130] In 2010, *The Sixth Sense* director M. Night Shyamalan helmed a big-budget, live-action film adaptation of *Avatar* that met with widespread derision.[131] Two years later, Nickelodeon aired the sequel series *The Legend of Korra* but pulled the show midway through season 4, releasing the final five episodes digitally online.[132] The *Avatar* universe lives on in comic books published by Dark Horse Comics,[133] and in September 2018 Netflix announced a live-action reboot.[134]

Commentary

By the early twenty-first century, Japanese anime and manga had made enough of an inroad in the United States to demonstrate that ambitious, epic-storytelling was possible in cartoons. Throughout the 1990s, animated series such as *Batman: The Animated Series* and *Gargoyles* suggested that action-adventure cartoons could emphasize dramatic stories over merely selling toys. These cartoons presented new approaches to blending genres in children's entertainment, but *Avatar: The Last Airbender* took this tactic even further, adapting Japanese anime tropes to a Western animation style. While varied in terms of narrative and aesthetics, anime often contains formulaic designs, characters, and storytelling conventions, including large eyes, exaggerated expressions, intense action sequences, and complicated villains. These tropes occur throughout *Avatar* (for example, see Aang's impish reactions to the world and Zuko's redemption arc). The animation also looks similar, featuring clean lines but detailed settings and fluid motion. In many ways, *Avatar* showcased how much Japanese animation imports impacted American producers and audiences as Nickelodeon sought to capitalize on high interest in Japanese cartoons and comics like *Dragon Ball Z* and *Sailor Moon*.

At the same time, *Avatar*'s use of anime-inspired tropes helped American producers and audiences realize that cartoons can do more than one thing at a time. *Avatar* pioneered the blending of genres to produce its epic story. The series writers combined the adventure of Aang's journey to become the Avatar; the action of combatting the Fire Nation; a romantic triangle between three central characters; the comedy of sidekicks Sokka and Momo; and the drama of family relationships and struggles with destiny. All these genres worked together to produce immense pathos for the characters, prompting audiences to develop an intense emotional attachment to them. More than that, every genre and storyline felt necessary rather than tacked on. The various genres and tropes worked together to seamlessly create a complex longform tale that rewarded multiple viewings. *Avatar*'s success helped the American animation industry realize that children's

Aang (left) and his friends Katara (center) and Sokka set out to protect the world from the evil forces of the Fire Nation. *Nickelodeon Network/Photofest*

entertainment can be complicated while remaining totally appealing, thus securing for the show a place on the list of all-time greatest cult TV shows.

See also *Adventure Time* (2010–2018), *Steven Universe* (2013–Present)

THE AVENGERS (1961–1969)

Creator: Sydney Newman
Cast: Patrick Macnee (John Steed), Honor Blackman (Catherine Gale), Diana Rigg (Emma Peel), Linda Thorson (Tara King), Ian Hendry (Dr. David Keel), Patrick Newell (Mother)
Genre: Action, Comedy, Mystery, Romance, Science Fiction, Thriller

---

Synopsis

A rotating cast of stylish secret agents defend the United Kingdom from threats both internal and external.

Production History

In 1960, Howard Thomas, managing director of ITV broadcaster ABC, asked Canadian film and television producer Sydney Newman to develop a lighthearted crime thriller series as counterprogramming to ABC's more serious dramas.[135] Newman decided to refashion the flailing cops-and-robbers show *Police Surgeon* into a lightweight thriller teaming a shadowy secret agent with a doctor out to avenge his wife's murder.[136] Newman tapped *Police Surgeon* star Ian Hendry to headline the new series and cast a reluctant Patrick Macnee (on the verge of quitting acting until lured back in front of the camera with the promise of a good salary) as undercover British Secret Service agent John Steed.[137] Newman then hired writer and producer Brian Clemens, who proved integral to the show's success during its eight years on the air.[138] The new series, titled *The Avengers*, debuted on January 7, 1961, and ran for 161 episodes.[139]

Hendry left after the first series, at which point Macnee transitioned from sidekick to leading man.[140] Hendry's departure also paved the way for Steed's first female partner, Catherine Gale, played by Honor Blackman.[141] Unfinished scripts were refashioned to accommodate the series' new direction.[142] In 1964, *The Avengers* switched from shooting on tape to shooting on film just in time for Blackman to announce her own departure from the series.[143] Producers cast Diana Rigg as Steed's second (and arguably most popular) partner, Emma Peel.[144] In 1966, *The Avengers* debuted in the Unites States as part of the so-called British Invasion.[145] Around that time, Rigg threatened to walk, claiming poor treatment from producers.[146] She left after two seasons and Macnee almost joined her but producers convinced him to stay by increasing his salary.[147] Eventually American viewers stopped tuning in to the show, which wrapped soon after.[148] In 1976, Clemens launched a sequel series, *New Avengers*, which ran for just two seasons.[149] Twenty years later, Warner Bros. tried to relaunch the franchise with an abysmal film adaptation starring Ralph Fiennes, Uma Thurman, and Sean Connery. Despite that film's failure, legions of hardcore fans still love *The Avengers*.

Commentary

One year before *Dr. No* introduced film audiences to suave superspy James Bond,[150] *The Avengers* helped usher the spy genre to the small screen. In a world gripped by fear over the Cold War, nuclear annihilation, and political assassinations, movies and television shows starring debonair secret agents soothed such anxieties by presenting shadowy figures who worked tirelessly to prevent such catastrophes. In *The Avengers*, John Steed and his various partners provided this reassurance with style, marrying mod fashion with classic British haberdashery. Bond brought the martini and the tuxedo, but Steed sported a bowler and umbrella. While the episodes sometimes offered more style than substance,[151] the style—most notably in the case of Emma Peel—proved both influential and fun.

More importantly, whereas Bond often objectified women and treated them as little more than sexual conquests, Steed treated his female partners as complete equals. Of course, Steed and his sidekicks frequently shared a relationship marked

Stylish secret agents Emma Peel (Diana Rigg, left) and John Steed (Patrick Macnee) protect England from weird threats and quirky villains. *ITV/ABC/Photofest*

by sexual tension—especially once Peel entered the picture—so much so that the "Will they, won't they?" storyline served as one of the series' most prominent features. Yet the sexual tension worked in large part due to the empowerment of Steed's partners. The show positioned each woman as an essential member of the team, portraying them as every bit as smart and capable as their male co-worker. Significantly, this portrayal commenced with the introduction of Steed's first partner, Cathy Gale, who was based on *Life* magazine photographer Margaret Bourke-White and anthropologist Margaret Mead[152] (Honor Blackman essentially played a leather-clad anthropologist long before Lara Croft).[153] In fact, scholar Angelina I. Karpovich considers Gale "perhaps the first strong female character in popular culture who was genuinely accessible as a role model."[154]

People recall the 1960s as a tumultuous time defined by various types of revolutions that occurred around the world, including the sexual revolution, which saw women gain more control over their lives and enter the workforce at higher rates. *The Avengers* captured that rebellious spirit as it refused to shy away from portraying men and women as equals.[155] As such, it continues to resonate with fans even now, more than fifty years after leaving the airwaves.

See also *The Prisoner* (1967–1968)

B

BABYLON 5 (1994–1998)

Creator: J. Michael Straczynski
Cast: Bruce Boxleitner (Captain John Sheridan), Richard Biggs (Dr. Stephen Franklin),
    Claudia Christian (Commander Susan Ivanova), Jeff Conaway (Zack Allan), Jerry
    Doyle (Michael Garibaldi), Mira Furlan (Delenn), Stephen Furst (Vir Cotto), Peter
    Jurasik (Londo Mollari), Andreas Katsulas (G'Kar), Bill Mumy (Lennier)
Genre: Action, Drama, Science Fiction

Synopsis

In the far future, the crew of the Earth Alliance space station Babylon 5 deal with political intrigue, racial tensions, and interstellar war.

Production History

Writer J. Michael Straczynski created *Babylon 5* in the late 1980s because he felt television lacked a quality science fiction series that mixed thoughtful, speculative concepts with gripping drama.[1] Straczynski came up with the idea for the show in 1986 and wrote the pilot script in 1987.[2] Two years later, he wrote the series bible,[3] setting the ambitious new show in one central location to make it more budget-friendly.[4] Yet *Babylon 5* remained in limbo for five years because network executives refused to take a chance on a new, untested, science fiction property.[5] Undaunted, Straczynski hired artist Peter Ledger to develop conceptual artwork and teamed with producers Douglas Netter and John Copeland to find a studio willing to distribute the show. Netter and Copeland brought Straczynski's idea to HBO, Paramount Television, and ABC before finally securing a deal with Warner Bros.[6] In 1989, studio executives commissioned a feature-length *Babylon 5* pilot three months before Paramount announced plans for a new *Star Trek* series called *Deep Space Nine*, which was similarly set on a space station.[7]

The *Babylon 5* pilot movie aired in February 1993 and earned big ratings,[8] leading Warner Bros. to greenlight a full series that debuted in January 1994.[9] Straczynski served as executive producer[10] and wrote 92 of the show's 110 episodes,[11] while famous science fiction writers like D. C. Fontana and Peter David also contributed scripts.[12] In addition, legendary author Harlan Ellison, a close friend of Starczynski,

The intrepid crew aboard the space station Babylon 5 navigate interstellar political intrigue while standing fast against a variety of intergalactic threats. *Warner Bros. Television/Photofest*

served as a consultant on the series.[13] The effects artists at Optic Nerve designed all the aliens and provided the makeup effects, which earned them an Emmy Award in 1994.[14] Anticipating the future of high-definition television sets, Straczynski ordered each episode shot in a 16:9 aspect ratio, meaning that the director of each episode needed to stage scenes so that important information remained in the space offered by the 4:3 aspect ratio of the time.[15] The last episode of *Babylon 5* aired in November 1998,[16] but the show spawned four TV movies and the short-lived spinoff series *Crusade*. In 2014, Straczynski teased a theatrical *Babylon 5* reboot,[17] though Warner Bros. seems disinterested in such a project.[18]

Commentary

Released amid a wave of science fiction and speculative fiction shows that included the relaunched *Star Trek* franchise (which had just launched the spinoff series *Star Trek: Deep Space Nine* the previous year), *Babylon 5* set out to redefine science fiction on television. In the process, the show developed a small but fervent cult audience drawn in by the compelling characters, gripping storylines, impressive effects, and deft handling of sensitive topics like religion, war, homosexuality, and more. Though it seemed destined to live in the long shadow cast by Gene Roddenberry's pop culture juggernaut, *Babylon 5* nevertheless carved out its own distinct identity. Whereas other shows of the time often seemed to make things up as they went along, series creator J. Michael Straczynski developed a five-year plan for *Babylon 5* and made the other writers and directors stick to it, thus ensuring a strict continuity from beginning to end. Therefore, while the show started off a bit weak as it struggled to find its footing, *Babylon 5* nevertheless helped pave the way (along with *The X-Files*) for the sort of meticulous seriality that defines weekly television in the early years of the twenty-first century. For that reason alone, it deserves a spot on any list of the all-time great cult TV shows.

At the same time, *Babylon 5* offered viewers more than just trailblazing continuity. It also featured complex characters and intriguing storylines alongside pioneering computer-generated effects more advanced than anything else on television at the time. As David Bassom put it in his book *Creating* Babylon 5, "*Babylon 5* was the first series to use Computer-Generated Imagery (CGI) and to win an Emmy for CGI."[19] The show set the stage for subsequent effects-heavy science fiction series like *seaQuest DSV*, *Space: Above and Beyond*, *Farscape*, and *Star Trek: Voyager*—all of which used similar techniques to realize their fantastic seascapes and breathtaking intergalactic vistas. In addition, *Babylon 5* introduced viewers to multilayered human characters like Captain John Sheridan, Commander Susan Ivanova, and Security Chief Michael Garibaldi, who all served to reinforce the importance of imperfect humans in science fiction stories. The show also featured fascinating alien races and cultures, including the Minbari, the Narns, and the Vorlons, all beautifully designed extraterrestrials who brought their otherworldly customs and enthralling intrigues to the station.

In many ways, *Babylon 5* signaled the expansion of space sci-fi on television in the 1990s because it presented a new universe beyond the one offered by *Star Trek*, which had dominated the genre since the 1960s. Numerous other space operas emerged in its wake, and while the show failed to achieve the same sort of longevity as its more popular forerunner, *Babylon 5* still deserves recognition as a groundbreaking cult series that left a lasting imprint on science fiction television.

See also *Farscape* (1999–2003)

BATTLESTAR GALACTICA (1978–1979)

Creator: Glen A. Larson
Cast: Richard Hatch (Captain Apollo), Dirk Benedict (Lieutenant Starbuck), Lorne Greene (Commander Adama), Herbert Jefferson Jr. (Lieutenant Boomer), John Colicos (Count Baltar), Maren Jensen (Lieutenant Athena), Noah Hathaway (Boxey), Laurette Spang (Cassiopeia), Terry Carter (Colonel Tigh)
Genre: Action, Drama, Science Fiction

Synopsis

After a devastating attack by the evil Cylons, the last remnants of humanity set off on a desperate interstellar search for the legendary planet Earth.

Production History

Glen A. Larson claims he came up with the idea for *Battlestar Galactica* in the late 1960s.[20] His original concept featured a wealthy man learning about the impending destruction of the world and trying to launch as many people as possible into space aboard a massive starship.[21] Larson titled his idea *Adam's Ark* but put it on the shelf until science fiction proved more marketable.[22] In the late 1970s, executives at ABC snatched up Larson's idea because they wanted to capitalize on the success of *Star Wars*. Initially, Larson pitched *Adam's Ark* as a seven-hour miniseries, but the network gave him a $7 million budget to expand it to a weekly series. ABC hired John Dykstra, who worked on *Star Wars*, to provide the special effects.[23] The network also cast Lorne Greene to headline the new show, likely to exploit his legacy as patriarch of the *Bonanza* clan.[24] During production, cast and crew worked six eighteen-hour days a week, and each episode took ten days to film,[25] leaving the cast exhausted and frustrated.[26]

The show, now called *Battlestar Galactica*, premiered on September 17, 1978, and initially earned big ratings. However, egos clashed behind the scenes as ABC fought with parent company Universal over the series' profits, and producers quarreled with the marketing team.[27] In addition, 20th Century Fox sued

Capt. Apollo (Richard Hatch, left), Lt. Starbuck (Dirk Benedict), and the crew of the Battlestar Galactica battle the evil cylons while searching for the legendary planet Earth. *ABC/Photofest*

ABC and Universal for copyright infringement,[28] but Universal countersued for copyright infringement on their film *Silent Running*.[29] The case eventually settled out of court.[30] Despite all that, *Battlestar Galactica* consistently landed in the top 20 during its first year.[31] It also earned several award nominations, including the Saturn Award for Best Costumes, a Grammy for Best Album or Original Score, and two Emmys.[32] Ratings soon declined, however, and ABC canceled *Battlestar Galactica* after just one season. In 1980, the network tried to revive the show with *Galactica 1980*, which failed to attract viewers.[33] In the years after, Berkley Science Fiction published fourteen official *Battlestar Galactica* novels,[34] while Dynamite Entertainment published comic books based on the show starting in 2006.[35] Most recently, Ronald D. Moore launched an acclaimed reboot of *Battlestar Galactica* that aired on the Sci-Fi Channel from 2003 to 2009,[36] but the original series remains a fan favorite.

Commentary

Though inspired by *Star Trek* and *Star Wars*, *Battlestar Galactica* nevertheless plotted its own course and developed an original mythos embraced by science fiction enthusiasts around the world. Each week, the show offered up complex storylines and compelling characters along with stunning visual effects, thrilling space battles, and intriguing alien races (like the insectoid Ovions, the noncorporeal Seraphs, and, of course, the robotic Cylons). Rooted in both Mormonism (the ancient human home-world is called Kobol) and Greek myth (many of the characters are named after Greek gods), *Battlestar Galactica* takes viewers on an epic intergalactic journey that follows the last remaining humans as they set off on a search for a new home, all while pursued by the Cylons, machinelike beings determined to wipe out all biological life. While highly derivative, the show still developed a fervent following largely due to talented and charismatic cast members like Lorne Greene, Richard Hatch, and Dirk Benedict (sometimes credited as *Battlestar Galactica*'s main draw due to his matinee idol looks and abundant charm).[37] It also helped that *Battlestar Galactica* debuted when sci-fi fans looking for a weekly dose of ambitious space opera had far fewer choices. As such, the show seemed ready-made for a cult audience.

Battlestar Galactica only lasted one season consisting of just twenty-one episodes, but it still produced lasting stories and memorable moments during its brief lifespan. The pilot episode, "Saga of a Star World," kicked things off in grand fashion, showing the annihilation of the Twelve Colonies of Man and following the survivors as they embarked on their desperate search for a new home. This episode (which cost nearly $3 million and soared into theaters outside the United States) enticed viewers with impressive effects and gripping drama that the remaining episodes sadly lacked. Nevertheless, *Battlestar Galactica* served up plenty of fun exploits and exciting action throughout its abbreviated run as in "The Lost Warrior" (S1E4), which sees Apollo crash-land on a planet that resembles the Wild West and run afoul of a cruel Cylon gunfighter. Meanwhile, the two-part "Guns on Ice Planet Zero" (S1E6, S1E7) alludes to both *Star Wars* and *The Dirty Dozen* with its story about a group of convicts setting out on a suicide mission to destroy a powerful Cylon weapon. Episodes such as these helped *Battlestar Galactica* spark the imagination of sci-fi fans everywhere, cementing its status as a cherished cult classic that launched a whole new universe of adventure.

See also *Lost in Space* (1965–1968), *Star Trek* (1966–1969)

BAYWATCH (1989–2001)

Creators: Michael Berk, Gregory J. Bonann, Douglas Schwartz
Cast: David Hasselhoff (Mitch Buchannon), Jeremy Jackson (Hobie Buchannon), Pamela Anderson (C. J. Parker), Yasmine Bleeth (Caroline Holden), Michael Newman (Michael "Newmie" Newman), Gregory Alan Williams (Garner Ellerbee), Alexandra Paul (Stephanie Holden)
Genre: Action, Crime, Drama, Romance

Synopsis

The lifeguards of Baywatch protect the beaches of Los Angeles while also dealing with crime on the city's streets.

Production History

Inspired by his experiences as a Los Angeles County lifeguard,[38] Gregory J. Bonann developed the idea for a TV show called *Baywatch*, which he initially pitched to Grant Tinker of MTM Enterprises in 1977.[39] Tinker turned it down so Bonann sat on the idea until 1981 when he once again shopped the concept to networks around Hollywood.[40] In 1988, Bonnan decided to make a 16mm short film to illustrate his idea.[41] By then Tinker had left MTM and created GTG with newspaper syndicator Gannett.[42] GTG worked with Bonann to develop *Baywatch* for CBS[43] though the project ultimately landed at NBC,[44] with executives purchasing a two-hour pilot but demanding script approval.[45] David Hasselhoff landed the lead role of Mitch Buchanan after producers considered William Katt, Tom Wopat, and Adrian Paul.[46]

Production commenced on January 4, 1989,[47] with the pilot episode premiering on April 23, 1989, as a highly rated movie-of-the-week.[48] The next month, NBC picked up *Baywatch* for the 1990–1991 season, ordering twelve episodes with a promise of nine more if the series did well.[49] By May 1990, however, NBC had canceled *Baywatch*,[50] citing high production costs, low ratings, and the impending split between Gannett and GTG.[51] Later that summer, Bonann, Michael Berk, and Douglas Schwartz bought the rights from Tinker for $10,[52] though Gannett asked $5,000 per episode for any future series.[53]

Bonann and Hasselhoff then looked for ways to finance and distribute the series,[54] eventually striking a deal with Fremantle Corporation, which had distributed *Baywatch* overseas when it was with NBC.[55] Domestically, broadcast and cable networks refused to show *Baywatch* so the producers decided to sell the show in syndication to independent television stations through Pearson All American Television.[56] Filming resumed on July 8, 1991.[57] Pamela Anderson joined the cast during the second season in syndication,[58] and at that point *Baywatch* was doing so well that Pearson asked for a second drama series in 1994, resulting in the spinoff series *Baywatch Nights*.[59] In 1999, rising production costs inspired the producers to consider moving the series to Australia, but they ran into resistance from the locals.[60] Instead, production moved to Hawaii for the last two seasons.[61] *Baywatch* ended its run in 2001 when Pearson declined to renew it for financial reasons.[62] In 2017, Paramount Pictures released a critically derided film reboot starring Dwayne Johnson.[63]

Commentary

A winning combination of playful sexiness, gripping melodrama, and captivating mysteries turned *Baywatch* into a worldwide hit and one of the most popular syndicated television series of all time. The show boasted a cast comprised of some of the most attractive performers of the 1990s, all of whom routinely put their taut, tanned bodies on display. Whether running on the beach in slow motion or engaging in some hot and heavy after-hours action, the stars of *Baywatch* served as the show's primary draw. The series turned Pamela Anderson, Yasmine Bleeth, and Erika Eleniak into internationally renowned sex symbols who graced the covers of magazines around the world. Meanwhile, *Baywatch* also featured a bevy of shirtless studs led by David Hasselhoff, who watched over the beaches of Los Angeles alongside hot hunks like Billy Warlock, Jeremy Jackson, and David Charvet. More than anything, sex appeal helped *Baywatch* build a massive global fanbase.

Yet the show also offered engaging stories and exciting adventures. Each week, *Baywatch* mixed soap-opera-style plots with over-the-top action sequences, all set against the picturesque backdrop of some of the most beautiful beaches in Los Angeles. In "If Looks Could Kill" (S2E11), Mitch saves and promptly falls in love with a woman (played by Shannon Tweet, star of numerous softcore thrillers produced throughout the 1990s) only to learn she harbors murderous tendencies. Meanwhile "Nevermore" (S7E22) riffs on *The Phantom of the Opera* as C. J. lands in the clutches of a mysterious, disfigured admirer who lurks under the Malibu pier. "Eel Niño" (S8E8) sees Mitch descend into an underwater cave to kill an oversized electric eel with a defibrillator. In addition, *Baywatch* featured delightfully hammy dialogue and exuberant guest stars (in one episode, World Championship Wrestling stars Hulk Hogan, Ric Flair, and "Macho Man" Randy Savage all pay a visit to the beach). Throughout its run, *Baywatch* offered dopey, sexy fun, which explains why fans love it even now.

> ## *BEAUTY AND THE BEAST* (1987–1990)
>
> *Creator*: Ron Koslow
> *Cast*: Ron Perlman (Vincent), Linda Hamilton (Catherine Chandler), Roy Dotrice
> (Jacob "Father" Wells), Jay Acovone (Deputy D.A. Joe Maxwell), Renn Woods
> (Edie), Stephen McHattie (Gabriel), Edward Albert (Elliot Burch), Jo Anderson
> (Diana Bennett)
> *Genre*: Drama, Fantasy, Romance

Synopsis

The French fairytale is updated for the twentieth century as a beautiful, young assistant district attorney falls in love with a gentle beast-man who dwells in the sewers beneath New York City.

Production History

In the 1980s, Ron Koslow of Witt-Thomas Productions developed an adaptation of the 1740 French fairytale *La Belle et la Bête*, turning it into a "contemporary fable" by bringing the characters into modern-day New York City.[64] Seeing the city as a "mythic place," Koslow wrote the pilot script, which sparked interest among executives at CBS.[65] To oversee the make-up for the show, the network hired Academy-award winner Rick Baker,[66] who suggested Ron Perlman for the lead role based on the actor's performances in *Quest for Fire* (1981) and *The Name of the Rose* (1986), both of which required heavy make-up work.[67] Perlman prepared for the role by repeatedly watching Jean Cocteau's film adaptation of the fairy tale and recalling the work of Charles Laughton in *The Hunchback of Notre Dame* (1939).[68]

Beauty and the Beast (B&B) premiered on September 25, 1987,[69] with critics praising the show but panning the violence.[70] The producers fought with CBS over the show's sexuality, politics, and violence.[71] In the second season, which aired on Friday evenings at 8:00 p.m., CBS responded to criticism with a gentler Beast and an increased focus on the romance.[72] Along with these content struggles, B&B struggled to find an audience,[73] though it won its specific time slot.[74] CBS ordered a third season of twelve episodes but put the show on hiatus soon after.[75] In response, fans (known as "Helpers" and "Beasties") organized a petition to save the show,[76] sending over 4,200 letters to CBS, but network executives mostly ignored the impassioned pleas.[77]

After season 2, costar Linda Hamilton left the series due to her pregnancy and a desire to pursue other projects. Producers killed off her character in a two-part episode and introduced a new love interest for season 3.[78] CBS then moved B&B to Wednesdays at 8:00 p.m.,[79] where it continued to struggle in the ratings until its cancelation in 1990.[80] In 2012, the CW Network rebooted the series with co-showrunners Sherri Cooper-Landsman and Jennifer Levin,[81] and the new show ran until 2016.[82]

Commentary

Television shows that blend fantasy and romance are common today but they were much rarer in 1987 when *Beauty and the Beast* debuted on CBS. The show brought Gothic romance to primetime, offering viewers a weekly dose of lush visuals, melodramatic stories, and inflamed passion. In each episode, B&B contrasted the grimy reality of pre-Giuliani New York with the fantastic imagery of the subterranean society the leonine Vincent calls home. The show also dazzled viewers with enthralling tales in which the title characters deal with various threats while nurturing their growing desire. B&B attracted a cult following thanks in large part to the chemistry of its two leads. Ron Perlman (acting under heavy makeup provided by legendary FX-guru Rick Baker) plays Vincent, a physically powerful brute who possesses a gentle soul and refined tastes. He also purrs every line in a low, growly voice that set many fans' hearts aflutter. Meanwhile, Linda Hamilton (still a few years from her role as a badass, butt-kicking mom in James Cameron's 1992 blockbuster *Terminator 2*) turns Catherine into more than just a standard damsel-in-distress even though she frequently lands in the bad guys' clutches. Throughout B&B's three seasons, Catherine rescued Vincent almost as often as he saved her, thus establishing herself as a tough, modern woman.

The show also boasted an incredible array of talent in the writer's room. In addition to *Homeland* creators Howard Gordon and Alex Gansa, a pre-fame George R. R. Martin—best known for writing the bestselling fantasy series *A Song of Ice and Fire*, the basis for the smash hit HBO show *Game of Thrones*—served on the writing staff, penning fourteen of B&B's fifty-five episodes. Series star (and avid jazz enthusiast) Perlman once compared Martin's scripts to "John Coltrane on acid—primal, but with incredible elegance,"[83] an apt description of installments like "Ozymandias" (S1E21) and "What Rough Beast" (S2E20), which took daring risks while advancing the show's central narrative (the former installment featured Vincent reading the title poem in its entirety). Like many shows before and since, B&B took a little while to find its footing, and many first-season episodes feel somewhat formulaic. By season 2, however, the show had established itself as one of the most captivating dramas on TV at that time. Season 3 even introduced a season-long arc that centered on a new archvillain named Gabriel (played with gusto by Stephen McHattie), thus blazing a trail for later serialized supernatural romances like *Buffy the Vampire Slayer*, *Grimm*, and *Once Upon a Time*. While never a huge hit, B&B cast a long shadow, and its spirit lives on in books like Stephanie Meyer's *Twilight* and films such as Guillermo Del Toro's *The Shape of Water*, in which strong-willed, beautiful women fall for beastly but sensitive men.

See also *Beauty and the Beast* (1987–1990), *Buffy the Vampire Slayer* (1997–2003), *Outlander* (2014–Present), *True Blood* (2008–2014)

THE BLACK ADDER (1982–1983)

Creator: Rowan Atkinson, Richard Curtis
Cast: Rowan Atkinson (Edmund, Duke of Edinburgh), Tony Robinson (Baldrick), Elspet Gray (The Queen), Brian Blessed (King Richard IV), Tim McInnerny (Percy), Robert East (Harry, Prince of Wales)
Genre: Comedy

Synopsis

During the Middle Ages, the craven Duke of Edinburgh schemes to capture the throne of England.

Production History

While attending Oxford University in the late 1970s, Rowan Atkinson met Richard Curtis, thus planting the seeds for a long and fruitful partnership.[84] Shortly after graduating, the duo landed gigs on the satirical sketch program *Not the Nine O'Clock News*.[85] When that show ceased production, BBC executives asked Atkinson and Curtis to develop a sitcom.[86] Though intimidated by the success of *Fawlty Towers*,[87] the pair agreed and hatched an idea for a period comedy about a king and his friends.[88] Drawing inspiration from films about Medieval England, Atkinson and Curtis changed the protagonist from a handsome and honorable hero to a cowardly antihero.[89] Upon completing the script for the pilot episode, which they called "Prince Edmund and His Two Friends," they brought it to BBC producer John Lloyd, who greenlit the show.[90] Atkinson and Curtis wrote the character of Percy for their friend Tim McInnerny,[91] but casting Baldrick proved more difficult. After a long audition process, they offered the part to Tony Robinson, who gratefully accepted.[92]

The first episode of *The Black Adder* began shooting in February 1983 at Alnwick Castle in Northumberland.[93] Atkinson and Curtis received a hefty budget for the show, which went primarily toward location shooting and period costumes.[94] Network executives almost cancelled *The Black Adder* after the first series but Lloyd promised big changes including budget cuts and stage-based production. He also hired Ben Elton to co-write the second series, set during the Elizabethan period based on a suggestion from Elton and Curtis.[95] *Blackadder II* earned big ratings so Lloyd decided to continue moving each new series to a different historical period, placing *Blackadder the Third* during the Regency era.[96] In 1989, *Blackadder Goes Forth*, which took place during World War I, earned high ratings, drawing 11.7 million viewers.[97] The series first arrived in the United States on A&E in the late 1980s[98] before airing on PBS. In the years since, Atkinson and pals kicked around several ideas for a fifth *Blackadder* series, including *The Blackadder Five*, a satirical look at a 1960s rock group with a drummer named Bald Rick.[99] In 2019, rumors surfaced that the BBC had commissioned a fifth series set in the early twenty-first century with Atkinson playing a smug university professor who mocks the younger generation.[100]

Commentary

Over the years, the various *Blackadder* series have offered up satirical takes on different periods of British history, but the first series took dead aim at the Middle Ages. By upending the events that occurred during England's fabled War of the Roses, *The Black Adder* earned a permanent place in the hearts of comedy fans and history nerds alike. The series showcased several talented comedic performers including Rowan Atkinson, Tony Robinson, Tim McInnerny, and Brian Blessed, all of whom delivered manic performances as some truly despicable people. Atkinson played the title character as a sniveling schemer intent on killing his own father and assuming the throne but who repeatedly thwarts his own efforts out of incompetence and cowardice. Blessed, meanwhile, turned King Richard IV into a blustery and self-absorbed royal whose thoughts rarely stray from food, sex, and extreme violence. Robinson played Baldrick as a devious and opportunistic boot-licker, while McInnerny portrayed Percy as a loyal but dimwitted accomplice who frequently sabotages Prince Edmund's conspiracies. The actors all dialed their performances far beyond eleven, evoking huge laughs even as they performed dastardly acts (such as trying to prevent a wedding by deflowering the bride-to-be). As such, *The Black Adder* earned a devoted worldwide fanbase.

With scripts written by series co-creators Atkinson and Curtis, each episode of *The Black Adder* featured sharp wit and amusing one-liners. For example, in "Born to be King" (S1E2), King Richard declares, "As the good Lord said: 'Love thy neighbor as thyself . . . unless he's Turkish, in which case, kill the bastard.'" Later in that same episode, Prince Edmund learns that the eunuchs he has hired for the evening's entertainment have canceled and declares, "I'm gonna teach them a lesson they'll never forget. I'll remove whatever extraneous parts of their bodies still remain." A few episodes later, in "Witchsmeller Pursuivant" (S1E5), the titular witchfinder explains his method for judging those accused of witch-craft: "The suspected witch has his head placed upon a block and an axe aimed at his neck. If the man is guilty, the axe will bounce off his neck, so we burn him; if he is not guilty, the axe will simply slice his head off." The show also featured uproarious visual gags (as in S1E3, "The Archbishop," in which Edmund wears an ostentatious metal helmet, an enormous protruding black codpiece, and ridicu-lous boots) and sidesplittingly awkward situations (see Edmund trying to herd a flock of sheep in S1E2, "Born to be King"). Overall, *The Black Adder* served up an intoxicating mixture of dry wit, comically loathsome characters, and hilariously over-the-top situations.

See also *Fawlty Towers* (1975–1979), *The Young Ones* (1982–1984)

BUFFY THE VAMPIRE SLAYER (1997–2003)

Creator: Joss Whedon
Cast: Sarah Michelle Gellar (Buffy Summers), Nicholas Brendon (Xander Harris), Alyson Hannigan (Willow Rosenberg), Anthony Head (Rupert Giles), Angel (David Boreanaz), Spike (James Marsters), Charisma Carpenter (Cordelia Chase), Emma Caulfield Ford (Anya), Michelle Trachtenberg (Dawn Summers)
Genre: Action, Drama, Fantasy, Romance

Synopsis

A teenage girl learns she is the Chosen One who must save the world from vampires and other demonic forces.

Teenage vampire-slayer Buffy Summers (Sarah Michelle Gellar) defends the world from monsters, madmen, and other nefarious types. *WB Television/Photofest*

Production History

Aspiring writer Joss Whedon came up with the idea for *Buffy the Vampire Slayer* while watching a horror movie that sparked in him a desire to show the typical ditzy blonde besting the monster rather than falling victim to it.[101] While writing for the popular television series *Roseanne*, Whedon penned a *Buffy* screenplay that he sold to Dolly Parton's Sandollar Productions in 1992. The resulting film disappointed Whedon, but five years later executives at the WB Television Network approached him about adapting the movie as a TV series.[102] Suzanne Daniels, president of programming at the WB, asked Whedon to shoot a presentation reel,[103] which proved good enough to secure a greenlight from the network.[104] The WB announced the series would debut during mid-season in 1997, requiring Whedon and his production team to shoot twelve episodes before any installments aired.[105]

Buffy premiered on March 10, 1997,[106] instantly becoming a fan favorite.[107] During the show's third season, the Columbine shooting led to increased censorship on television, prompting the WB executives to delay potentially controversial episodes like "Earshot" (S3E18) and "Graduation Day, Part II" (S3E22).[108] Nevertheless, the network extended to Whedon a great deal of creative freedom.[109] Following the end of season 5, the series moved from the WB Network, which opted to focus on the spinoff series *Angel* instead,[110] to fledgling UPN, which hyped *Buffy*'s arrival to drive ratings.[111] The show ended after seven seasons because many people involved felt it had run its course and Sarah Michelle Gellar wanted to move on to other projects.[112] *Buffy* continues to slay demons in comic books published by BOOM! Studios,[113] and talk of a reboot series persists.[114]

Commentary

Much has already been written about *Buffy the Vampire Slayer*. The show's popularity has even resulted in a field of academic study: Whedon Studies. Hundreds of articles, chapters, and even entire books analyze the characters, the setting, the stories, the arcs, the production, the reception, the themes, and so on. Any commentary on the series must seemingly comment on its presentation of "grrl power," which emerged with third-wave feminism in the 1990s, and the creation of the unlikely heroine Buffy Summers. While Whedon frequently returned to the trope of the waifish superpowered girl in the years after changing the pop culture landscape with *Buffy*, this initial depiction seemed groundbreaking in 1997 as did the show's later presentation of lesbian characters in Willow and Tara. These representations spoke to an audience of teenagers and queer viewers who felt like outsiders but who saw a strong portrayal of otherness in the series' stories and characters.[115]

Whedon's work also introduced innovative techniques now common in television. Audiences have long formed an emotional attachment to characters, but Whedon created characters who experienced the same emotional ups and downs as the show's viewers, who in turn came to dread seeing their favorite characters happy because they knew that something horrible would befall Buffy and her friends. Though Whedon seemingly delighted in such emotional torment, he also cared about his fans, often interacting with them online (he was one of the first producers to cultivate such a close relationship with his fanbase). Additionally, while the series drew on *The X-Files* with its mix of standalone episodes and installments that furthered a larger mythology, *Buffy* also helped television evolve by introducing the concept of the "Big Bad," which became a buzzword within the industry as television executives sought to develop their own complex narratives.[116] In addition, *Buffy* launched the careers of David Greenwalt, Jose Molina, David Fury, Marti Noxon, Dan Vebber, and Steven S. DeKnight, who all went on to produce more innovative television and film that pushed the boundaries of storytelling. *Buffy* irrevocably changed television and pop culture and for this reason alone deserves a spot among the greatest cult TV shows of all time.

See also *Charmed* (1998–2006), *Smallville* (2001–2011), *Supernatural* (2005–2020), *True Blood* (2008–2014), *Veronica Mars* (2004–Present)

SPOTLIGHT: JOSS WHEDON

With the success of the *Buffy the Vampire Slayer* television adaptation, Joss Whedon emerged as one of the most influential—and at times controversial—figures in American popular culture. Born June 23, 1964, in New York City,[117] Whedon graduated from Wesleyan University with a degree in film studies and a focus on women's studies. Soon after, he joined the writing staff for *Roseanne*.[118] During that time, he sold the screenplay to *Buffy the Vampire Slayer*. He later worked as a script doctor on films like *Toy Story*, *Alien: Resurrection*, and *Waterworld* before making a splash with the wildly popular *Buffy* TV series. From there, he created other cult shows including *Firefly*, *Dollhouse*, and the *Buffy* spin-off *Angel*. In addition, Whedon wrote and directed the webseries *Dr. Horrible's Sing-Along Blog*, authored comic books like *Astonishing X-Men* and *Runaways*, co-wrote the film *The Cabin in the Woods*, helped launch the Marvel Cinematic Universe, and co-created the television series *Agents of S.H.I.E.L.D.*[119]

C

CHARMED (1998–2006)

Creator: Constance M. Burge
Cast: Holly Marie Combs (Piper Halliwell), Alyssa Milano (Phoebe Halliwell), Shannen Doherty (Prue Halliwell), Rose McGowan (Paige Matthews), Brian Kraus (Leo Wyatt), Dorian Gregory (Darryl Morris), Julian McMahon (Cole Turner)
Genre: Drama, Fantasy, Mystery

Synopsis

Three sisters learn about their family history and discover their true destiny as witches tasked with protecting the world from dark forces.

Production History

Looking to cash in on the success of *Buffy the Vampire Slayer*,[1] Garth Ancier, chief programmer for the WB Network, worked with Aaron Spelling to launch a new supernatural series called *Charmed*.[2] They asked Constance Burge to develop a show about witches.[3] Unfamiliar with the topic, Burge researched Wiccan practice and came up with an idea centered on three sisters.[4] In casting the series, Spelling suggested Shannon Doherty even though they shared a rocky relationship while making *Beverly Hills 90210*.[5] Producers then cast Lori Rom as Phoebe[6] but she left after shooting the pilot,[7] claiming her church objected to the series.[8] Alyssa Milano stepped in to replace her[9] despite objections from Doherty who worried that Milano might assume a more prominent position within the show.[10] Meanwhile, Doherty's friend Holly Marie Combs landed the role of the third sister, Piper.[11] With the cast in place, *Charmed* premiered on October 7, 1998, earning the highest ratings of any the WB Network show at the time.[12]

From the start, producers wanted to focus more on the family element than the supernatural component.[13] However, *Charmed* struggled to find its identity during the first season,[14] especially as the WB's marketing efforts consistently emphasized the sex appeal of the main characters.[15] The problems continued after Burge left the show following the second season due to the increased focus on romantic storylines.[16] Additionally, Doherty left because of behind-the-scenes tension with Milano so producers killed off her character at the end of the third season.[17] They considered replacing her with Tiffani Amber-Thiessen or Jennifer Love Hewitt but both performers declined the offer,[18] paving the way for Rose McGowan to assume the role of the youngest Halliwell sister, Paige.[19] The WB slashed the show's budget during the eighth season thereby preventing location shoots, cutting back on visual effects and guest stars, and forcing production to move to the Paramount lot.[20] The series finale aired on May 21, 2006.[21] By that point, *Charmed* had produced 178 episodes, thus beating *Laverne & Shirley* as "the longest-running series with female leads."[22] In 2013, CBS announced a reboot that failed to launch.[23] Five years later, the CW successfully relaunched the show.[24]

Commentary

With its attractive leads and hip sensibility, *Charmed* defined the short-lived WB Network while also reflecting the feminist and pop cultural sensibilities of the 1990s.[25] Inspired in part by the popular teen-witch film *The Craft* (1996), *Charmed* followed the Halliwell sisters as they battled dark forces intent on using the "Power of Three" for their own nefarious purposes. The series recalled *Buffy the Vampire Slayer* in that it also featured young women empowered by a combination of independence and literal magical abilities. Yet *Charmed* often sexualized the Halliwell sisters, who routinely pranced around in skimpy costumes.[26] While the show revolved around a trio of empowered feminine women, it also contained the hallmarks of executive producer Aaron Spelling, the man behind *Charlie's Angels*, the pinnacle of so-called jiggle TV.[27] Like that camp classic, *Charmed* paid lip service to feminist ideals while balancing silliness and sexiness, only with more 1990s window-dressing.

After learning of their witchy heritage, the Halliwell sisters band together to fight evil. *The WB/ Photofest*

During its run, *Charmed* advanced a powerful message of sisterhood, making it unique among other grrl-power TV series of that era, including *Buffy*. Despite the presence of her pals (affectionately known as the Scooby Gang), Buffy Summers frequently faced evil alone. In *Charmed*, however, the Halliwell sisters relied on each other to reach their full potential, as demonstrated in episodes like "From Fear to Eternity" (S1E13), in which the Charmed Ones first meet the demon Barbas (Billy Drago), who kills his victims by preying on their deepest fears. Other examples include "That 70s Episode" (S1E17) as the Halliwell sisters travel back in time to meet their long-dead mother, and "Chick Flick" (S2E18), which sees the Charmed Ones square off against a bevy of iconic movie monsters unleashed by the Demon of Illusion. From beginning to end, *Charmed* emphasized family as its most important theme. The writers even incorporated Holly Marie Combs's real-life pregnancy in the narrative, allowing the show to portray motherhood and femininity as equally important as independence and butt-kicking. Across eight seasons, *Charmed* served up silly, sexy thrills that delight fans even now, making it one of the greatest cult TV shows of all time.

See also *Beauty and the Beast* (1987–1990), *Buffy the Vampire Slayer* (1997–2003)

COMMUNITY (2009–2015)

Creator: Dan Harmon
Cast: Joel McHale (Jeff Winger), Gillian Jacobs (Britta Perry), Danny Pudi (Abed Nadir), Alison Brie (Annie Edison), Yvette Nicole Brown (Shirley Bennett), Jim Rash (Dean Pelton), Donald Glover (Troy Barnes), Chevy Chase (Pierce Hawthorne)
Genre: Comedy

Synopsis

A group of misfit students embark on a series of bizarre adventures at their local community college.

Production History

While in his early thirties, comedian Dan Harmon attended Glendale Community College, where he enrolled in a Spanish class to spend more time with his girlfriend. During that time, he joined a study group and forged friendships with the other students.[28] Years later, Harmon turned that real-life experience into the plot for *Community*, a sitcom he pitched to executives at NBC.[29] The show premiered on September 17, 2009, and aired as part of NBC's Must-See-TV Thursday night line-up but it earned low ratings even as it received praise from critics and developed a passionate fanbase.[30]

Jeff Winger (Joel McHale, left) and the other misfits at Glendale Community College learn life lessons as they embark on various madcap adventures. *NBC/Photofest*

From the start, Harmon clashed with NBC and their production partner Sony Pictures Television as both parties jockeyed for creative control.[31] Additionally, because of Harmon's self-admitted anger management problems, several of the show's writers defected during the first three seasons.[32] Harmon also frequently quarreled with Chevy Chase on set.[33] In time, the feud between the two drew negative publicity while the scripts grew increasingly fantastical (including an episode done entirely in 8-bit videogame graphics), so NBC fired Harmon at the end of season 3.[34] The network then appointed *Happy Endings* writers David Guarascio and Moses Port as the new showrunners right around the time Chevy Chase decided to quit the series.[35] NBC then moved *Community* to Friday nights and ordered just thirteen episodes when scheduling season 4.[36]

The change in showrunners hurt the series, which lost 11 percent of its viewers.[37] Network executives quickly rehired Harmon (who dismissed season 4 as "the gas leak season") to oversee the series' fifth season, the last to air on NBC.[38] Yahoo! briefly revived *Community* for a sixth season that aired on their fledgling Yahoo Screen video hub, granting Harmon full creative control.[39] Unfortunately, the platform proved unsustainable and *Community* ended for good in 2016.[40] Since then, Harmon has discussed the possibility of a *Community* movie (thus fulfilling lead character Abed's winking prophecy of "six seasons and a movie").[41]

Commentary

Despite a troubled production history and consistently low ratings, *Community* inspired fierce loyalty among its fans. The show offered up smart pop-culture references and pitch-perfect parodies of movies and TV shows, thus inspiring devotion among nerds, geeks, and outcasts who saw themselves in characters like Abed, Annie, and Troy. For instance, fan-favorite episode "Modern Warfare" (S1E23) includes nods to numerous action films, including *The Warriors*, *28 Days Later*, *Terminator*, *Die Hard*, and John Woo's entire filmography. Meanwhile, "Basic Rocket Science" (S2E4) riffs on both *The Right Stuff* and *Apollo 13*. Episodes like these also established *Community* as a live-action cartoon in which anything could (and often did) happen. Consider "Abed's Uncontrollable Christmas" (S2E11), which transports the characters into a Claymation holiday musical reminiscent of the Rankin-Bass Christmas specials of the late 1960s and early 1970s, or "Digital Estate Planning" (S3E20), in which the characters enter an 8-bit computer game to fight for Pierce's inheritance. Yet these episodes also reveal the show's heart: the creators clearly care for the characters, and this love allows fans to invest in the foibles of the lovable misfits attending Greendale Community College.

Community also launched the careers of numerous people who went on to develop or star in other acclaimed projects, starting with series creator Dan Harmon, co-creator of the cult phenomenon *Rick and Morty*. Alison Brie went on to headline the critically acclaimed Netflix series *GLOW* based on the cult classic wrestling and variety show *Gorgeous Ladies of Wrestling*. Gillian Anderson and Joel McHale also made the leap to Netflix, with Anderson starring in Judd Apatow's comedy series *Love* while McHale hosted *The Joel McHale Show with Joel McHale*. Danny Pudi and Jim Rash both joined the cast of the *DuckTales* reboot while Yvette Nicole Brown voiced Amanda Waller in the animated series *DC Super Hero Girls*. Donald Glover created and stars in the smash hit FX series *Atlanta* while juggling a successful hip hop career under the name Childish Gambino. Finally, Joseph and Anthony Russo, known as the Russo Brothers, went from directing episodes of *Community* to helming four installments of the massively popular Marvel Cinematic Universe. While *Community* only attracted a niche audience, the cast and crew changed the face of popular culture in many ways.

The show weathered many highs and lows during its six seasons (season 4, produced after NBC fired Harmon, remains an especially abysmal low point), but

SPOTLIGHT: DAN HARMON

Born in Milwaukee, Wisconsin, on January 3, 1973, Daniel James Harmon grew up obsessed with television.[42] While attending Marquette University in Milwaukee,[43] he joined Milwaukee's ComedySportz improv group and helped found a sketch troupe called the Dead Alewives.[44] He also collaborated with fellow Alewife Rob Schrab on the acclaimed independent comic book *Scud: The Disposable Assassin*.[45] In the late 1990s, Harmon and Schrab moved to Los Angeles and co-founded the online TV network Channel 101 in 2003.[46] In the years after they co-created the TV show *The Sarah Silverman Program* and co-wrote the film *Monster House*.[47] Harmon then struck out on his own to create the NBC series *Community*.[48] In 2011, Harmon launched the weekly podcast *Harmontown*, and two years later he teamed with Justin Roiland to create the popular, adult-oriented, animated series *Rick and Morty* for Adult Swim.[49] In 2015, Harmon's company, Starburn Industries, produced Charlie Kaufman's stop-motion animated feature *Anomalisa*.[50]

fans still clamor for the long-rumored movie, proving that the highly influential show remains much loved long after graduating from the airwaves.

See also *Arrested Development* (2003–2019), *It's Always Sunny in Philadelphia* (2005–Present), *Parks and Recreation* (2009–2015)

COWBOY BEBOP (1998–1999)

Creator: Shinichirô Watanabe
Cast: Kôichi Yamadera/Steve Blum (Spike Spiegel), Megumi Hayashibara/Wendee Lee (Faye Valentine), Unshô Ishizuka/Beau Billingslea (Jet Black), Aoi Tada/Melizza Fahn (Edward Wong Hau Pepelu Tivruski IV)
Genre: Action, Drama, Science Fiction

Synopsis

An eccentric group of bounty hunters, thieves, and adolescent tech geniuses learn to trust one another as they hunt criminal types throughout the galaxy.

Production History

After co-directing the space-age battle series *Macross Plus* and directing episodes of *Mobile Suit Gundam 0083: Stardust Memory* for the Japanese animation studio Sunrise, animator Shinichirô Watanabe landed a gig directing the anime series *Cowboy Bebop*.[51] Namco Bandai originally developed the show to promote their new spaceship toy line but ultimately granted Watanabe complete creative control.[52] Watanabe worked with Sunrise to produce four episodes[53] but Namco disliked them and ended the relationship, leaving the series' future uncertain until Bandai Visual stepped in as a sponsor.[54]

From the beginning, Watanabe wanted to mix elements of different genres, drawing inspiration from Bruce Lee flicks, Clint Eastwood Westerns, Blaxploitation movies, anime series like *Lupin the 3rd*, and more.[55] He worked with Yoko Kanno to produce the soundtrack, which similarly blended various music styles including jazz, blues, techno, and heavy metal.[56] Watanabe and Kanno worked together to develop their creative ideas, with Kanno composing music that led Watanabe to devise new scenes, which in turn led Kanno to create new music, sometimes before Watanabe asked for it.[57]

Cowboy Bebop originally aired on Japan's TV Tokyo from April 3, 1998, to June 26, 1998, but only twelve of the total twenty-six episodes ran at the time due to concerns over the series' violence.[58] Watanabe never expected the show to catch on in the United States[59] but *Cowboy Bebop* attained massive popularity among American viewers after debuting as part of Cartoon Network's Adult Swim programming block on September 2, 2001.[60] Three years later, *Cowboy Bebop: The Movie* opened in the United States, two years after premiering in Japan.[61] In November 2018, Netflix

The easygoing crew of the Bebop traverse the galaxy searching for high-priced fugitives to bag but often wind up inadvertently saving the universe from various intergalactic threats. *Destination Films/Photofest*

ordered ten episodes of a live-action adaptation of *Cowboy Bebop* with Watanabe serving as creative consultant and Christopher Yost as executive producer.[62]

Commentary

With its mix of complex storylines, compelling characters, and loving homage to everything from samurai cinema to Spaghetti Westerns, *Cowboy Bebop* appealed to science fiction fans and pop culture nerds while paving the way for an anime explosion in the United States during the early years of the twenty-first century. While films like *Akira* and *Ghost in the Shell* and shows like *Sailor Moon* and *Dragon Ball Z* helped popularize Japanese animation during the 1980s and 1990s (decades after shows like *Astro Boy*, *Speed Racer*, and *Kimba the White Lion* first landed on U.S. shores), *Cowboy Bebop* introduced anime to many Western viewers when it appeared as part of Cartoon Network's Adult Swim block in 2001. The show featured stunning animation, gritty action, and witty humor, all wrapped in a cyberpunk space opera set in a crime-ridden galaxy populated by flawed but lovable characters. *Cowboy Bebop* approached science fiction with the sort of 1970s cool that epitomizes Quentin Tarantino's oeuvre, and the show dealt in the same sort of genre remixing, alluding to everything from *Seven Samurai* to *Coffy* and from *Django* to *Alien*. As such, the show resonated with genre aficionados who appreciated the references to other media as well as anime fanatics who enjoyed the vibrant animation, fun characters, and engaging storylines.

Cowboy Bebop also incorporated jazz sensibilities that gave it a hip swagger rarely found in other anime series of the time (though one incorporated by numerous shows in the years after). Thanks to composer Yoko Kanno and her band Seatbelts, *Cowboy Bebop* boasts a unique sound that emphasizes the "bebop" part of the title. From the boisterous "Tank!" which plays over the opening credits to the song that closes every episode, "The Real Folk Blues," the show features some of the best music in all of anime. Yet *Cowboy Bebop*'s soundtrack is every bit as eclectic as its film and TV references, evoking rock and roll, country, the blues, and more. The music informs and reflects the show's chaotic sensibilities and helps establish the characters' identities; for instance, lively but moody Spike Spiegel can go from fighting a man twice his size (in a reference to the climax of *Game of Death*) as an upbeat jazz tune wails on the soundtrack to moping through rain-slicked streets accompanied by a sad requiem. Meanwhile, the show sets sly but sentimental Faye Valentine's efforts to rob an intergalactic casino to a rocking melody then later elicits emotion via a downbeat ballad as the character explores the ruins of her family home. Ultimately, *Cowboy Bebop* offers something for everyone thanks to its impressive technical achievements, diverse soundtrack, and brash attitude, which explains why it remains revered even today.

SPOTLIGHT: SHINICHIRÔ WATANABE

Born in Kyoto on May 24, 1965,[63] Shinichirô Watanabe gravitated toward 1970s Hollywood films, particularly Blaxploitation films.[64] He also read Philip K. Dick, Robert H. Heinlein, and Isaac Asimov and watched anime series like *Lupin the 3rd*.[65] Watanabe joined Sunrise animation studio as a production manager and worked his way up to director,[66] co-directing *Macross Plus* and directing episodes of *Mobile Suit Gundam 0083: Stardust Memory* and *Escaflowne* before creating *Cowboy Bebop*.[67] After that series wrapped, Watanabe directed two segments in the Wachowskis' *The Animatrix* (2003). In the years after, he created *Samurai Champloo* (2004–2005) and *Space Dandy* (2014). In 2018, Watanabe began developing an animated *Blade Runner* series for Adult Swim,[68] and the following year he agreed to serve as a consultant on Netflix's live-action *Cowboy Bebop* series.[69] In 2019, Watanabe launched *Carole & Tuesday*, an animated musical sci-fi series that continues to blend genres and musical styles.

CRAZY EX-GIRLFRIEND (2015–2019)

Creators: Rachel Bloom, Aline Brosh McKenna
Cast: Rachel Bloom (Rebecca Bunch), Donna Lynne Champlin (Paula Proctor), Vincent Rodriguez III (Josh Chan), Pete Gardner (Darryl Whitefeather), Vella Lovell (Heather Davis), Gabrielle Ruiz (Valencia Perez), Scott Michael Foster (Nathaniel Plimpton III), Santino Fontana (Greg Serrano, 2015–2016), Skylar Astin (Greg Serrano, 2018–2019)
Genre: Comedy, Drama, Musical

Synopsis

Unhappy with her life, a New York lawyer moves to West Covina, California, to pursue her ex-boyfriend and her vision of a better existence.

Production History

In 2010, Rachel Bloom caused a sensation with her viral YouTube music video "Fuck Me, Ray Bradbury."[70] Three years later, her "Historically Accurate Princess Song" caught the attention of Aline Brosh McKenna, screenwriter of *The Devil Wears Prada*.[71] With the help of Kate Adler, an executive at CBS Television Studios, McKenna arranged a meeting with Bloom, and together they brainstormed ideas for a new TV series.[72] Bloom originally suggested a musical set in the entertainment world but McKenna wanted to reclaim the term "crazy ex-girlfriend" so the duo married their ideas and spent several months fleshing out the concept.[73] From the beginning, they wanted to do a series about the four cycles in a woman's life: denial, love, nasty turn, and rebuilding.[74]

Several networks expressed interest in the idea but Bloom and McKenna settled on Showtime.[75] In 2014, they worked with director Marc Webb to shoot a pilot episode,[76] and their efforts resulted in a "comedy pilot with musical elements."[77] Showtime ultimately passed on the series claiming it did not fit with their network.[78] Bloom and McKenna then tried pitching the show to other networks but failed to drum up interest. McKenna then watched *Jane the Virgin* on the CW Network and suggested pitching to them.[79] CW executives liked what they saw and greenlit the series in spring 2015,[80] at which point the producers decided to change the format to an hour-long musical drama given the subject matter.[81]

Crazy Ex-Girlfriend debuted on October 12, 2015, as the lead-in for *Jane the Virgin*.[82] The CW initially ordered thirteen episodes, but after the show debuted to solid ratings the network requested five additional episodes for the first season.[83] The ratings soon dropped but the show received a great deal of critical praise so in March 2016 the CW Network executives renewed *Crazy Ex-Girlfriend* for a second season.[84] Critics hailed the show for its music, choreography, and treatment of mental health issues, and Bloom even won a Golden Globe for Best Actress in a Television Series in 2016.[85] While seasons 2 and 3 spanned just thirteen episodes, the CW gave the creators eighteen episodes for the final season to wrap up the story.[86] *Crazy Ex-Girlfriend* remains a critical darling with a fervent fan following.

Commentary

With *Crazy Ex-Girlfriend*, writer and comedian Rachel Bloom successfully revived the television musical, which seemed dead following the end of *Glee*. The show, which appealed to theater kids and comedy nerds alike, mixed genres with unmatched ease, balancing comedy, drama, and catchy songs in every episode. In addition, *Crazy Ex-Girlfriend* offered up nuanced portrayals of women's relationships and mental health issues. The show regularly tackled complex topics like anxiety, depression, suicide, and substance abuse with a combination of frankness, sensitivity, and compassion. It wrapped these serious issues in a colorful, bubbly package filled with witty observational humor, quirky characters, and lavish musical numbers. From the opening theme song that changed with every new season (sample lyric: "Meet Rebecca, she's too hard to summarize"), *Crazy Ex-Girlfriend* promised big fun tempered with brutal honesty and plenty of touching moments, thereby eliciting equal amounts of laughs and tears from the show's devoted audience. Over the course of four tune-filled seasons, Rebecca and her pals struggled to find happiness while dealing with a variety of emotional traumas including heartbreak, disappointment, and general uncertainty.

While *Crazy Ex-Girlfriend* often dealt with heavy subject matter (including Greg's alcoholism and Rebecca's diagnosis of borderline personality disorder), the show never failed to bring the laughs with its uproarious dialogue and boisterous musical numbers. Starting with the first episode, "Josh Just Happens to Live Here," *Crazy Ex-Girlfriend* established itself as one of the funniest and most original TV series of all time thanks to humorous one-liners like "You're pretty, and you're smart, and you're ignoring me, so you're obviously my type." This episode also features the gut-busting musical number "The Sexy Getting Ready Song," a clever and candid peek into the reality that lies behind the fantasy of a woman getting dolled up to go out on a date. Other standout episodes include "Josh Is the Man of My Dreams, Right?" (S2E11), which features "The Santa Ana Winds" (a breezy tune performed by Eric Michael Roy in the style of Frankie Valli and the Four Seasons) and "Getting over Jeff" (S3E7), in which Donna briefly reconnects with an old flame and pays tribute to Abba with the toe-tapping (not to mention utterly sidesplitting) song "The First Penis I Saw." Brash humor, cheeky tunes, and heartwarming drama all turned *Crazy Ex-Girlfriend* into a dearly loved cult smash.

See also *Veronica Mars* (2004–Present)

THE CRITIC (1994–2001)

Creators: Al Jean, Mike Reiss
Cast: Jon Lovitz (Jay Sherman), Christine Cavanaugh (Marty Sherman), Nancy Cartwright (Margo Sherman), Charles Napier (Duke Phillips), Doris Grau (Doris Grossman), Maurice LaMarche (Jeremy Hawke), Gerritt Graham (Franklin Sherman), Judith Ivey (Eleanor Sherman), Tress MacNeille (Various)
Genre: Comedy

Synopsis

Snobbish New York film critic Jay Sherman deals with his dysfunctional family and wacky co-workers while reviewing films for his show *Coming Attractions*.

Production History

While working as showrunners on *The Simpsons,* Al Jean and Mike Reiss wanted to produce their own series.[87] They developed an idea with James L. Brooks for a live-action television series about the exploits of a snooty film critic, envisioning Jon Lovitz in the role.[88] They wrote the pilot script before approaching Lovitz,[89] who refused to commit to a live-action series.[90] At that point, Jean and Reiss decided to do an animated series instead[91] but one unlike *The Simpsons* and its 1990s copycats.[92] Working backward, the duo hired David Silverman, who developed lead character Jay Sherman, basing his looks on Andy Kaufman.[93] Brooks helped Jean and Reiss secure a deal with ABC, negotiating an order for thirteen episodes.[94]

Titled *The Critic,* the series premiered on January 26, 1994, and aired Wednesday nights after the successful *Home Improvement.*[95] However, with jokes poking fun at Manhattan and popular movies, combined with an unlikable main character, the series failed to catch on with viewers,[96] some of whom even sent hate mail to the network during the first season.[97] Unable to capitalize on its lead-in, ABC cancelled *The Critic* mid-season so Reiss and Jean brought it to Fox, where it aired after *The Simpsons.*[98] While it fared better in the ratings, the network's new president, John Matoian, hated the show.[99] After five episodes, Fox moved the series to a different time slot[100] and before canceling it in May 1995.[101] *The Critic* occasionally appears in syndication on Comedy Central and even generated a "poorly received webseries" in 2000–2001.[102] Despite the show's failure with viewers, Lovitz remains committed to reviving the show and has even pitched a live-action version to Netflix.[103]

Commentary

Despite its brief run, *The Critic* inspired intense devotion from fans, who recite lines from the show to this day. With its madcap characters, knowing pop culture parodies, and hilarious jokes ("You got a very valid point. But on the other hand, shut up"), *The Critic* seemed destined for cult status from the start. Created by *The Simpsons* showrunners Al Jean and Mike Reiss (who both contributed several scripts to the show during its two-year run), *The Critic* boasted an incredible lineup of writers, performers, and directors, all of whom helped turn the show into a cherished cult classic. In addition to Jean and Reiss, the writer's room included the likes of Judd Apatow, Steven Levitan, and Nell Scovell. Meanwhile, the voice cast included *Saturday Night Live* star Jon Lovitz as lead character Jay Sherman, *The Simpsons* alum Nancy Cartwright as Jay's loving sister Margo, veteran character actor Gerrit Graham as Jay's eccentric dad Franklin, and voice-acting legends Maurice LaMarche and Tress MacNeille as various characters who popped up throughout the show's run. In addition, animators Gregg Vanzo, Rich Moore, and David Cutler all directed episodes of *The Critic,* while celebrated composer Hans Zimmer wrote the theme song. Though short-lived, *The Critic* nevertheless endures as one of the most beloved animated comedies of all time thanks to the talent involved in its creation.

Of course, while the show cultivated a rabid cult audience, it failed to catch on with a wide audience due its singular sense of humor, a mixture of deft observational comedy and extreme wackiness. Set mainly in Manhattan, *The Critic* lovingly mocked that fabled metropolis with gags about television shows designed to teach English to cab drivers or *New York Daily News* columnist Jimmy Breslin overseeing a pre-school classroom. Such jokes helped establish the show's identity as rooted in the New York comedy tradition of both Woody Allen and *Seinfeld*. The series also served up zany parodies of popular movies, including *Home Alone 5* (a twenty-three-year-old Kevin McAllister discovers that his parents have left him behind yet again), *Forrest Gump 2: Gump Harder* (the titular character meets President Bill Clinton), and *Jurassic Park 2: Revenge of the Raptors* (the title beasts develop arrogant intelligence). In addition, *The Critic* delivered memorable zingers like "I'm about to take off my shirt. A feeling of mild nausea is normal" (Jay delivers this warning before bedding a paramour in S1E4, "Miserable") and "We'll just have to find out what you are good at. In my case, it's complaining about movies that bring happiness to idiots" (Jay offers this fatherly advice to Marty in S1E11, "A Day at the Race and a Night at the Opera"). While some jokes aged poorly (the show frequently fat-shames Jay), many fans still consider *The Critic* one of the funniest animated sitcoms ever made.

See also *Family Guy* (1999–Present), *Futurama* (1999–2013), *Home Movies* (1999–2004)

D

DARIA (1997–2001)

Creators: Glenn Eichler, Susie Lewis Lynn
Cast: Tracy Grandstaff (Daria Morgendorffer), Wendy Hoopes (Jane Lane/Quinn Morgendorffer/Helen Morgendorffer), Julian Rebolledo (Jake Morgendorffer), Lisa Kathleen Collins (Brittany Taylor), Marc Thompson (Kevin Thompson), Jessica Cydnee Jackson (Jodie Landon), Paul Williams (Michael Jordan Mackenzie), Alvaro J. Gonzalez (Trent Lane), Geoffrey Arend (Charles "Upchuck" Ruttheimer III), John Lynn (Sick Sad World Announcer)
Genre: Comedy, Drama, Romance

Synopsis

Two cynical teenage girls experience high school from an outsider perspective.

Production History

The Daria Morgendorffer character first appeared on the MTV series *Beavis and Butt-Head* in 1996 in an episode that saw the demented duo mock her with a taunt of "Diarrhea, cha cha cha," thereby demonstrating MTV's problem attracting a female audience.[1] Around that same time, MTV executives set out to greenlight pilots for shows intended to reach girls and young women, and they asked Abby Terkuhle, president of MTV Animation, to create a spinoff centered on Daria.[2] Writers Glenn Eichler and Susie Lewis originally created the character, and when *Beavis and Butt-Head* wrapped, series creator Mike Judge left Eichler and Lewis in charge of the spinoff show.[3] The *Daria* pilot tested well with audiences[4] so MTV ordered thirteen episodes.[5] The new series debuted on the network on March 3, 1997.[6]

Daria aired on Monday nights at 10:30, earning high ratings for much of its run.[7] During its five years on air, the show consistently averaged just 1 to 2 million viewers, but *Daria* nevertheless "became a signature show for MTV" as it scored "better among television critics and female viewers" than *Beavis and Butt-Head*.[8] Indeed, *Daria* eventually emerged as MTV's longest-running animated series.[9] At the beginning of 2002, MTV aired *Daria*'s final made-for-TV movie in which the gang graduated from high school,[10] bringing an end to their trials and tribulations as high schoolers.[11] In 2019, MTV developed a spin-off focused on Daria's friend Jodie Landon and plans to create other spinoffs designed to expand the "*Daria*-verse."[12]

Commentary

Spinning out of the pop culture phenomenon *Beavis and Butt-Head*, the sweetly sardonic *Daria* ditched the gross-out stoner humor of its iconic predecessor and instead offered a tongue-in-cheek look at teenage life in the late 1990s. The show, which mixed a laid-back vibe with keen observational humor, reflected the concerns of an entire generation through its story of an intelligent young outsider trying to carve out her own identity while navigating a world that leaves her feeling disappointed. The title character, a gifted but cynical teenage girl possessed of a profound intellect and a razor-sharp wit, struggles to make her way through a hostile high school landscape filled with shallow preppies and meat-headed jocks. Meanwhile, her upwardly mobile parents and fashion-conscious (and ultimately more popular) younger sister leave her feeling every bit as alienated. Luckily, Daria soon finds Jane, an equally acerbic young woman with a similar sense of humor and misanthropic outlook. Throughout the show's first three seasons, the disgruntled duo spent most of their time mocking their classmates and complaining about the world around them, but over time they both grew emotionally as they faced various difficult situations and personal revelations. *Daria* packed plenty of laughs into each episode, but it also served up relatable characters and situations.

Of course, the series also made sure to bring the funny thanks to witty writing provided by the likes of Peggy Nicoll, Neena Beber, and series co-creator Glenn Eichler (who went on to write for both *The Colbert Report* and *The Late Show with Stephen Colbert*). During its run, *Daria* delivered hundreds of delightfully scathing zingers that left viewers guffawing with laughter. For instance, in "Quinn the Brain" (S2E3), Daria ridicules her sister with the biting insult "Sometimes your shallowness is so thorough it's almost like depth." Meanwhile, in "The Old and the Beautiful" (S3E3), Daria mocks Jane's excitement about teaching arts and crafts to elderly hospital patients by asking, "Do you think if you breathe on me, I might catch your enthusiasm?" And in "Pinch Sitter" (S1E8), when asked to babysit a pair of creepily nice children, Daria explains, "I don't like kids. I didn't even like kids when I was a kid." Such humor endeared the show to Generation X viewers, who loved the title character's caustic attitude. However, *Daria* made sure to temper the scorn with sweetness, especially in later seasons as Daria sought to better understand her family and classmates. Ultimately, *Daria* offered a lighthearted look at some heavy topics, which may explain why fans love it to this day.

See also *Freaks and Geeks* (1999–2000), *Home Movies* (1999–2004), *My So-Called Life* (1994–1995)

DARK SHADOWS (1966–1971)

Creator: Dan Curtis
Cast: Jonathan Frid (Barnabas Collins), Grayson Hall (Julia Hoffman), Alexandra
    Isles (Victoria Winters), Nancy Barrett (Carolyn Stoddard), Joan Bennett (Elizabeth
    Collins Stoddard), Louis Edmonds (Roger Collins), David Selby (Quentin Collins)
Genre: Drama, Fantasy, Horror, Mystery, Romance, Science Fiction, Thriller

---

Synopsis

A cursed family confronts its supernatural history.

Production History

Dan Curtis reportedly came up with the idea for *Dark Shadows* in the summer
of 1965 when he dreamed about a girl with long dark hair visiting a large, bleak
house.[13] With encouragement from his wife, Curtis turned the idea into a television show, incorporating the imagery from his eerie dream into the script for the
first episode.[14] Curtis pitched the show to executives at ABC, who greenlit the
production as a daytime soap opera.[15] Television stalwart Art Wallace (who later
claimed that the show arose out of a script he previously wrote for an anthology
series[16]) wrote the series' story bible and served as head writer while Lela Swift,
John Sedwick, and Henry Kaplan all accepted offers to direct episodes. Meanwhile,
Curtis served as the series' primary ideas man though he wrote and directed few
episodes.[17] The first episode of *Dark Shadows* premiered June 27, 1966, to lackluster ratings, but the series nevertheless amassed a devoted fanbase of housewives,
younger viewers, and celebrities like Joanne Woodward and Neil Simon.[18]

The show suffered from a low budget, and episodes routinely featured flubbed
lines, stray insects, wobbly sets, and careless technicians wandering in the background.[19] To combat the first season's low ratings, Curtis took the advice of his
children and increased the supernatural elements, leading to the appearance of
fan-favorite character Barnabas Collins in April 1967.[20] From then on, the show
borrowed from horror classics written by genre luminaries like Henry James, Edgar Allan Poe, and H. P. Lovecraft.[21] At that point, ratings doubled, with roughly
20 million viewers tuning in by the end of the decade.[22] At its peak, *Dark Shadows*
spawned board games, Halloween costumes, trading cards, soundtrack records,
paperback tie-ins, and even a comic book series.[23] It also inspired two feature films
that hit theaters in 1970 and 1971, but they failed to prevent the show's ratings from
declining to season 1 levels.[24] In 1991, NBC revived *Dark Shadows* as a nighttime
drama but cancelled it after just twelve episodes, while in 2004 the WB Network
announced another revival that never aired.[25] In 2012, Warner Bros. released a
critically reviled *Dark Shadows* feature film adaptation directed by Tim Burton and
starring Johnny Depp as Barnabas but it bombed at the box office. The property has
lain dormant since, though the original series continues to bewitch fans to this day.

Commentary

By replacing the standard conventions of melodrama with overtly supernatural storylines, *Dark Shadows* radically changed the landscape of daytime television. The show contributed to the rise of gothic storytelling and helped establish the vampire as both a sympathetic character and an antiheroic sex symbol.[26] Each week, *Dark Shadows* served up spooky, serialized tales that nevertheless emphasized the same sort of themes found in other daytime dramas, namely, "family life, personal relationships, sexual dramas, emotional and moral conflicts."[27] As such, the show made history as "the first soap opera to incorporate genuinely supernatural elements into its storyline."[28] Despite the darkness of the stories, the show kept things light by adopting a campy, playful tone that prevented episodes from becoming too gloomy. By drawing heavily on the horror tales and gothic literature of the nineteenth and early twentieth centuries, *Dark Shadows* broke the mold of the traditional soap opera and influenced horror shows for decades afterward.

Of course, the introduction of Barnabas Collins transformed the show from a campy curiosity into an enduring cult phenomenon. As portrayed by Shakespearean actor Jonathan Frid, Barnabas helped establish the trope of the tragic vampire who loathes his existence and actively seeks a way to end it yet continues living. Over nearly six hundred episodes, Frid, with his haunted eyes and cadaverous good looks, imbued Barnabas with both pathos and sex appeal, turning the character into one of the most popular bloodsuckers of all time. Sporting a swirling

After two hundred years in the grave, suave vampire Barnabas Collins (Jonathan Frid, left) returns to deal with the curse placed upon his family by a jealous witch. *ABC/Photofest*

cape, severe eyebrows, and a refined air, Frid hammed it up while delivering excessively purple dialogue like "For most men, time moves slowly, oh so slowly, they don't even realize it. But time has revealed itself to me in a very special way. Time is a rushing, howling wind that rages past me, withering me in a single, relentless blast, and then continues on." Yet *Dark Shadows* also offered other captivating characters (including mysterious psychologist Julia Hoffman and the goodhearted Victoria Winters) and engrossing storylines that featured zombies, ghosts, time travel, and other fantastical elements. These ingredients all guarantee *Dark Shadows* a long afterlife as one of the all-time great cult TV shows.

See also *Kolchak: The Night Stalker* (1974–1975), *Supernatural* (2005–2020), *True Blood* (2008–2014)

DARKWING DUCK (1991–1992)

Creator: Tad Stones
Cast: Jim Cummings (Darkwing Duck/Negaduck), Terence McGovern (Launchpad McQuack), Christine Cavanaugh (Gosalyn Waddlemeyer-Mallard), Katie Leigh (Honker Muddlefoot), Susan Tolsky (Binkie Muddlefoot), Dan Castellaneta (Megavolt), Tino Insana (Dr. Reginald Bushroot), Kath Soucie (Morgana Macawber)
Genre: Action, Comedy, Mystery, Science Fiction

Synopsis

By day, wealthy playboy Drake Mallard raises his adopted daughter Gosalyn, but by night he defends the city of St. Canard from evil as the superhero Darkwing Duck.

Production History

In 1989, Walt Disney executive Jeffrey Katzenberg tasked Tad Stones with developing a new series inspired by the *DuckTales* episode "Double-O-Duck," which parodied the James Bond films.[29] However, Stones soon learned that the producers of the Bond franchise owned the "Double-O" name, thus preventing Disney from using it in the title.[30] Stones retooled the idea, turning the lead character into a superhero named Darkwing Duck.[31] Inspired by pulp adventurers like Doc Savage, the Green Hornet, and the Shadow, Stones came up with the idea of a superhero raising a brave little girl who refuses to stay at home.[32] He then created the catchphrase "Let's get dangerous!" and told his story editor to include it in every episode.[33] Disney executives initially worried about the show's slapstick-style humor, but they settled down after seeing the success of Warner Bros.' *Tiny Toon Adventures*, a silly homage to the cartoons of the past.[34]

After a trial run on the Disney Channel,[35] *Darkwing Duck* premiered on the second season of the Disney Afternoon in 1991.[36] Later that year the show made the leap to ABC's Saturday morning line-up.[37] Not long after, *Darkwing Duck* made history by becoming the first American cartoon broadcast in the Soviet Union.[38] The show also earned nominations for Outstanding Animated Programming Emmys in 1992 and 1993.[39] Despite all that acclaim, *Darkwing Duck* consistently earned low ratings, leading Disney to cancel it after just two years.[40] Nevertheless, Disney produced a total of ninety-one episodes because ABC ordered two additional thirteen-episode seasons to air on Saturday mornings.[41] In 2011, BOOM! Studios launched an ongoing *Darkwing Duck* comic book series, while Joe Books released their own series in 2016.[42] Three years later, the rebooted *DuckTales* revived the character in the 2019 episode "The Duck Knight Returns!"[43]

Commentary

Long before superheroes dominated popular culture, *Darkwing Duck* offered viewers a tongue-in-cheek sendup of Silver Age comic books.[44] Using the same blend of comedy and action that helped make *DuckTales* a huge success, *Darkwing Duck* married the grittiness of 1990s comics with the goofiness of 1950s comics and the family-relationship focus of 1960s comics. The series deconstructed caped crusaders and their exploits, a common tactic in the comic book industry but something entirely new to television at that time. More importantly, though, *Darkwing Duck* poked fun at superheroes without undermining the forthright values that made them so important to fans (especially children). Though a bit of a bumbling blowhard prone to comedic mishaps, Drake Mallard refuses to back down when facing off against nefarious evildoers such as Megavolt, Bushroot, or Negaduck. *Darkwing Duck* turned many 1990s kids into superhero fanatics by portraying the wacky adventures of a terror that flaps in the night but one possessed of a heart of gold and a fighting spirit.

Each episode of *Darkwing Duck* mixed the grim tone of *Batman: The Animated Series* with the extreme silliness of Looney Tunes. The show also introduced viewers to an entire universe of bizarre characters that lampooned the colorful heroes and villains found in the pages of comic books. Together with his misfit sidekicks Gosalyn Waddlemeyer-Mallard and Launchpad McQuack, Darkwing defended his hometown of St. Canard from a cavalcade of wacky villains led by Negaduck, the Duck Knight's dark doppelgänger introduced in a self-titled episode that sees Megavolt split Darkwing into good and evil versions. Other villains include Bushroot, a meek scientist who gains the ability to communicate with and control plants. First introduced in "Beauty and the Beet" (S1E3), the character pays homage to floral-based supervillains such as Poison Ivy and the Floronic Man. In addition to parodying comic books, *Darkwing Duck* also satirized other TV shows, including *Twin Peaks* (S1E44, "Twin Beaks"), and even poked some good-natured fun at parent company Disney (S1E42, "Twitching Channels"). Self-aware humor and memorable characters make *Darkwing Duck* a great cult TV show.

See also *Gargoyles* (1994–1996), *The Tick* (1994–1997)

SPOTLIGHT: DISNEY AFTERNOON

In late 1984, Michael Eisner sought to reinvigorate the Walt Disney Company's animation division.[45] In 1985, the studio produced cartoons specifically for television starting with *Adventures of the Gummi Bears* followed by *DuckTales* two years later.[46] In 1989, Disney created an hour-long block of syndicated original animation for weekly afternoon broadcasts, which they later expanded to a two-hour block called the Disney Afternoon.[47] The initial line-up consisted of *Chip 'n' Dale Rescue Rangers, Disney's Adventures of the Gummi Bears, DuckTales*, and *TaleSpin*.[48] Other new series soon followed, including *Darkwing Duck* (1991), *Goof Troop* (1992), and *Gargoyles* (1994).[49] In 1997, Disney decided to move their original animated series to the Disney Channel, thus bringing an end to the Disney Afternoon.[50]

DEADWOOD (2004–2006)

Creator: David Milch
Cast: Ian McShane (Al Swearengen), Timothy Olyphant (Seth Bullock), Brad Dourif (Doc Cochran), Molly Parker (Alma Garret), John Hawkes (Sol Starr), Paula Malcomson (Trixie), W. Earl Brown (Dan Dority), William Sanderson (E. B. Farnum), Robin Weigert (Calamity Jane), Jeffrey Jones (A. W. Merrick), Kim Dickens (Joanie Stubbs), Powers Boothe (Cy Tolliver), Dayton Callie (Charlie Utter), Jim Beaver (Whitney Ellsworth)
Genre: Drama, Western

Synopsis

A former U.S. marshal moves to the newly settled town of Deadwood, South Dakota, to start a hardware business but instead finds only deep-rooted corruption.

Production History

In 2002, David Milch, previously a writer and producer on gritty cop shows like *Hill Street Blues* and *NYPD Blue*,[51] approached HBO with an idea for a show about cops set in Ancient Rome. The network was already developing *Rome*, but executives asked Milch to rework his idea as a Western set in the mining town of Deadwood, South Dakota.[52] Milch agreed and spent the next two years researching his new series, turning some historical figures into characters and basing others on real people or on the types of folks who had lived in Deadwood in the past. He also investigated the life of newspaper magnate William Randolph Hearst and incorporated the tycoon's story into the narrative by tweaking some historical events.[53] Famed action director Walter Hill helmed the pilot episode of *Deadwood*, which premiered on HBO on March 21, 2004.[54]

Milch originally wanted *Deadwood* to run for four years, the same amount of time that the eponymous town remained an unincorporated city before joining the Dakota territory.[55] However, at the start of the third season, HBO opted not to renew contracts and instead announced plans for two two-hour *Deadwood* movies scheduled to air on the network in 2008 following negotiations with the show's producers.[56] The network announced *Deadwood*'s cancelation soon after. By that point, the show had emerged as the most expensive weekly series on TV, with each episode budgeted at around $6 million due to the elaborate sets, period costumes, and meticulous production design.[57] Actors also expressed frustration with Milch's methods, which included writing or rewriting scripts minutes before shooting them as well as scrapping or recasting entire sequences or episodes on a whim (for example, Milch ordered much of the third season completely reshot).[58] These days, *Deadwood* enjoys a reputation as one of TV's best shows, and in 2019 HBO aired *Deadwood: The Movie*, written by Milch (who a few weeks before the movie's debut revealed his struggle with Alzheimer's) and directed by series regular Daniel Minahan.[59]

Commentary

Filled with complex characters, florid dialogue, and equal amounts of pathos and humor, *Deadwood* serves up an enthralling tale about the founding of the United States as told through the microcosm of one small South Dakota mining town. The show features dozens of regular or recurring characters, all struggling to reconcile their own base impulses with their desire to create a civilized society while reciting some of the most lyrically filthy dialogue ever written. Premiering in 2004, *Deadwood* helped revitalize the Western genre for the twenty-first century

Ruthless brothel owner Al Swearengen (Ian McShane) keeps a watchful eye on the lawless mining town of Deadwood, South Dakota. *HBO/Photofest*

despite failing to capture a broad audience (which may explain why it rode off into the sunset after just three seasons). Indeed, in the years after the show first aired, dozens of Westerns and neo-Westerns popped up on TV and cinema screens, including *Justified, Hatfields & McCoys, The Assassination of Jesse James by the Coward Robert Ford*, and a remake of *The Magnificent Seven*.

Like all great Westerns, *Deadwood* concerns the tension between civilization and the frontier, a clash that plays out in the heart and mind of every single character on the show. A true ensemble series, *Deadwood* boasts an incredible cast and gives every performer a chance to shine. Standouts include Ian McShane, who portrays brothel owner Al Swearengen as a power-hungry man driven by kindness and a code of honor. Meanwhile, Timothy Olyphant imbues former U.S. marshal Seth Bullock with a seething rage balanced by his desire to help others and enact justice. Robin Weigert plays Calamity Jane as a woman with a tough exterior who cannot hide her fear of abandonment and the emotional scars left by her past pain and trauma. Conversely, Paula Malcolmson's Trixie initially seems like little more than a battered whore-with-a-heart-of-gold, but she quickly establishes herself as a powerful woman fully in charge of her own fate. While many of the performers appeared in numerous other acclaimed projects in the years after, *Deadwood* features some of their best work.

Of course, *Deadwood* is perhaps most famous for its dialogue, which sounds like nothing else on television. Critics often called it Shakespearean,[60] and indeed, creator David Milch wrote many of the lines in iambic pentameter. More importantly, though, he used the dialogue to give voice to the characters' internal tension between their aspiration toward civilization and their baser nature. Many lines feature lyrical turns of phrase that are then contrasted with some of the most creative profanity ever conceived, as when Swearengen describes the businessmen interested in Deadwood as "hypocrite cocksuckers," explaining that "the fuckin' lyin' instruments and tactics they use to fuck people up the ass can be turned against them." Overall, *Deadwood* remains both respected and adored to this day due to its gripping stories, captivating scripts, and lavish production values.

DEGRASSI JUNIOR HIGH (1987–1989)

Creators: Linda Schuyler, Kit Hood
Cast: Pat Mastroianni (Joey Jeremiah), Stefan Brogren (Archie Simpson), Duncan Waugh (Arthur Kobalewscuy), Maureen Deiseach (Heather Farrell), Angela Deiseach (Erica Farrell), Siluck Saysanasy (Yick Yu), Arlene Lott (Nancy Kramer)
Genre: Drama, Romance

Synopsis

Canadian teenagers face daily problems and successes in high school.

Production History

In 1979, school teacher Linda Schuyler produced a half-hour television program based on the children's book *Ida Makes a Movie* but she changed the characters from cats to kids.[61] That special served as the basis for the twenty-six-episode TV series *The Kids of Degrassi Street*, which chronicled the everyday lives of kids in Toronto's East End.[62] A "quasi-documentary project that emerged out of theater workshops with local kids," the show ran for five years before evolving "into the more tightly scripted *Degrassi Junior High*."[63] Co-produced by the Canadian Broadcasting Corporation and Kate Taylor of PBS flagship station WGBH,[64] *Degrassi Junior High* featured a cast of kids chosen from Schuyler's Playing with Time repertory company.[65] More than fifty kids participated in the workshop, and each season "about twenty more kids would go through workshops and a handful would be added to the cast."[66]

During the series, the producers and writers developed the characters specifically for the actors, often creating or expanding roles for certain performers.[67] In addition, they frequently incorporated elements from the kids' own lives into the narrative.[68] In 1987, *Degrassi Junior High* won a Gemini Award for Children's Series and an International Emmy for an episode about pregnancy.[69] The following year, numerous PBS stations across the United States started airing the show,[70] which faced increased censorship outside Canada.[71] For instance, PBS edited an episode about abortion, removing scenes featuring anti-abortion protests at an abortion clinic.[72] Meanwhile, the BBC stopped airing *Degrassi Junior High* after viewers complained about episodes centered around teenage pregnancy and lesbian daydreams.[73]

Over the years, the series went through several permutations as the kids aged and the cast changed.[74] The various versions of the show include *The Kids of Degrassi St.* (1980–1986), *Degrassi Junior High* (1987–1989), *Degrassi High* (1989–1992), *Degrassi: The Next Generation* (2001–2009), *Degrassi* (2010–2015), and *Degrassi: Next Class* (2016–Present). *Degrassi Junior High* remains one of the most popular iterations and boasts famous fans such as filmmaker Kevin Smith, comedian Nick Kroll, and actress Ellen Page.[75]

Commentary

Years before shows like *My So-Called Life*, *Daria*, and *Freaks and Geeks* appeared on the scene, *Degrassi Junior High* tackled the topic of teenage angst in a thoughtful, nuanced, and brutally honest fashion. Each week, the show served up authentic stories about real kids confronting serious issues like teen pregnancy, homosexuality, drugs, abuse, epilepsy, and more. *Degrassi Junior High* often felt more like a documentary thanks to its intimate aesthetic and unflinching exploration of sensitive subject matter. The show blazed a trail for all the other teen-oriented dramas that emerged in its wake mainly because it understood teenage culture better than almost any other show produced before or since. *Degrassi Junior High* featured complex characters and cast age-appropriate (and often non-professional) performers in the roles. Young viewers recognized themselves in the show's protagonists and thus developed an intense emotional attachment to them. Throughout the series, characters dealt with various challenges affecting young people including bullying, child abuse, and divorce, all portrayed with an intense realism absent from many other shows about teens. These depictions earned *Degrassi Junior High* numerous awards, but more importantly they ensured the show a long legacy as one of the most acclaimed cult TV series of all time.

Despite some outdated fashions and slang, *Degrassi Junior High* remains relevant thanks to its compassionate and genuine exploration of teen life as well as its willingness to tackle complex topics that still affect young people today. Every episode of the show entertained adolescent viewers while educating them about such sensitive issues as teen sex, drug use, and peer pressure. For example, "The Cover Up" (S1E4) deals with Joey's attempts to help school bully Rick Munro, who suffers abuse at the hands of his cruel father. In "The Great Race" (S1E5), the boys' soccer team challenges the girls' swim team to a swimming race, resulting in a sympathetic examination of body issues that result from teasing. "It Creeps" (S1E14) revolves around resident loner Lucy's efforts to direct an independent feminist horror film starring her pals Simon and Caitlin (collectively known as the Zits). In perhaps the show's most harrowing storyline, the two-part "Bad Blood" (S2E1, S2E2), Dwayne contracts HIV, meaning his classmates must now confront the specter of AIDS head on. A combination of fearlessness and authenticity make *Degrassi Junior High* a lasting fan favorite as well as a great cult TV show.

See also *Buffy the Vampire Slayer* (1997–2003), *Daria* (1997–2001), *Freaks and Geeks* (1999–2000), *My So-Called Life* (1994–1995)

A DIFFERENT WORLD (1987–1993)

Creator: Bill Cosby
Cast: Jasmine Guy (Whitley Gilbert), Kadeem Hardison (Dwayne Wayne), Darryl M. Bell (Ron Johnson), Charnele Brown (Kim Reese), Dawnn Lewis (Jaleesa Vinson), Cree Summer (Freddie Brooks), Lou Myers (Vernon Gaines), Glynn Turman (Colonel Brad Taylor), Sinbad (Coach Walter Oakes), Jada Pinkett-Smith (Lena James), Lisa Bonet (Denise Huxtable)
Genre: Comedy, Drama

Synopsis

Students at a historically black college navigate coursework, relationships, and the social issues facing the United States.

Whitley Gilbert (Jasmine Guy, right) and Dwayne Wayne (Kadeem Hardison, second from right) learn important life lessons while navigating college. *NBC/Photofest*

Production History

Following the success of *The Cosby Show*, NBC executives requested a spinoff series.[76] Bill Cosby responded with *A Different World*, in which eldest Huxtable daughter Denise leaves home to attend a historically black college where she shares a room with a young white woman, thus reversing typical Hollywood tropes.[77] Problems arose almost immediately as the network fired most of the writing staff and hired Anne Beatts to create new material for the first episodes.[78] This new content included creating the characters Whitley Gilbert and Dwayne Wayne and splicing them into already completed episodes.[79] In addition, during the first season, the network ordered the showrunners to avoid referencing race and forgo showing anything academic, resulting in a show "about a black college that wasn't about college and couldn't be black."[80]

A Different World premiered on September 24, 1987, finishing second in the ratings.[81] Critics dismissed the show as boring, juvenile, and unrealistic.[82] At first Cosby took a hands-off approach to the series' production but Phylicia Rashad urged him to get more involved after meeting with the disaffected cast.[83] Additionally, Beatts and Bonet clashed behind the scenes, leading to Beatts's departure in March 1988.[84] Meanwhile, Bonet left the series when she became pregnant largely because Cosby refused to produce a show featuring an unwed mother.[85]

As the show entered its second season, Debbie Allen, an alum of histori-cally black college Howard University, stepped in as showrunner, providing "a much-needed insider perspective on Black college life that spoke intimately to both Black and non-Black audiences."[86] Allen took the writers to several historically black colleges and universities (HBCU) and had them speak with students.[87] At that point, *A Different World* became the "most watched program by African-Americans,"[88] racking up "accolades in the form of over sixteen industry award nominations, as well as an Emmy Award, a People's Choice Award, and numerous NAACP Image Awards in a variety of categories."[89] Nonetheless, falling ratings prompted ABC to put the show on hiatus before canceling it on July 9, 1993.[90] *A Different World*, which featured positive images of African Americans in college, contributed to an increase in HBCU enrollment.[91]

Commentary

When it premiered in 1987, *A Different World* owed its success to its lead-in, *The Cosby Show*. However, the series established its own identity during the second season, which reflected on sociocultural issues such as race, gender, and class. For instance, "Ms. Understanding" (S4E17) explored the treatment of black women by black men. Meanwhile, "Mammy Dearest" (S5E11) considered the racist nature of the Mammy image. "Cat's in the Cradle" (S514) confronted racial prejudice while the season 6 premiere "Honeymoon in L.A." (S6E1) directly addressed the Rodney King beating and the subsequent 1992 Los Angeles riots following the acquittal of the four responsible white officers. *A Different World* also included references to sexual harassment, domestic violence, rape, the AIDS crisis, and even the Per-sian Gulf War.[92] For audiences accustomed to sitcoms that comforted them with escapist fluff, *A Different World* presented a truly different world by addressing the realities its viewers faced every day.

The series also offered black viewers aspirational images and characters because *A Different World* represented college life more realistically than other television shows or films at that time. Seeing a black college experience inspired many fans to attend college and thus work toward the upper-class lifestyle seen on *The Cosby Show*. More significantly, the characters modeled how to handle the tough issues of modern life. While the show's moralizing occasion-ally turned into preachiness,[93] the messages were conveyed by identifiable characters who often generated intense emotional attachment among viewers. For example, Dwayne Wayne modeled how to evolve from a socially awkward nerd to a suave, self-confident scholar. Similarly, Whitley Gilbert demonstrated how to transition from an upper-class snob to an empathic and powerful leader. Each episode of *A Different World* featured multifaceted characters dealing with complex problems, which explains why fans consider it one of the best cult TV shows ever made.

> # *DOCTOR WHO* (1963–PRESENT)
>
> *Creator*: Sydney Newman
> *Cast*: William Hartnell (The Doctor, 1963–1966), Patrick Troughton (The Doctor, 1966–1969), Jon Pertwee (The Doctor, 1970–1974), Tom Baker (The Doctor, 1974–1981), Peter Davison (The Doctor, 1981–1984), Colin Baker (The Doctor, 1984–1986), Sylvester McCoy (The Doctor, 1987–1989), Paul McGann (The Doctor, 1996), Christopher Eccleston (The Doctor, 2005), David Tennant (The Doctor, 2005–2010), Matt Smith (The Doctor, 2010–2013), Peter Capaldi (The Doctor, 2014–2017), Jodie Whittaker (The Doctor, 2018–Present)
> *Genre*: Science Fiction, Drama

Synopsis

A mischievous Time Lord from the planet Gallifrey traverses time and space alongside companions from various worlds and historical periods.

Production History

In December 1962, Sydney Newman, the new head of drama at the BBC, sought to bring more attention to common life in England.[94] Caring little for classical literature and preferring science fiction, Newman developed a program that would "follow the old BBC adage that broadcast programming was meant 'to inform, educate, and entertain.'"[95] Consulting experts, Newman and his team created a series that blended original stories with adaptations of classical literature and science fiction stories.[96] The original pitch contained three characters[97] but Newman rejected it in April 1963 because he wanted to make the dialogue and concepts more understandable to children.[98] Newman then turned the older of the three characters into an alien scientist who absconded with a spaceship that doubles as a time machine.[99] He named this character the Doctor and titled the series *Dr. Who*.[100]

While British television writer and playwright C. E. Webber continued to work on the pitch, Newman assembled his production team,[101] starting with producer Verity Lambert, who agreed on the need to include "morality lessons at the center of the stories."[102] Lambert then cast William Hartnell as the Doctor.[103] At that point, Newman retitled the series *Doctor Who*[104] but Lambert rejected Webber's first script as unproducible (though producers later recycled his idea).[105] Following some rewrites, the first episode, "An Unearthly Child," commenced shooting, though the finished product suffered from numerous technical difficulties, poor direction choices, and underwhelming cast performances.[106] Newman ordered the episode "redone from scratch, even though this would delay the intended November 16 airdate."[107] The first episode of *Doctor Who* finally aired on November 23, 1963, after adjusting for a delay caused by coverage of the Kennedy assassination.[108]

Before its cancelation in 1989, *Doctor Who* ran for a record-breaking twenty-six years, drawing a whopping 110 million viewers around the world at the height of

Renegade Timelord the Doctor (William Hartnell, right) embarks on exciting adventures throughout time and space. *BBC/Photofest*

its popularity.[109] The series arrived in the United States in the 1970s, drawing big ratings by the mid-1980s.[110] Not long after the cancelation of the original series, during the course of which seven different actors played the Doctor, Fox aired a made-for-TV movie starring Paul McGann as the eighth incarnation of the Doctor, seeing it as a possible pilot for a U.S. relaunch of the series.[111] That project failed to materialize, but in September 2003 the BBC announced a reboot overseen by longtime *Doctor Who* fan Russell T. Davies.[112] Produced by BBC Wales and the Canadian Broadcasting Corporation, the new series debuted on March 25, 2005.[113] The show remains popular with viewers around the world.

Commentary

From the beginning, *Doctor Who* appealed to both adults and children because it refused to "patronize or insult the intelligence of children—and therefore is adult enough to appeal to 'grown-ups.'"[114] With each new installment the show served up exciting adventures that educated even as they entertained. While the show's budget often resulted in cheesy effects and stilted action, *Doctor Who* nevertheless boasted smart stories that took viewers on thrilling journeys through time and space. During the show's long history, the writers routinely crafted scripts that explored serious topics and included references designed to appeal to a wide range of viewers. For instance, the Doctor and his companions regularly meet famous historical figures such as William Shakespeare or visit ancient locations like Pompeii. These references use historical, cultural, and social touchstones to reach a broad audience.

Doctor Who also uses politics to connect people. The political ambiguity of both the series and its title character speaks to audiences with different or even opposing political positions. Yet the Doctor frequently espouses liberal and humanist values as he seeks to help others. *Doctor Who* frequently comments on British history, society, and culture via its characters and stories, using the militaristic Daleks to highlight the connections between racism and war, or critiquing the dangers of pre-emptive military strikes via the Silurians, a race of aggressive, reptilian humanoids.[115] Since 1963, *Doctor Who* has presented a progressive viewpoint while exploring complex issues like environmentalism, racism, and sexism.

The most recent revival put this progressivism front and center, featuring a more diverse cast of Doctors and companions. This diversity served as a sly commentary on contemporary British culture, as well as a recognition of how the show's fandom had changed since 1963. To ensure the series' success, producers now acknowledged a range of perspectives, positions, and audiences beyond that of the traditional and stereotypical white male science fiction fan. *Doctor Who* initially set out to educate children on historical and scientific concepts, but over time it evolved to explore thorny sociocultural issues and give voice to marginalized groups, thereby demonstrating why the Doctor continues to captivate audiences even now.

DRAGON BALL Z (1996–2003)

Creator: Akira Toriyama
Cast: Masako Nozawa/Sean Schemmel (Goku), Toshio Furukawa/Christopher Sabat (Piccolo), Mayumi Tanaka/Sonny Strait (Krillin), Ryō Horikawa/Brian Drummond (Vegeta), Masako Nozawa/Stephanie Nadolny (Gohan), Hiromi Tsuru/Tiffany Vollmer (Bulma), Takeshi Kusao/Laura Bailey (Trunks), Kōhei Miyauchi/Mike McFarland (Master Roshi)
Genre: Action, Fantasy, Science Fiction, Thriller

Synopsis

In this long-running martial arts fantasy series, powerful hero Goku embarks on various misadventures as he seeks out the magical wish-granting dragon balls. Along the way, he meets friends, clashes with enemies, and eventually discovers his true origins.

Production History

Animator Akira Toriyama came up with the idea for the original *Dragon Ball* series while watching Jackie Chan movies.[116] Toriyama launched the *Dragon Ball* comic book series in 1984, melding tropes from martial arts cinema with elements from the ancient Chinese legend of the monkey king.[117] The following year, the series made the leap to animation with a show that produced 153 episodes in Japan.[118] However, ratings soon slumped, at which point Kōzō Morishita and Takao Koyama stepped in to reboot the series,[119] making it much more serious and turning the protagonist Goku into an adult.[120] In addition, Toriyama added a Z (the last letter of the alphabet) to the title to suggest an impending end.[121] Premiering on Fuji TV in Japan on April 26, 1989,[122] *Dragon Ball Z* ran longer than its predecessor, airing hundreds of episodes and three movies.[123]

In 1996, Funimation Productions picked up the license to release an English dub of *Dragon Ball Z* in North America, tapping Saban Entertainment to handle television distribution while Pioneer Entertainment oversaw home video distribution.[124] The show debuted in the United States on September 13, 1996, running in syndication on Fox Kids.[125] Two years later, on August 31, 1998, *Dragon Ball Z* moved to Cartoon Network's Toonami block of programming aimed at children ages 6–12.[126] Episodes that aired in the United States were censored and altered from their original versions as Saban refused to distribute the series without changes to cut down on what they perceived as excessive violence.[127] Despite all that, *Dragon Ball Z* attained an unprecedented level of popularity throughout the West largely because it featured "sprawling sagas full of drama, character development, and overblown fight scenes" absent from other children's cartoons of the time.[128] Fans love the show to this day.

Commentary

A combination of gripping, melodramatic storylines and action-packed spectacle helped *Dragon Ball Z* build a massive fan following around the world but especially in the United States, where the show helped usher in a massive manga and anime boom. Ostensibly an animated soap opera,[129] the show appealed to boys, teenagers, and young men thanks to its exhilarating mix of dense mythology, over-the-top action, and captivating characters. Influenced by everything from Chinese folklore to martial arts movies to professional wrestling, *Dragon Ball Z* told a sprawling story that followed dozens of characters as they embarked on exciting adventures and learned valuable lessons about teamwork, loyalty, and trust. The show contributed to the emergence of American anime fanboys who embraced the once-negative designation "otaku," a Japanese term for people with obsessive interests. Western fans flocked to *Dragon Ball Z* because it offered exciting action not found in movies or television shows (animated or otherwise) at that time. The show even inspired several copycats such as *Yu Yu Hakusho*, *Naruto*, and *One Punch Man*, many of which boast huge fan bases of their own (though none ever attained the same level of popularity). In the years since it first burst on the scene, *Dragon Ball Z* continues to spawn numerous memes (including the ubiquitous "It's over 9000!"), thus demonstrating its lasting impact on popular culture.

Over the course of nine seasons and 219 episodes, *Dragon Ball Z* dazzled viewers with dynamic fight sequences and thrilling set pieces while also serving up plenty of rib-tickling comedy and heart-wrenching drama. For instance, in "Goku's Unusual Journey" (S1E4), lead character Goku battles the evil Raditz, leading to a conclusion that left the show's fans reeling. Season 1 culminates with the exciting finale "The Battle Ends" (S1E26), in which Goku's son Gohan uses his newfound ability to transform into a giant ape known as an Oozaru to defeat the powerful villain Vegeta. "The Ultimate Battle" (S3E12) features the first of many clashes between Goku and the nefarious Frieza, a fight that leaves an entire planet in ruins. Meanwhile, in "Spirit Bomb Triumphant" (S9E33), Goku summons a Super Spirit Bomb to stop the absurdly overpowered Majin Buu, who manages to fend off the attack, necessitating Goku's transformation into a Super Saiyan. In the show's touching finale, "Goku's Next Journey" (S9E38), Goku sets off in search of a successor and winds up squaring off against a powerful but unskilled young warrior named Uub. Along the way, *Dragon Ball Z* introduces dozens of unforgettable characters, including Piccolo, Trunks, Krillin, Cell, and Bulma. Subsequent *Dragon Ball* series offered diminishing returns, but *Dragon Ball Z* continues to thrill fans years after the final battle ended.

F

FAMILY GUY (1998–PRESENT)

Creators: Seth McFarlane, David Zuckerman
Cast: Seth McFarlane (Peter Griffin/Stewie Griffin/Brian Griffin/Glenn Quagmire),
   Alex Borstein (Lois Griffin), Seth Green (Chris Griffin), Mila Kunis (Meg Griffin)
Genre: Comedy

Synopsis

A buffoonish but well-meaning husband and father bumbles his way through life with the help of his zany family and screwball neighbors.

Production History

While in college, aspiring animator Seth MacFarlane created the animated short film *Life of Larry* about a schlubby husband, his attractive wife, and their talking dog for his senior thesis.[1] That work landed MacFarlane an offer to work for Hanna-Barbera.[2] While there, the young animator worked on *Dexter's Laboratory* and *Johnny Bravo* until 1996, when he produced a sequel to his thesis film that aired on Cartoon Network.[3] From there, Fox Television hired him to animate interstitials on *MADtv*, and a few years later gave him $50,000 to develop a pilot episode for a new animated series.[4] MacFarlane created the seven-minute pilot in three months, doing all the animation and voice work himself.[5] In May 1998, Fox ordered thirteen episodes of *Family Guy*,[6] making the twenty-five-year-old McFarlane the youngest executive producer in history.[7]

The new show premiered on January 31, 1999, after Super Bowl XXXIII,[8] and that April it entered Fox's Sunday night line-up following *The Simpsons*.[9] Despite initial high ratings, Fox repeatedly shuffled the series around the schedule.[10] Network executives renewed *Family Guy* in 2000 but scheduled it against *Friends*, causing the ratings to nosedive.[11] The network canceled the show the following year,[12] at which point Cartoon Network picked up the series for its Adult Swim programming block and scored huge ratings.[13] This success, combined with strong DVD sales, inspired Fox TV president Gary Newman to renew the show for another season of thirty-five new episodes.[14] *Family Guy* returned to Fox's line-up on May 1, 2005, in the Sunday 9:00 p.m. time slot and has remained there ever since,[15] consistently earning high ratings among males aged 18–49.[16]

Commentary

Family Guy, the foul-mouthed offspring of adult-oriented animated sitcoms like *The Simpsons* and *King of the Hill*, elicits big laughs thanks to a combination of whip-smart jokes and goofy cutaway gags. The show, which survived not one but two cancelations, features a cast of screwy characters who wind up in all sorts of outrageous situations, all while cracking wise and spouting catchphrases like "Freakin' sweet!" or "Whose leg do you have to hump to get a dry martini around here?" As such, *Family Guy* endeared itself to viewers who enjoyed the show's absurd humor and hilarious non-sequiturs. In each episode, the Griffin clan and their pals partake in silly escapades that grow wilder with each season. For instance, in "Da Boom" (S2E3), the Y2K bug leaves the fictional town of Quahog, Rhode Island, a post-apocalyptic wasteland populated by nuclear mutants (and singer/songwriter Randy Newman). A few seasons later, "Meet the Quagmires" (S5E18) sees Peter travel back in time and accidentally change the future so that Lois winds up married to their sex-crazed neighbor Glenn Quagmire. Uproarious exploits like these leave viewers in stitches, and they helped *Family Guy* build a fervent fanbase among animation fans who love nonsensical comedy and risqué entertainment.

The show also features witty writing, with talented comedic writers such as Andrew Goldberg, Teresa Hsiao, Patrick Meighan, Alex Borstein (who also voices Lois), and series creators Seth McFarlane and David Zuckerman all churning out hundreds of sidesplitting (not to mention lewd) jokes on a weekly basis. Every episode of *Family Guy* features gut-busting gags like Stewie's outburst of "Hey, you know this old woman who lived in a shoe, she had so many children, she didn't know what to do? I got something she could do: Get your tubes tied, you kook!" (S13E17, "Fighting Irish"), or Quagmire's observation that when "you're banging eight strangers who responded to a flyer, at some point you're going to look out a window and question every decision you've ever made" (S11E16, "12 and a Half Angry Men"). The show also served up numerous raucous pop culture parodies during its more than twenty years on the air, including a pitch-perfect recreation of the infamous training montage from the film *Rocky IV* (S4E15, "Brian Goes Back to College") and a riff on *Back to the Future* that reveals Doc Brown's racist tendencies (S4E16, "The Courtship of Stewie's Father"). These elements helped turn *Family Guy*—which put series co-creator McFarlane on the map and ushered in a raunchier future for animated comedies—into an enduring cult phenomenon.

See also *The Critic* (1994–2001), *South Park* (1997–Present)

FARSCAPE (1999–2003)

Creator: Rockne S. O'Bannon
Cast: Ben Browder (John Crichton), Claudia Black (Aeryn Sun), Anthony Simcoe (Ka D'Argo), Virginia Hey (Pa'u Zotoh Zhaan), Jonathan Hardy (Dominar Rygel XVI), Gigi Edgley (Chiana), Lani John Tupu (Captain Bialar Crais/Pilot), Wayne Pygram (Scorpius), Paul Goddard (Stark), Melissa Jaffer (Utu-Noranti Pralatong), Raelee Hill (Sikozu Svala Shanti Sugaysi Shanu), Tammy Macintosh (Joolushko Tunai Fenta Hovalis)
Genre: Action, Drama, Science Fiction

Synopsis

During an experimental space mission, an American astronaut is blasted to a distant part of the universe where he teams up with a group of escaped political prisoners to stop an evil empire from conquering the entire galaxy.

Production History

In 1993, Brian Henson and Rockne S. O'Bannon developed a space series focused more on alien characters and less on spaceship fights, thus utilizing all the abilities of the Jim Henson Creature Shop.[17] Rather than another *Star Trek* clone, the duo wanted something along the lines of the Mos Eisley Cantina sequence from *Star Wars* on a weekly basis.[18] In the fall of 1993, they brought this idea, originally called *Space Chase*, to Fox Network. Executives asked for a pilot episode but refused to pay for it, instead providing just enough money to develop four more scripts and the creature designs.[19] Henson and O'Bannon returned to Fox in June 1994 only to discover new executives who no longer wanted the show.[20]

Undeterred, Henson continued pitching the series until the Sci-Fi Channel picked it up.[21] After reading two of O'Bannon's scripts, network president Rod Perth decided the show seemed like a good fit for the channel.[22] Network executives granted the producers creative freedom but stressed that they wanted a show aimed at adults rather than kids.[23] At the same time, Australian film and television producer Matt Carroll helped Henson and O'Bannon secure production in Australia.[24] The Jim Henson Company teamed with Hallmark Entertainment (a regular Henson Company co-production partner) and Australia's Nine Films and Television to produce the new show.[25] With the deal made official in January 1998, production on the series began May 1, 1998,[26] at which point the title changed from *Space Chase* to *Farscape*.[27]

The first episode debuted on March 19, 1999.[28] *Farscape* immediately developed a cult fanbase but struggled to find popularity with a wider American audience.[29] Additionally, the show proved expensive, costing about $1.2 million per episode. Despite ordering a fourth and fifth season simultaneously, Sci-Fi unexpectedly canceled *Farscape* after season 4, airing the last episode on March 21, 2003.[30] Around that time, a group of German investors bought the Henson Company and decided to pull the plug on the expensive series.[31] Fans launched a "Save

Farscape" campaign, prompting the Sci-Fi Channel to produce and air the miniseries *Farscape: Peacekeeper Wars* in 2004.[32] In the years since, *Farscape* has spawned tie-in novels, comic books, games, action figures, and more.

Commentary

While something of an acquired taste, *Farscape* offered viewers a fun romp through a distant galaxy filled with memorable characters, thrilling stories, and cutting-edge (for the time) effects. Due to the involvement of the Jim Henson Company, the show featured highly detailed animatronic puppets starting with lead characters Rygel and Pilot (who both grew more expressive and convincing with each season). From the creepy Halosians to the reptilian Scarrans, *Farscape* boasted some of the most impressive practical effects ever on television. Yet the show also used some thoroughly convincing computer-generated imagery to create epic space vistas, tense intergalactic battles, and even some of the aliens that the crew encounter (such as the massive Budong, a gigantic predatory beast that swallows starships whole). Through a combination of convincing puppets and dazzling computer graphics, *Farscape* transported viewers to a spectacular new universe every single week.

Of course, even the best effects cannot compensate for a lack of compelling characters and interesting stories. Thankfully, *Farscape* featured both, offering up sympathetic heroes and complex villains who all took part in wild adventures both exciting and heart wrenching. Ben Browder played central character John

After a wormhole sends him to the other side of the universe, dashing astronaut John Crichton (Ben Browder, left) searches for a way home with the help of his extraterrestrial companions. *SCI FI Channel/Photofest*

Crichton as an affable lunkhead whose dashing good looks belied a brilliant mind and a compassionate soul. Claudia Black, meanwhile, brought pathos to her role as former Peacekeeper Officer Aeryn Sun, expertly conveying the character's inner conflict as she struggled to navigate her newfound emotions. Browder and Black also used their scorching chemistry to turn the burgeoning attraction between their characters into one of the sexiest slow-burn romances in science fiction history. They were supported by Anthony Simcoe, Virginia Hey, and Gigi Edgley, who all turned in excellent performances under heavy makeup, while Lani John Tupu and Wayne Pygram delivered multifaceted turns as the series' central antagonists. Throughout *Farscape*'s four seasons, the characters embarked on exciting adventures as when Crichton and his pals try to rob a heavily guarded interstellar bank, or when Crichton and Chiana find themselves trapped inside a virtual world populated by alternate versions of their friends. More than a showcase for trailblazing special effects, *Farscape* also featured captivating characters and thrilling tales.

Farscape appealed to sci-fi fans looking for fun stories, exhilarating action, scary situations, and romantic relationships. Despite failing to attract a wide audience, the show nevertheless helped establish the Sci-Fi Channel (or as it is known these days, the Syfy Channel) as a home for amusingly original science fiction series that push the envelope in terms of effects and storytelling.

See also *Babylon 5* (1994–1998)

FAWLTY TOWERS (1975–1979)

Creators: John Cleese, Connie Booth
Cast: John Cleese (Basil Fawlty), Prunella Scales (Sybil Fawlty), Andrew Sachs (Manuel), Connie Booth (Polly Sherman), Ballard Berkeley (Major Gowen), Gilly Flower (Miss Agatha Tibbs), Renee Roberts (Miss Ursula Gatsby)
Genre: Comedy

Synopsis

A put-upon hotel owner hatches hair-brained schemes while dealing with his domineering wife, wacky staff, and misfit guests.

Production History

John Cleese reportedly developed the idea for *Fawlty Towers* after he and other members of Monty Python visited a hotel run by a manager who openly scorned his guests.[33] When Cleese left Monty Python to collaborate on other projects with his wife Connie Booth, he used this experience as the basis for a new sitcom that he pitched to executives at the BBC.[34] While writing the first episode, Cleese repurposed an idea he previously wrote for a 1971 sitcom called *Doctor at Large*.[35] He sent the script for the pilot episode to a script editor at the BBC, who informed his bosses that the new sitcom sounded like a potential disaster.[36] Luckily for Cleese,

Impatient hotel owner Basil Fawlty (John Cleese, left) grows increasingly exasperated as he deals with his overbearing wife, oddball staff, and irritating guests. *BBC/Photofest*

BBC executives ignored this warning and greenlit *Fawlty Towers*.[37] The pilot episode, starring Cleese as smug hotelier Basil Fawlty, filmed in December 1974 and aired on BBC2 at 9:00 p.m. on September 19, 1975.[38]

The first episode of *Fawlty Towers* left critics unimpressed; for instance, the reviewer at the *Daily Mirror* declared that the show lacked humor.[39] However, in an unprecedented move BBC2 rebroadcast the episode less than three months later while BBC1 aired it seven months after that,[40] helping the show build an audience. Cleese and Booth wrote the entire first series, working hard to bring the laughs while also making Basil somewhat sympathetic.[41] The BBC commissioned a second series that aired in 1979, four years after the first series ended.[42] Cleese and Booth separated in 1976 but spent the following year writing series 2.[43] Around that time, public TV stations in the United States picked up *Fawlty Towers*, which earned a cult following among American viewers.[44] Cleese and Booth divorced in September 1978,[45] just a few months before the second series of *Fawlty Towers* premiered on February 19, 1979.[46] Despite its rocky start and tumultuous behind-the-scenes drama, *Fawlty Towers*, which came back briefly in 2016 as a live stage show written by Cleese,[47] delights fans even now.

Commentary

Though it initially struggled to find an audience, *Fawlty Towers* eventually emerged as a classic British comedy beloved by audiences on both sides of the Atlantic. The show especially resonated with Monty Python fans outside the United Kingdom, who helped turn it into a cult smash. Every episode of *Fawlty Towers* elicits uproarious laughter thanks to the singular comedic sensibilities of co-creator John Cleese, who plays lead character Basil Fawlty, a blustering incompetent who dreams of giving a touch of class to his rundown hotel but repeatedly sabotages his own efforts. Of course, one cannot overlook Connie Booth's contribution to the show as she reportedly wrote much of the dialogue spoken by Basil's stern wife, Sybil (Prunella Scales). Indeed, while *Fawlty Towers* focuses mainly on Basil and his hilariously inept schemes (and specifically the fallout caused by them), the show was a true ensemble comedy, with each member of the cast contributing to the laughs (especially Andrew Sachs as the lovable but culturally insensitive bellboy, Manuel). Yet audiences mainly tuned in to see Basil fail spectacularly, and Cleese delivered huge laughs with a manic performance that veered from loudmouthed anger to simpering fear to resigned sadness, often in a single line. *Fawlty Towers* served as a showcase for the outspoken Monty Python alum, who turned a show viewed as a risky venture into an enduring cult hit.[48]

With its high-strung lead character who often berated both hotel staff and guests, *Fawlty Towers* also demonstrated the importance of the unlikeable but sympathetic protagonist, a model followed by numerous other shows in the years after, including hit dramas like *The Sopranos*, *Mad Men*, and *Breaking Bad*. Cleese played Basil as a truly loathsome character who belittled others just to make himself feel important. He routinely spat out blistering insults like "Sounds like somebody machine-gunning a seal" (referring to his wife's laugh) or "Can't we get you on *Mastermind*, Sybil? Next contestant: Sybil Fawlty from Torquay. Specialist subject: The Bleeding Obvious." He also repeatedly demeaned Manuel with culturally specific putdowns like "We have a Spanish porter at the moment, he's from Barcelona. It'd be quicker to train an ape." and "Stupidissimo! Continental cretin!" As such, audiences loved to see the character get his comeuppance when his conniving inevitably went awry. For instance, in "The Builders" (S1E2), Basil winds up paying double for renovations because he ignores Sybil's advice not to hire the inexpensive but incompetent O'Reilly and his equally daft crew. Meanwhile, "The Hotel Inspectors" (S1E4) sees Basil's abusive tendencies once again come back to bite him when he mistreats a guest in front of three hotel inspectors. *Fawlty Towers* achieved cult status because it featured riotously funny humor and a gifted comedian playing a character that viewers loved to hate.

See also *Monty Python's Flying Circus* (1969–1974)

FRAGGLE ROCK (1983–1987)

Creator: Jim Henson
Cast: Jerry Nelson (Gobo/Pa Gorg/Marjory the Trash Heap), Steve Whitmire (Wembley/Sprocket the Dog), Dave Goelz (Boober/Uncle Traveling Matt), Karen Prell (Red), Kathryn Mullen (Mokey), Gerard Parkes (Doc), Richard Hunt (Junior Gorg), Myra Fried (Ma Gorg, 1983), Cheryl Wagner (Ma Gorg, 1984–1987)
Genre: Adventure, Comedy, Fantasy, Musical

Gobo (center) and his pals sing, play, and learn important life lessons down in Fraggle Rock. *HBO/ Photofest*

Synopsis

The denizens of Fraggle Rock embark on various adventures and learn important life lessons along the way.

Production History

In October 1980, legendary puppeteer Jim Henson came up with an idea for a new children's show in between finishing *The Great Muppet Caper* and starting *The Dark Crystal*.[49] In May 1981, Henson and his team brainstormed the new series that would feature three different Muppet species living together in harmony.[50] Henson used the notes from these brainstorming sessions to create *Woozle World*. He tasked his team with developing the world of the new series, but first they needed to think up a new title since A. A. Milne used "woozles" in his book *Winnie-the-Pooh*.[51] The team eventually came up with "Fraggles" and spent the summer of 1981 creating the world of *Fraggle Rock*.[52] While shooting the show, Henson and his team employed new puppeteering technologies developed during the making of *The Dark Crystal*.[53] Michael Frith, creative director for Jim Henson Productions, designed the five main characters, and in November Henson asked the major Muppet performers to develop their characters. Bernie Brillstein pitched the series to different television networks but ordered *Fraggle Rock* put into pre-production before securing a firm deal with any of them.[54]

Brillstein eventually sold the series to HBO. Network executives thought *Fraggle Rock* could help expand the channel's base, and they offered to co-produce the show with Henson Associates, Britain's Television South, and the Canadian Broadcasting Corporation.[55] HBO wanted the show to debut in January 1983 so in March 1982 Henson traveled to Toronto to oversee production.[56] He directed seven episodes and performed several recurring characters during the first season but eventually handed full control over to the *Fraggle* team.[57] He even gave Frith more creative freedom over the designs for the series.[58] *Fraggle Rock* premiered on January 10, 1983, earning high ratings and much critical praise. The show ran for five years and aired in more than ninety countries including the Soviet Union starting in 1989.[59] HBO broadcast the final episode of *Fraggle Rock* in May 1987, though Henson produced four additional episodes to meet the numbers for syndication and wrap up the storyline.[60] The show ended long ago, but the Fraggles continue to dance and frolic in the hearts of viewers.

Commentary

With *Fraggle Rock*, Jim Henson moved beyond the boundaries of the Muppets, the characters that turned him into a household name, and created a show that offered the same sort of wacky humor and memorable songs melded with a gentle spirit and wide-eyed sense of discovery. The show features endearing characters who set off on all sorts of adventures in each episode, sometimes thrilling, sometimes touching, but always lighthearted and fun. As with other Henson productions, *Fraggle Rock* features top-notch puppetry, and the expressive characters frolic through highly detailed sets, cracking wise (in "I Don't Care," S1E15, after accidentally spilling juice on Boober's speech, Wembley tries to decipher page 62: "I think it says, uh, 'bliffenstimmers'"), imparting wisdom ("The magic is always there, as long as we keep looking for it," Uncle Traveling Matt explains in "Junior Faces the Music," S4E5), and singing catchy tunes (such as the upbeat "Pukka Pukka Pukka Squeetily Boink"). Viewers of all ages embraced *Fraggle Rock* because it contained equal amounts of thrilling adventure, heartfelt emotion, and pleasant humor.

The show also focused on educating its young viewers but in a much less direct way than its long-running forebear, *Sesame Street*. In *Fraggle Rock*, the character Traveling Matt embarks on adventures in "outer space," the name the Fraggles give to the realm that exists beyond the boundaries of their cavernous home. Throughout the series, Matt observes the humans around him, sending Gobo postcards detailing their actions. Matt served as a surrogate for young viewers (the character was about the same size as the average four- or five-year-old) as he explored the world with a sense of wonder and curiosity. *Fraggle Rock* thereby helped children understand the world and their place in it. More importantly, *Fraggle Rock* left Matt's whereabouts ambiguous, allowing children around the world to identify with the character and his experiences. Indeed, the show went to great lengths to appeal to an international audience of children and adults as everyone involved in the production wanted to entertain and educate viewers of all ages on a global scale. Though the Fraggles seem forever destined to live in the shadow of their far more popular counterparts the Muppets, *Fraggle Rock* nevertheless remains cherished by fans who opt to dance their cares away and set their worries aside for another day.

See also *Farscape* (1999–2003)

SPOTLIGHT: JIM HENSON

Born in Mississippi on September 24, 1936, Jim Henson was two when his family moved to Maryland[61] only to return to Mississippi when he entered first grade.[62] When not playing outside with his older brother, Henson built crystal radios or listened to radio shows.[63] After experiencing television for the first time in 1948, Henson pleaded with his family to buy a set, finally getting his wish in 1950.[64] In 1954, Henson built his first puppets for local television station WTOP.[65] He developed the term "Muppet" in December 1954 and introduced these new characters to TV audiences during the *Afternoon with Inga* show on WRC-TV in 1955,[66] which led to Henson landing his own show, *Sam and Friends*.[67] As the Muppets' popularity grew, Henson received more offers to work on shows around the country, but in the summer of 1968 he settled on the Children's Television Workshop, where he developed *Sesame Street*.[68] From there, Henson launched numerous beloved projects until his death May 16, 1990.

FREAKS AND GEEKS (1999–2000)

Creator: Paul Feig
Cast: Linda Cardellini (Lindsey Weir), John Francis Daley (Sam Weir), James Franco (Daniel Desario), Samm Levine (Neal Schweiber), Seth Rogen (Ken Miller), Jason Segel (Nick Andopolis), Martin Starr (Bill Haverchuck), Becky Ann Baker (Jean Weir), Joe Flahrety (Harold Weir), Busy Philipps (Kim Kelly), Thomas F. Wilson (Ben Fredricks)
Genre: Comedy, Drama

Synopsis

Set in the fictional Midwestern town of Chippewa, Michigan, this melancholic series follows a disparate group of nerds and outsiders who band together to survive high school during the early 1980s.

Production History

Judd Apatow met Paul Feig in the mid-1980s, years before they broke into Hollywood as a writer/director and actor respectively.[69] After watching the pilot for *Felicity*, co-created by his friend Matt Reeves, Feig recalled his own high school experience as a lonely nerd, something most movies or television shows failed to portray correctly.[70] Feig spent two weeks writing a pilot script for a semi-autobiographical high-school show that he showed to Apatow, who brought the project to DreamWorks Television.[71] The studio shopped the script around but only Scott Sassa, president of NBC West Coast, expressed any interest.[72] He picked up the series, granting Feig and Apatow complete creative control.[73] In early 1999, the duo shot the pilot episode of *Freaks and Geeks* at Raleigh Studios in Hollywood, and in May of that year NBC ordered thirteen episodes for the upcoming fall season.[74]

Around that time, Garth Ancier, who attended a boarding school as a child and therefore failed to understand the show's premise, became president of NBC Entertainment.[75] *Freaks and Geeks* premiered on Saturday, September 25 at 8:00 p.m.[76] The pilot earned strong ratings and positive reviews but the ratings soon declined until the show earned a reputation as the lowest-rated program on NBC.[77] Network executives disliked the show's "serious, dark, and uncomfortable" tone, and Ancier wanted Feig and Apatow to provide more happy endings.[78] For the remainder of the show's life, NBC shuffled *Freaks and Geeks* around the schedule, airing episodes out of order and even pulling the show for weeks on end. These actions left the cast and crew worrying about the show's imminent cancellation so they worked to make the stories bolder.[79]

NBC eventually moved *Freaks and Geeks* to Monday nights but ratings failed to improve.[80] On March 19, 2000, the network cancelled the series, leaving six episodes unaired.[81] That summer, NBC aired three additional episodes in response to a fan campaign called "Operation Haverchuck," and the Fox Family Channel aired the final three later that year.[82] Fans organized an online petition to have the series released on DVD,[83] sales of which helped *Freaks and Geeks* build a cult audience, which grew even bigger after the show's sole season streamed on Netflix.[84]

Commentary

With *Freaks and Geeks*, series creator Paul Feig took a nostalgic look back at his own awkward teen years but refused to don rose-colored glasses, instead serving up a realistic and unflinching consideration of nerdiness before the emergence of geek chic. The show transported viewers to a past not that far removed yet radically different from the present to follow several teenagers as they dealt with puberty, cliques, dating, humiliation, and more. In each episode of *Freaks and Geeks*, the characters struggled to establish their own identities while experiencing the ups and downs of growing up. Along the way, they laughed, cried, and learned important life lessons (sometimes harsh, sometimes hilarious). The show often elicited awkward laughter from the characters' foibles (as in S1E6, "I'm with the Band," when shy Sam finally works up the courage to shower after gym class only to have someone to steal his clothes, forcing him to run naked through the halls) but also served up plenty of tender, melancholy moments that left many viewers feeling wistful (in S1E17, "Dead Dogs and Gym Teachers," for example, lonely latchkey kid Bill arrives home, makes a grilled cheese sandwich, and laughs uproariously while watching Garry Shandling perform stand-up). *Freaks and Geeks* understood the teenage experience better than almost any other show ever produced.

The series also changed the face of the entertainment industry by launching the career of several people who went on to produce or appear in other popular films and TV shows, including Feig, Apatow, Linda Cardellini, Seth Rogen, James Franco, Jason Segel, and Martin Starr. In addition, *Freaks and Geeks* featured great comedic performers in small or supporting roles such as Joe Flahrety, Joel Hodgson, Trace Beaulieu, Lizzy Caplan, Rashida Jones, and Thomas F. Wilson. The series also nailed the period details, from the clothes to the decor, and from the music to the slang. Reportedly the crew even used tinted lights to replicate a Midwestern color scheme and avoided shooting outdoors as much as possible because production took place in sunny California.[85] More than anything, though, *Freaks and Geeks* accurately portrayed pop culture–obsessed teens struggling to navigate a hostile high school environment seemingly comprised of cliques and bullies. The show followed the characters as they forged bonds and enjoyed the occasional success but refused to shy away from the uncomfortable moments and embarrassing failures. This deft handling of youth culture and adolescent feelings helped *Freaks and Geeks* find a small but loyal audience and ensures that the show will continue to resonate with young viewers for years to come.

See also *My So-Called Life* (1994–1995), *Veronica Mars* (2004–Present)

FRISKY DINGO (2006–2008)

Creator: Adam Reed, Matt Thompson
Cast: Adam Reed (Xander Crews/Killface/Wendell T. Stamps), Stuart Culpepper (Stan), Christian Danley (Simon), Kate Miller (Grace Ryan), Amber Nash (Valerie), Kelly Jenrette (Sinn), Killer Mike (Taqu'il), Mr. Ford (Mr. Ford)
Genre: Comedy, Science Fiction

Synopsis

Billionaire playboy Xander Cage, who moonlights as superhero Awesome X, faces comedic situations while battling his arch-nemesis Killface.

Production History

After scoring a hit with the fan-favorite Adult Swim series *Sealab 2021*, the crew at 70/30 Productions turned their attention to creating a new animated series about a superhero team led by a dysfunctional husband and wife duo.[86] Initially called *Whiskey Tango Six*, the show revolved around a crack team of heroes trying to save the world from the cadaverous supervillain Killface.[87] During development, copyright questions led series co-creators Adam Reed and Matt Thompson to change the title of the show to *Frisky Dingo,* which Cartoon Network executives ultimately found much funnier.[88] *Frisky Dingo* utilized entirely original animation and therefore proved costlier than *Sealab 2021,* which repurposed an old Hanna-Barbera cartoon.[89] For the look of the show, which now centered on the conflict between Killface and narcissistic superhero Awesome X, Reed and Thompson drew inspiration from the video game *Grand Theft Auto: San Andreas.*[90] When designing the characters, the 70/30 crew photographed real people and animated over them using Adobe Illustrator.[91]

During production, Reed and Thompson directed the voiceover sessions and edited the audio tracks[92] while designers Neal Holman, Christian Danley, Casey Willis, David Caicedo, and Eric Sims drew the show's visual elements, with Atlanta-based Soapbox Studio handling post-production.[93] *Frisky Dingo* premiered on October 15, 2006,[94] doing well enough in the ratings that Cartoon Network ordered a second season, which debuted on August 26, 2007, and aired on Sunday nights.[95] During its short run, the show built up a small but loyal fanbase, but low ratings led Cartoon Network to pull the plug at the end of the second season. The final episode of *Frisky Dingo* aired on March 23, 2008,[96] and two days later Cartoon Network released the show's first season on DVD via Warner Home Video.[97] A few months later, on January 6, 2009, the series' second season landed on DVD.[98] Though *Frisky Dingo* failed to catch on with a wide audience, it nevertheless laid the groundwork for Reed's later hit *Archer.*[99]

Commentary

Emerging just prior to a deluge of films and television series centered on costumed crusaders, *Frisky Dingo* served up an outrageous parody of superheroes. Co-creators Adam Reed and Matt Thompson hilariously lampooned wealthy crimefighters like Batman and Iron Man via the character of Xander Crews, a philandering billionaire playboy who doubled as the self-absorbed superhero Awesome X. As voiced by Reed, Crews embodies all the worst traits of spoiled rich kids who grow up without ever facing any consequences for their actions, no matter how harmful. Crews, who cares more about marketing his image than he does about fighting crime or saving lives, treats everyone around him like dirt, including his long-suffering girlfriend, intrepid reporter Grace Ryan. Meanwhile, the evil Killface (also voiced by Reed) hilariously struggles to establish himself as a top-tier supervillain while also raising his weird son, Simon, who enjoys traveling to Chinatown to participate in illegal underground death rabbit fights. Other characters include Crews's scheming employee Stan, Killface's high-strung assistant Valerie, and weaselly CIA agent Wendell Stamps. With their outsized personalities and reprehensible attitudes, these characters established *Frisky Dingo* as an adored cult hit.

During its brief run, *Frisky Dingo* featured uproarious dialogue and over-the-top situations. For example, in "Meet Awesome X" (S1E2), after accidentally revealing his secret identity to a prostitute and paying her to keep quiet, Xander can no longer afford to pay his private army, the Xtacles, and fires them. Upon learning of their dismissal and the loss of their health insurance, one of the Xtacles asks, "Are we at least eligible for COBRA?" to which Xander replies, "What, the little . . . the G.I. Joe dolls?" Later, in "XPO" (S1E4), after genetically modified crab man Watley inadvertently lays a clutch of eggs, a mortified Killface mutters, "That's . . . something you don't see every day . . . one hopes." Meanwhile, in "Blind Faith" (S1E8), Crews escapes from the Xtacles, who now work for former henchwoman Sinn, only to stumble upon a blind and concussed Killface. When asked his identity, Crews haltingly responds, "Barnaby Jones," prompting a delirious Killface to sing, "People, let me tell ya 'bout my new best friend, Barnaby Jones!" After a long pause, Killface exclaims, "Nap!" and then passes out. Filled with riotous humor and raucous situations and characters, *Frisky Dingo* helped set the stage for all the adult-oriented animated comedies that followed, making it one of the funniest and most significant cult TV shows of all time.

See also *Aqua Teen Hunger Force* (2000–2015), *Space Ghost Coast to Coast* (1994–2008)

FUTURAMA (1999–2013)

Creator: David X. Cohen, Matt Groening
Cast: Billy West (Philip J. Fry/Hubert J. Farnsworth/John A. Zoidberg), Katey Sagal (Turanga Leela), John DiMaggio (Bender), Lauren Tom (Amy Wong), Phil LaMarr (Hermes Conrad), Tress MacNeille (Carol "Mom" Miller), Maurice LaMarche (Morbo), David Herman (Scruffy), Frank Welker (Nibbler)
Genre: Comedy, Science Fiction

Synopsis

After accidentally stumbling into a cryogenic pod that leaves him frozen for one thousand years, hapless pizza delivery boy Philip J. Fry wakes up in the year 3000 and joins the wacky staff of an interstellar delivery service.

Production History

A science fiction fan since childhood,[100] *The Simpsons* creator Matt Groening decided after ten seasons that he wanted to do something different.[101] Inspired by Isaac Asimov novels and 1950s B-movies, Groening came up with an idea for a sci-fi cartoon.[102] He teamed with fellow sci-fi fan David X. Cohen to develop the new series.[103] Groening pitched the idea to executives at Fox Network, who eagerly ordered thirteen episodes.[104] Unfortunately, the executives found the resulting series "too dark and mean-spirited, and thought they had made a huge mistake," leading them to seek changes that Groening resisted.[105] The series, titled *Futurama*, premiered after *The Simpsons* on March 28, 1999, earning high ratings in key demographics.[106] However, this placement only lasted for two weeks, after

One thousand years in the future, the zany crew of the Planet Express delivery service embark on uproarious adventures throughout the universe. *Fox Network/Photofest*

which Fox moved *Futurama* to its new Toon Tuesday lineup along with *King of the Hill* and *The PJs*, which Groening called a programming blunder.[107] As the ratings declined, Fox placed *Futurama* on hiatus in February 2002, and even a fan petition with 130,000 signatures failed to save the show.[108]

Starting in 2004, Cartoon Network added reruns of *Futurama* to their Adult Swim block of programming and aggressively marketed the series.[109] When Groening and Cohen saw the ratings, along with the success of the *Family Guy* direct-to-DVD movies, they talked to Fox about producing a series of *Futurama* movies.[110] Network executives agreed, and later repurposed the DVD movies, which earned $32 million between 2007 and 2009, as the show's fifth season.[111] Four months after the final DVD movie, Comedy Central ordered twenty-six new episodes of *Futurama*, the first of which premiered June 24, 2010, to become the "highest-rated Thursday prime-time rating in the network's history."[112] The cable network ran new episodes until April 2013, at which point the series officially ended.[113] In June 2017, game developers TinyCo and Jam City released *Futurama: Worlds of Tomorrow*, a mobile game featuring the original voice cast, while Nerdist Industries produced a forty-two-minute radio play titled *Radiorama* later that same year.[114]

Commentary

Though it lived in the shadow of *The Simpsons*, creator Matt Groening's previous cultural juggernaut, *Futurama* nevertheless built up a devoted cult following thanks to its smart humor, big heart, and deft handling of complex sci-fi concepts.

Fans heralded the show for its zany characters (such as standouts Bender and Dr. Zoidberg) and hilarious dialogue ("Oh, no room for Bender, huh? Fine! I'll go build my own lunar lander, with blackjack and hookers. In fact, forget the lunar lander and the blackjack. Ahh, screw the whole thing!"). Yet they also loved how *Futurama* tackled sci-fi clichés like time travel (the Planet Express crew journeys to Roswell, New Mexico, in 1947 and Fry becomes his own grandfather), alternate dimensions (Professor Farnsworth invents a device that lets the crew look in on parallel universes), and out-of-control technology (Bender gains the ability to self-replicate and his increasingly smaller copies threaten to engulf Earth). Indeed, despite the silliness, *Futurama* often emphasized the "science" in science fiction as the writers' room boasted three doctoral degrees and seven master's degrees.[115]

Of course, the funny gags, wacky situations, and madcap characters also helped endear the show to a fiercely loyal cult audience. With *Futurama*, Groening blasted his signature comedic style into outer space, peppering his screwy universe with vaudevillian witticisms and wry observational comedy that extrapolated today's concerns into the far future. For instance, "Attack of the Killer App" (S6E3) sees the villainous Mom develop a social media app capable of infecting users' brains with a virus. Meanwhile, in "The Problem with Popplers" (S2E18), the Planet Express crew travel to another planet and discover an addictive snack food that turns out to be infant aliens. The episode critiques everything from crass consumerism to eating meat to militant veganism, all while tossing out sidesplitting one-liners like "Well, it's a type-M planet, so it should at least have Roddenberries." Episodes like these reveal how *Futurama* balances smart satire with silly humor and demonstrate just why the series cultivated such a loyal fanbase.

Despite all that, *Futurama* failed to catch on with a wider audience but still rocketed to an impressive seven seasons. While that number falls far short of *Futurama*'s sister show *The Simpsons* (which stands at a whopping 31 seasons and counting), the shorter lifespan ensures that *Futurama* will hold up better as it never had the chance to descend into self-parody as *The Simpsons* has done during its later years. No matter the reason, *Futurama* remains one of the most adored sci-fi comedies in the entire universe.

See also *Mystery Science Theater 3000* (1988–2018), *Red Dwarf* (1988–2017)

SPOTLIGHT: MATT GROENING

Born on February 15, 1964, in Portland, Oregon,[116] Matt Groening knew from an early age that he wanted to work in animation.[117] He studied journalism at Evergreen State College,[118] after which he moved to Los Angeles, where he worked odd jobs until alternative newspaper *The Los Angeles Reader* agreed to run his comic strip *Life in Hell*.[119] In 1984 Groening released the first *Life in Hell* collection.[120] Three years later, James L. Brooks asked Groening to create *Life in Hell* animated shorts for *The Tracy Ullman Show*, but the cartoonist worried about losing the copyright to the strip.[121] Instead, he created the Simpsons,[122] a dysfunctional family that appeared in a handful of popular shorts before spinning off into their own show that premiered in 1989 and continues to run to this day.[123] Groening's second animated series, *Futurama*, premiered in 1999, while his third, *Disenchantment*, arrived on Netflix in 2018.[124]

G

GARGOYLES (1994–1996)

Creator: Greg Weisman
Cast: Keith David (Goliath), Salli Richardson-Whitfield (Elisa Maza), Jeff Bennett (Brooklyn), Frank Welker (Bronx), Edward Asner (Hudson), Bill Fagerbakke (Broadway), Thom Adcox-Hernandez (Lexington), Jonathan Frakes (David Xanatos), Marina Sirtis (Demona), Brigitte Bako (Angela)
Genre: Action, Drama, Fantasy, Mystery, Romance, Thriller

Synopsis

One thousand years after a wizard transformed them into lifeless stone statues, six heroic gargoyles reawaken in modern New York and resume their battle against the forces of evil.

Production History

The success of the Disney Afternoon syndicated block of animated shows revolved around funny animal shows like *DuckTales* and *Goof Troop*, but by 1992 producers at Disney Animation wanted to try something different to prevent audiences from experiencing "funny animal fatigue."[1] That same year, *Batman: The Animated Series* debuted and built an audience of pre-teens and teenagers so the folks at Disney decided to develop a fantasy series à la *Gummi Bears* but with a darker, more mature edge.[2] Development executive Greg Weisman hatched the idea for a comedic series about a group of medieval gargoyles reawakening in modern times and setting out to battle evil.[3] Disney CEO Michael Eisner passed on the idea[4] so Weisman revised it to feature a more dramatic tone and revolve around a new gargoyle named Goliath.[5] Nonetheless, Eisner continued to reject the idea until Weisman reworked the pitch to focus on the relationship between Goliath and Elisa Maza, a human police officer.[6] At that point, Eisner greenlit the show,[7] which debuted on October 24, 1994.[8]

Michael Reaves and Brynne Chandler wrote most of episodes during the first year,[9] with Weisman serving as producer.[10] Based on the success of the thirteen-episode first season, Disney ordered a second season of fifty-two episodes.[11] Around that time, several of the show's supporters, including Jeffrey Katzenberg,

Trapped in stone for one thousand years, a clan of medieval gargoyles awakens in present-day Manhattan and pledges to defend their new home from evil. *Disney/Photofest*

left Disney.[12] In addition, ratings dropped when the studio scheduled *Gargoyles* against the massively popular *Mighty Morphin' Power Rangers*.[13] During season 3, Disney demoted Weisman from producer to story editor, outsourced production to Nelvana, moved the series to ABC's Saturday morning block, and renamed it *The Goliath Chronicles*, implementing changes in the tone and characters.[14] The show ended soon after, with Weisman dismissing the final thirteen episodes as non-canonical.[15] Despite recent attempts to relaunch the franchise,[16] *Gargoyles* currently remains dormant.

Commentary

With *Gargoyles*, Disney added a much darker fantasy adventure animated series aimed at teenagers and young adults to its afternoon lineup. Existing alongside *DuckTales*, *Darkwing Duck*, *Chip 'n Dale Rescue Rangers*, *TaleSpin*, *Goof Troop*, and other kid-oriented series, *Gargoyles* stood out thanks to its deep mythology and more mature themes. In addition to serving up thrilling adventures and amusing dialogue during its three seasons, the show also tackled complex issues such as racism, gun violence, and conspiracy theories. Unlike a lot of other cartoons at the time, *Gargoyles* featured a diverse cast of characters (placing a woman of color in a prominent role) and gritty urban settings, allowing a wide variety of viewers to identify with the show. The series also featured stunning animation and an absorbing mixture of mythology, science, literature, and action that appealed to audiences of all ages. Critics often compared *Gargoyles* to *Batman: The Animated Series* (a comparison that apparently irked *Batman* co-creator Bruce Timm[17]) but *Gargoyles* managed to establish its own singular identity by taking daring risks while also telling an imaginative tale rooted in Celtic folklore and high fantasy.

Though short-lived, *Gargoyles* still served up plenty of fanciful adventures as the eponymous creatures learned to navigate late-twentieth-century New York alongside their friend NYPD detective Elisa Maza. In each episode, the Manhattan Clan squared off against nefarious villains alongside colorful allies. The thrills begin in the first episode, "The Awakening: Part 1," which sees the wicked David Xanatos (played with mustache-twirling glee by Jonathan Frakes, best known for his role as Will Riker in *Star Trek: The Next Generation*) free the gargoyles from their stone prison after transporting a Scottish castle to the roof of his skyscraper. Later, in "Reawakening," Xanatos and his accomplice Demona (a rogue gargoyle voiced by Frakes's *Star Trek* costar Marina Sirtis) use a combination of science and sorcery to resurrect a gargoyle from a rival clan. The two-part "City of Stone" (S2E9, S2E10) takes viewers back in time to reveal Demona's backstory, detailing her rivalry with the villainous Macbeth, an immortal Scottish nobleman intent on wiping out the gargoyles. Episodes such as these helped *Gargoyles* establish a reputation as an exciting animated fantasy series but also one that featured intricate storylines intended for kids and grownups alike.

See also *Beauty and the Beast* (1987–1990), *The Tick* (1994–1997)

GILLIGAN'S ISLAND (1964–1967)

Creator: Sherwood Schwartz
Cast: Bob Denver (Gilligan), Alan Hale Jr. (Jonas "The Skipper" Grumby), Jim Backus (Thurston Howell III), Natalie Schafer (Lovey Howell), Tina Louise (Ginger Grant), Russell Johnson (Professor Roy Hinkley), Dawn Wells (Mary Ann Summers)
Genre: Comedy

Synopsis

A three-hour tour turns into a three-year ordeal after a storm leaves a ragtag group of strangers shipwrecked on a deserted island, where they embark on wacky adventures as they strive to return to the mainland.

Production History

On May 13, 1963, Sherwood Schwartz inked a deal with United Artists, CBS, and Phil Silvers' Gladasya Productions to produce a new television series called *Gilligan's Island*.[18] The following month, Schwartz met with William Paley, chairman of CBS, as well as executives for the network's east- and west-coast divisions, and presented them with an eight-page presentation and bible for the show.[19] Schwartz originally intended *Gilligan's Island* as a mix of social satire and slapstick comedy, a sort of humorous primetime fable about people from different classes and backgrounds trapped in a jungle purgatory learning to live together.[20] However, CBS wanted the castaways to fix the boat and set off on new trips in each episode, and Schwartz soon found himself negotiating requests for changes from executives at both CBS and United Artists.[21] The network and the studio wanted to shoot the pilot episode close to Los Angeles but scouting locations failed to turn up a place with the appropriate South Seas appearance.[22] They eventually settled on shooting in Hawaii,[23] with pre-production taking place on the 20th Century Fox Studios lot.[24] Schwartz considered Jerry Van Dyke for the role of Gilligan but changed his mind after meeting with Bob Denver.[25] Schwartz then hired Alan Hale to play Skipper after seeing him at a restaurant,[26] and the rest of the cast fell into place soon after. Production commenced on November 19, 1963,[27] but by early 1964 CBS had yet to pick up the pilot for broadcast,[28] despite numerous re-edits.[29] Finally, after submission of a version complete with the now-iconic theme song and new casting for the characters of the Professor, Ginger, and Mary Ann, CBS aired the first episode of *Gilligan's Island*, which tested well with audiences.[30] The show landed in the top ten during its first two years despite moving around the schedule, but ratings dipped in the third year,[31] leading CBS to pull the series and replace it with *Gunsmoke*.[32] In 1971, Filmation Associates asked Schwartz to produce an animated version of *Gilligan's Island* but he declined, only for *Gilligan's Planet* to premiere years later in 1982.[33] In 1978, NBC aired the two-hour TV movie *Rescue from Gilligan's Island*,[34] which proved popular with viewers.[35] The network followed it with the less successful *The Castaways of Gilligan's Island* in 1979,[36]

Gilligan (Bob Denver, third from left) and the rest of the castaways hatch wacky schemes to escape from a deserted island and return home. *CBS/Photofest*

and finally *The Harlem Globetrotters on Gilligan's Island* in 1981.[37] Though often dismissed by critics, *Gilligan's Island* still looms large in popular culture, with Dan Harmon citing it as influence on *Community*.[38]

Commentary

Gilligan's Island charmed viewers young and old with its irreverent, illogical humor and ensemble of lovable misfit castaways who soon reached iconic status around the world. When it debuted in the mid-1960s, critics savaged the show, dismissing it as little more than a frivolous distraction. Similarly, CBS executives seemed eager to rid themselves of the quirky series as they repeatedly shuffled it around the schedule before finally ending its run after just three years. Yet *Gilligan's Island* survived both the critical drubbing and the network meddling to become a staple of syndicated television, delighting solitary retirees, lonesome latchkey kids, and bored potheads to this day. In the more than five decades since its initial cancelation, the show remains a near constant presence on television not just in the United States but around the world. Few other series can match the lasting power or cultural ubiquity of *Gilligan's Island*, which continues to inspire retrospective articles and heated discussion (much of it centered on debating the attractiveness of Ginger and Mary Ann) long after the crew of the S.S. *Minnow* sailed off into the sunset. While the show never really offered much insight into society or the human condition (though creator Sherwood Schwartz certainly wanted it to), *Gilligan's Island* still enchanted a global audience with its goofy humor and amiable characters, both of which appeal to viewers even now.

Over three years, the show produced ninety-nine episodes filled with goofball antics and amusing (but often groan-inducing) gags that still provoke big laughs in audiences of all ages. The show often took viewers on wacky and sometimes fantastic adventures as the castaways unsuccessfully plotted to escape the island and return home. Along the way, they ran into all sorts of zany characters (including several culturally insensitive islanders and racist caricatures) and the occasional weird beastie (such as the giant spider that menaces the gang in S3E28, "The Pigeon"). For instance, in "Don't Bug the Mosquitoes" (S2E12), an overworked mop-top American singing group travels to the deserted island for some rest and relaxation only to fall victim to the castaways' wacky shenanigans. Later, in "The Friendly Physician" (S2E29), hijinks ensue when a mad scientist swaps the castaways' brains. Perhaps most famously, "The Producer" (S3E4) sees Hollywood bigshot Harold Hecuba (played by legendary ham Phil Silvers) wind up on the island, prompting the castaways to stage a musical version of Shakespeare's *Hamlet*. In addition, each episode featured screwball physical comedy and rib-tickling zingers like "There's a space up there, there's a space down here, and there's a space between your ears." (S2E4, "Smile, You're on Mars Camera") and "I wouldn't be a good vampire. I faint at the sight of blood. I'll starve to death" (S3E1, "Up at Bat"). These elements helped turn *Gilligan's Island* into an enduring cult classic.

See also *Community* (2009–2015), *Lost* (2004–2010)

GILMORE GIRLS (2000–2007)

Creator: Amy Sherman-Palladino
Cast: Lauren Graham (Lorelai Gilmore), Alexis Bledel (Rory Gilmore), Keiko Agena (Lane Kim), Scott Patterson (Luke Dane), Yanic Truesdale (Michel Gerard), Kelly Bishop (Emily Gilmore), Edward Herrmann (Richard Gilmore), Melissa McCarthy (Sookie St. James)
Genre: Comedy, Drama

Synopsis

A mother and teenage daughter develop a close relationship as they learn how to grow up together.

Production History

Amy Sherman-Palladino joined the writing team of *Roseanne* in 1990 during the hit sitcom's third season, first as a writer then as a story editor, but she left

Quick-witted single mom Lorelai Gilmore (Lauren Graham, right) shares a close relationship with her teenage daughter Rory (Alexis Bledel). *WB Television Photographer: Mitchell Haddad/Photofest*

after a year because Barr treated the writers poorly.[39] In 1999, Sherman-Palladino approached both NBC and the WB Network with two different ideas for a new series, one about her father and one for an hour-long show based on a magazine article about a fifteen-year-old girl living in Los Angeles.[40] Meanwhile, Sherman-Palladino's agent Gavin Polone had recently produced the movie *Drop Dead Gorgeous* and wanted to do a show inspired by the mother-daughter relationship in that film. WB Network president Susan Daniels and executive vice president Jordan Levin liked that idea best and picked it up,[41] meaning that Sherman-Palladino and Polone now needed to flesh out the details.[42] A trip to New England helped Sherman-Palladino develop the story while Polone focused on securing the deal with the network.[43] The WB eventually teamed with the Association of National Advertiser's Family Friendly Programming Forum to fund the pilot episode of *Gilmore Girls*[44] though the network considered it a low priority.[45]

Casting commenced in February 2000.[46] Casting director Alison Goodman first hired newcomer Alexis Bledel after looking at her head shot[47] and later cast Lauren Graham as Lorelai after meeting with three other actresses.[48] To save on production costs, the WB shot the first episode of *Gilmore Girls* in the Toronto suburb of Unionville in Markham, Ontario, but the series eventually relocated to the Warner Brothers lot.[49] The pilot episode of *Gilmore Girls* aired on October 5, 2000, and the series ran for seven seasons,[50] but Sherman-Palladino left after season 6 due to tension between her and the network.[51] Writer David S. Rosenthal stepped in as showrunner starting in season 7[52] but hardcore fans disliked his work.[53] As such, *Gilmore Girls* ended with a lack of closure, disappointing fans and those involved in making the series.[54] In 2016, Sherman-Palladino teamed with streaming giant Netflix to produce *Gilmore Girls: A Year in the Life*,[55] a disappointing four-episode miniseries that took fans back to Stars Hollow one last time.[56]

Commentary

Relatively few American television shows focus on women's relationships. Even shows about women regularly place their husbands, sons, fathers, boyfriends, colleagues, bosses, and so on in prominent positions. Shows like *I Love Lucy*, *The Mary Tyler Moore Show*, *Roseanne*, and *30 Rock* starred talented comediennes, but often their relationships with men overshadowed any bonding with women. *Gilmore Girls* put these women-focused relationships front and center, showing three generations of women learning how to live with one another. The series remained true to its focus on mother-daughter relationships from beginning to end, a rare feat outside daily soap operas. *Gilmore Girls* showed these relationships without descending into the melodramatic exaggeration common to daytime dramas while also providing frank, realistic portrayals of friendship and romance.

The show's main draw lay in its fully formed characters. In Rory, teenage girls found a friend and a role model who showed them how to handle the angsty struggles of growing up. Meanwhile, Lorelai provided young women with a sympathetic portrayal of a woman trying to balance motherhood and a career all while looking for romance. This mother-daughter team directly addressed the struggles of single mothers both in American culture and in terms of personal conflicts between desires and responsibilities. Furthermore, it did so with smart, sarcastic, dramatic, and heartfelt writing.

The men in *Gilmore Girls* served to further the lead character's personal development, thus occupying the role usually inhabited by women in television and popular culture. In a sense, these men remained tertiary to the women, a complete flip of the script that felt refreshing yet appropriate for a series that helped usher in the twenty-first century. In addition, the show's success helped demonstrate that media featuring women in lead roles could draw a sizeable audience and fanbase not just of women but anyone who could relate to the characters and their foibles. *Gilmore Girls* showed that viewers will watch shows featuring fully realized characters who possess complex motivations and demonstrate realistic reactions to events that could happen to anyone. As such, *Gilmore Girls* drew a wide audience and remains intensely loved to this day.

See also *Buffy the Vampire Slayer* (1997–2003), *Crazy Ex-Girlfriend* (2015–2019), *Veronica Mars* (2004–Present)

THE GOLDEN GIRLS (1985–1992)

Creator: Susan Harris
Cast: Bea Arthur (Dorothy Zbornak), Betty White (Rose Nylund), Rue McClanahan
   (Blanche Devereaux), Estelle Getty (Sophia Petrillo)
Genre: Comedy, Drama

Synopsis

Four sassy elderly women live together and experience the senior citizen scene
in Miami.

Production History

After watching the film *How to Marry a Millionaire* (and after seeing actresses
Selma Diamond and Doris Roberts perform an awards show skit in which they
ogled *Miami Vice* star Don Johnson), NBC chief Brandon Tartikoff decided to
create a new show about a group of senior women living together.[57] Tartikoff
and Warren Littlefield, vice president of comedy programs at NBC, conferred
with other executives about adding the new sitcom—titled *Miami Nice*—to the
upcoming 1985–1986 season.[58] A meeting with producers Paul Junger Witt and
Tony Thomas led to Witt's wife, Susan Harris (who created the gay character
Jodie Dallas on *Soap*), taking on the idea.[59] The trio then set about brainstorming
the series, which initially featured three women, a mother, and a gay houseboy
all living together.[60] They rechristened the show *The Golden Girls* and commenced assembling the cast.[61]

In February 1985, the showrunners cast sixty-one-year-old Estelle Getty as the
eighty-year-old mother Sophia, and the actress immediately worked on developing her character.[62] Soon after, Betty White auditioned for the role of Southern
sexpot Blanche while Rue McClanahan read for naive Midwesterner Rose.[63]
However, Jay Sandrich, who directed the show's pilot, later suggested that they
swap roles.[64] Harris approached veteran TV actor Bea Arthur to play Dorothy but
she turned down the role.[65] Tartikoff also had misgivings about Arthur because
audiences disliked the performer due to her role on *Maude* so he suggested Broadway legend Elaine Stritch.[66] Yet Harris persevered, and McClanhan ultimately
convinced Arthur to join the cast just in time for rehearsals to begin on April 8.[67]
Finally Tartikoff suggested Charles Levin as the gay houseboy[68] but the showrunners cut the character when Witt decided his storylines felt unnecessary.[69]

The Golden Girls premiered on September 14, 1985, at 9:00 p.m., drawing an
audience of different ages from around the country.[70] In 1992, after Arthur left the
series, the remaining cast appeared in a short-lived spinoff, *The Golden Palace*.[71]
Between 1997 and 2009, Lifetime cable network aired repeats of *The Golden Girls*,
drawing 11 million viewers per week and 30 million per month. On June 2, 2003,
Lifetime aired *The Golden Girls Reunion*, which drew 4.2 million viewers, making
it the network's highest-rated special ever.[72] In 2009, Hallmark acquired the rights
to the show and aired it every day until 2013, when *The Golden Girls* moved to TV
Land and Logo.[73] By 2015, the show's Facebook page had amassed over 1.6 mil-

lion Likes, while Twitter hosts over a dozen accounts that tweet daily about *Golden Girls* news and quotes, all boasting thousands of followers.[74] *The Golden Girls* also enjoys a substantial queer following, with drag queens regularly performing tributes to the show.[75] In 2016, a puppet show parody premiered off-Broadway.[76]

Commentary

The 1980s saw many different types of family sitcoms, from the traditional, such as *Family Ties* and *The Cosby Show*, to the unusual, such as *The Facts of Life* and *Perfect Strangers*. *The Golden Girls* presented yet another nontraditional family sitcom and one that aged better than others. Of course, much of its staying power resulted from its innovative portrayal of elderly women as funny, sexy, successful, and sassy. Rather than rely on outdated stereotypes about crones, hags, or women long past their prime, *The Golden Girls* put the sex lives of senior citizens front and center, never shying away from dealing with the sociocultural issues faced by their generation. All the while, the series remained uproarious due largely to the strength of its writing but also because of the four leading ladies. Each performer delivered an iconic performance, offering up a complex portrayal of senior life. As such, *The Golden Girls* helped dispel longstanding misconceptions about the elderly.

Interestingly, the cult around the series contains a variety of people, from young Millennials to older queer fans. Generation X viewers, especially those still too young to date, grew up watching *The Golden Girls* on Saturday nights. Millennials

Elderly pals Sophia (Estelle Getty, left), Blanche (Rue McClanahan, second from left), Rose (Betty White, third from left) and Dorothy (Bea Arthur) navigate the singles scene in Miami, Florida. *NBC/Photofest*

embraced the series when it reached cable, and their fascination with *The Golden Girls* contributed to the show's rebirth, with companies cranking out new merchandise to meet young fans' desire for all things *Golden*. The portrayal of the four women creating a family unit also sent an important message to queer viewers looking for validation of their nontraditional way of life. *The Golden Girls* emerged before the AIDS crisis reached mainstream America and thus well before gay civil rights truly made significant strides. The presence of the show and its portrayals, as well as the support of the actors themselves, helped queer audiences feel heard and valued. Of course, *The Golden Girls* also kick-started the careers of many people who went on change the landscape of American television including Christopher Lloyd, Mitchell Hurwitz, and Marc Cherry. All this explains why, even now, viewers continue to see *The Golden Girls* and its characters as dear friends.

H

HANNIBAL (2013–2015)

Creator: Bryan Fuller
Cast: Hugh Dancy (Will Graham), Mads Mikkelsen (Hannibal Lecter), Carolinie Dhavernas (Alana Bloom), Laurence Fishburne (Jack Crawford), Scott Thompson (Jimmy Price), Aaron Abrams (Brian Zeller), Gillian Anderson (Bedelia Du Maurier), Michael Pitt (Mason Verger)
Genre: Drama, Horror, Mystery, Thriller

Synopsis

A gifted young FBI criminal profiler befriends a renowned psychiatrist who just happens to be a cannibalistic serial killer.

Production History

Following a chance meeting with his old friend Katie O'Connell of the Gaumont Film Company,[1] writer and producer Bryan Fuller set about developing a television series about Hannibal Lecter, the notorious serial killer introduced in a series of novels by author Thomas Harris.[2] Fuller, a fan of the books, wanted to explore the relationship between Lecter and gifted FBI profiler Will Graham.[3] He plotted for seven seasons, with season 4 drawing from the novel *Red Dragon*, season 5 from *Silence of the Lambs*, and season 6 from *Hannibal*.[4] Season 7 would then expand on the books.[5] Fuller brought the idea to Martha De Laurentiis, head of De Laurentiis Entertainment Group, who liked his take on the material.[6] Fuller and De Laurentiis then pitched the show to Jennifer Salke at NBC Entertainment, who picked it up and agreed to let Fuller develop the series as he saw fit.[7]

In February 2012, NBC ordered thirteen episodes based solely on Fuller's pilot script.[8] During production, Fuller worked with the network's Standards and Practices Department to avoid censorship.[9] When casting the show, Fuller met with *Doctor Who* actor David Tennant about playing the lead role[10] but Danish actor Mads Mikkelsen ultimately landed the part.[11] Titled *Hannibal*, the show premiered on April 4, 2013, at 10:00 p.m.[12] The first episode drew 4.3 million viewers but ratings soon declined, with fewer than 3 million viewers tuning in to the second season finale.[13] In addition *Hannibal* often courted controversy because it pushed

Gifted FBI profiler Will Graham (Hugh Dancy, right) confronts suave serial killer Hannibal Lecter (Mads Mikkelsen). *NBC/Photofest*

the boundaries of violence on TV.[14] Fuller even pulled the fourth episode of season 1 because it featured children murdering children.[15] NBC canceled *Hannibal* after three seasons[16] but fans still hold out hope for a revival.

Commentary

Filled with haunting imagery and compelling characters, *Hannibal* is the darkest of series creator Byran Fuller's visions, not to mention the least comedic. While it failed to catch on with a broad audience, the show nevertheless built a fervent cult following thanks to an exhilarating combination of disturbing-yet-beautiful aesthetics, captivating storylines, and absorbing relationships. Using Thomas Harris's popular novels as a springboard, Fuller crafted a weird and wonderful series that pushed the envelope in terms of brutality and shocking imagery. In addition, *Hannibal* featured a top-notch cast led by international superstar Mads Mikkelsen, who put a new and original spin on title character Hannibal Lecter, previously portrayed by Brian Cox and (most famously) Anthony Hopkins. Mikkelsen turned the cannibalistic Lecter into a soft-spoken and sophisticated psychopath who oozed charisma, dignity, and sex appeal. Hugh Dancy, meanwhile, portrayed FBI profiler Will Graham as a quietly intense man driven by obsession. The chemistry between Dancy and Mikkelsen (the pairing that launched a thousand ships) helped turn *Hannibal* into one of the most adored cult television shows ever made. In addition, while the show routinely featured creative gore (in one episode, a killer flays his victims' backs and perches the skin to resemble wings), it expertly walked the line between the grotesque and the beautiful.

With each episode, *Hannibal* reinterpreted familiar material in creative ways, giving viewers a terrifying glimpse inside the title character's mind to reveal the motivations behind his actions. The show also relied heavily on dream sequences to create some truly unsettling imagery that lingered in the minds of viewers long after the end credits rolled. The show regularly served up imaginative thrills and chills, starting with the first episode, "Apéritif," in which Will Graham searches for a maniac named Garret Jacob Hobbs (who sometimes impales his victims on deer antlers) but comes face-to-face with the smooth and conniving Lecter. A few episodes later, in "Rôti" (S1E11), Lecter drives Graham (who struggles with empathy disorder and advanced encephalitis) over the edge with the help of the murderous Dr. Abel Gideon (played by comedian Eddie Izzard). Season 2 took the show to new extremes with episodes like "Mizumono" (S2E13), a shocking season finale that sees Lecter set out on a deranged killing spree that thins the show's regular cast. Episodes such as these explain why *Hannibal* lured an audience of engaged and devoted fans (known affectionately as "Fannibals") who continue to clamor for a fourth season.

See also *Twin Peaks* (1990–1991)

SPOTLIGHT: BRYAN FULLER

Born July 27, 1969, Bryan Fuller grew up a fan of horror and science fiction.[17] Upon graduating from college, he sent spec scripts to the producers of the *Star Trek: Deep Space Nine*, landing a gig writing for that show and *Star Trek: Voyager*.[18] During his last year on *Voyager*, Fuller wrote the spec pilot that served as the basis for *Dead Like Me*.[19] From there, Fuller created *Wonderfalls* with Todd Holland before assuming a position as a writer and co-executive producer on the first season of *Heroes*, which he left to create *Pushing Daisies*.[20] He then created the show *Hannibal* and wrote the screenplay for a live-action version of *Pinocchio* for Warner Bros.[21] Fuller also served as showrunner on *American Gods* and *Star Trek: Discovery* but left both shows after one season due to various conflicts.[22]

HE-MAN AND THE MASTERS OF THE UNIVERSE (1983–1985)

Creators: Roger Sweet, Mark Taylor, Mark Ellis, Lou Scheimer
Cast: John Erwin (He-Man/Prince Adam), Alan Oppenheimer (Skeletor/Man-at-Arms), Linda Gary (Teela), Lou Scheimer (Orko)
Genre: Action, Fantasy, Science Fiction

Synopsis

Meek Prince Adam periodically transforms into the powerful warrior He-Man to protect the planet Eternia from the forces of the evil Skeletor.

Production History

Seeking to cash in on branded toy lines after the success of Kenner's *Star Wars* toys, Mattel teamed with Conan Properties in 1980 to develop a toy line for the upcoming film adaptation of Robert E. Howard's classic pulp character Conan the Barbarian, redressing a male action figure called "Big Jim" that had failed to catch on with kids. However, Mattel executives dropped the license after seeing early screenings of the excessively violent film.[23] Rather than wait for another Hollywood film brand to license, Mattel commenced testing both a space-military and barbarian-fantasy toy line but ultimately decided to combine the two ideas.[24] Mattel toy designer Roger Sweet and graphic artist Mark Taylor developed the new character, with Sweet christening their creation He-Man to align with Mattel's wish for a generic hero who fought alongside other characters in a mix of space-opera clichés, military action, and fantasy tropes.[25] Dubbed "Masters of the Universe," the toy line debuted in 1982 with Mattel spending an unprecedented $19 million on advertising[26] and approaching Filmation in 1980 to develop animation for the commercials.[27]

Mattel soon realized the franchise's storytelling potential,[28] leading executives to take advantage of recently relaxed FCC regulations and develop a cartoon series inspired by the toys.[29] Senior Vice President of Marketing Thomas Kalinske approached Filmation founder Lou Scheimer, who expressed interest in the property but wanted to tone down the violence. Together they rewrote the concept,[30] tapping writer Michael Halperin to develop the idea by adding moral lessons

The heroic He-Man and his friends defend Eternia from the forces of the evil warlord Skeletor. *Group W Productions/Photofest*

and giving the main character an alter ego and enemies to fight.[31] Mattel sold the property in foreign markets but ABC and NBC rejected it due to the violence and the issue of blurring the line between children's programming and advertising.[32] Kalinske and Scheimer sold the show through syndication, allowing Filmation to work around governmental restrictions on content.[33]

He-Man and the Masters of the Universe debuted on September 26, 1983.[34] Less than two months later, the group Action for Children's Television filed a complaint with the FCC decrying the show as nothing but "program-length commercials,"[35] while other organizations similarly criticized the series' advertising aspect.[36] By 1984, *He-Man* had been syndicated by 120 television stations in the United States and appeared in over thirty countries.[37] That same year, Conan Properties sued Mattel for copyright infringement but a judge ruled in favor of Mattel and declared Conan a public domain character.[38] Despite all that, kids turned *He-Man* into a hit,[39] and the property spawned the spinoff series (and accompanying toy line) *She-Ra: Princess of Power* as well as a live-action film adaptation and a handful of reboots.

Commentary

He-Man and the Masters of the Universe transported kids to a brightly colored world filled with instantly recognizable characters embarking on fun and thrilling adventures, and in the process it kicked off a wave of cartoons inspired by toy lines. The show proved so successful that it spawned numerous imitators and parodies,[40] paving the way for dozens of other beloved syndicated weekly cartoons like *DuckTales* and *Batman: The Animated Series*. In addition, *He-Man* took risks and pioneered new techniques, including the production of longer seasons and granting the show's creators more leeway to experiment with characters and storylines.[41] The show also capitalized on relaxed governmental regulation of children's programming to push the envelope in terms of violence (though the series appears tame when compared to other shows that appeared in its wake like *G.I. Joe: A Real American Hero* or *Gargoyles*). Overall, *He-Man* struck a chord with 1980s kids because it featured memorable characters and thrilling stories that blended science fiction, fantasy, and humor. The show benefited greatly from the contributions of talented speculative writers like Paul Dini and J. Michael Straczynski, both of whom contributed scripts and helped flesh out the world of Eternia.[42] Producers designed *He-Man* to sell toys, but the show still took kids on an exciting journey to a world of imagination and wonder.

Critics often dismissed *He-Man* as a juvenile power fantasy that revolved around a muscular paragon of violent and regressive machismo. While not unfounded, such critiques miss the fact that *He-Man* (both the show and the character) helped empower lonely latchkey kids while also teaching them important lessons about morality and personal responsibility. Each episode ended with the various characters breaking the fourth wall to talk directly to young viewers about the ethical underpinnings in that week's episode.[43] While *He-Man* and other shows of the period used these codas to work around FCC regulations regarding the educational needs of children age sixteen and younger, the lessons neverthe-less helped many kids develop their moral compasses. Of course, kids loved *He-Man* because it featured cool (and highly marketable) characters like He-Man, Skeletor, Man-at-Arms, Beast Man, and Trap Jaw along with nifty weapons and vehicles such as the Battle Ram, the Attack Trak, and the Bashasaurus (a tank shaped like a triceratops). The show also featured thrilling (not to mention weird) storylines such as "The Cosmic Comet" (S1E1), in which Skeletor enlists the help of a sentient comet to defeat He-Man, or "Happy Birthday Roboto" (S2E48), which sees nefarious, multi-headed villain Modulok attempt to steal Man-at-Arms's brain. These elements and more ensure that *He-Man* will continue to find new fans well into the future.

HOME MOVIES (1999–2004)

Creators: Loren Bouchard, Brendon Small
Cast: Brendon Small (Brendon Small), H. Jon Benjamin (Jason Penopolis/Coach McGuirk), Melissa Bardin Galsky (Melissa Robbins), Ron Lynch (Ronald Lynch), Paula Poundstone (Paula Small, 1999), Janine Ditullio (Paula Small, 2001–2004), Jonathan Katz (Erik Robbins)
Genre: Comedy

Synopsis

A bright but unmotivated eight-year-old navigates adolescence while making movies with his best friends.

Production History

Following a stint as a producer on the Comedy Central series *Dr. Katz: Profes-sional Therapist*, Loren Bouchard met Brendon Small, an aspiring standup comic attending Berklee College of Music.[44] Bouchard asked Small to play the child in the pilot episode of an animated series that Tom Snyder Productions was devel-oping for UPN in which veteran comedian Paula Poundstone played a single mother raising a precocious kid.[45] Bouchard and Small developed the series through brainstorming, with Small introducing somewhat autobiographical ele-ments based on his childhood when he forced his friends to act in his no-budget movies.[46] Small voiced the main character (named after him) although producers altered his voice to a higher pitch.[47] Additionally, Small drew on his musical train-ing to write and perform music for the series.[48]

During the first season, *Home Movies* used the "Squigglevision" technique created by Tom Snyder for *Dr. Katz*. The performers improvised much of the dialogue, especially in the first season, which relied on a procedure known as

Movie-obsessed nine-year-old Brendan Small (center) navigates adolescence with the help of his best friends Melissa (left) and Jason. *Cartoon Network/Photofest*

retroscripting: the scripts merely outlined plot points, thus allowing the actors to create the dialogue and humorous situations.[49] The entire cast gathered in the recording booth to record the dialogue together, creating a conversational tone that encouraged such improvisation.[50] Producers even tossed out scripts in favor of the improvisations done during those sessions,[51] which were then edited down to a soundtrack for the animators to work with.[52]

Home Movies premiered on April 26 at 8:30 p.m. after *Dilbert*[53] but the show only ran for five episodes before UPN pulled it from the schedule.[54] Cartoon Network quickly acquired the unaired episodes of *Home Movies* for its newly launched Adult Swim programming block and renewed the show for another season.[55] With the change in networks came a change in animation as Small and Bouchard switched to using Flash, which cost the same but looked better.[56] The series ran for an additional three seasons and fifty-two episodes before Adult Swim canceled it, with producers waiting to announce the termination until after the last episode aired.[57]

Commentary

With *Home Movies*, series creators Brendon Small and Loren Bouchard introduced audiences to the sort of relaxed, heavily improvised comedy that would inform subsequent animated efforts like *Metalocalypse* and *Bob's Burgers*. The show features hilariously awkward comedic situations and sidesplitting dialogue, neither of which the crude animation (characters barely move, and the backgrounds often appear poorly drawn) detract from. *Home Movies* boasts a cast of talented voice actors culled from the worlds of standup and sketch comedy, starting with Small, who voices lead character Brendon as an eight-year-old Woody Allen analog full of neurotic energy and self-deprecating humor. H. Jon Benjamin, meanwhile, pulls double duty as Brendon's best friend Jason, a soft-spoken misfit dealing with lots of bottled-up rage, and soccer coach John McGuirk, an obnoxious yet big-hearted dimwit who usually acts before he thinks. They are backed by some of the funniest people around, including Melissa Bardin Galsky (as Brendan's other bestie, Melissa), Ron Lynch (as put-upon grade school teacher Mr. Lynch), and Jonathan Katz (as Melissa's jovial father, Erik). These gifted players helped *Home Movies* find a devoted audience, thereby giving the show a second chance at life following its initial cancelation.

In addition to the rib-tickling comedy, *Home Movies* likely appealed to many viewers because it tapped into a very specific vein of nostalgia, offering an adult take on both childhood and imagination. When creating the show, Small drew inspiration from both his childhood and early adulthood, which may explain why the kids in *Home Movies* speak and quip like grown-ups (thus aligning the series with long-running pop cultural institution *South Park*). At the same time, the show provides keen insight into childhood anxieties (as in "Brendon's Choice," S1E13, in which Brendon asks about his estranged father) as well as a peek into the boundless imagination and creative process of visionary youngsters, usually via the movies made by Brendon and his friends. Yet even here the series' humor shines through thanks to several riotously funny sendups of specific films and cinematic genres (though viewers only see snippets of most of these). For example, "Time to Pay the Price" (S3E10) features parodies of *Mad Max*, *The Man Who Wasn't There*, *Godzilla*, and more while "History" (S2E10) serves up "Starboy and the Captain of Outer Space," a sci-fi musical that alludes to *Star Wars* and *Superman*. Gags like these made *Home Movies* a cult hit with comedy nerds and pop culture obsessives alike.

H.R. PUFNSTUF (1969–1970)

Creators: Marty Krofft, Sid Krofft
Cast: Jack Wild (Jimmy), Billie Hayes (Witchiepoo), Lennie Weinrib (H.R. Pufnstuf), Joan Gerber (Freddy the Flute), Walker Edmiston (Dr. Blinkey), Sharon Baird (Lady Boyd), Johnny Silver (Ludicrous Lion)
Genre: Adventure, Fantasy

Synopsis

Whisked away to a colorful fantasy land by an evil witch, a young boy sets off on surreal adventures with a friendly dragon.

Production History

In 1960, brothers Sid and Marty Krofft launched a risqué puppet review called *Les Poupees de Paris*, which they performed in various nightclubs before taking the act to television on series like *The Dean Martin Show*.[58] Their big break came in 1968 when they designed the costumes for the live action Hanna-Barbera series *The Banana Splits Adventure Hour*.[59] Impressed by the show's imagination and ratings success, Larry White, head of programming at NBC, asked the brothers to develop a series of their own.[60] The Kroffts decided to revamp a character they previously created for San Antonio's 1968 World's Fair, adding just "a dash of Puff the Magic Dragon."[61] Working with their workshop crew, they spent a week putting together a presentation that consisted of a series bible and concept art.[62] That presentation convinced NBC executives to pick up the show under the title *H.R. Pufnstuf*.[63]

Upon receiving word that NBC had greenlit the series, Marty Krofft set about researching how to run such a show because he and his brother possessed no knowledge about the business side of television production.[64] The network provided little money to produce the series,[65] giving the Kroffts just $54,000 per episode. However, the brothers spent twice that amount on each installment, meaning they lost $1 million and therefore relied on the profits generated by their other puppet shows to afford to make *Pufnstuf*.[66] They shot the series on film at a soundstage located at Paramount Studios[67]—all expensive production features. The series premiered on September 6, 1968, earning high enough ratings for Universal Pictures and Kellogg's to invest in a feature film version that debuted in 1970.[68] The series ran on NBC from 1969 to 1972 and ABC from 1972 to 1983 but consisted of just seventeen episodes.[69] While NBC wanted to renew *Pufnstuf* after the first season, White's replacement only offered to increase the budget by 5 percent, meaning the Kroffts would lose another $1 million.[70] The series then entered into syndication and languished there until July 2016 when several of the characters reappeared on Nickelodeon's preschool live-action show *Mutt & Stuff*, also produced by the Kroffts.[71]

Commentary

With *H.R. Pufnstuf*, brothers Sid and Marty Krofft introduced a whole new level of psychedelic surrealness to Saturday morning children's programming. Featuring vivid colors and bizarre characters, the show perfectly captured the hallucinogenic aesthetics of the era—so much so that many viewers considered it a product of the stoner counterculture (though the Krofft brothers reportedly abstained from using hard drugs). According to authors Timothy and Kevin Burke, "The general setting and goings-on in *H.R. Pufnstuf* were so oddly psychedelic that people have joked that 'H.R.' stood for 'hand rolled.'"[72] Yet the Krofft brothers intended the show as a homage to the classic Peter, Paul, and Mary song "Puff, the Magic Dragon," which told a similar story of a young boy traveling to a magical land where he meets an amiable fire-breather. *Pufnstuf* evokes the spirit of this beloved folk song and the two animated specials it inspired via phantasmagoric, hand-painted sets, whimsical adventures, and quirky characters. Each week, the show took kids and bored stoners alike on a journey to a magical island filled with unlikely heroes, spooky but laughable villains, and imaginative hijinks, which may explain why *Pufnstuf* remains so fondly remembered even now.

Though the show only produced seventeen episodes, it still managed to serve up plenty of delightfully fun exploits during its short life. Consider "The Mechanical Boy" (S1E4), in which the villainous Witchiepoo turns lead character Jimmy into a robot after she catches him trying to steal her boat. Meanwhile, in "The Show-Biz Witch" (S1E4), Pufnstuf wants to raise enough buttons (the currency used on Living Island) to purchase a supersonic pogo stick for Jimmy, so he organizes a talent show that draws the attention of Witchiepoo and her incompetent henchmen, who don disguises to infiltrate the contest and abscond with Freddy the Magic Flute. "The Stand-In" (S1E9) introduces viewers to Pufnstuf's younger sister, Shirley, a famous film actress who visits the island to shoot her latest movie, providing the title character with an opportunity to lure the fame-obsessed Witchiepoo out of her castle so Jimmy can sneak in and steal her Vroom-Broom. The show closed its run with "Jimmy Who?" (S1E17), which sees Jimmy bump his head and lose his memory, leading Pufnstuf, Dr. Blinkey, and Freddie to try to refresh the boy's memory via flashbacks from previous episodes. Though short-lived, *Pufnstuf* transported viewers to an amusing land full of whimsy and imagination. No wonder fans consider it one of the grooviest cult TV shows of all time.

See also *Pee-wee's Playhouse* (1986–1991)

I

IRON CHEF (1993–1999)

Creator: Fuji TV
Cast: Takeshi Kaga (Chairman Kaga), Kenji Fukui (Announcer), Yukio Hattori (Commentator), Shinichiro Ohta (Kitchen Report)
Genre: Game Show, Reality

Synopsis

Talented cooks from around the world journey to Kitchen Stadium to battle one of Chairman Kaga's three Iron Chefs.

Production History

Fuji TV's Yoshiaki Yamada ordered Director of Programming Osamu Kanemitsu to develop a culinary program for Sunday nights at 10:30 p.m. Yamada decided to marry the cooking show template with a fast-paced game show format, creating a series marked by an intense atmosphere that recalled Harrod's food emporium.[1] Kyouichi Tanaka agreed to create the new culinary competition program, and he considered pitting five chefs against amateur challengers,[2] noting that the avant-garde approach of cuisine versus cuisine emerged at the right time for Japanese culture.[3] Takashi Ishihara of the Programming and Production Department at Fuji TV suggested incorporating a theme ingredient that would rise up from below the stage and be introduced by an imperious host played by Takeshi Kaga.[4] Tanaka came up with the title *The Iron Chef of the Ovens* and suggested setting each two-hour episode inside what he called "Kitchen Stadium." He then combined these different ideas to create *Iron Chef* (*Ryōri no Tetsujin*, or "Ironmen of Cooking"),[5] which went on to become a worldwide phenomenon in the 1990s.

Yutaka Ishinabe, who specialized in French cuisine, initially rejected an offer to appear on the show but changed his mind after Tanaka suggested that each installment involve a new culinary discovery.[6] Meanwhile, Rokusaburo Michiba, a master of Japanese cuisine, agreed to participate after producers assured him it would only run for six months.[7] Chen Kenichi, well-versed in Chinese cuisine, thought the idea strange but ultimately decided to take the opportunity to venture outside his comfort zone and cook new dishes.[8] *Iron Chef* premiered on October 10,

Chairman Kaga (Takeshi Kaga) prepares to unleash another secret ingredient on the Iron Chefs who compete in Kitchen Stadium. *Fuji TV/Photofest*

1993, at 11:00 p.m.,[9] and for the first two months it earned weak ratings, leading the network to retool the series so that each episode featured one battle between an Iron Chef and a challenger rather than a series of preliminary battles.[10] In 1999,[11] Food Network picked up the show and worked with Fuji TV to tailor it for American audiences, including trimming episodes down to one hour and adding subtitles.[12] The last episode of *Iron Chef* aired on September 24, 1999, with specials running until 2002, producing a total of 309 episodes. In the United States, the show failed to find a wide audience until 2000[13] when Bobby Flay unsuccessfully challenged Iron Chef Masahura Morimoto, increasing viewership threefold.[14] *Iron Chef* spawned several spinoffs and remakes including *Iron Chef USA* (2001) and *Iron Chef America* (2005–2014),[15] while a reboot launched in Japan in 2012.[16]

Commentary

Given the current proliferation of cooking competition shows, it is difficult to imagine a time before chefs battled in stylized fashion for the viewing pleasure of television audiences. Before there were master chefs, top chefs, or even British bakers, *Iron Chef* provided audiences with a new way to watch food on television. Instead of watching a chef teach viewers how to prepare a dish, this Japanese program made the act of watching someone else cook into entertainment rather than education. Shows like *Iron Chef* possibly inspired viewers to try new ingredients, cooking techniques, dishes, or cuisine. However, the goal was to leave audiences amazed at the skills of the master chefs.

In every episode of *Iron Chef*, the experienced cooks who battled it out in Kitchen Stadium faced a surprise ingredient, and each contestant rose to the challenge, creating new dishes that combined ingredients and cuisines in ways previously unimagined. Part of the excitement lay in learning the surprise ingredient and seeing how the chefs used it in their dishes. During the ninety fast-paced minutes, the cooks went from surprise to inspiration to planning their dish to carrying out that plan and finally to presenting their new creation to the judges. The entertainment stemmed from watching that process, witnessing the drama of dealing with problems, cheering on the underdogs, and laughing at the comedic moments that lightened the mood. By the end of each episode, beautiful dishes emerged to tempt viewers' eyes and stomachs. Overall, *Iron Chef* encouraged viewers take their own creative culinary risks and try something new.

Of course, the industry itself took up this encouragement. *Iron Chef* spawned a franchise that captivated viewers around the globe, from *Iron Chef America* and *Iron Chef UK* to *Iron Chef Australia* and *Iron Chef Vietnam*. Beyond this one franchise, *Iron Chef* kicked off a trend for food on television, helping the Food Network ascend while further changing viewers' relationship with food.[17] Since the rise of this genre, foodies and food porn have become common fixtures in the United States as has the regular American's willingness to try new food brought over by immigrants hailing from outside European cultures. With that willingness comes the possibility of connecting with others, as argued by chefs like Andrew Zimmern and Anthony Bourdain.[18] *Iron Chef* helped spread awareness of cultural cuisines from around the world, and many viewers continue to take up that call to creativity and connectivity.

> ## IT'S ALWAYS SUNNY IN PHILADELPHIA (2005–PRESENT)
>
> *Creators*: Rob McElhenney, Glenn Howerton
> *Cast*: Glenn Howerton (Dennis Reynolds), Kaitlin Olson (Dee Reynolds), Danny De-
>   Vito (Frank Reynolds), Rob McElhenney (Mac), Charlie Day (Charlie Kelly)
> *Genre*: Comedy

Synopsis

A group of social misfits own and operate a rundown bar where they hatch insane get-rich-quick schemes and wacky adventures.

Production History

In 2004, struggling young Hollywood actor Rob McElhenney developed an idea for a short film about a guy and his insensitive friend.[19] Later, with the help of his girlfriend Jordan Reid and friends Charlie Day and Glenn Howerton, McElhenney adapted that short into a television pilot about struggling Hollywood actors called *It's Always Sunny on TV*.[20] The quartet shot a twenty-six-minute pilot using two video cameras and $85 worth of blank tapes.[21] McElhenney, along with his manager and his agent, pitched the idea to various networks until they received an offer from John Landgraf, president of FX.[22] Landgraf gave the group $400,000 to reshoot the pilot, ordering them to change the setting and characters to set the show apart from other series set in Los Angeles.[23] McElhenney moved the setting from Hollywood to Philadelphia and made the characters co-owners of a dive bar.[24] FX appointed McElhenney showrunner but the actor nevertheless kept his waiter job just in case the show failed.[25] In addition, McElhenney, Day, and Howerton served as executive producers.[26] Around that time, Reid ended her relationship with McElhenney[27] so the guys (rather unceremoniously) replaced her with Kaitlin Olson.[28]

Based on the reshot pilot, Landgraf ordered a first season of seven episodes with a budget of $450,000 per episode.[29] Now titled *It's Always Sunny in Philadelphia*, the show premiered on August 4, 2005, earning low ratings despite critical acclaim.[30] Landgraf suggested adding Danny Devito to the cast to increase ratings.[31] The producers reluctantly agreed after FX threatened to cancel the show.[32] The addition of DeVito helped *It's Always Sunny* reach an audience of 1.3 million viewers during its second season, prompting FX to order a third.[33] That season kicked off "The Nightman Cometh" storyline, which culminated with a musical episode that premiered on November 20, 2008, during the show's fourth season.[34] Soon after, the cast toured the country performing *The Nightman Cometh* live onstage to promote the fifth season.[35] *It's Always Sunny*, which recently entered its fourteenth season,[36] continues to draw big ratings and shows no signs of stopping anytime soon.[37]

Commentary

With its degenerate characters and twisted sense of humor, *It's Always Sunny in Philadelphia* serves up outrageous, over-the-top situations and mean-spirited (though cartoonish) jokes in each episode. The show mines much of its extremely dark humor from the sociopathic tendencies displayed by the core characters, who show little regard for their own well-being much less that of others. *It's Always Sunny* portrays Dennis, Mac, Dee, Charlie, and Frank as selfish assholes whose short-sightedness often leads to sidesplittingly tragic outcomes, as when the gang's actions drive their old pal Matthew Mara (aka "Rickety Cricket") to abandon the priesthood and develop a raging heroin habit. Similarly, Charlie's incessant stalking causes the object of his unwanted affection, a former alcoholic known only as the Waitress (played by Day's wife, Mary Elizabeth Ellis), to relapse. *It's Always Sunny* lacks any sort of sympathy for its characters (though the creators appear to harbor at least some empathy for these pathetic sad sacks) and puts them through the emotional wringer in each episode, much to the delight of the show's most devoted fans.

The show elicits big laughs from fans of dark comedy via harsh gags and shocking situations that push the envelope of acceptability. For example, in "The Gang Gets Held Hostage" (S3E4) the core characters land in the clutches of their hated rivals the McPoyles, causing Frank to declare, "When we get out of this, I'm gonna

The dysfunctional misfits of Paddy's Pub hatch harebrained schemes that constantly backfire. *FX Networks/Photofest*

shove my fist right into your ass, hard and fast! Not in the sexual way! In the 'I am pissed off' sort of way!" Later, in "Frank's Pretty Woman" (S7E1), the gang offers to makeover Frank's prostitute fiancée, with Mac stating, "People change, Frank. Look at me: I went from a tiny twink to the muscle-bound freak you see before you." In addition to the rib-tickling dialogue, *It's Always Sunny* also featured riotous situations, as in the fan-favorite episode "The Nightman Cometh" (S4E13), which sees Charlie convince his pals to help him stage an amusingly inept rock opera. The show also offered up biting social commentary via episodes like "Gun Fever: Still Too Hot" (S9E2), in which the gang tackles the gun control debate, and "Mac Finds His Pride" (S13E10), which features Mac coming out to his father through interpretive dance. Such episodes turned *It's Always Sunny* into one of the funniest and most topical cult TV shows ever made.

See also *The League* (2009–2015)

J

THE JOY OF PAINTING (1983–1994)

Creator: Bob Ross
Cast: Bob Ross
Genre: Documentary, Instructional

Synopsis

Soft-spoken artist Bob Ross paints happy little trees and inviting natural land-scapes.

Production History

In 1981, after a personal loss, Annette Kowalski met Bob Ross at a painting class. Mesmerized by his presence,[1] she became Ross's manager to set up his teaching gigs and even a hotline, 1–800-BOB-ROSS.[2] In that first year, Ross and his wife, Jane, went into business with the Kowalskis, with both couples losing $20,000.[3] In 1982, to promote his struggling teaching classes, the quartet produced a commercial featuring Ross and PBS celebrity William Alexander, who mentored Ross in the wet-on-wet painting style, and brought it to their local PBS station, WNVC in Fairfax, Virginia.[4] The folks at WNVC were so impressed they offered Ross a show.[5] Together they developed a thirteen-week, televised painting class called *The Joy of Painting*,[6] which ran on sixty PBS stations during the first year.[7]

Ross's original idea for the set was a hunter's log-cabin but he ultimately decided to go with a minimalist set to generate more intimacy with viewers.[8] This first series drew a small audience so the station dropped *The Joy of Painting*.[9] In 1983, WIPB in Muncie, Indiana, aired an advertisement for Ross's teaching class, which proved so successful that Ross approached the station about a series.[10] At that point, Alexander handed over his technique to Ross for *The Joy of Painting* to continue with a national audience.[11] The series would continue from Muncie until 1994, producing a total of 403 episodes over thirty-one seasons.[12] During the show, Ross lived in Florida and traveled to Muncie every three months to produce the series, shooting all thirteen episodes at a fast pace (at one point he even completed eight episodes in a single day).[13] He produced the paintings live on tape using previously finished reference paintings to guide him.[14]

Over time the series aired on 95 percent of public television stations in the United States, reaching almost 100 million households every week.[15] The series also became a hit with international audiences, particularly in Europe, Canada, Mexico, and Japan.[16] In 1994, Ross was diagnosed with lymphoma, and he eventually became too weak to travel to Indiana to complete series 32.[17] Ross died on July 4, 1995,[18] but his painting style continues to influence fans around the world,[19] including attendees of the 2019 San Diego Comic-Con.[20] The Internet streaming site Twitch recently launched a Bob Ross marathon that drew 5.6 million viewers, and the service plans to redo the marathon every October 29 to celebrate Ross's birthday.[21]

Commentary

With his infectious positivity and calming demeanor (not to mention his impressive Afro, which he reportedly hated), Bob Ross became an icon for an entire generation of retirees, latchkey kids, and bored pot smokers thanks to his long-running PBS series *The Joy of Painting*. Ross, a former military man who learned to paint while stationed in Alaska, used his platform to convey his love of painting to viewers for over ten years. Yet his quiet personality and laid-back style turned him into a beloved cult figure whose likeness adorns tee shirts, mugs, pillows, toys, and more to this day. When *The Joy of Painting* debuted in 1983, Ross immediately established himself as unique among both art instructors and television hosts thanks to his look, cheery optimism, and gentle air, all of which endeared him to audiences around the world. As a painter, Ross churned out lovely but unexceptional landscapes of the sort found in the average motel lobby, but his soothing voice and encouraging attitude (he once remarked that anyone could paint if they had "a few tools, a little instruction, and a vision in [their] mind") made him a hit with fans from all walks of life even if they never picked up a paintbrush. For many viewers, *The Joy of Painting* felt like a little island of tranquility in a sea of screeching advertisements, depressing news stories, and overbearing sitcoms, which may explain why people still love the show even now.

The Joy of Painting truly revolves around Ross and his personality given that it consists almost entirely of the artist painting one of his many landscapes (according to at least one estimate, Ross completed thirty thousand paintings during his lifetime).[22] Ross proved a mellow but strong personality, one filled with delightful quirks and boundless enthusiasm. His joyful smile and dancing eyes revealed a playful side that made him difficult to dislike. While painting, Ross often talked about his own life, sharing brief anecdotes that revealed his delight in even the simplest things, and he exhorted viewers to do the same. He also offered up plenty of quote-worthy aphorisms such as "We don't make mistakes, just happy little accidents," "You need the dark in order to show the light," and "There's nothing wrong with having a tree as a friend." Such sayings helped Ross later attain meme status on the Internet, which is littered with his image along with some sarcastic or profound comment. Without Ross and his relaxed disposition, *The Joy of Painting* likely would have failed to attain widespread pop cultural recognition it currently enjoys.

The Joy of Painting lives on today thanks to sites like YouTube and Netflix, both of which stream episodes of the series for viewers young and old. Despite his peaceful character and relaxing voice, Ross left behind a quiet legacy that rings loud to this day.

K

KEY & PEELE (2012–2015)

Creators: Keegan-Michael Key, Jordan Peele
Cast: Keegan-Michael Key, Jordan Peele
Genre: Comedy

Synopsis

This hip, hilarious sketch show spoofs politics, sociocultural issues, pop cultural icons, and more.

Production History

Keegan-Michael Key met Jordan Peele in 2003 when Key worked with Chicago's Second City and Peele toured with Amsterdam's Boom Chicago.[1] The two talented improv comics "fell in comedy love," and later that year they each auditioned for spots on Fox's sketch comedy series *MADtv*.[2] Both men landed gigs with the show, and during their time in the cast, they mostly impersonated black celebrities but also honed their sketch-writing skills.[3] When Peele's contract expired in 2009, he and Key developed an idea for their own sketch show.[4] Their mutual manager pitched them as a comedy duo to Fox and Comedy Central, with the latter offering to fund a pilot.[5] Key and Peele used the money to produce a pilot episode, and in June 2011 Comedy Central picked up the then untitled sketch-comedy series.[6]

For the first season, Key and Peele wrote 260 sketches but later whittled that number down to 54 they wanted to produce.[7] Comedy Central wanted the show to follow the formula Dave Chappelle developed for his own self-titled show, with the duo introducing their sketches on stage in front of a live audience.[8] Before the series premiered, the two comics released a series of videos called "Key & Peele: Obama Anger Translator" on their *Key & Peele* YouTube channel.[9] The sketch series, now titled *Key & Peele*, premiered January 31, 2012, at 10:30 p.m.,[10] and it did so well that Comedy Central quickly ordered a second season of ten episodes.[11]

As the series progressed it continued to earn strong ratings, so Comedy Central executives grew more relaxed about the racially charged comedy and offered fewer notes.[12] In 2013, the series won a Peabody Award for its handling of racial issues.[13] The following year, Comedy Central ordered a fourth season of twenty-two episodes and even considered creating an animated spin-off based on the recurring characters Vandaveon and Mike.[14] *Key & Peele* ended after the fifth season when the titular duo decided to move on to other projects.[15] Since then Key and Peele have each produced or appeared in numerous other television series and movies, both together and apart.

Commentary

Key & Peele introduced the world to the uproarious comedy of Keegan-Michael Key and Jordan Peele, both of whom would go on to change not just the face of comedy but popular culture itself. Over the course of five brief seasons, the show produced several hilarious skits and unforgettable characters that quickly attained viral status, most notably Luther (Barack Obama's high-strung "anger translator") and the "East/West College Bowl" trilogy (which introduces football players with increasingly silly names). *Key & Peele* brought a rarely seen perspective to the realm of sketch comedy, that of the biracial black nerd, an identity that both performers embrace.[16] Each week, the duo translated their dweeby interests (e.g., movies, television, science fiction, horror) into comedy gold, using their obsessions as the basis for hilariously incisive skits like "Alien Imposters" (the survivors of an alien invasion use long-standing racial biases to identify their fellow humans); "Sexy Vampires" (a newly turned bloodsucker fails to fit in with his extremely goth compatriots); and "'Gremlins 2' Brainstorm" (the titular twosome imagine the pitch for the campy sequel to Joe Dante's holiday classic *Gremlins*).

In their self-titled sketch show, Keegan-Michael Key (left) and Jordan Peele serve up hilarious skits filled with wacky characters. *Comedy Central/Photofest*

Every episode of *Key & Peele* unleashed new hilarity that felt like nothing else on TV at the time and audiences responded enthusiastically, turning the show into one of the most buzzed-about sketch comedies of all time.

Key & Peele also resonated with viewers and critics because it offered up sharp political, social, and cultural commentary. Each episode tackled tough topics like racism, sexism, consent, inequality, homophobia, bullying, toxic masculinity, and other hot-button issues with keen wit and striking candor. Consider "Bitch" (S1E1), in which two deeply insecure men try to impress one another by lying about how they each refer to their wives as "bitch." The insightful "School Bully" (S2E7) revolves around a schoolyard tough inadvertently revealing his own deep-seated fear, uncertainty, and self-hatred while confronting one of his victims. "Pirate Chantey" (S5E1) sees a group of cutthroat pirates sing a jolly song about treating women with respect, while "Town Hall Meeting" (S5E1) tackles homophobia and misrepresentation when a C-SPAN cameraman mistakes a heterosexual man for gay during a discussion about same-sex marriage. The show bowed out in grand style with the frank and funny "Negrotown" (S5E11), a lively musical about police brutality. *Key & Peele* pokes fun at America's worst tendencies but never makes light of them, instead using comedy to help viewers confront their own biases, racial or otherwise. At the same time, the eponymous comics also laugh at themselves, using characters like the Valets (two overzealous parking attendants who ceaselessly discuss pop culture) and Wendell Sanders (an obese, nerdy shut-in) to lightly mock their own interests and personalities. Overall, a combination of knowing wit, sly pop culture parody, and sociopolitical satire turned *Key & Peele* into a cult smash.

See also *Mr. Show with Bob and David* (1995–1998)

SPOTLIGHT: JORDAN PEELE

Born February 21, 1979,[17] Jordan Peele, a shy nerd interested in musical theater and movies, grew up on Manhattan's Upper West Side.[18] He eventually landed a scholarship to attend the Calhoun School, an independent performing arts school.[19] Later, he studied puppetry at Sarah Lawrence College but dropped out to move to Amsterdam, where he performed with the improv troupe Boom Chicago.[20] After returning to the United States, Peele joined the cast of the sketch show *MADtv* before teaming with castmate and friend Keegan-Michael Key to create *Key & Peele*. Since then, Peele has written and directed the acclaimed horror films *Get Out* (2017) and *Us* (2019), while his production company, Monkeypaw, produced Spike Lee's 2018 film *BlackKklansman* and a critically acclaimed reboot of *The Twilight Zone* for CBS All Access.

THE KIDS IN THE HALL (1988–1994)

Creator: Lorne Michaels
Cast: Dave Foley, Bruce McCulloch, Kevin McDonald, Mark McKinney, Scott Thompson
Genre: Comedy

Canadian comedy troupe the Kids in the Hall elicits big laughs from viewers with their bizarre skits and outrageous characters. *HBO/Photofest*

Synopsis

In this uproarious variety show, a troupe of Canadian comics serves up outrageous skits filled with absurdist humor and weird characters.

Production History

In 1981, Bruce McCulloch met Mark McKinney in Calgary at the Loose Moose Theater, where they developed the improv team the Audience.[21] A year later, Dave Foley and Kevin McDonald met at Second City improv workshops in Toronto,[22] later forming a sketch troupe called the Kids in the Hall (KITH). In 1983, the Audience moved to Toronto and met KITH,[23] and the two groups soon decided to merge.[24] Scott Thompson saw their act in the fall of 1983 and enthusiastically introduced himself,[25] and he officially joined the troupe in early 1984.[26] In the summer of 1986,[27] *Saturday Night Live* producer Lorne Michaels saw KITH perform at the Rivoli rock club in Toronto.[28] Impressed, Michaels helped the group secure their own television show.[29]

Michael Fuchs, head of programming at HBO, expressed interest in the project and offered a "moderately priced pilot, with an option toward a full series."[30] In 1987, KITH relocated to Manhattan to write and perform an HBO showcase that would serve as the pilot, but their edgy comedy style alienated the Manhattan crowd.[31] It took a while for audiences to warm to the group, who continued performing showcases to drum up interest among HBO executives.[32] The cable service aired an hour-long special in October 16, 1988,[33] but it took the Canadian

Broadcasting Corporation (CBC) offering to co-produce the show to secure a greenlight.[34] Based on the success of the special, the two networks ordered a full season of twenty episodes.[35]

The self-titled series shot in Toronto,[36] with episodes budgeted at around $300,000.[37] *The Kids in the Hall* premiered July 21, 1989, on HBO and September 4 of that same year on CBC.[38] From there, CBC aired the series on Thursday evenings at 9:30 p.m. while HBO ran it Fridays at midnight.[39] In 1993, the networks slashed the budget as the show headed into season 4 so Michaels took it to CBS, which broadcast *The Kids in the Hall* on Fridays at 12:30 a.m. though many affiliates broadcast it much later.[40] CBS cancelled the series after season 5,[41] and the troupe decided to quit while they were ahead.[42] In 1996, they produced the troubled and poorly received 1996 film *Brain Candy* and broke up soon after.[43] KITH reunited in 2000 for a live tour, followed by another in 2008, the CBC miniseries *Death Comes to Town* in 2010,[44] and another tour in 2015.[45]

Commentary

Following in the footsteps of the legendary *Monty Python's Flying Circus*, the riotously funny skit show *The Kids in the Hall* delighted audiences around the world with its droll wit, bizarre characters, surreal situations, and abundant cross-dressing. Like *SCTV* before it, the show offered up a distinctly Canadian style of absurdism that left many viewers scratching their heads while others laughed until their sides ached. As the titular kids, Dave Foley, Bruce McCulloch, Kevin McDonald, Mark McKinney, and Scott Thompson used their singular comedic sensibilities to create memorable recurring characters (like the Chicken Lady and Buddy Cole); surreal situations (see "Love and Sausages," a hysterically funny riff on both David Lynch films and Franz Kafka stories); and unforgettable lines such as "An optimist says, 'The drink is half full.' A pessimist says, 'The drink is half full, but I might have bowel cancer.'" Despite the involvement of *Saturday Night Live* creator Lorne Michaels, *The Kids in the Hall* offered sketch comedy fans a distinctly peculiar alternative to a long-running *Saturday Night Live*, which attracted a much broader audience. With bizarre skits like "The Pear Dream" (a parody of pompous art films) and "My Pen!" (a meek bank employee goes to great lengths to retrieve his favorite pen), *The Kids in the Hall* seemed destined for cult status.

Fans consider *The Kids in the Hall* one of the best sketch comedy series of all time thanks in large part to its quote-worthiness. During its seven-year run, the show spawned numerous lines that devotees recite to this day. For instance, cries of "I'm crushing your head!" (the repeated declaration of McKinney's Head Crusher) or "Now we're cooking with evil gas!" (as uttered by horror show host Sir Simon Milligan, played to fey perfection by McDonald) allow *The Kids in the Hall* fanatics to identify one another more than twenty years after the show left the air. Meanwhile, skits like "Sarcastic Guy" (in which a character played by Dave Foley claims to have a speech impediment that makes him sound sarcastic) and "Citizen Kane" (a film fanatic fails to remember the title of Orson Welles's masterpiece, much to the annoyance of his friend) appear tailor-made for quoting thanks to lines like "Oh, I'm not being sarcastic. No! This is just a little speech impediment. I can't help it." In addition, along with the jaunty theme song provided by Shadowy Men on a Shadowy Planet, *The Kids in the Hall* featured several toe-tapping tunes written and performed by the show's stars, including "Daves I Know" (McCulloch lists all the Daves he knows), "The Terrier Song" (McCulloch again, this time extolling the virtues of a certain breed of dog), and "Do Re Mi" (the entire cast pays homage to *The Sound of Music* with an elaborate musical number set in Toronto's business district). Songs like these, along with the sharp writing and outrageous characters, helped transform *The Kids in the Hall* into a beloved cult classic.

See also *Monty Python's Flying Circus* (1969–1974), *Mr. Show with Bob and David* (1995–1998), *SCTV* (1976–1984), *The State* (1993–1995), *Upright Citizens Brigade* (1998–2000)

KOLCHAK: THE NIGHT STALKER (1974–1975)

Creator: Jeffrey Grant Rice
Cast: Darren McGavin (Carl Kolchak), Simon Oakland (Tony Vincenzo), Jack Grinnage (Ron Updyke), Ruth McDevitt (Miss Emily Cowles)
Genre: Horror, Mystery, Thriller

Synopsis

A Chicago newspaper reporter investigates the paranormal.

Production History

In the early 1970s, producer Dan Curtis read reporter Jeff Rice's unpublished novel *The Night Stalker* in which an intrepid journalist named Carl Kolchak encounters a vampire in modern-day Las Vegas.[46] Curtis purchased the property and asked author Richard Matheson, who penned several episodes of *The Twilight Zone* and the 1972 film *Ghost Story*, to write a teleplay based on the story.[47] The resulting script served as the basis for a made-for-TV movie that aired on ABC on January 11, 1972.[48] That telefilm earned huge ratings, prompting ABC to commission a sequel, *The Night Strangler* (also scripted by Matheson), that debuted the following year.[49] The sequel did well enough that the network ordered a third telefilm called *The Night Walkers*. Not long after, ABC announced a weekly *Kolchak: The Night Stalker* series, minus the involvement of either Rice or Curtis.[50]

Throughout production, series lead Darrin McGavin, whose production company owned 50 percent of the show, often clashed with producers, network executives, and studio heads over the scripts, violence, and tone, which veered increasingly into comedy with each new episode.[51] The show's low budget also meant that the crew often cut corners when creating the monsters and special effects.[52] The first episode premiered on September 13, 1974, and ABC scheduled *Kolchak* to air on Fridays at 10:00 p.m., resulting in low ratings especially when the show was put up against similarly named series like *Kodiak* and *Kojak*.[53] Meanwhile, Rice, who claimed he never authorized a *Kolchak* series, threatened to sue ABC, though the lawsuit never made it to court. Finally, in 1975, ABC's new programming executive, Fred Silverman, pulled the plug on *Kolchak* after just twenty episodes.[54] CBS reran the series in 1979–1980 as part of their late-night schedule, while the Sci-Fi Channel briefly aired *Kolchak* years later.[55] Though short-lived, the show left an indelible imprint on popular culture, with Chris Carter citing it as an influence on *The X-Files*.[56]

Commentary

Despite lasting only a single season of just twenty hour-long episodes (preceded by three well-received made-for-TV movies), *Kolchak: The Night Stalker* neverthe-less kicked off a wave of paranormal investigation shows including *The X-Files*, *Buffy the Vampire Slayer*, and *Fringe*. Like its numerous offspring, *Kolchak* served up genre-bending stories that mixed cop show clichés with well-worn horror tropes, occasionally adding a dash of comedy. The show also pioneered the monster-of-the-week format that later became standard in genre fare like *Smallville* and *Supernatural*. Sadly, as author John Kenneth Muir observes, the stories sometimes suffered because David Chase, producer Cy Chermak, and star Darren McGavin often tweaked scripts at the last minute, making each episode "clever and witty, but not particularly unique or imaginative."[57] Nonetheless, *Kolchak* endeared itself to viewers thanks to well-rounded characters who stood apart from the one-note caricatures found in other horror shows of the time.[58] The charismatic McGavin portrayed the title character as an eccentric, determined, obsessive, funny, some-what incompetent coward who comes face-to-face with the supernatural, thus imbuing Kolchak with a sense of authenticity.[59] Overall, *Kolchak* served as a master class in how to mismanage a popular property given that it developed a fervent fanbase but left network executives confused and seemingly unsure of how to market the program to a wider audience.

Each week, *Kolchak* served up spooky procedurals that saw the title character square off against various supernatural beasties including vampires, werewolves, demons, and even a reincarnated Jack the Ripper. In "The Zombie" (S1E2), a voo-doo priestess resurrects her dead grandson so he can enact revenge on the mob-sters who murdered him. In the next episode, "They Have Been, They Are, They Will Be . . ." (S1E3), Kolchak encounters otherworldly visitors who suck the bone marrow out of their human victims. Later, in "Firefall" (S1E6), Kolchak tries to prevent a dead gangster's ghost from possessing a popular music conductor. The following week, in perhaps the show's wildest episode, "The Devil's Platform" (S1E7), Kolchak meets a popular politician granted the ability to transform into a demonic hellhound by the Devil himself. In addition, Kolchak occasionally bat-tled earthly (but equally fantastic) antagonists as in "Mr. R.I.N.G." (S1E12), which sees the exasperated reporter confront a homicidal robot. The series concluded its run with "The Sentry" (S1E20), in which Kolchak travels to an underground facil-ity to investigate a series of murders committed by a prehistoric reptilian creature. Thrilling adventures such as these helped *Kolchak* build a devoted fanbase and shape the future of science fiction and fantasy on television.

See also *Dark Shadows* (1966–1971), *Supernatural* (2005–2020), *The X-Files* (1993–2018)

L

THE LEAGUE (2009–2015)

Creators: Jackie Marcus Schaffer, Jeff Schaffer
Cast: Mark Duplass (Pete Eckhart), Stephen Rannazzisi (Kevin MacArthur), Paul Scheer (Andre Nowzick), Katie Aselton (Jenny MacArthur), Nick Kroll (Rodney Ruxin), Jonathan Lajoie (Taco MacArthur), Jason Mantzoukas (Rafi), Nadine Velazquez (Sofia Ruxin)
Genre: Comedy

Synopsis

A group of former high school pals try to maintain their tenuous friendships into adulthood via their fantasy football league.

Production History

In December 2005, husband and wife producing duo Jeff and Jackie Schaffer traveled to the French Alps for Christmas.[1] One night, Jackie found Jeff standing in the snow screaming into his cell phone as he tried to coordinate two fantasy football Super Bowls,[2] thus giving her an idea for a television show. Soon after, HBO commissioned the Schaffers to write a pilot[3] but wanted to delay the start of production for a year.[4] Rather than wait, the Schaffers sent the treatment to Nick Grad, president of original programming at FX and a fellow fantasy football fanatic.[5] FX picked up the show, ordering six episodes for the 2009–2010 season,[6] and the Schaffers filled the cast with comedic performers who brought their own sensibilities to the series, including YouTube stars, independent filmmakers, and improv artists.[7]

The Schaffers shot the pilot episode in the summer of 2009.[8] They allowed the actors to improvise and essentially create each episode, starting with the pilot, which Jeff Schaffer equated to "shooting a live comedy sporting event."[9] Every episode started with a 10–11-page outline developed by the Schaffers,[10] who struggled to turn episodes in on time as they needed to edit everything they recorded down to the 21-minute 50-second length required by commercial television.[11] Titled *The League*, the series quietly debuted on October 29, 2009. FX quickly renewed the series with a thirteen-episode order.[12] By the third season, the show routinely drew around 1.7 million viewers, making it a ratings success.[13] In 2013, during the show's fifth season, *The League* moved to the recently launched FXX comedy network.[14] The series ended after seven seasons[15] but remains popular among sports fans and comedy nerds.

Commentary

Filled with raunchy humor and amusingly despicable characters, *The League* serves up big laughs while poking good-natured fun at the worlds of sports fandom and bro culture. The show helped launch the careers of several funny and talented people including Mark Duplass, Nick Kroll, Jonathan Lajoie, Paul Scheer, and Jason Mantzoukas. Each member of the cast brought their own singular style of humor to *The League*, which featured an abundance of crude jokes and awkward situations. For instance, in "The Bounce Test" (S1E2), Ruxin explains why he refuses to leave his beautiful Latina wife Sophia, declaring, "If we got a divorce, she would get half of my money, making me ostensibly poor, yet still paying her to just get pounded by other dudes, which will happen, because she is still smoking hot, whereas I look like a Nazi propaganda cartoon of a Jew." Meanwhile, in "12. 12. 12" (S4E11), football star Deion Sanders unwittingly stumbles onto a porn set overseen by inveterate perverts Dirty Randy (Seth Rogen) and Rafi, and Rafi bluntly states, "Buddy, I don't know who you are, but you're about to get chlamydia." Lines like these, along with funny cameos from popular sports stars, helped *The League* build a devoted audience.

The show mined much of its humor from the relationships shared by the core group of dudes as they jockey for position and repeatedly try to one-up each other in both fantasy football and life. For example, in "The Anniversary Party" (S2E6), Taco goads an increasingly angry Ruxin into throwing a lavish anniversary party for Sophia and hijinks ensue when Pete engages in a battle of wills with his ex-wife's new boyfriend. Later, in "High School Reunion" (S2E10), the gang sets out to impress their former classmates, resulting in a series of wacky shenanigans. Meanwhile, "Yobogoya!" (S3E6) sees Kevin suffer food poisoning after eating cheap meat from a fast food joint while Andre participates in the new fad of "urban foraging" and fails spectacularly. "Rafi and Dirty Randy" (S5E4) sees the eponymous duo travel to Los Angeles to avenge a friend's death only to wind up on the wrong side of the law in hilariously over-the-top fashion. Such episodes helped *The League* score a big following among fans of vulgar comedy, but the amusingly loathsome characters and awkward situations guarantee that the series will remain a cult favorite for years to come.

See also *Arrested Development* (2003–2019), *It's Always Sunny in Philadelphia* (2005–Present)

LOST (2004–2010)

Creators: J. J. Abrams, Jeffrey Lieber, Damon Lindelof
Cast: Matthew Fox (Jack Shephard), Evangeline Lilly (Katherine Austen), Josh Holloway (James Ford), Jorge Garcia (Hugo Reyes), Terry O'Quinn (John Locke), Naveen Andrews (Sayid Jarrah), Yunjin Kim (Sun-Hwa Kwon), Daniel Dae Kim (Jin-Soo Kwon)
Genre: Drama, Fantasy, Mystery, Science Fiction, Thriller

Synopsis

The survivors of an airplane crash must band together to escape a mysterious deserted island that seems determined to finish what the crash started.

Production History

In 2001, ABC chairman Lloyd Braun watched a reality series produced by Conan O'Brien called *Lost*.[16] A few years later, while on vacation in Hawaii, Braun saw the film *Cast Away*, which inspired him to create a scripted series about people stranded on a deserted island.[17] He asked Jeffrey Lieber to write a pilot script, which Braun wound up hating.[18] An ABC executive then suggested J. J. Abrams, who spent five days co-writing an outline with screenwriter Damon Lindelof.[19] Braun received the outline on a Friday night and greenlit the two-hour pilot the next morning.[20] Production took place between March and April 2004[21] but Walt Disney executives fired Braun after he spent $14 million on the pilot (the most expensive in history).[22] Nonetheless, the pilot episode of *Lost* debuted on September 22, 2004, to huge ratings,[23] leading ABC to pick up the series.

Around that time, Abrams departed the show to direct *Mission: Impossible III*, leaving Lindelof to oversee *Lost* on his own.[24] However, by episode 11, Lindelof had decided he needed help[25] so he asked Carlton Cuse to join him as co-showrunner.[26] Over the next two years, the duo clashed with ABC over the series' length: Cuse and Lindelof planned to end the show after four years while network executives wanted to keep it going for at least ten.[27] Eventually, both parties settled on six years.[28] During the first season, ABC lost about $11 million on *Lost* as each episode cost $2.8 million to produce.[29] The show only became financially lucrative once it reached one hundred episodes, allowing the network to syndicate it.[30] Midway through the third season, ratings slumped and critics turned on the show.[31] The divisive finale of *Lost* aired on May 23, 2010, drawing just 13 million viewers.[32] Fans continue to engage in heated discussions about the show to this day.

Commentary

With its twisty narrative and captivating (if sometimes frustrating) cliffhangers, *Lost* signaled the rise of series co-creator J. J. Abrams's so-called mystery box style of storytelling. The show turned the multi-talented Abrams into a pop culture icon and altered the television landscape for years to come. Upon its debut in

In *Lost*, a group of strangers struggles to survive on a mysterious island that holds many secrets.
ABC/Photofest

September 2004, *Lost* caused a sensation, earning huge ratings and wide critical acclaim. It also unleashed a wave of imitators as other networks scrambled to find the next big longform serialized drama, launching shows such as *Heroes*, *Fringe*, *The Nine*, and *Revolution*, all of which tried (often unsuccessfully) to replicate the formula that made *Lost* such a massive hit. The show also developed a zealous fanbase, and producers embraced these enthusiasts, essentially turning them into another stream of marketing for the series. Abrams's production company Bad Robot even set up a website called "The Fuselage" that allowed fans to interact with the show's actors and writers. The site's message boards quickly "exploded with viewer-generated threads that attempted to track the island's history, the content and source of the whispers in the jungle, and potential explanations for all the surprising connections among the characters' lives."[33] A labyrinthine plot and the producers' shrewd exploitation of fans turned *Lost* into one of the most buzzed-about TV shows of all time.

Every week *Lost* served up compelling mysteries and shocking revelations that frequently left viewers reeling. The thrills began with the first episode, "Pilot," which set up the show's premise and introduced all fifteen central characters in an exciting manner, dropping tantalizing hints about the series' mythology while staging one of the most intense plane-crash sequences ever seen on television. A few episodes later, *Lost* truly established itself as must-see TV with "Walkabout" (S1E4), a breathtaking installment that revealed the backstory of fan-favorite character John Locke, upending everything viewers thought they knew about the show and its island setting. Season 3 ramped up the mystery and deepened the show's already dense lore with a two-part season finale, "Through the Looking Glass" (S3E22, S3E23), offering fans a glimpse into the future via a flash forward that reveals the fate of some of the castaways. *Lost* even delved into the complex history of its villains as in "Whatever Happened, Happened" (S5E11), which divulges the backstory of arch nemesis Benjamin Linus (played with evil relish by Michael Emerson) while also considering the metaphysical implications of the castaways' time-hopping exploits. During the last few seasons, episodes tended to drag while the increasingly convoluted storylines muddied the mythology, culminating with a finale that left many viewers feeling unsatisfied (if not outright angry). Despite all that, *Lost* deserves a spot on any list of the greatest cult TV shows ever made.

See also *Twin Peaks* (1990–1991), *The X-Files* (1993–2018)

SPOTLIGHT: J. J. ABRAMS

Born in New York City on June 27, 1966, Jeffrey Jacob Abrams transitioned from making short Super-8 films as a boy to working on the low-budget sci-fi film *Nightbeast* in 1982.[34] After graduating from Sarah Lawrence College in 1988, Abrams co-wrote the screenplay for *Taking Care of Business* (1990).[35] He then wrote or co-wrote the screenplays for *Regarding Henry* (1991), *Forever Young* (1992), *Gone Fishin'* (1997), and *Armageddon* (1998).[36] In 1998, Abrams co-created the television show *Felicity*, which ran for four seasons.[37] From there, he created or co-created *Alias* in 2001, *Lost* in 2004, and *Fringe* in 2008.[38] In addition to his television work, Abrams directed the films *Mission: Impossible III* (2006), *Star Trek* (2009), *Super 8* (2011), *Star Trek Into Darkness* (2013), *Star Wars: Episode VII—The Force Awakens* (2015), and *Star Wars: Episode IX—The Rise of Skywalker* (2019).[39]

LOST IN SPACE (1965–1968)

Creator: Irwin Allen
Cast: Guy Williams (John Robinson), June Lockhart (Maureen Robinson), Mark Goddard (Don West), Marta Kristen (Judy Robinson), Bill Mumy (Will Robinson), Angela Cartwright (Penny Robinson), Jonathan Harris (Zachary Smith)
Genre: Comedy, Fantasy, Science Fiction

Synopsis

An explorer takes his family on an interstellar mission that goes drastically off course.

The crew of the *Jupiter 2* encounters weird aliens and other intergalactic threats as they try to find their way back to Earth. *CBS/Photofest*

Production History

Writer Ib Melchior claimed that in 1960 he planned to adapt *Swiss Family Robinson* as *Space Family Robinson*.[40] He then worked to bring his new project to fruition,[41] first as a weekly show with CBS[42] and then as a motion picture in 1964.[43] Meanwhile in 1963, Hilda Bohem wrote a screenplay titled *Swiss Family 3000*, which Allied Artists hoped to produce the following year.[44] Finally, in August 1964 Irwin Allen developed a series called *Space Family Robinson* for 20th Century Fox and CBS.[45] However, comic book publisher Gold Key distributed a monthly series under that title[46] so Allen renamed his show *Lost in Space*.[47] Melchior worried that Allen's work might interfere with his upcoming film,[48] which he believed informed Allen's property.[49] Even Bohem thought Allen based his series on her script, though Allen's idea had more in common with Melchior's screenplay.[50]

Despite all this, production on the pilot episode of *Lost in Space*, which cost $600,000 and took twenty days to shoot, commenced in December 1964.[51] After suing Allen and CBS for copyright infringement, Bohem settled for $20,000.[52] Meanwhile, Melchior failed to receive any money related to the project.[53] In the end, Allen succeeded in bringing *Lost in Space* to the screen first because he "had established business ties in the industry."[54] Shimon Wincelberg wrote the unaired pilot's script, which lacked the characters of Dr. Smith and the robot.[55] They only appeared once story editor Tony Wilson decided the show needed more "internal conflict."[56] Overall, casting went smoothly, though Jonathan Harris refused to provide examples of his previous work.[57] Nevertheless, he landed the role of Dr. Smith "without even having to read for the part."[58] Adding Harris helped Allen sell the series to CBS.[59]

Lost in Space premiered on September 15, 1965.[60] The first season shot in black and white before moving to color in the second season.[61] *Lost in Space* ran for three seasons comprised of eighty-three episodes. While the series started strong, its quality diminished after adopting a campier tone in the second and third seasons to compete with *Batman*.[62] At that point, *Lost in Space* earned higher ratings but the producers and cast disliked the departure from the logical plots of the first season.[63] However, Dr. Smith's buffoonish antics helped increase ratings, prompting CBS to request a fourth season but only if producers reduced the cost of the series.[64] Allen refused this request, and the network responded by canceling *Lost in Space*.[65] In the years since, the show has generated numerous tie-in products as well as a short-lived animated series,[66] a disastrous theatrical film adaptation,[67] and a reboot that premiered on Netflix in 2018.[68]

Commentary

One year before the premiere of *Star Trek*, Irwin Allen launched *Lost in Space*, a family-friendly adventure series that showed that strong family bonds could overcome any challenge. While the show initially focused more on realistic scientific concepts, network executives eventually encouraged sillier stories and broader characterizations. Nevertheless, from the start, *Lost in Space* remained a family-friendly show recalling the film serials of the 1930s and 1940s that brought science fiction adventures to life in sanitized stories aimed at children. As such, *Lost in Space* recalled the earlier episodes of *Doctor Who*, which debuted just two years before in the United Kingdom. *Lost in Space* inspired young fans to become "fighter pilots, computer technicians, and science fiction writers."[69] While *Star Trek* ultimately proved more popular with grownups thanks to its more mature approach to space travel, *Lost in Space* remained dear to younger viewers.

Though somewhat less well-remembered than *Star Trek*, *Lost in Space* nevertheless deserves accolades as a pioneering science fiction show and perhaps in television storytelling generally as Allen claimed his show was the first to incorporate cliffhanger endings in prime-time television.[70] Each week, *Lost in Space* served up unforgettable adventures that transported viewers to distant worlds filled with weird aliens as in "The Ghost Planet" (S2E3), which sees the crew of the *Jupiter 2* stumble upon a mysterious world inhabited by a cybernetic brain that commands an army of spooky robots. Later, in "The Great Vegetable Rebellion" (S3E23), the Robinsons land on a lush planet and encounter a giant humanoid carrot that turns Dr. Smith into a sentient stalk of celery. Despite such goofiness, *Lost in Space* successfully depicted space on television through engaging stories and likeable characters, setting the stage for an entire genre. This explains why fans still consider it one of the all-time great cult TV shows.

See also *Doctor Who* (1963–Present), *Star Trek* (1966–1969)

LUCHA UNDERGROUND (2014–PRESENT)

Creators: Robert Rodriguez, Mark Burnett

Cast: Luis Fernandez-Gil (Dario Cueto), Matthew Kaye (Matt Striker), Ian Hodgkinson (Vampiro), Melissa Santos (Herself), Óscar Gutiérrez (Rey Mysterio), John Hennigan (Johnny Mundo), Trevor Mann (Prince Puma), Dulce María García (Sexy Star), Salvador Guerrero IV (Chavo Guerrero Jr.), Gilbert Cosme (Mil Muertes), Karlee Perez (Catrina), Ivelisse Vélez (Ivelisse), Matt Capiccioni (Son of Havoc), Adam Birdle (Angélico), Pentagón Jr. (Himself), Fénix (Himself), Jeff Cobb (Matanza), Brian Cage (Cage)

Genre: Action, Drama, Sport

Synopsis

Nefarious fight promoter Dario Cueto oversees an underground wrestling promotion that attracts various shady, supernatural competitors from around the world.

Production History

In 2014, reality television guru Mark Burnett teamed with filmmaker Robert Rodriguez to produce a weekly professional wrestling show for Rodriguez's recently launched El Rey cable network.[71] Originally titled *Lucha: Uprising*, the show was intended to introduce American audiences to the high-flying superstars of the Mexican professional wrestling promotion Lucha Libre AAA (*Asistencia Asesoría y Administracíon*).[72] Production began on September 6, 2014,[73] with matches taking place inside a one-hundred-year-old rail warehouse in Boyle Heights, Los Angeles, that could seat 350–400 spectators.[74] The first episode of the series, renamed *Lucha Underground*, premiered at 8:00 p.m. on October 29, 2014, with Univision Corporation's UniMás cable network rebroadcasting the episode in Spanish the following Saturday.[75] During that first season of thirty-nine episodes, *Lucha Underground* earned critical acclaim and built a fervent cult following.[76]

Problems arrived quickly for the new series. During season 2, AAA performers revealed that the wrestling federation took a portion of their earnings from *Lucha Underground* bookings.[77] In addition, UniMás dropped the show at the end of that season.[78] Without those viewers and advertising revenue, and because of the high production cost, the show experienced financial troubles, leaving producers scrambling to secure funds for a fourth season.[79] They managed to raise enough for a shortened season,[80] but the decreased budget necessitated a move to the Union Central Cold Storage site just south of downtown Los Angeles.[81] The problems worsened when several wrestlers, hoping to obtain more competitive contracts and permission to work all year, sued the production companies.[82] In June 2019, MGM Television and El Rey Network clashed over ownership rights, leaving the future of *Lucha Underground* uncertain.[83]

Commentary

Lucha Underground offered a different type of professional wrestling that combined various genres (including telenovelas, exploitation, horror, and science fiction) and embraced an over-the-top fantasy version of "kayfabe" (the technique of presenting staged performances as genuine, or "real"). With its complex characters, deep mythology, and full-season format, the series recalled tightly plotted serialized dramas such as *Breaking Bad* or *Game of Thrones* rather than weekly wrestling shows like *Monday Night Raw* or *SmackDown Live*. While *Lucha Underground* experienced its share of unintended mishaps (Ivelisse suffered a broken ankle that left her sitting on the sidelines for much of season 1 while Angélico missed most of season 3 due to an injured elbow), the showrunners still managed to create captivating longform storylines. For instance, fan favorite Pentagón Jr. rose to prominence thanks to his tendency to break his opponents' arms as a sacrifice to his mysterious dark master, all leading to one of the bloodiest and most unforgettable matches in *Lucha Underground*'s short history, the infamous "Cero Miedo" match. Similarly, despite numerous setbacks, Ivelisse embarked on a multi-season journey from ringside valet to contender for the company's top title. All the while, Dario Cueto plotted to unleash ancient Aztec gods upon an unsuspecting world. Stories like these helped distinguish *Lucha Underground* from other wrestling promotions as the show's seemingly bottomless mythos and tense cliffhangers left fans clamoring for more.

Lucha Underground also offered some of the most exhilarating wrestling ever shown on television (at least in the United States). Dynamic performers like Prince Puma, Fénix, Son of Havoc, and Angélico thrilled audiences with their high-flying acrobatics and daredevil stunts, as when Angélico leapt from the roof of Cueto's office all the way to the ring to dropkick his opponent off a ladder, or when Prince Puma tackled Johnny Mundo off a balcony and they both crashed into a stack of tables below. Other matches proved incredibly brutal, as in the "Hell of War" match that left competitors Dante Fox and Killshot emotionally drained and physically scarred. *Lucha Underground* offered wrestling fans an experience far more intense than the watered-down sports entertainment offered by the likes of larger promotions. The show also blazed a trail in terms of equality and representation, portraying women wrestlers like Ivelisse and Sexy Star and queer wrestlers such as Pimpinela Escarlata and XO Lishus (aka Sonny Kiss) as tough and capable. At the time of this writing, it is unknown whether *Lucha Underground* will return for a fifth season, but one thing remains certain: the show forever altered the professional wrestling landscape by bringing hot new stars to the fore and introducing new ways of presenting the artform to audiences.

M

MAX HEADROOM (1987–1988)

Creators: George Stone, Annabel Jankel, Rocky Morton
Cast: Matt Frewer (Edison Carter/Max Headroom), Amanda Pays (Theora Jones),
Jeffrey Tambor (Murray McKenzie), Chris Young (Bryce Lynch), Charles Rocket
(Ned Grossberg), W. Morgan Sheppard (Blank Reg)
Genre: Comedy, Science Fiction

Synopsis

Twenty minutes into the future, two journalists join forces with an oddball artificial intelligence to expose corruption in a dystopian city ruled by unethical television networks.

Production History

In 1981, Andrew Park of England's Channel Four asked Peter Wagg, head of Creative Services for London's Chrysalis Records, to develop a half-hour music video show.[1] Wagg agreed and set about looking for someone to host the new series. His friend, advertising copywriter George Stone, suggested a computer-based format and recommended calling the show *Max Headroom*, an abbreviation of "Maximum Headroom."[2] Though he disliked the idea of a computer-generated host,[3] Wagg nevertheless brought in animation and video directing team Rocky Morton and Annabel Jankel to create the Max character, and together they conceived the show as a paranoid thriller about an investigative reporter who injures himself while fleeing from villainous types, only for someone to upload his consciousness to a computer network.[4] Channel Four lacked money for the project so in 1984 Wagg convinced HBO/Cinemax to invest $500,000 in a pilot film.[5] Steve Roberts wrote the script while Wagg focused on casting the title character, settling on Matt Frewer after an extensive international casting call.[6] Roberts finished the script in October 1984, and production began in November at an abandoned gasworks in Wembley.

Max Headroom premiered on Channel Four in early 1985 and the video series debuted soon after. Cinemax aired the show in the United States under the title *The Max Headroom Show* around the same time that Roberts released a humorous companion book, *Max Headroom's Guide to Life.*[7] The Cinemax series featured guests like Jack Lemmon, Michael Caine, Sting, and Vidal Sassoon, and Max himself soon emerged as a pop icon, even landing a gig as the spokesperson for Coca-Cola.[8] The character's success inspired Wagg to approach both NBC and CBS with the idea for an ongoing one-hour dramatic series built around Max, but they turned him down. He then brought the idea to executives at ABC, who picked up the series and gave Wagg full creative control.[9] Producer Philip DeGuere agreed to head the project but he worried that ABC failed to fully

A reporter teams up with the madcap artificial intelligence Max Headroom (Matt Frewer) to investigate corruption in a futuristic society. *ABC/Photofest*

comprehend the show and bowed out after the pilot episode.[10] ABC initially provided *Max Headroom* with a hefty budget[11] though the show still managed to go $4 million over.[12] The network scaled back the budget after the show's first season received low ratings, at which point *Max Headroom* grew increasingly gimmicky and formulaic.[13] The series ended soon after, but the character stayed in the public consciousness for years after.

Commentary

Upon its debut in 1986, *Max Headroom* brought cyberpunk to primetime television (at least in the United States). While it only attracted a small audience, the show introduced many viewers to the sort of cerebral science fiction pioneered by the likes of William Gibson and Bruce Sterling. During its short run, *Max Headroom* featured well-worn genre tropes such as artificial intelligence, corporate espionage, cool computer hackers, brain uploading, and genetic engineering. Each week the show took viewers to a grimy, near-future world that recalled the one seen in director Ridley Scott's *Blade Runner* though far less somber. *Max Headroom* posited a society ruled by TV networks so powerful that even the federal government bowed before them, with politicians seeking to curry the favor of influential executives by ramming through legislation designed to increase their authority and their reach, including banning television sets fitted with Off switches. The series presented itself as satire, marrying dystopian imagery and sardonic humor. Indeed, *Max Headroom* provided series star Matt Frewer with plenty of opportunities to crack wise as both intrepid reporter Edison Carter and his digital doppelgänger Max Headroom even as they investigated serious issues like organ harvesting (S1E3, "Body Banks") and censorship (S2E13, "Lessons"). These days, however, the show appears positively prescient as giant multinational media corporations pay billions of dollars to buy up their competition and exert undue influence over lawmakers.

In the tradition of other thoughtful science fiction series like *The Twilight Zone* and *Star Trek*, *Max Headroom* routinely offered intriguing sociocultural commentary on contemporary issues by extrapolating them into the future and exaggerating them. For instance, "Security Systems" (S1E4) tackles issues surrounding cybersecurity as a shady security firm erases Carter's identity and frames him for a crime he did not commit. Similarly, "The Blanks" (S1E6) presents a story in which a techno-terrorist threatens to infect the city's computer network with a powerful virus. Meanwhile, "Deities" (S2E2) deals with whole brain emulation, or mind uploading, as the leader of a New Age church preys on parishioners by promising to transfer their brain patterns to a neural grid. In "Whackets" (S2E5), unsuspecting viewers become hopelessly addicted to a new game show that broadcasts a subliminal signal. Episodes such as these inspired fans to think about their own world and the one just over the horizon. The show also portrayed technologies that have now become commonplace, including the Internet (the unnamed city relies on a network of computers that presages the World Wide Web) and artificial assistants (Max himself foreshadows bots like Siri, Alexa, and Cortana). Despite low ratings, *Max Headroom* left a lasting impact on society: the show helped turn Frewer into a cult figure on par with Bruce Campbell and Jeffrey Combs while the title character enjoyed a brief stint as a worldwide icon. As such, *Max Headroom* has earned its place in the pantheon of great cult TV shows.

MONTY PYTHON'S FLYING CIRCUS (1969–1974)

Creators: Graham Chapman, John Cleese, Terry Gilliam, Eric Idle, Terry Jones, Michael Palin

Cast: Graham Chapman, John Cleese, Terry Gilliam, Eric Idle, Terry Jones, Michael Palin

Genre: Comedy

Synopsis

In this classic British sketch comedy series, the irreverent comedy collective known as Monty Python serves up hilariously surreal skits and wacky absurdist humor.

Production History

In May 1969, Graham Chapman, John Cleese, Terry Gilliam, Eric Idle, Terry Jones, and Michael Palin gathered at Cleese's Basil Street apartment to develop a new comedy show.[14] Two months later, they started shooting the first episode under the working title *Bunn, Wackett, Buzzard, Stubble, and Boot*.[15] Later when BBC executives asked for a formal title, Cleese and his pals replied with *Flying Circus*.[16] However, the network wanted to know whose *Flying Circus*, leading to another brainstorm session during which the group came up with the name *Monty Python*.[17] Production on the first series then resumed, continuing through August and September.[18] During that time, the BBC basically gave the troupe carte blanche to do what they wanted, though public pressure groups, politicians, and BBC administrators frequently mounted opposition to the language and subject matter.[19] Nevertheless, the first episode of *Monty Python's Flying* Circus premiered on October 5, 1969,[20] with the first series wrapping up its run on January 11, 1970.[21]

The show proved a hit, and the BBC ordered a second series that ran from September 15 through December 22, 1970. Not long after, *Monty Python's Flying Circus* debuted on the Canadian Broadcasting Corporation,[22] though the network dropped it from the schedule in February 1971, prompting protests from fans in Montreal, Toronto, and Winnipeg.[23] The first Monty Python feature film, *And Now for Something Completely Different*, opened in London on September 28, 1971, and it received a limited release in the United States the following year.[24] However, the show failed to develop a fanbase in the United States until 1974,[25]

With their kooky characters and absurd skits, British comedy troupe Monty Python helped blaze a trail for surreal comedy. *BBC/Photofest*

when PBS affiliate KERA in Dallas, Texas, aired *Monty Python* reruns with the other 113 PBS stations following suit by the summer of 1975.[26] Series 3, which featured Cleese's last appearance, ran from October 19, 1972 to January 18, 1973, but internal tensions threatened to tear the group apart.[27] The remaining Pythons shot a six-episode fourth series that premiered on October 31, 1975 (this time on BBC2 rather than BBC1).[28] In November 1975, the Pythons sued ABC because the network aired three edited episodes of *Monty Python*.[29] The court initially sided with ABC, but the Pythons successfully appealed, preventing ABC from airing the show and establishing their ownership over the scripts.[30] In the years since, both the group and the show have become international institutions, with fans spouting quotes to this day.

Commentary

Upon its debut on October 5, 1969, *Monty Python's Flying Circus* contributed mightily to the rise of absurdist comedy around the world, exerting a huge influence on nearly every sketch comedy series that came after. From the start, the show challenged traditional notions of comedy with bizarre skits such as "The Dead Parrot" (S1E8), "The Death of Mary Queen of Scots" (S2E9), "Election Night Special" (S2E6), and "Spam" (S2E12). *Monty Python* also tickled viewers' ribs with some of the silliest sketches ever produced, including "The Funniest Joke in the World" (S1E1), "The Ministry of Silly Walks" (S2E1), and "The Spanish Inquisition" (S2E2). In addition, the show unleashed a handful of sidesplitting tunes, including "The Money Song," "The Spam Song," and perhaps most famously, "The Lumberjack Song." *Monty Python* served as a launching pad for its core performers, who all went on to create or star in numerous other hilarious projects including beloved TV series like *Fawlty Towers* and *Ripping Yarns* and acclaimed films such as *Brazil* and *A Fish Called Wanda*. The show left many viewers scratching their heads, but Monty Python nevertheless changed comedy for decades to come and continues to inspire young comics to this day.

Monty Python spawned numerous films, spinoffs, albums, books, and more. Moreover, both the show and its cast remain beloved even now, more than five decades after first bursting on the comedy scene. The troupe appeared together in five theatrical movies and released several comedy albums over the years and toured the world performing live shows for enthusiastic audiences. Sadly, Graham Chapman died on October 4, 1989, following a long battle with cancer,[31] but the following month BBC1 aired *Parrot Sketch Not Included: Twenty Years of Monty Python*, a reunion show filmed in September 1989 that featured the final reunion of all six Pythons.[32] Nearly ten years later, the remaining Pythons reunited for the U.S. Comedy Arts Festival Tribute to Monty Python, which aired as an hour-long show on HBO.[33] Over the years, the show has inspired all sorts of merchandise, from card games (such as Looney Labs' *Monty Python Fluxx*) to T-shirts (including the official Airspeed Velocity of an Unladen Swallow T-shirt) to toys (like Toy Vault's Black Knight plush figure with detachable limbs). *Monty Python* unquestionably has earned its reputation as an oft-quoted and highly influential cult TV series.

See also *Fawlty Towers* (1975–1979), *The Kids in the Hall* (1988–1994), *Mr. Show with Bob and David* (1995–1998)

MR. SHOW WITH BOB AND DAVID (1995–1998)

Creators: David Cross, Bob Odenkirk
Cast: Bob Odenkirk, David Cross, John Ennis, Jay Johnston, Tom Kenny, Karen Kilgariff, Brett Paesel, Brian Posehn, Jill Talley, Paul F. Tompkins
Genre: Comedy

Synopsis

Each episode of this hilariously surreal variety show uses weird humor and an edgy attitude to poke fun at everything from politics to popular culture.

Production History

Quirky standup comics David Cross and Bob Odenkirk first met via their mutual friend Janeane Garofalo and then reconnected a few years later while writing for

The Ben Stiller Show.[34] However, their friendship really coalesced when they saw each other perform stand-up.[35] Starting in 1994, the duo performed together at the Diamond Club, where they created a sketch show called *The 3 Goofballz* with Brian Posehn.[36] The following year, Cross and Odenkirk moved the show to the Upfront Theater, changing the title first to *Mr. Show* then *Grand National Championships* and finally to *The Cross/Odenkirk Problem.*[37] After seeing the show, Carolyn Strauss, then director of development for HBO, helped Cross and Odenkirk land a deal to develop a live stage show,[38] meaning the two comics no longer needed to invest their own money (upward of $18,000) for the performances.[39] The new show premiered in 1995 at HBO's inaugural comedy festival in Aspen, Colorado.[40] Afterward, Cross and Odenkirk's new manager Bernie Brillstein convinced HBO head of programming Chris Albrecht to take a chance on a full *Mr. Show* series.[41] Strauss and Albrecht backed the program even without the full support from HBO.[42]

The network initially ordered just two episodes but Cross and Odenkirk worked around this restriction by producing a four-episode pilot done on a two-episode budget.[43] The duo followed the template established by *Monty Python's Flying Circus,*[44] mixing pre-taped vignettes and live sketches in each episode.[45] Cross and Odenkirk filled the cast with performers who had worked on previous versions of *Mr. Show,* including John Ennis,[46] Jill Talley,[47] and Brian Posehn.[48] They also hired standup comics Jay Johnston and Tom Kenny.[49] Other writers and performers included Dino Stamatopoulos, Sarah Silverman, Karen Kilgariff, Paul F. Tompkins, Scott Adsit, Jack Black, and Scott Aukerman.[50] Each episode took about three weeks to write and produce.[51] The troupe usually taped two live shows a week on a single night, creating a club-like atmosphere.[52] They shot the pre-taped segments for little money and without permits, working fast and lean and shooting out of order.[53]

The show premiered on November 3, 1995, at midnight.[54] Cross and Odenkirk struggled to fill seats during season 1 so they bused people in and sent out production assistants to find others but the show eventually built a devoted audience.[55] *Mr. Show* ran for four seasons but HBO routinely shuffled it around the schedule before moving it to Mondays at midnight during the fourth season.[56] After that season, Cross was exhausted and wanted to move on in his career, so with no more money coming from HBO, the series ended.[57] The show toured with a theatrical revue called *Mr. Show: Hooray for America!* in 2002 and continues to find fans and influence young comedians to this day.[58]

Commentary

Despite poor marketing and erratic scheduling, *Mr. Show with Bob and David* established itself as an all-time great sketch show thanks to the people involved. The series boasted an incredible ensemble of funny folks, beginning with creators Bob Odenkirk and David Cross, who spent years toiling on the standup circuit before the series finally put them and their cast members on the map (despite HBO's mishandling of the show). The duo surrounded themselves with a cast of fantastic supporting players who shared their peculiar comedic sensibilities, including hilarious performers like Tom Kenny, Paul F. Tompkins, John Ennis, Jay Johnston, and Jill Talley. In addition to performing, everyone involved contributed to the scripts, lending the show an outrageous identity and an un-predictable sense of humor that attracted a loyal audience of misfits, weirdos, and stoners. Every episode of *Mr. Show* featured several thematically linked skits that mocked a wide array of subjects, from politics (usually via recurring character Senator Howell Tankerbell, an uptight Southern Dixiecrat played by Bob Odenkirk) to religion (the "Hail Satan Network" sketch features Kenny and Talley as a pair of satanic televangelists) to popular culture ("Coupon: The Movie" offers a pitch-perfect sendup of Hollywood marketing efforts). Its sardonic wit and uproarious brashness set *Mr. Show* apart from more conventional skit shows such as *Saturday Night Live* and *MADtv*.

Beyond its nonsensical comedy, *Mr. Show* also served up several socially and culturally relevant skits during its abbreviated run. For instance, "Goin' on a Holiday" (S3E6) features an extended sketch in which a group of American scientists set out to blow up the moon for unstated reasons. When a chimp capable of communicating in sign language questions the mission, jingoistic country singer C. S. Lewis Jr. (Odenkirk) pens a retaliatory tune called "Big Dumb Ape," which features the lyric "Hey Mr. Monkey / Don't be asking why / Don't you know you can't mess / With American pride?" While excessively silly, the song also sends up aggressively patriotic country jams like "Courtesy of the Red, White and Blue (The Angry American)" by Toby Keith and "It's America" by Rodney Atkins. Other episodes take aim at hot-button issues such as censorship as in "What to Think" (S1E2), which sees Senator Tankerbell campaign to strip funding from the arts. While both episodes remain firmly rooted in the mid-1990s due to the fashion and slang, they nevertheless address issues that remain relevant even now. More importantly, though, *Mr. Show* tackled these topics with its trademark bizarre humor ("Gentlemen, I propose that this arts funding is like a milking machine and unless we shut it down, it's gonna rip our dicks right off!"), which make it a lasting cult hit revered by hipsters and comedy nerds everywhere.

See also *The Kids in the Hall* (1988–1994), *The State* (1993–1995), *Tenacious D* (1997–2000)

MY LITTLE PONY: FRIENDSHIP IS MAGIC (2010–2019)

Creator: Lauren Faust
Cast: Tara Strong (Twilight Sparkle), Ashleigh Ball (Applejac/Rainbow Dash), Tabitha St. Germain (Rarity/Princess Luna), Andrea Libman (Fluttershy/Pinkie Pie), Spike (Cathy Weseluck)
Genre: Comedy, Drama, Fantasy, Musical, Science Fiction

Synopsis

A diverse group of adventurous ponies learns about the meaning of friendship and work to teach all Equestria about this magic.

Production History

Following the success of the first *Transformers* movie in 2007, Hasbro sought to reinvent their other properties.[59] In 2008, Lisa Licht of Hasbro Studios met with Lauren Faust, who pitched an animated series based on her Milky Way and the Galaxy Girl characters.[60] Instead, Licht asked Faust to reboot the My Little Pony franchise.[61] A fan of the franchise since childhood, Faust spent six weeks writing a forty-page series bible that included sketches illustrating her vision.[62] Over the next several months, Hasbro worked with Faust to secure DHX Media in Vancouver as the production studio, auditioned voice actors, and finalized the series format.[63] In April 2009, Hasbro partnered with Discovery Communications to create the Hub network, and in June 2010 the company officially announced a new series titled *My Little Pony: Friendship Is Magic*.[64]

My Little Pony debuted on October 10, 2010, as part of Hub's Sneak Peek Sunday.[65] After season 1, Faust left to pursue other projects and supervising director Jayson Thiessen stepped in to replace her.[66] The show soon attracted an adult fanbase of men calling themselves "Bronies" and women known as "Pegasisters."[67] This fanbase raised $322,000 in a Kickstarter campaign in 2012 to make the documentary *Bronies: The Extremely Unexpected Adult Fans of* My Little Pony.[68] In a bid to attract teenagers, Hasbro released a series of spinoff movies featuring the ponies changed into teenage girls beginning with *My Little Pony: Equestria Girls* in 2013. By 2014, *My Little* Pony was airing in 170 countries and drawing over 12 million American viewers.[69] An animated feature titled *My Little Pony: The Movie* performed well enough in 2017 for Hasbro to announce a second film slated for a 2021 release.[70] In 2020, following the ninth and final season of the series, Hasbro produced a live *My Little Pony* touring musical.[71]

Commentary

The *My Little Pony* franchise delighted young girls of the 1980s so much that the company sold millions of toys around the world. Fast forward three decades, and the state of children's television has changed with more programming attempting to reach an audience of both boys and girls. Action-adventure shows, traditionally for boys, incorporate more romance (à la *Gargoyles*) while feminine bonding shows, traditionally aimed at girls, integrate action and adventure (such as *The Powerpuff Girls*). *My Little Pony* took this genre-blurring even further, creating a unique series that developed a unique cult following.

My Little Pony attracted a wide audience of boys and girls of all ages as well as adults of both sexes. Adult male fans embraced the series for many reasons, and they gathered online and in person to share their love of the series and its characters. Beginning in 2011, these fans have organized an annual BronyCon, a family-friendly event that welcomes anyone who loves *My Little Pony*. Girls and women also love the series, but male fans attracted the most attention due to their adoration of a so-called girlie show focused on pastel-colored ponies, feminine bonding, and messages of friendship, collaboration, and peace

Of course, *My Little Pony* also contains action and adventure set in a mythologically rich world and presents humorous Easter Eggs for pop culture fans, all while creating complex characters with deep emotions and passions. Viewers identify with Twilight Sparkle and her friends as they embark on heartwarming adventures and learn valuable life lessons. More importantly, perhaps, the ponies survive the worst threats because of their friendship and thus the show imparts an important message about empathy and camaraderie to viewers of all ages, sexes, and genders. Indeed, if Discord, the show's spirit of chaos and harmony (voiced by John de Lancie), can learn about friendship, anyone can. Because of this all-inclusive message, *My Little Pony* moved beyond being a girlie cartoon reboot into a great cult TV show.

See also *Adventure Time* (2010–2018)

SPOTLIGHT: LAUREN FAUST

Born on July 25, 1974, in San Jose, California, Lauren Faust bought her first My Little Pony figure at seven years old.[72] Years later, Faust, who grew up interested in animation, attended the California Institute of Arts.[73] After graduating, she landed a job at Turner Feature Animation animating characters on *Cats Don't Dance, Quest for Camelot,* and *Iron Giant.*[74] She met her husband, Craig McCracken, while working on *The Powerpuff Girls,* during which time she learned how to direct animation.[75] Faust then served as the head writer and supervising producer for *Foster's Home for Imaginary Friends* before creating *My Little Pony: Friendship Is Magic.* From there, she developed *Super Best Friends Forever, Wander over Yonder,* and *DC Super Hero Girls.*

MY SO-CALLED LIFE (1994–1995)

Creator: Winnie Holzman
Cast: Claire Danes (Angela Chase), A. J. Langer (Rayanne Graff), Bess Armstrong (Patty Chase), Jared Leto (Jordan Catalano), Wilson Cruz (Rickie Vasquez), Devon Gummersall (Brian Krakow), Devon Odessa (Sharon Cherski), Lisa Wilhoit (Danielle Chase), Tom Irwin (Graham Chase)
Genre: Comedy, Drama, Romance

Synopsis

Angst-ridden suburban teenager Angela Chase tries to find her way through high school and life.

Production History

Looking to follow up their smash hit *thirtysomething*, Marshall Herskovitz and Ed Zwick teamed with up-and-coming writer Winnie Holzman to create a new

Angst-ridden teenager Angela Chase (Claire Danes, right) endures the trials and tribulations of high school. *ABC/Photofest*

show for ABC's family lineup.[76] The trio came up with an idea for an authentic, uncensored series about an angst-ridden teenage girl growing up in the suburbs, which they titled *My So-Called Life*.[77] However, network executives expressed reluctance over catering to a teen demographic, especially one comprised mainly of teenage girls, and they pressured the series' writers and producers to focus on the show's more adult-oriented aspects.[78] Yet Ted Harbert, ABC's president of entertainment, considered the pilot script "brilliant"[79] and decided to take a chance on the show. When it came time to cast *My So-Called Life*, Herskovitz, Zwick, and Holzman wanted an actual teenager in the lead role, but only sixteen-year-old Alicia Silverstone and thirteen-year-old Claire Danes auditioned, with Danes ultimately landing the part.[80]

Production on the pilot took place in May 1993 with the episode set to air in spring 1994 provided the network liked it. Unfortunately, executives at ABC considered the pilot too dark and therefore waited until the fall to order a full season, leaving cast and crew scrambling to produce the additional eighteen episodes.[81] The first episode of *My So-Called Life* premiered on August 25, 1994, at 8:00 p.m. opposite the smash hit *Friends*.[82] The show generated low advertising revenues, earning just $50,000 per commercial spot, but Harbert's support combined with a massive fan campaign kept the series alive during the first season.[83] Eventually, though, Danes decided she wanted to move on and pursue a film career.[84] The final episode of *My So-Called Life*, which Holzman wrote as a series finale due to the network's continued uncertainty, aired on January 26, 1995.[85] In an unusual move, ABC licensed the show to MTV, where it ran in reruns until 1997.[86] While the move failed to improve ratings, it did help *My So-Called Life* reach its intended audience.[87] It remains beloved by fans to this day.

Commentary

With its touching and brutally honest portrait of Generation X teenage angst, *My So-Called Life* appealed to younger viewers who identified deeply with protagonist Angela Chase (expertly portrayed by then-newcomer Claire Danes). Despite its all-too-brief life, the show nevertheless helped kick off a wave of programming aimed at teenagers.[88] *My So-Called Life* sympathetically explored concerns relevant to both late Generation Xers and early Millennials, offering up chances for identification and emotional attachment because of how it dealt with real issues affecting high schoolers of the mid-1990s. In addition, the show tackled serious topics including substance abuse, homelessness, and LGBTQ issues. Unlike other teen-oriented shows such as *Saved by the Bell* or *Beverly Hills 90210*, *My So-Called Life* captured the zeitgeist of the era while also setting the tone for all the other series that emerged in its wake, including *Buffy the Vampire Slayer* and *Freaks and Geeks*. The show depicted teenage life as a confusing, difficult, and often miserable time and thus it spoke to a generation of disaffected young viewers who felt aimless and uncertain about the future. Such authenticity helped turn the show into an enduring cult classic that still resonates with fans.

From the start, *My So-Called Life* served up touching drama, genuine humor, and powerful pathos in each episode. In "Pilot" (S1E1), Angela sets out to shed her good girl image and embrace her darker side after striking up a friendship with troubled teens Rayanne Graff and Rickie Vasquez. From there, the show explored teenage life in a nuanced and introspective way that still resonates with teenagers decades later as in "The Zit" (S1E5), which sees a pimple send Angela's already tenuous self-esteem into a downward spiral, especially once she learns about the existence of a list rating the attractiveness of all the sophomore girls at Liberty High School. Other episodes deal with thornier issues such as "Guns and Gossip" (S1E3), which tackles the topic of gun violence (making it incredibly relevant today), or Rickie's multi-episode coming-out story, which involves topical subjects like homelessness, bullying, and sexual identity. The show also boasted smart dialogue ("My parents keep asking how school was. It's like saying, 'How was that drive-by shooting?' You don't care how it was, you're lucky to get out alive") and hip guest stars (alternative rocker Juliana Hatfield appears as a homeless woman in the critically derided Christmas episode). *My So-Called Life* graduated too soon, but it lives on in the hearts and minds of fans everywhere.

See also *Daria* (1997–2001), *Degrassi Junior High* (1987–1989), *Freaks and Geeks* (1999–2000)

MYSTERY SCIENCE THEATER 3000 (1988–2018)

Creators: Joel Hodgson and Jim Mallon

Cast: Joel Hodgson (Joel Robinson, 1988–1994), Trace Beaulieu (Dr. Clayton Forrester/Crow T. Robot, 1988–1996), J. Elvis Weinstein (Dr. Laurence Erhardt/Tom Servo/Gypsy, 1988–1990), Kevin Murphy (Tom Servo, 1988–1999), Frank Conniff (TV's Frank, 1990–1999), Jim Mallon (Gypsy, 1989–1998), Mary Jo Pehl (Pearl Forrester, 1992–1999), Bill Corbett (Observer/Crow T. Robot, 1997–1999), Jonah Ray Rodriguez (Jonah Heston, 2017–2019), Felicia Day (Kinga Forrester, 2017–2019), Patton Oswalt (Max aka TV's Son of TV's Frank, 2017–2019), Baron Vaughn (Tom Servo, 2017–2019), Hampton Yount (Crow T. Robot, 2017–2019)

Genre: Comedy, Science Fiction

Synopsis

Marooned in space aboard the Satellite of Love, a man and his robot companions are forced by a rotating cast of evil mad scientists to watch bad movies, and they can only maintain their sanity by cracking jokes nonstop during each film.

Production History

In 1988, comedian Joel Hodgson teamed with Jim Mallon to develop *Mystery Science Theater 3000* (*MST3K*) for the struggling UHF station KTMA Channel 23 of St. Paul, Minnesota.[89] Drawing inspiration from the 1972 science fiction film *Silent Running*,[90] Hodgson came up with a premise in which two evil scientists launch a hapless janitor (played by Hodgson himself) into space and force him to watch bad movies. To ease his loneliness, the janitor creates three robot companions, two of which watch the movies along with him. This format allowed Hodgson and Mallon to use the station's library of licensed films, airing one movie in its entirety per episode while Joel and the bots crack jokes the entire time.[91]

Hodgson and Mallon enlisted KTMA employee (and future Tom Servo) Kevin Murphy and local comics Josh Weinstein (later J. Elvis Weinstein) and Trace Beaulieu to help develop and shoot a thirty-minute pilot episode,[92] which landed them a thirteen-episode deal at KTMA.[93] The first episode of *MST3K* premiered on November 24, 1988 (Thanksgiving Day, which would become an important part of the show's legacy).[94] The show became an instant cult hit, prompting station owner Donald W. O'Connor to order eight additional episodes.[95] Hodgson and Mallon then secured the rights to the show and split them equally.[96]

Despite *MST3K*'s success, KTMA filed for bankruptcy in July of 1989.[97] Seeking to keep the show alive, Hodgson and Mallon sent a demo reel to executives at HBO, who were looking for content for their new cable network, the Comedy Channel (which later merged with comedy network HA! to become Comedy Central).[98] *MST3K* soon became the network's flagship show.[99] Over time, the series developed a rabid audience, prompting executives to keep it on the air despite middling ratings.[100] Nevertheless, Comedy Central finally cancelled *MST3K* in 1996.[101] Fans (known as "Misties") staged a letter-writing campaign to save the show, leading executives at the fledgling Sci-Fi Channel to produce three more seasons before pulling the plug yet again.[102]

Despite the show's absence, *MST3K*'s fanbase continued to grow, and in 2015 Hodgson launched a highly successful Kickstarter campaign to revive the series, raising over $6 million in just a few months.[103] The first season of the rebooted *MST3K* debuted on Netflix in April of 2017,[104] and it proved so popular that the streaming giant ordered a second season, which aired on Thanksgiving Day 2018.[105]

Commentary

It is easy to see why the original incarnation of *MST3K* briefly became the signature show of Comedy Central (as well as a beloved cult hit): it is consistently hilarious thanks to the brilliant comedic sensibilities of Hodgson and his accomplices, who draw on decades of popular culture (and their own experiences living in the Midwest) to generate some of the funniest gags ever aired on television. However, Hodgson and his crew of dedicated riffers had help from some of the most sidesplittingly inept movies ever made, including *Eegah!*, *Santa Claus Conquers the Martians*, and (perhaps most famously) *Manos: The Hands of Fate*, all of which provided plenty of opportunities for laughs. This tradition continues with the Satellite of Love's new crew, who have managed to keep the spirit of the original series alive while also carving out their own comic identity in new episodes produced for Netflix.

MST3K endures for many reasons but mainly because Hodgson and his team avoided topical humor (though they included the occasional timely political joke

Joel Robinson (Joel Hodgson, center) and his robot pals use their sharp wit to mock some of the worst movies ever made. *Comedy Central/Photofest*

such as the oft-used "John Sununu goes for a haircut" whenever a plane takes to the sky). This grants *MST3K* a timelessness that allows it to remain funny for audiences of all ages. Of course, the show sometimes dabbles in mature comedy (as in *Mystery Science Theater 3000: The Movie*, when Servo demands, "What kind of shithole planet is this?" while watching a spaceship land in *This Island Earth*), but overall its brand of silliness appeals to kids (who no doubt enjoy the antics of the bots) and adults (who can appreciate the slyly smart jokes that fly at a rapid-fire pace). The show also proved immensely influential and made riffing somewhat commonplace in the twenty-first century; for instance, horrorcore rap group Insane Clown Posse riffed on music videos in the webseries *Insane Clown Posse Theater* while wrestler, podcaster, and comedian Colt Cabana riffs on wrestling in *Colt Cabana and Friends Sit in a Theater and Watch Bad Wrestling!* More than just a beloved cult show, *MST3K* changed the face of both comedy and popular culture.

See also *Freaks & Geeks* (1999–2000)

SPOTLIGHT: JOEL HODGSON

Born in Stevens Point, Wisconsin, on February 20, 1960,[106] Joel Hodgson spent his childhood in Green Bay.[107] In the early 1980s, he left Wisconsin to embark on a career as a prop comic, appearing on *Saturday Night Live* and *Late Night with David Letterman*. He retired from stand-up comedy at the ripe old age of twenty-four only to turn his gizmo-inventing style into the show *Mystery Science Theater 3000*.[108] After leaving the show in 1995, Hodgson kept a low profile, working with his brother, Jim, to found Visual Story Tools in Los Angeles and to focus on scriptwriting and creating special effects.[109] He also made appearances on cult TV shows like *Freaks and Geeks*, *Arrested Development*, and *Other Space*. In the fall of 2015, Hodgson launched a Kickstarter campaign to bring back *Mystery Science Theater 3000*, going on to serve as executive producer, writer, director, and occasional guest star for the revival.

O

THE OFFICE (2001–2003)

Creators: Ricky Gervais, Stephen Merchant
Cast: Ricky Gervais (David Brent), Martin Freeman (Tim Canterbury), Mackenzie Crook (Gareth Keenan), Lucy Davis (Dawn Tinsley)
Genre: Comedy, Drama

Synopsis

In this hilariously awkward mockumentary series, a documentary crew chronicles the daily activities of a paper company in Slough, England.

Production History

In 1996, Ricky Gervais and Stephen Merchant met while they both worked at XFM, a London radio station.[1] Three years later, they co-wrote an episode of the Channel 4 comedy anthology series *Comedy Lab*, which starred Gervais.[2] Inspired by this work, the duo created the David Brent character and wrote a pilot script for a new show, which the BBC initially rejected.[3] However, network executives changed their mind after Gervais and Merchant sent them a short video that showed Brent in action.[4] Titled *The Office*, the new show premiered on BBC2 on July 9, 2001.[5] Critics praised the series but it left British audiences indifferent.[6]

Despite this cool reception, *The Office* changed the face of television production for years to come thanks to its faux-documentary aesthetic, which allowed Merchant to produce content at a much faster rate.[7] The show evoked then-popular "fly-on-the-wall" documentaries that showcased ordinary people.[8] Though it often appeared unscripted, *The Office*, which shot at a real office in Teddington Film Studios, relied heavily on scripted dialogue that incorporated controlled improvisation.[9] During writing sessions, Merchant and Gervais worked together to develop ideas that they then recorded, transcribed, and reworked into scripts.[10] Due to the amount of work they put into producing each episode, Gervais and Merchant only produced two short seasons and a two-part Christmas special.[11]

Despite its brief life, *The Office* won several awards, including the 2002 British Comedy Award.[12] It also became the first British comedy ever nominated for a Golden Globe for Best TV Series: Musical or Comedy, which it won.[13] The series

Overbearing office manager David Brent (Ricky Gervais) oversees a staff of misfits at the Slough branch of the fictional Wernham Hogg Paper Company. *BBC/Photofest*

aired in the United States on BBC America starting in January 2003,[14] followed by an American remake that launched in 2005.[15] The original series appears in syndication in over eighty countries and has spawned numerous culturally specific adaptions around the world.[16] In 2016, Gervais reprised his role as David Brent in the feature film *David Brent: Life on the Road.*[17]

Commentary

The Office brought the awkward humor and mockumentary aesthetic of such films as *Real Life* and *This Is Spinal Tap* to the small screen, in the process emerging as a worldwide hit that kicked off a wave of imitators both official and otherwise. The series served up a wickedly funny exploration of social norms and cultural values, all centered around the character of David Brent (played with overbearing obnoxiousness by controversial comic Ricky Gervais), an unlikeable, unsympathetic protagonist who nevertheless displays an innate ability to empathize with his put-upon employees. In addition to Gervais, *The Office* introduced audiences around the world to the comedic stylings of Martin Freeman, Mackenzie Crook, and Lucy Davis, each of whom went on to appear in hit films such as *Shaun of the Dead, The World's End, The Black Panther,* and *Pirates of the Caribbean.* The show also launched the career of series co-creator Stephen Merchant, who in the years since has been involved in shows like *Extras, An Idiot Abroad,* and the American adaptation of *The Office.* With its hilariously uncomfortable situations, unpleasant characters, and faux-documentary format, the original version of *The Office* established a new template for situation comedies during the early years of the twenty-first century.

The show only lasted two seasons comprised of twelve episodes (and a two-part Christmas special), but in that time it served up plenty of embarrassing scenarios and witty dialogue. *The Office* kicked things off in sidesplitting style with "Downsize" (S1E1), which suffers from a mostly aimless plot but still features such laugh-out-loud zingers as "I haven't got a sign on the door that says, 'White people only.' I don't care if you're black, brown, yellow . . . Orientals make very good workers." A few episodes later, in "Training" (S1E4), the increasingly disillusioned staff of Wernham Hogg's Slough branch attend a mandatory day-long training session that features David Brent singing some outrageously inappropriate songs. "Charity" (S2E5) features quite possibly the show's funniest moment as David tries to upstage two of his coworkers by performing a comically cringe-inducing dance during the company's annual fundraiser. The show also boasted such hilariously dry one-liners as "I'm 30 today. My mum got me up really early this morning to give me my present" (S1E3, "The Quiz") and "If you want the rainbow, you've gotta put up with the rain. Do you know which philosopher said that? Dolly Parton. And people say she's just a big pair of tits" (S2E6, "The Interview"). Such gags and its worldwide pop cultural influence secured *The Office* a spot among the greatest cult TV shows of all time.

See also *Parks and Recreation* (2009–2015)

OUTLANDER (2014–PRESENT)

Creator: Ronald D. Moore
Cast: Caitriona Balfe (Claire Randall), Sam Heughan (Jamie Fraser), Duncan Lacroix (Murtagh Fraser), Tobias Menzies (Frank Randall/Jack Randall), Grant O'Rourke (Rupert MacKenzie), Graham McTavish (Dougal MacKenzie)
Genre: Drama, Fantasy, Romance

Synopsis

During World War II, an English combat nurse is mysteriously transported back in time to the Scottish Highlands in the year 1743.

Production History

Starting in 1991, Diana Gabaldon began writing the bestselling fantasy-romance-adventure book series *Outlander*.[18] Over the years, various studios sought to option the rights to Gabaldon's wildly popular series, but the property eventually landed in the hands of Ronald D. Moore, the man behind the *Battlestar Galactica* reboot. Moore's wife, an ardent *Outlander* fan, suggested he read the series, which he wound up loving. He then pitched the project as a television series to Starz CEO Chris Albright, who committed to producing a faithful adaptation of the novels.[19] In July 2013, Sam Heughan landed the role of sexy Scotsman Jamie Fraser,[20] and two months later producers cast Caitriona Balfe as lead character Claire Randall following a long audition process.[21] Production on the pilot began soon after, with most of the shooting taking place inside a Scottish warehouse converted into a studio.[22]

While developing *Outlander*, showrunners planned to base each season on one of the books in the series,[23] and they even asked Gabaldon to factcheck their scripts.[24] In addition, the network hired expert Gaelic speaker Àdhamh Ó Broin to serve as a consultant on the show.[25] The first episode of *Outlander* premiered on August 9, 2014, at 9:00 p.m. on the Starz cable network, and the first season consisted of sixteen episodes.[26] In time, the first episode "surpassed 5 million views across all platforms" and "drew roughly equal male and female viewership,"[27] prompting Starz to almost immediately renew the series for a second season. During its run, *Outlander* filmed in Scotland, Prague, and Cape Town, and the series proved so popular that it increased tourism to Scotland.[28] The series returned with season 5, and a commitment for a sixth season, in February 2020.[29]

Commentary

Deftly mixing fantasy and romance, *Outlander* often feels like a steamy Harlequin novel brought to life, though one with a dash of science fiction thrown in for good measure. While it involves a rather torrid love story, the show refuses to romanticize the past, instead offering viewers a multifaceted look at both history and intimate relationships. Indeed, *Outlander* tackles difficult issues like rape and violence while offering up a modern commentary on the past. In addition, the series features complex characters, starting with protagonist Claire Randall, a complex, independent woman who defies long-standing female stereotypes without stepping into more traditional male roles. *Outlander* also features plenty of racy sex scenes that cater specifically to a female or queer gaze, which likely contribute to its massive popularity. At the same time, the show follows the characters as their relationships evolve over the course of more than two decades. *Outlander* moves beyond the courtship and the sex to show the central couple working through the many phases of their relationship as they deal with various hardships. As such the show offers a far more mature look at romantic love than most other fantasy shows and therefore resonates deeply with fans.

Showrunner Ronald D. Moore and his team of talented writers (which includes Ira Steven Behr, Matthew B. Roberts, Toni Graphia, and author Diana Gabaldon herself) craft gripping stories that deal with complicated issues like misogyny, classism, and racism. Claire refuses to accept such injustices while her eighteenth-century husband, Jamie Fraser, embraces her unconventional ideas. Yet both characters also understand and accept the difficulty of trying to change the world around them given how ingrained such issues are during that historical period. Thus each episode of *Outlander* forces viewers to examine their own prejudices and assumptions. Aside from the explicit eroticism, much of the show's appeal lies in its picturesque setting and exhaustively researched period detail, which lend a sense of authenticity missing in a lot of other series set in the past (real or imagined). *Outlander* routinely dazzles viewers with spellbinding tales set against the lush backdrop of the Scottish Highlands circa the 1700s. For instance, "The Wedding" (S1E7) sees Jamie wed the time-displaced Claire to prevent her from falling into the clutches of the nefarious Black Jack Randall. Meanwhile "Prestonpans" (S2E10) deals with an actual historical battle in exhilarating fashion, with Jamie hatching a cunning plan to defeat the British while Claire uses her skills to treat the wounded. In each episode, *Outlander* juggles sexy romance, enthralling drama, and historical thrills, much to the delight of its hardcore fans.

OZ (1997–2003)

Creator: Tom Fontana
Cast: Ernie Hudson (Leo Glynn), J. K. Simmons (Vern Schillinger), Lee Tergesen (Tobias Beecher), Dean Winters (Ryan O'Reily), George Morfogen (Bob Rebadow), Terry Kinney (Tim McManus), Rita Moreno (Sister Peter Marie Reimondo), Harold Perrineau (Augustus Hill)
Genre: Drama, Thriller

Synopsis

The inmates, guards, and wardens of an experimental prison wing known as Emerald City deal with the harsh conditions behind bars.

Production History

While working as a writer on the gritty cop show *Homicide: Life on the Street*, Tom Fontana created *Oz*, which would become the "first ever hour-long cable drama."[30] Fontana wanted to use the series to explore what happens to criminals after they wind up in prison.[31] He teamed with Barry Levinson to develop the idea and then took it to the four major broadcast networks, which all rejected it.[32] Fontana and Levinson then approached Chris Albrecht of HBO, who gave them $1 million to shoot a fifteen-minute presentation as proof of concept to establish the show's tone.[33] Fontana shot the presentation in Baltimore while working on *Homicide*, and it proved good enough to land him an eight-episode order with the network.[34]

During production, Fontana penned 75 percent of the scripts,[35] writing them in long hand.[36] In addition, he wrote parts for specific actors such as Dean Winters and Lee Tergesen although casting the character of Kareem Saïd proved difficult until one of Fontana's associates recommended Eamonn Walker.[37] Fontana and his team shot the pilot episode and the first season in Manhattan on sets constructed inside an old Oreo cookie factory located in what is now Chelsea

The inmates of the Oswald State Correctional Facility try to survive prison life. *HBO/Photofest*

Market.[38] Darnell Martin's work as director on the pilot established the visual language and production design for the rest of the series as she shot everything on 16mm film to improve camera mobility.[39] *Oz* premiered on July 12, 1997, at 11:30 p.m., and it went on to win three CableACE awards in its first season, including one for best dramatic series.[40] HBO never shared ratings information with Fontana, but Albrecht seemed happy with the attention *Oz* received from critics and viewers.[41] In the fall of 2002,[42] HBO canceled *Oz* after six seasons and fifty-six episodes as the stories became increasingly unrealistic and even absurd.[43] The last episode aired on Sunday February 23, 2003.[44]

Commentary

With *Oz*, HBO launched their first original drama series, in the process kick-starting the so-called golden age of television of the late twentieth and early twenty-first centuries.[45] During its six seasons, *Oz* earned critical praise and built a devoted fanbase thanks to a combination of terrific performances, gritty realism, and a willingness to explore often ignored areas of American society and culture. As media scholar Michele Malach notes, "*Oz* attempts to contextualize the penal system within the larger ideology of contemporary, mainstream American culture and to foreground economic and political issues most of us ignore in the same way that we ignore prisons themselves."[46] Of course, *Oz* also featured outrageously melodramatic storylines and copious amounts of violence and male nudity, which likely contributed to the show's popularity among viewers looking for something a little different from standard network dramas. Regardless of why it resonated with viewers and critics, *Oz* signaled a profound shift in televised dramas, inspiring a host of prestige TV shows that focused on complicated characters (often of the anti-heroic variety), intricate serialized narratives, and mature themes, including *The Sopranos*, *The Wire*, and *Breaking Bad*.

Oz featured a sprawling, ever-changing ensemble cast led by veteran performers such as Ernie Hudson and Rita Moreno as well as future stars like Chris Meloni, J. K. Simmons, and Harold Perrineau. The show also mixed stark realism with over-the-top storylines and situations, often involving bizarre premises and fantasy sequences. The first episode, "X," introduced viewers to the harsh conditions inside the Emerald City experimental unit of Oswald State Penitentiary and immediately established the pecking order that exists among the inmates. The first season culminated with "A Game of Checkers" (S1E8), in which a riot breaks out and irrevocably changes the prison and its inhabitants. Other episodes explored the complex relationships between the characters, as in "Ancient Tribes" (S2E2), which sees Emerald City's idealistic manager Tim McManus create a council of group representatives to maintain order inside the prison and initiates classes designed to help the inmates secure high school equivalency credentials. The show also pioneered the use of musical episodes with "Variety" (S5E6), which included several fantasy interludes sung by the show's cast members. Unfortunately, *Oz* jumped the shark in the sixth season thanks to the introduction of dubious plots and baffling scenarios, including one involving the use of an experimental aging pill to ease overcrowding. Nonetheless, the show deserves a spot among the greatest cult TV shows because it altered the television landscape and still enjoys a fervent fan following today.

See also *Deadwood* (2004–2006), *The Wire* (2002–2008)

P

PARKS AND RECREATION (2009–2015)

Creators: Greg Daniels, Michael Schur
Cast: Amy Poehler (Leslie Knope), Nick Offerman (Ron Swanson), Aubrey Plaza
(April Ludgate), Chris Pratt (Andy Dwyer), Aziz Ansari (Tom Haverford), Jim
O'Heir (Jerry Gergich), Retta (Donna Meagle), Adam Scott (Ben Dwyer), Rashida
Jones (Ann Perkins), Rob Lowe (Chris Traeger)
Genre: Comedy

Synopsis

An upbeat civil servant and her crew of misfits work to make Pawnee, Indiana,
the best possible town in the Midwest.

Production History

In 2008, executives at NBC asked Greg Daniels to develop a spinoff of the
American remake of *The Office*.[1] Daniels instead teamed with Michael Schur to
create *Parks and Recreation*, a mockumentary-style show about an overly optimistic
civil servant attempting to make a difference in a small-town government.[2] Due
to a pre-existing deal between the duo and NBC, network executives ordered
Parks and Recreation straight to series with a thirteen-episode guarantee.[3] Daniels
and Schur then contacted Amy Poehler, who Schur knew from his days working on *Saturday Night Live*, and asked her to play lead character Leslie Knope.[4]
Though pregnant at the time, Poehler accepted the role.[5] Daniels and Schur then
cast Rashida Jones, Aubrey Plaza, Aziz Ansari, Chris Pratt, Nick Offerman, Retta,
Jim O'Heir, and Paul Schneider in supporting roles.[6] Production began soon after,
with NBC promising to air the first episode after Super Bowl XLIII.[7] Cast and crew
shot six episodes in a row but Poehler's pregnancy delayed production, causing
the show to lose its coveted post–Super Bowl slot.[8]

Parks and Recreation premiered on April 9, 2009,[9] with the first episode earning solid ratings.[10] Unfortunately, ratings soon declined, and critics compared
the show unfavorably to *The Office*.[11] However, *Parks and Recreation* established
its own identity in season 2, at which point it earned critical praise and award

nominations.[12] Nonetheless, the show continued to pull low ratings, prompting the creators to write every season finale as a possible series finale.[13] The first six episodes drew an average of 6.1 million viewers, but by season 5 that number had fallen to an average of 4.1 million viewers. NBC's tendency to shuffle the show around the schedule likely contributed to the low ratings.[14] Nonetheless the show maintained a loyal and consistent audience mainly of the 18–34-year-olds coveted by advertisers.[15] Producers decided to end the series after season 7,[16] and the final episode aired on February 24, 2015,[17] but Leslie and her misfit co-workers live on in Internet memes and the hearts of fans.

Commentary

Bursting with optimism and laughs, *Parks and Recreation* introduced viewers to cheerful over-achiever Leslie Knope and her zany co-workers at the Parks Department of the fictional city of Pawnee, Indiana. The series showcased several hilarious performers who went on to shape the comedy landscape including Nick Offerman, Aubrey Plaza, Chris Pratt, Adam Scott, and Rashida Jones. The show also boasted incredible talent behind the camera, with funny folks like Rob Schrab, Jorma Taccone, Nicole Holfcener, and Paul Feig directing episodes, while Harris Wittels, Megan Amram, Chelsea Peretti, and Katie Dippold all provided scripts. As such, each installment of *Parks and Recreation* contained both big laughs

Mid-level bureaucrat Leslie Knope (Amy Poehler, center) tries to enlist her kooky co-workers to help her improve her beloved hometown of Pawnee, Indiana. *NBC Universal/Photofest*

and touching moments. The show also took daring risks, as when the final season jumped forward in time (to the far-flung future of 2017!) to offer up a winking critique of tech culture and Silicon Valley as an Internet startup called Gryzzl tries to set up a corporate office in Pawnee to hilarious results. While it started on shaky ground (fans often dismiss the first season as terrible[18]), *Parks and Recreation* nevertheless developed a loyal following thanks to a mix of amiable humor, cartoonish situations, and delightful characters.

Every episode of *Parks and Recreation* featured laugh-out-loud dialogue and over-the-top situations, all of which endeared the show to fans of good-natured (yet slightly warped) comedy. For example, in "Flu Season" (S3E2), antisocial misanthrope Ron Swanson dismisses Andy Dwyer's attempts at bonding by flatly stating, "I once worked with a guy for three years and never learned his name. Best friend I ever had. We still never talk sometimes." Later, in "The Fight" (S3E13), Leslie tells her bestie, Ann Perkins, that they need to focus on the important things in life: "Friends, waffles, and work. Or waffles, friends, work. It doesn't matter. But work is third." In "Bus Tour" (S4E21), the athletic and handsome Chris Traeger explains how he staves off depression: "If I keep my body moving, and my mind occupied at all times, I will avoid falling into a bottomless pit of despair." The show often mined humor from the characters' misery, as when Andy declares, "I'm fine. It's just that life is pointless, and nothing matters and I'm always tired" in "Correspondent's Lunch" (S5E15). In the end, an abundance of heartfelt humor and appealing characters turned *Parks and Recreation* into a beloved cult favorite of fans who *literally* could not imagine life without it.

See also *Arrested Development* (2003–2019), *Community* (2009–2015), *The Office* (2001–2003)

PEE-WEE'S PLAYHOUSE (1986–1991)

Creator: Paul Reubens
Cast: Pee-wee Herman (Paul Reubens), Lynne Marie Stewart (Miss Yvonne), William Marshall (King of Cartoons), John Paragon (Jambi), Laurence Fishburne (Cowboy Curtis), S. Epatha Merkerson (Reba the Mail Lady), Phil Hartman (Captain Carl)
Genre: Comedy, Musical

Synopsis

Impish man-child Pee-wee Herman invites viewers to visit his madcap playhouse where anything can happen.

Production History

Comedian Paul Reubens created the Pee-wee Herman character in 1978 while a member of the famed Los Angeles improv group the Groundlings.[19] A few years later, Reubens launched *The Pee-wee Herman Show*,[20] a live stage show that

Puckish manchild Pee-wee Herman invites viewers to join him in his unique playhouse to partake in wacky, imaginative fun. *CBS/Photofest*

eventually gained the attention of executives at HBO,[21] who in 1981 agreed to air a recording of the show's final performance.[22] Reubens then toured the country as his alter ego until 1985, at which point Warner Bros. approached him about headlining a Pee-wee Herman movie called *Pee-wee's Big Adventure*.[23] Michael Chase Walker, director of children's programming for CBS, saw an advanced screening of the film and decided to build a Saturday morning children's show around the character. Reubens initially declined because he wanted to focus on his film career,[24] but Walker eventually convinced the comic to set his sights on TV stardom instead.[25] In January 1986, Reubens agreed to appear in the show[26] but he wanted to change it from animation to live action.[27] The network gave him the freedom to express his vision however he wanted, and both parties committed to a September 1986 release.[28]

While developing *Pee-wee's Playhouse*, Reubens looked to the children's shows of the 1950s.[29] Production began in February 1986 with a budget of $325,000–$525,000 per episode.[30] Lynne Stewart, Phil Hartman, and John Paragon all reprised their roles from the stage show but Hartman soon left for *Saturday Night Live*.[31] Casting Cowboy Curtis proved difficult until Reubens remembered Larry Fishburne from his days with the Groundlings[32] (Fishburne used to hang out with the kid who ran lights).[33] Broadcast Arts and Aardman Studios provided animation for the show,[34] while the art directors from the original live show oversaw the puppets.[35] *Pee-wee's Playhouse* premiered at 10:00 a.m. on September 13, 1986, and tanked in the ratings.[36] However, positive word of mouth soon caused the show's ratings to skyrocket, prompting the network to order two additional seasons.[37] When it came time to renew the series, an exhausted Reubens agreed to film twenty more episodes split into two seasons[38] but he declined to keep the show going through 1993.[39] The final episode of *Pee-wee's Playhouse* aired on November 10, 1990.[40]

Commentary

By repackaging his popular stage show as a surrealist Saturday morning kids' show, comedian Paul Reubens brought his singularly weird brand of comedy into the realm of children's programming. As the puckish Pee-wee Herman, Reubens played the unhinged embodiment of childhood, letting his overactive imagination run wild in a weekly series that featured screwy puppets, weird cartoons, and slyly subversive humor. *Pee-wee's Playhouse* often felt like it leapt straight from the mind of a manic twelve-year-old riding a sugar rush brought on by eating too many bowls of Cap'n Crunch. The show captured the spirit of children's programs like *The Howdy Doody Show* and *Captain Kangaroo* but with the volume turned up way past eleven. Each week, Pee-wee interacted with a cast of bizarre characters both puppet and human, and together they embarked on wacky adventures through the title character's boundless imagination. In addition, the show featured amusing clay animation sequences (some provided by Aardman Animations, of *Wallace & Gromit* fame) along with excerpts from old cartoons produced between the 1920s and 1960s. Throughout, Pee-wee served as a sort of madcap Mr. Rogers, taking his young viewers on a wild journey to Puppetland, a fantastic place that recalled Winsor McKay's Slumberland. There, kids (and bored stoners) met zany characters like Chairry (an armchair with eyes and a mouth), Conky 2000 (a stuttering robot), and Pterri (a childish Pteranodon). *Pee-wee's Playhouse* offered weird fun for everyone.

Throughout the show's five-year run, Pee-wee served as a beacon of positivity, always finding the good in every situation. Kids responded to the mischievous character because he smiled and laughed often, and they chortled right along with him. In addition, Pee-wee played the same games and engaged in similar shenanigans as the show's preadolescent audience such as making ice cream soup, putting on a magic show, or pretending to shop at a store. The show also featured a lot of "naughty" humor, using cunning innuendo to cover up numerous poop and fart jokes that no doubt left many kids rolling on the floor laughing. For instance, Pee-wee once returned from the grocery store with two bottles of milk and a bottle of lemonade, prompting him to blurt out, "Around the corner fudge is made!" before offering a knowing wink to the camera. Parents may not get the joke but kids who had heard the phrase spoken on the playground likely laughed out loud. *Pee-wee's Playhouse* also served up loads of quotable dialogue, such as "Why don't you take a picture? It'll last longer," Jambi's repeated refrain of "Mekka lekka hi, mekka hiney ho," and, of course, Pee-wee's catchphrase "I know you are but what am I?" *Pee-wee's Playhouse* had its run cut short due to Reubens's offscreen behavior, but it still produced forty-five hilariously chaotic episodes that delighted viewers of all ages and remain cherished to this day.

See also *H.R. PufnStuf* (1969–1970)

> ## PINKY AND THE BRAIN (1995–1998)
>
> *Creator*: Steven Spielberg
> *Cast*: Rob Paulsen (Pinky), Maurice LaMarche (the Brain), Tress MacNeille (Various),
>   Frank Welker (Various)
> *Genre*: Comedy, Science Fiction

Synopsis

Two genetically engineered lab mice hatch wacky schemes as they plot to take over the world.

Production History

Beloved animated characters Pinky and the Brain first appeared in the *Animaniacs* episode "Win Big" (S1E2).[41] Producer Tom Ruegger based the cartoon duo on the *Animaniacs* writing team of Tom Minton and Eddie Fitzgerald (who reportedly exclaimed things like "narf" and "poit").[42] Casting director Andrea Romano offered the role of Brain to standup comic Maurice LaMarche after hearing his Orson Welles impression.[43] Meanwhile, Rob Paulson, a fan of Monty Python, affected a British accent while auditioning for Pinky, a choice that ultimately landed him the gig.[44] The characters' popularity with fans of *Animaniacs* led Amblin Entertainment and Warner Bros. to create a spinoff series for the WB Network in 1995.[45] Jamie Kellner, president of the WB, put great faith in the series,[46] and Steven Spielberg gave the writers the freedom to do whatever they wanted.[47]

Pinky and the Brain premiered on September 9, 1995, as part of the WB's primetime lineup, but it soon moved to the Kids WB block on Saturday mornings, where it ran for four years.[48] The show featured smart writing intended for both children and adults, with the WB advertising it as their version of *The Simpsons*.[49] *Pinky and the Brain* proved a hit with both viewers and critics, and it won an Emmy in 1996.[50] In 1997, Kids WB executives decided to add a third character, prompting Ruegger to create Larry (inspired by Larry Fine of the Three Stooges and voiced by Billy West), who appeared in one episode as a joke and caused the executives to back off. However, in 1998 they again requested a larger cast, so this time Ruegger added *Tiny Toons* character Elmyra and retooled the series as *Pinky, Elmyra, and the Brain*.[51] However, fans disliked the change, complaining that adding Elmyra ruined both the characters' chemistry and the show's format.[52] The show reverted to *Pinky and the Brain* shortly before the last episode, "Star Warners" (S4E7), aired in 1998, reuniting the entire cast of *Animaniacs* for an affectionate spoof of *Star Wars*.[53]

Commentary

Steven Spielberg rejuvenated Warner Brothers Looney Tunes cartoons and their descendants in *Tiny Toon Adventures* (*TTA*) and then built on that success with *Animaniacs*, which introduced new characters in the Merrie Melodies style. And

Genetically engineered lab mice Pinky (left) and the Brain plot to take over the world. *WB/Photofest*

while Wakko, Yakko, and their sister Dot were undoubtedly the stars of *Animaniacs*, their co-stars Pinky and the Brain consistently stole the show whenever an episode featured one of their animated skits. Of all these new characters, only Pinky and the Brain succeeded enough to deserve their own spin-off show. While Plucky Duck also got a spinoff from *TTA*, his lasted only 13 episodes, while *Pinky and the Brain* lasted 65—or 90 if you count the misguided episodes that added Elmyra from *TTA*. That 90 episodes is almost as much as *TTA* (98) and *Animaniacs* (99), showing that the spinoff was as popular as its predecessors, which is an immensely rare occurrence in television let alone animated television.

What made the laboratory mice such fan favorites in *Animaniacs* easily translated to their own series, which would run as shorts or full twenty-one-minute episodes. The antics remained the same, only sometimes they were more complex, more fully developed, and even more absurd. The "Fly" (S1E12) begins with the Brain having purchased all the property in the world above the 39th floor, then he and Pinky travel to the Hubble telescope in a plot to use it to melt the polar ice-caps, thereby flooding the Earth and forcing all the survivors to live on his property.[54] In "It's Only a Paper World" (S1E15), the Brain recreates the Earth in papier-mâché and lures all of humanity there with an offer of free T-shirts. Such absurdist comedy harkens back to the glory days of Merrie Melodies as well as Monty Python.

The plots to take over the world always mattered less than the humor and the relationship between the Brain and his enthusiastically incapable sidekick. Pinky was the heart of the series, a lovable idiot who continually offered up some of the series' most quotable lines, from his exclamations like "Narf!" and "Troz!" (which is "Zort!" backward, as he tells us in S1E10, "Snowball") to his non-sequiturs in response to Brain's perennial and meme-worthy question "Pinky, are you pondering what I'm pondering?" At times, Pinky's response would emphasize the adultness of the absurd comedy; for example, "Well, I think so, Brain, but Kevin Costner with an English accent?" (S2E8, "Robin Brain"). Children unaware of Kevin Costner's portrayal of Robin Hood would not understand the joke, but adult viewers would, and the series routinely offered such content for older viewers, such as parodying Orson Welles in *The Third Man* in the episode "The Third Mouse" (S1E14) or having Pinky become an Indian guru in the 1960s in "All You Need Is Narf" (S3E6) to lampoon the Beatles. With humor aimed at children and adults, *Pinky and the Brain* showed how a spinoff can be as successful as its predecessors.

See also *Rocko's Modern Life* (1993–1996)

POLICE SQUAD! (1982)

Creators: Jim Abrahams, David Zucker, Jerry Zucker
Cast: Leslie Nielsen (Frank Drebin), Alan North (Ed Hocken), Rex Hamilton (Abraham Lincoln), Ed Williams (Mr. Olson), William Duell (Johnny), Peter Lupus (Norberg)
Genre: Comedy

Synopsis

Two bumbling police detectives investigate wacky crimes in this hilarious spoof of cop shows.

Production History

Following the success of *Airplane!* Jim Abrahams, David Zucker, and Jerry Zucker (known collectively as ZAZ) landed a deal to produce *Police Squad!*, a television series that would spoof cop shows. The trio wrote the lead role for Leslie Nielsen[55] because they wanted him to send up his own roles in *The Bold Ones: The Protectors* and *S.W.A.T.*[56] However, during preproduction, executives at ABC worried that Nielsen was too old to play Drebin and wanted the character recast, but ZAZ threatened to walk unless the network relented.[57] Instead of making a pilot, ZAZ sold the series on the strength of the opening credits sequence, arguing that the series would be like *Airplane!* only focusing on the police procedural genre.[58] ZAZ set out to mock police procedurals, and they even copied lines from gritty cop show *M Squad* and had the actors deliver them straight in the pilot episode.[59] The show's writing staff consisted of two three-person teams, with ZAZ acting as the first team while David Misch, Robert Wuhl, and Tino Insana made up the other.[60] ABC ordered six episodes shot over the course of six weeks on a small budget, asking for a laugh track, but ZAZ argued that audience research did not support having one.[61]

Police Squad! debuted on Thursday, March 4, 1982, at 8:00 p.m., opposite *Magnum P.I.* and *Fame*.[62] ABC agreed to run the show for six weeks as a trial run but pulled the plug after only four weeks.[63] The network delayed airing the remaining two episodes until that July before finally canceling the series outright,[64] claiming it required "too much attention" from viewers.[65] During its brief lifespan, *Police Squad!* featured several guest stars including Lorne Greene, Robert Goulet, William Shatner, Dick Clark, Florence Henderson, and Dr. Joyce Brothers, whose characters died during the opening credits sequence. The show also received a handful of Emmy nominations, including Outstanding Lead Actor in a Comedy Series and Outstanding Writing in a Comedy Series. Most importantly, the show spawned three theatrical films: *The Naked Gun: From the Files of Police Squad!* (1988), *The Naked Gun 2 1/2: The Smell of Fear* (1991), and *Naked Gun 33 1/3: The Final Insult* (1994). In 2018, David Zucker announced a *Naked Gun* reboot focusing on Drebin's son but that project has yet to materialize.[66]

Commentary

With *Police Squad!* Jim Abrahams and the Zucker brothers brought their zany style of spoof comedy to primetime television though neither network executives nor viewers seemed prepared for such extreme wackiness. The show suffered a quick cancelation but it nevertheless changed the comedy landscape for decades afterward, spawning three successful spinoff films and inspiring a wave of similar parodies. It also helped revive the career of Leslie Nielsen and turned him into a comedy icon during the last two decades of the twentieth century.

In its six episodes, *Police Squad!* expertly deconstructed the crime genre, sending up such well-worn cop show clichés as the gritty voiceover narration, tense interrogation scenes, and even the show-closing freeze frame (but rather than a still shot, in *Police Squad!* the actors simply stopped moving). As daft detective Frank Drebin, Nielsen brought all his dramatic chops to bear, portraying the character as a cross between Joe Friday (as portrayed by Jack Webb in *Dragnet*) and Joe Mannix (Mike Connors). However, by playing everything extremely straight, Nielsen ratcheted the comedy up, infusing every situation with outrageous hilarity (as in the first episode, which sees Frank shoot it out with a suspect just five feet away). *Police Squad!* provided big laughs to viewers eager for someone to pop the bubble of self-importance that had surrounded most crime dramas up to that point.

Starting with its first episode, "A Substantial Gift (The Broken Promise)," *Police Squad!* served up a bevy of nonsensical jokes and loads of witty visual gags that left many viewers in stitches while others merely scratched their heads in bewilderment. For instance, in "A Substantial Gift," Drebin and his partner, Ed Hocken (brilliantly underplayed by Alan North), investigate a shooting at a bank, and when they arrive one of the chalk outlines recreates an Egyptian hieroglyph.

Later, in "Rendezvous at Big Gulch (Terror in the Neighborhood)" (S1E5), a group of thugs try to shake down an undercover Drebin posing as a shop owner but not before putting up a sign that says "Sorry. Owner being beaten. Back in 5 minutes." In other episodes, Drebin uses live ammunition during a crime reenactment, visits an informant who explains the Cinderella complex to Dr. Joyce Brothers, and then debates existentialism with a priest. Each episode of *Police Squad!* also features sidesplitting dialogue, as in "Revenge and Remorse (The Guilty Alibi)" (S1E4) when scantily clad showgirl Mimi Du Jour asks, "Is this some kind of bust?" to which Drebin responds, "Yes, it's very impressive, but we'd just like to ask you a few questions." Likewise, in the premiere episode, Drebin consoles a grieving widow by saying, "We're sorry to bother you at such a time like this, Mrs. Twice. We would have come earlier, but your husband wasn't dead then." Jokes such as these helped make *Police Squad!* an enduring cult classic.

THE PRISONER (1967–1968)

Creators: Patrick McGoohan, George Markstein
Cast: Patrick McGoohan (Number Six), Angelo Muscat (the Butler), Peter Swanwick (Supervisor), Leo McKern (Number Two), Peter Cargill (Number Two), Colin Gordon (Number Two), Kenneth Griffith (Number Two)
Genre: Drama, Mystery, Science Fiction

Synopsis

A retired secret agent awakens to find himself trapped in a picturesque English village that doubles as a high-tech Kafkaesque prison staffed by despotic wardens.

Production History

In the early 1960s Patrick McGoohan starred in *Danger Man*, a short-lived British spy series that followed the exploits of secret agent John Drake. Both the show and McGoohan proved popular enough that Lew Grade, head of Incorporated Television Company (ITC), greenlit a follow-up show called *Secret Agent* for the United States market that aired from 1964 to 1967, at which point an increasingly disenchanted McGoohan decided to move on.[67] Around that time, McGoohan was reading a book about retired secret agents. In it, the author theorized that nefarious forces abduct such agents and bring them to a secret village or town staffed by overseers who try to extract information the agents gathered during their missions.[68] McGoohan liked the concept and wanted his *Danger Man* character to suffer a similar fate.[69] He brought the idea to Grade,[70] who enthusiastically agreed to produce the show under the title *The Prisoner*.[71]

Producer David Tomblin spent a month writing the script for the first episode of *The Prisoner*.[72] Filming took place at MGM British Studios in Borehamwood,

A captive secret agent known only as Number Six (Patrick McGoohan, left) encounters bizarre characters as he tries to escape from a surreal island prison called the Village. *CBS/Photofest*

England, with exteriors shot at the Hotel Portmeirion in North Wales.[73] In addition to starring in every episode as lead character Number Six, McGoohan's production company, Everyman Films, owned the series, and he wrote and/or directed several episodes.[74] McGoohan wanted to end *The Prisoner* after seven episodes[75] but Grade convinced him to shoot twenty-six installments.[76] However, increasing production costs led Grade to end the series after seventeen episodes.[77] The series premiered in the United Kingdom on September 29, 1967, on ITV and in the United States on June 1, 1968, on CBS.[78] While many involved wanted a conclusive ending, McGoohan instead opted for something more metaphorical,[79] which outraged many fans.[80] The series nevertheless remained popular, and in 1986 CBS and ITC announced an Americanized sequel series without McGoohan's involvement.[81] That show failed to materialize, but in 1988 DC Comics released a four-part graphic novel set twenty years after the last episode.[82] In 2009, ITV and AMC produced a critically panned six-episode reboot of *The Prisoner*,[83] and rumors continue to swirl about a big-screen adaptation.[84]

Commentary

Patrick McGoohan followed up the popular spy show *Danger Man* with one of the weirdest and most paranoid television series ever produced. *The Prisoner* confused and delighted audiences on both sides of the Atlantic with a beguiling, psychedelic narrative that featured stylish secret agents, despicable villains, and trippy technology (such as Rover, a sentient white balloon that emerges from the ocean to capture escaping inmates). Filled with Orwellian overtones, *The Pris-*

oner follows captive spy Number Six as he plots to flee a pastoral island prison known as the Village. His efforts are repeatedly thwarted by a rotating group of sinister wardens who employ various techniques (like hallucinogenic drugs and mind control) to extract information from him. Yet with its revolutionary, surrealist storyline and groundbreaking aesthetics, *The Prisoner* subverted the popular spy genre, which by then had grown somewhat stale. Dispensing with the usual cloak-and-dagger action of James Bond films or TV shows like *The Man from U.N.C.L.E.*, the series instead served up more cerebral stories about complex issues like identity, freedom, and scientific progress. Author Douglas L. Howard notes that "the ambiguous nature of the narrative and the metaphoric nature of the plots immediately lend themselves to such larger readings."[85] More than just another spy show, *The Prisoner* gave viewers much to think about during its short but memorable run.

In many ways, the series marked the beginning of high-concept television shows and "mystery box" serialized narratives (as in shows produced by J. J. Abrams) as well as the emergence of the auteur showrunner. McGoohan (along with script editor George Markstein) co-created *The Prisoner*, wrote six of the seventeen episodes, and directed five more. As Matthew Sweet of the *Telegraph* puts it, *The Prisoner* serves as "a mirror to McGoohan's volatile, malcontented imagination."[86] McGoohan reportedly exerted a great deal of control over the show, often acting like a dictator on set (he supposedly even punched fellow actors during fight scenes).[87] Several colleagues suspected he "was having a nervous breakdown and committing it to celluloid."[88] Yet the actor's behavior resulted in some truly fascinating experimental television, producing daring episodes like "The Girl Who Was Death" (a rambling, dreamy, chase narrative is revealed as a bedtime story recited by Number Six to a group of children) and the ambiguous series finale "Fall Out" (in which Number Six finally escapes from the Village . . . or does he?). With its tales of fragmented identities and constant surveillance,[89] along with narratives that blur the line between truth and fiction, *The Prisoner* laid much of the groundwork for the postmodern era of television.

See also *The Avengers* (1961–1969), *Lost* (2004–2010), *The Twilight Zone* (1959–1964), *Twin Peaks* (1990–1991)

Q

QUANTUM LEAP (1989–1993)

Creator: Donald P. Bellisario
Cast: Scott Bakula (Sam Beckett), Dean Stockwell (Al Calavicci), Dennis Wolfberg (Gooshie), Deborah Pratt (Narrator)
Genre: Action, Drama, Mystery, Science Fiction

Synopsis

Following a botched time-travel experiment, scientist Sam Beckett finds himself leaping into different people's bodies in the recent past, shaping their lives as he tries to return home.

Production History

Donald P. Bellisario created *Quantum Leap* while working on *Magnum P.I.*[1] He originally envisioned the series as an anthology but networks and studios alike rejected that concept.[2] Bellisario then retooled the show, turning it into a time-travel series with a lead character who leaped into new eras and places each week.[3] He pitched the idea to Brandon Tartikoff at NBC who expressed confusion about the concept but nevertheless greenlit the show.[4] Bellisario acted as a hands-on showrunner, overseeing all aspects of production.[5] He wrote a lengthy series bible that established firm rules designed to set the show apart from other time-travel series,[6] including an edict stating that Sam could only leap to periods within his own lifetime and only into non-famous people (though that changed over time).[7]

Scott Bakula and former child star Dean Stockwell landed the lead roles, and Stockwell, a staunch activist, convinced Bellisario to include more social issues in the stories.[8] *Quantum Leap* debuted on NBC on March 26, 1989, and almost immediately endeared itself to audiences and critics.[9] Yet the show struggled in the ratings and remained on the verge of cancelation throughout most of its run, only avoiding that fate thanks to an effective letter-writing campaign mounted by dedicated fans.[10] However, NBC shuffled the show around the schedule so often that fans eventually teamed with the organization Viewers for Quality Television to protest the decision to move the show from Wednesday to Friday evenings.[11] The show originally aired on Sunday nights, then it bounced between Friday and

Wednesday nights before briefly moving to Tuesday nights, finally landing on Wednesday nights for the remainder of its run.[12] During that time, *Quantum Leap* received several Emmy nominations, including one for Outstanding Drama Series as well as nods for both Bakula and Stockwell.[13] During its brief life, the show generated spinoff novels, comic books, and even a soundtrack that featured Bakula singing.[14] The series finale aired on May 5, 1993, and drew big ratings[15] as well as questions from its fans who still ask if Dr. Sam Beckett will ever find a way home.[16]

Commentary

Each week, *Quantum Leap* took viewers on a journey through the twentieth century as lead character Sam Beckett bounced back and forth through time, embarking on adventures big and small. The show served up thrilling action, gripping drama, and touching romance, offering a little something for everyone. During its five seasons, *Quantum Leap* tackled sociocultural issues like racism, homophobia, and women's liberation in episodes that helped build understanding and empathy for marginalized perspectives.[17] Moreover, the show frequently engaged in gender-bending, race-bending, and straight-bending. In each episode, Sam (a white, heterosexual male) finds himself viewing the world through different eyes, which sometimes belonged to women, people of color, or queer characters. Series star Bakula rose to the challenge, showing Sam's discomfort as he struggled to adjust to each new situation and his emotional growth as he experienced perspectives different from his own. As such, *Quantum Leap* advanced an ethos of tolerance and compassion while presenting gripping narratives that

Al Calavicci (Dean Stockwell, left) tries to help time-displaced scientist Sam Beckett (Scott Bakula) find his way home. *NBC/Photofest*

often unfolded against larger historical movements and events. For instance, "The Color of Truth" (S1E7) sees Sam leap into an aging black chauffeur in 1950s Alabama six months before Rosa Parks's defiant sit-in. Meanwhile, in the two-part "Lee Harvey Oswald" (S5E1, S5E2), Sam lands in Oswald's body, thus gaining an opportunity to change the past. *Quantum Leap* wrestled with big questions even as it sent audiences on a wild ride through time.

The show appeared around the same time as the nascent World Wide Web, which hosted early *Quantum Leap* discussion boards and websites. That fandom has only grown in the years since and now includes everything from fan-fiction archives to media tributes.[18] Because the show emerged during a time when few science fiction and fantasy series aired on TV, it inspired fierce devotion among its fans (known as "Leapers"), who organized *Quantum Leap* conventions, produced fanzines, and even raised money to fund Dean Stockwell's star on the Hollywood Walk of Fame.[19] *Quantum Leap* also contributed to the rise of fangirls, who were drawn in by the show's sci-fi elements, humanistic values, and attractive star. As Sam, Bakula displayed boyish good looks and roguish charm, a combination guaranteed to melt hearts and quicken pulses. More importantly, though, he openly showed emotion, often crying (as when he heard his dead father's voice for the first time in years) or expressing outrage over injustice (as when he strives to save a black civil rights lawyer while inhabiting the body of Klansman). The character championed values like respect and love, which endeared him to viewers of all sexes, genders, and orientations, and these elements helped make *Quantum Leap* a timeless cult classic.

See also *Doctor Who* (1963–Present), *Outlander* (2014–Present)

QUEER AS FOLK (1999–2000)

Creator: Russell T. Davies
Cast: Aidan Gillen (Stuart Jones), Craig Kelly (Vince Tyler), Charlie Hunnam (Nathan Maloney), Denise Black (Hazel Tyler), Andy Devine (Bernard Thomas), Esther Hall (Romey Sullivan)
Genre: Drama

Synopsis

Two gay friends lead lives filled with sex, drugs, and clubbing but things grow increasingly complicated after one of them meets a rebellious teenager.

Production History

Inspired by his own experiences in the Manchester gay scene, Russell T. Davies developed the pioneering drama series *Queer as Folk* for Britain's Channel 4.[20] He completed the first draft of the pilot script in February 1998.[21] Davies tried to avoid writing "something with a message" and instead focused on crafting an entertaining and captivating story about characters who just happened to be gay.[22] Channel 4 bought the series in March 1998, and filming took place between August 31 and December 19, 1998.[23] Davies wanted Christopher Eccleston as lead character Stuart Jones but Eccleston declined and instead suggested his friend Aidan Gillen.[24] Producers then cast Craig Kelly and Charlie Hunnam in the other lead roles.[25] Produced by Red Productions, the show shot mainly in Manchester on a £3 million budget.[26]

Queer as Folk premiered on February 23, 1999,[27] the same day Britain's House of Lords considered a bill to reduce the age of consent for homosexual couples to sixteen years old.[28] Channel 4 ordered a second season of ten episodes but Davies declined because he felt he had said everything he wanted to with the first series.[29] Nonetheless, he wrote a short, two-hour sequel that aired on February 22, 2000, and wrapped up the show to his liking.[30] Starting in August 2000, cable network C1TV aired an edited version of *Queer as Folk* in the United States.[31] Meanwhile, the uncut version of the show played at gay film festivals across the United States.[32] In December 2000, Showtime launched an American remake of *Queer as Folk*.[33] Bravo announced a reboot in 2015[34] but quickly scrapped the idea. Around the same time, NBCUniversal nabbed the rights to relaunch *Queer as Folk* on its dedicated streaming service.[35]

Commentary

Groundbreaking drama *Queer as Folk* shocked viewers with some of the most explicit gay sex ever seen on British television up to that point. The show even upset gay audiences who worried that it advanced predatory stereotypes, but queer viewers quickly fell in love with *Queer as Folk* because it featured "the first completely honest depiction of the ordinary lives twentysomething gay men lead in big cities everywhere—with absolutely nothing held back."[36] The series initiated a frank conversation about queer sexuality and gay relationships at the turn of the century, both in the United Kingdom and the United States. This conversation proved massively important considering a 1999 study "revealed that a staggering 49 percent of British people thought homosexual relationships were either 'always wrong' or 'mostly wrong.'"[37] In addition, the show emerged when "the gay community was still reeling from the AIDS crisis while continuing to navigate a hostile press."[38] *Queer as Folk* provided a sensitive, nuanced depiction of queer life that delighted its audience of mostly gay men and heterosexual women.[39]

Each episode of the show served up raw and uncompromising tales (all written by series creator Russell T. Davies, who later revived *Doctor Who*) about three adventurous young men navigating the gay scene in Manchester at the dawn of the new millennium. The revolutionary series produced bold episodes like "Meeting People Is Easy" (S1E1), in which a chance encounter changes the lives of arrogant lothario Stuart Jones and rebellious teenager Nathan Maloney. Soon after, in "Death and Remembrance" (S1E4), Nathan reveals his homosexuality to his mother to disastrous results. Such audacious and candid stories turned *Queer as Folk* into a pioneering hit that inspired an American remake that debuted the same year the original version ended. The remake's producers worried that American audiences might reject the show, but they nevertheless banked on the fact that the original series achieved "cult status among gay men on both sides of the Atlantic."[40] Indeed, *Queer as Folk* built a reputation in the United States via bootleg recordings passed among American friends within the show-business community before eventually making their way to "Chelsea, Fire Island, West Hollywood, and the Castro."[41] Both versions of the show remain important touchstones of queer representation.

SPOTLIGHT: RUSSELL T. DAVIES

Born April 27, 1963, in Wales, Stephen Russell Davies grew up immersing himself in television, particularly *Doctor Who*.[42] He earned a degree in English Literature from Oxford University and came out as gay while there.[43] Davies briefly worked in theater before breaking into children's television as a cartoonist[44] and then with the BBC's *Why Don't You?*[45] From there, he wrote the children's science fiction series *Dark Season* and *Century Falls*.[46] After winning a BAFTA in 1996 for *Children's Ward*, Davies focused on adult dramas, writing for *The House of Windsor* and *Coronation Street* before creating *Queer as Folk* in 1991.[47] In 2005, Davies served as showrunner for the regenerated *Doctor Who*, which he left in 2008[48] after creating its two spinoffs, *Torchwood* and *The Sarah Jane Adventures*.

R

RED DWARF (1988–2017)

Creators: Rob Grant, Doug Naylor
Cast: Craig Charles (Dave Lister), Danny John-Jules (Cat), Chris Barrie (Arnold Rimmer), Robert Llewellyn (Kryten), Chloë Annett (Kristine Kochanski), Norman Lovett (Holly, 1988–2017), Hattie Hayridge (Holly, 1988–2017)
Genre: Comedy, Science Fiction

Synopsis

Three million years in the future, the last living human drifts through deep space aboard the mining starship Red Dwarf with a fussy robot, an uptight hologram, an evolved cat, and a scatterbrained artificial intelligence as his only company.

Production History

In the mid-1980s, comedy writers Rob Grant and Doug Naylor set out to create their own sitcom,[1] which they based on a sketch they'd written years earlier called "Dave Hollins, Space Cadet."[2] They titled their new idea *Red Dwarf* and took it to executives at the BBC, who nearly rejected the show until producer Paul Jackson expressed his support. Jackson sent the pilot script to Commissioning Editor Peter Risdale-Scott, who gave it an enthusiastic thumbs up.[3] Nonetheless, *Red Dwarf* remained in limbo until 1986, with an electrician's strike in 1987 further delaying production of the first series.[4] Liverpudlian punk poet Craig Charles landed the lead role of Dave Lister despite a lack of acting experience while Chris Barrie, who had worked with Grant and Naylor on *Spitting Image*, played Lister's dead-roommate-turned-hologram, Arnold Rimmer. Laid-back standup comic Norman Lovett also auditioned for the role of Rimmer but producers thought him a better fit for the titular ship's absentminded artificial intelligence, Holly.[5] Danny John-Jules, a professional singer and dancer, rounded out the core cast as Cat, a vain lifeform that evolved from the ship's cat.

Red Dwarf premiered on February 15, 1988, with BBC2 airing fifty-two episodes between 1988 and 1999.[6] Grant and Naylor served as producers starting with series 3 just in time to replace a departing Lovett with Hattie Hayridge as a gender-swapped version of Holly.[7] The series began airing on PBS stations across the United States in the early 1990s.[8] In 1992, Hollywood producer (and fan of the show) Linwood Boomer proposed an American adaptation of *Red Dwarf* but the project quickly fell apart.[9] Soon after, director Ed Bye decided to leave *Red Dwarf* so Grant and Naylor directed every episode of series 6, which fans now consider the best despite a rushed schedule that resulted from changes dictated by the BBC.[10] Grant and Naylor ended their partnership shortly before the debut of series 7,[11] which proved so popular that BBC2 commissioned an eighth series.[12] The network rejected Naylor's idea for a ninth season, but *Red Dwarf* returned in 2009 when Channel Dave ordered a poorly reviewed but highly rated three-part special.[13] Channel Dave continued their support and aired series 12 in 2017,[14] and rumors of a thirteenth series continue to swirl.[15]

Commentary

Red Dwarf strikes the perfect balance between comedy and science fiction, presenting heady concepts in an outrageously funny fashion. The long-running British series paved the way for later shows like *Futurama*, *Other Space*, and *The Orville*, which also mix genuine science fiction ideas with laugh-out-loud comedic situations. *Red Dwarf* tackles well-worn genre tropes in a thoughtful and often original fashion. At the same time, the show pokes fun at these concepts, mining plenty of laughs from a variety of fantastical situations. Consider, for instance, the episode in which the crew travel to a parallel dimension and meet female versions of themselves (or, in Cat's case, a dog version) only for Lister to become impregnated by his sex-swapped doppelgänger. Another episode features the crew playing a virtual reality game that grants their every wish until Rimmer's low self-esteem corrupts the program. In *Red Dwarf*, such scenarios provide lots of laughs, but they are explored in a thoughtful way that recalls more straightforward science fiction series like *Star Trek* and *Babylon 5*.

Red Dwarf also features immensely quotable dialogue, much of which was written by series creators Rob Grant and Doug Naylor and delivered by a talented cast. As Dave Lister, Craig Charles delivers his lines with a laid-back gusto indicative of his slovenly character who would rather kick back and eat lamb vindaloo than work. For instance, in the episode "Holoship" (S5E1), Lister describes Rimmer as "a complete smeg pot. Brains in the anal region. Chin absent, presumed missing. Genitalia small and inoffensive. Of no value or interest." Chris Barrie's Rimmer, meanwhile, gets his own share of sidesplitting zingers: in "Stasis Leak" (S2E4), a series of wacky circumstances results in an intoxicated Rimmer telling the ship's captain (who is dressed as a giant chicken) to "kindly cluck off before I extract your giblets and shove a large seasoned onion between the lips you never kiss with." Meanwhile, Cat, played to perfection by Danny John-Jules, routinely offers up witty bon mots like "I'm so gorgeous, there's a six-month waiting list for birds to suddenly appear every time I am near."

In addition to the smart sci-fi and humorous dialogue, *Red Dwarf* also explores male relationships in an interesting and touching way as the characters learn to live together and care for one another. Given their situation, stranded in deep space 3 million years after the collapse of human civilization, the crew has no choice but to rely on each other, and over time they forge true friendships based on mutual love and respect (though none of them would ever admit to such feelings). As such, *Red Dwarf* adds a touch of sweetness to its impeccable mixture of sci-fi and comedy, ensuring that it will continue to find new fans far into the future.

See also *Farscape* (1999–2003), *Futurama* (1999–2013), *Mystery Science Theater 3000* (1988–2018)

THE REN & STIMPY SHOW (1991–1996)

Creators: John Kricfalusi, Bob Camp
Cast: John Kricfalusi (Ren Höek), Billy West (Stimpson J. Cat/Ren Höek)
Genre: Comedy

Synopsis

A psychotic chihuahua and a dimwitted cat experience madcap adventures.

Production History

In 1989, Nickelodeon president Gerry Laybourne wanted to create a new animated series that respected kids and their intelligence rather than one that merely doubled as another half-hour toy commercial.[16] Around that time, animator John Kricfalusi, one of the co-founders of the animation studio Spümcø, met with Vanessa Coffey of Nickelodeon, who asked Kricfalusi to create a series based on his characters Ren Höek and Stimpson J. Cat.[17] Kricfalusi agreed to hand over the copyright to Nickelodeon provided he retain the rights to another show they wanted, *Jimmy's Clubhouse*. In late 1989, production commenced on "Big House Blues," the pilot episode of what would eventually become *The Ren & Stimpy Show*,[18] with Kricfalusi playing Ren and his friend, actor Billy West, as Stimpy.[19] Initially network executives were skeptical of the show but Coffey defended it, saying they could fire her if the show failed.[20] Focus testing suggested the series would be a big hit with children, prompting Nickelodeon to order a six-episode first season in September 1990.[21]

Ren & Stimpy debuted on August 11, 1991,[22] and it proved so popular that Nickelodeon quickly ordered a second season.[23] However, production fell behind schedule due to Kricfalusi's perfectionism.[24] As such, Nickelodeon reran content, upsetting viewers who wanted new episodes of the outrageous series.[25] With production lagging, Nickelodeon executives went over Kricfalusi's head and started issuing orders directly to Spümcø personnel, causing strife within the studio.[26] In 1992, Nickelodeon ordered Kricfalusi to cut twenty seconds from the episode "Man's Best Friend" (S2E2b) to reduce violent content.[27] Kricfalusi

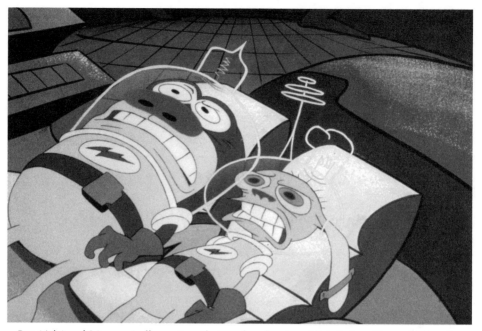

Ren (right) and Stimpy set off on yet another wacky adventure. *Nickelodeon Network/Photofest*

refused, so Nickelodeon pulled the episode entirely.[28] Kricfalusi circulated it on a bootleg VHS tape,[29] causing network executives to fire him and appoint Bob Camp as showrunner.[30] From there, Nickelodeon exerted more control over the show and increasingly censored content,[31] leading to a noticeable dip in quality. Nickelodeon stopped ordering new episodes in January 1995.[32] In 2003, Kricfalusi revived the show as *Ren & Stimpy's Adult Party Cartoon*, a critically derided adult animated series that aired on Spike TV for one season.[33]

Commentary

The Ren & Stimpy Show took children's entertainment in a whole new direction, one filled with scatological humor and outrageous characters. Understanding that kids love jokes about boogers and farts,[34] co-creator John Kricfalusi packed the show with gross sight gags and vulgar humor wrapped in a radical animation style unlike anything else on television at the time. *Ren & Stimpy* routinely pushed the envelope of good taste, assaulting viewers with all sorts of hilariously disgusting images, including rotting teeth, seeping wounds, and sentient fart clouds. In addition, the show delighted fans of all ages with its uproariously nonsensical dialogue; for instance, in "Space Madness" (S1E5), a crazed Ren, mistaking a bar of soap for an ice cream bar, salaciously intones, "Oh, my beloved ice cream bar! How I love to lick your creamy center!" Later, in "Stimpy's Invention" (S1E12), the dimwitted cat invents the Cheese-O-Phone, which allows the user to "communicate with various cheeses, regardless of their foreign tongue. Go ahead, Ren, say something in Limburger." The show also turned outbursts like "You idiot!" (or as Ren pronounces it, "You eediot!") and "Oh joy!" into ubiquitous catchphrases. While the bizarre humor and repugnant animation offended many grownups, those same qualities endeared *Ren & Stimpy* to legions of kids and stoned twentysomethings.

Ren & Stimpy, along with other beloved animated shows like *Rugrats* and *Doug*, signaled the rise of the Nicktoon. The series also helped mainstream the sort of bawdy comedy found in later Nicktoons like *Rocko's Modern Life*, *Angry Beavers*, *Invader Zim*, and *SpongeBob SquarePants*. Yet they all owe their existence to *Ren & Stimpy* because the show introduced many impressionable young kids to risqué, scatological humor—now a common feature in children's entertainment. Of course, *Ren & Stimpy* also appealed to twentysomething viewers because it featured the same sort of sarcastic wit and ironic detachment that defined Generation X. The show captured the sardonic spirit of the 1990s, portraying the title characters as disaffected slackers drifting from one weird situation to the next with little purpose or direction, commenting on everything with caustic humor and ironic detachment. *Ren & Stimpy* defined an era and became a cultural touchstone for impressionable young kids and disillusioned Gen-Xers alike. The show remains an important artifact within the history of animation as well as one of the most popular cult cartoons of all time.

See also *Aqua Teen Hunger Force* (2000–2015), *Rocko's Modern Life* (1993–1996)

ROCKO'S MODERN LIFE (1993–1996)

Creators: Joe Murray, Doug Osowski aka Mr. Lawrence
Cast: Carlos Alazraqui (Rocko), Tom Kenny (Heffer Wolfe), Doug Osowski aka Mr. Lawrence (Filburt Turtle), Charlie Adler (Ed Bighead/Bev Bighead)
Genre: Comedy

Synopsis

A soft-spoken Australian wallaby emigrates to the United States where he navigates modern adulthood alongside his loyal dog, wacky pals, and exasperated neighbors.

Production History

Upon graduating from college, animator Joe Murray started producing independent animated films.[35] While working on the short film *My Dog Zero*, he sent a copy of a pencil test to Nickelodeon to try to secure funding for his film.[36] Instead, Linda Simensky, head of animation development, asked Murray to develop a series.[37] Murray initially declined,[38] but Simensky promised him full creative control.[39] Murray then pitched a show centered around a character he had created for an unpublished comic strip about a nervous wallaby named Travis.[40] Three months later, Simensky asked for a pilot.[41] Murray, fully expecting Nickelodeon to reject the idea, wrote "Trash-O-Madness," which he animated with the help of his San Francisco animation crew.[42] To Murray's surprise, Nickelodeon liked what they saw and asked him to expand the episode to eleven minutes.[43] Murray agreed but demanded a clause in his contract preventing network executives from paying unannounced visits to his relocated animation studio in Los Angeles.[44] To produce the show, Murray assembled a team of experienced animators and hired local comedians as voice talent,[45] choosing performers who fit with his specific idea of how each character would sound.[46]

Production on the show, now titled *Rocko's Modern Life*, began in January 1993.[47] Murray and his team worked at a hectic pace, producing an episode a week and often clashing with the network over the show's content.[48] *Rocko's Modern Life* premiered on September 18, 1993,[49] with Murray expecting it to last just one season.[50] However, the first season earned solid ratings, leading Nickelodeon to order a second season in December 1993.[51] Before the third season, Murray stepped down from his position as showrunner.[52] He stayed on as an executive producer but Steve Hillenburg and Ken Kessell assumed producing and creative directing responsibilities starting with the fourth season.[53] Murray encouraged the network to order a fifth season, but Nickelodeon opted to cancel the series after fifty-two episodes.[54] More than twenty years later, the network produced a forty-five-minute *Rocko's Modern Life* special that premiered on Netflix on August 9, 2019.[55]

Commentary

Unleashed as part of the second wave of Nicktoons, *Rocko's Modern Life* introduced young viewers to the sort of existential crises that adults face daily, all while delighting both kids and grownups with witty observational humor, screwball characters, and subversive gags. The show parodied various aspects of modern life, from commuting (S2E5, "Commuted Sentence") to hosting a garage sale (S2E18, "Junk Junkies") to getting an eye exam (S2E23, "Eyes Capades"). At the same time it featured over-the-top situations and surreal comedy, assaulting viewers with fart jokes, gross sight gags, and boundary-pushing innuendo. For example, in "Flu-In-U-Enza" (S1E3), Rocko falls ill and visits Doctor Bendova, who prescribes a medication that causes Rocko to hallucinate sentient, half-eaten food items that offer him a remedy made from toe jam. Meanwhile, in "Leap Frogs" (S1E6), Rocko's lascivious neighbor, Bev Bighead, feels unwanted by her neglectful husband so she tries to seduce the title character. At one point, Bev even winds up naked, causing Rocko to zip his eyes shut. Other episodes get much weirder as characters go to Hell (S1E11, "To Heck and Back") or find themselves pursued by a demented tour guide (S3E4, "I See London, I See France"). *Rocko's Modern Life* amused viewers of all ages with a rib-tickling mix of comical situations and shocking humor.

Of course, the show connected with viewers of all ages due to its charmingly zany characters, who demonstrated recognizable foibles and relatable (if exaggerated) reactions as they navigated young adulthood. Both kids and twenty-somethings identified with Rocko (played with gentle enthusiasm by Carlos Alazraqui, who also appeared in the beloved cult series *Reno 911!*) as he struggled to find his place in the modern world of the chaotic 1990s. He was accompanied on this journey by his best pal, Heffer (Tom Kenny, later the voice of SpongeBob SquarePants), a self-involved but loyal slacker who was equally adrift but much less worried about his own lack of direction, and the neurotic Filburt, a pessimistic family man whose pent-up rage and endless anxieties often sent him flying off the rails. Rocko also enjoyed the companionship of his faithful dog, Spunky, a hyperactive bull terrier who frequently emits foul odors and secretes icky bodily fluids (which he then consumes) but also showers his owner with affection. These characters present viewers young and old with a familiar portrait of growing up and learning how to "adult." Of course, this portrait also contains silly circumstances and loads of yucky stuff, but then so does real life. *Rocko's Modern Life* understands this, which may explain why fans love it to this day.

See also *The Adventures of Pete & Pete* (1992–1996), *The Ren & Stimpy Show* (1991–1996)

ROSWELL (1999–2002)

Creator: Jason Katims
Cast: Shiri Appleby (Liz Parker), Jason Behr (Max Evans), Katherine Heigl (Isabel Evans), Majandra Delfino (Maria DeLuca), Brendan Fehr (Michael Guerin), Nick Wechsler (Kyle Valenti), William Sadler (Sheriff Jim Valenti), Colin Hanks (Alex Whitman)
Genre: Drama, Mystery, Science Fiction, Thriller

Synopsis

Three young alien-human hybrids with extraordinary powers navigate high school in Roswell, New Mexico.

Production History

Between 1998 and 2000, Pocket Books published ten *Roswell High* novels written by author Melinda Metz.[56] Fox Television purchased the rights to the property based on the first manuscript.[57] The network then hired Jason Katims to develop the series,[58] giving him twelve days and $2 million to make the pilot.[59] Katims hired David Nutter to direct,[60] and Heath Ledger auditioned for the lead role.[61] However, executives rejected Ledger due to the failure of his previous series, *Roar*.[62] Executives at Fox Network ultimately disliked the pilot, but the WB Network stepped in and ordered twenty-two episodes.[63] *Roswell* premiered on the WB at 9:00 p.m. on October 6, 1999, right after *Dawson's Creek*, earning high ratings.[64] However, viewership soon decreased and the network considered cancelation but a successful fan campaign encouraged WB executives to renew *Roswell* for a second season.[65]

While the first season focused mainly on the love story of a human girl and a half-alien boy, the second season emphasized the science fiction elements due to the influence of new co-executive producer Ronald D. Moore, who had worked on various *Star Trek* series.[66] With the conclusion of the second season, the WB dropped *Roswell*, which then moved to fledgling UPN after fans once more campaigned to save the series by sending more than twelve thousand bottles of Tabasco sauce (a favorite of the show's extraterrestrial characters)[67] to network execs, imploring them to "Spice Up Your Lineup—Add *Roswell* to UPN."[68] Despite all the fan activism, UPN canceled *Roswell* after the third season,[69] citing consistently low Nielsen ratings as the reason.[70] In 2019, the CW Network launched a poorly received reboot series titled *Roswell, New Mexico*.[71] Fans still prefer the original.

Commentary

Roswell successfully brought fantastic stories aimed at young adults to television years before adaptations of similar fare like *Harry Potter*, *The Hunger Games*, *Divergent*, *A Series of Unfortunate Events*, and *His Dark Materials* flooded screens both big and small. The show, which combined fantasy and teenage angst, helped establish the CW Network's emerging style and signaled a shift toward focusing on teenage girls as a core demographic. Unlike the novels that inspired it, *Roswell* all but dispensed with complicated mythologies and convoluted backstories and instead focused on relationships between the main characters,[72] creating an "ensemble melodrama" filled with sensitive and intelligent teenagers.[73] According to pop culture scholar Stan Beeler, *Roswell* resonated strongly with young viewers because it emerged at the start of a chaotic new millennium and featured "young-adult themes" that echoed real-world events such as "the Columbine incident, and the events of September 11, 2001."[74] In other words, the show "presents its target audience with characters and situations easily applicable to their own turbulent lives."[75] Thus while it only lasted three seasons spanning sixty-one episodes, *Roswell* still struck a chord with adolescent audiences and shaped TV for years to come.

During its brief life, *Roswell* served up exciting adventures that followed three superpowered alien teens as they navigated high school while trying to keep their true identities secret. The show kicked things off in breathtaking style with "Pilot," which opened with the instantly iconic line "I'm Liz Parker, and five days ago, I died." From there, the episode establishes the characters' personalities, introduces all the major relationships, and sets the series' central conflict in motion. The first season builds to the exhilarating finale "Destiny" (S1E22) as protagonists Max, Liz, and Isabel manage to elude their human pursuers only to capture the attention of hostile aliens. Season 2 continues the thrills in episodes like "Harvest" (S2E6), which sees the heroes embark on a mission to disable a factory operated by their enemies, and "Cry Your Name" (S2E17), a heart-wrenching installment that takes the core trio on an emotional journey as they uncover shocking revelations while dealing with the death of a friend.

Acting as a preview for the young adult genre that came to inform Hollywood a decade later, *Roswell* portrayed the struggles of its adolescent characters as potentially world-shattering events, which may explain why it resonated so deeply with young viewers who often see their own problems as potentially leading to the end of the world. Though it failed to generate big ratings, *Roswell* proved popular enough that fans rallied to save the show from impending cancelation. The series also spawned an uninspired reboot that launched in 2019,[76] but devotees still hold the original in high esteem for its innovative approach to the alien-invasion story.

See also *Buffy the Vampire Slayer* (1997–2003), *Smallville* (2001–2011)

S

SAILOR MOON (1992–1997)

Creator: Junichi Sato
Cast: Kotono Mitsuishi/Terri Hawkes/Linda Ballantyne (Sailor Moon), Keiko Han/
Jill Frappier (Luna), Aya Hisakawa/Karen Bernstein (Sailor Mercury), Michie To-
mizawa/Katie Griffin (Sailor Mars), Emi Shinohara/Susan Roman (Sailor Jupiter),
Rika Fukami/Emilie Claire-Barlow (Sailor Venus), Toru Furuya/Vince Corazza
(Mamoru Chiba)
Genre: Action, Comedy, Fantasy, Romance

Synopsis

A group of magical teenage girls defend the Earth from the evil forces of the
Dark Kingdom.

Production History

In October 1990, Naoko Takeuchi launched her first manga series, *The Cherry
Project*, which wrapped in December 1991,[1] at which point Takeuchi's editor decided "her next project would be a 'magical girl fighting for love and justice'"[2] and
suggested a superhero wearing a sailor uniform similar to those worn by Japanese
schoolgirls.[3] Drawing inspiration from the 1970s live-action series *Kyōryū Sentai
Zyuranger* (better known outside Japan as *Mighty Morphin' Power Rangers*),[4] Takeuchi created the manga series *Codename Sailor V* for *Run-Run* magazine.[5] At the
same time, Toei Animation and TV Asahi developed a *Sailor V* animated series,
but Takeuchi changed the focus from Sailor V to a five-person team led by Sailor
Moon.[6] The *Pretty Soldier Sailor Moon* manga debuted in 1992,[7] followed only a
month later by the anime.[8]

The anime series ran for two hundred episodes from March 1992 to February
1997 on TV Asahi and consisted of five story arcs: *Sailor Moon, Sailor Moon R, Sailor
Moon S, Sailor Moon Super S,* and *Sailor Moon Sailor Stars*.[9] The anime quickly out-
paced the manga and diverged from the story, much to Takeuchi's displeasure.[10]
Soon after, DIC Entertainment president Andy Heyward discovered the series and

decided to adapt it for an American audience,[11] which meant editing the episodes to remove extreme violence.[12] DIC's version premiered in September 1995[13] but aired at 6:30 a.m.,[14] meaning it failed to capture a substantial audience.[15] Meanwhile in Japan, the fifth and final season of *Sailor Moon* concluded on February 7, 1997, with the manga wrapping up several months later.[16] In 1998, Cartoon Network secured the rights to air the series as part of its Toonami block.[17] In 2003, a live-action version appeared on Japanese TV[18] while a staged "2.5D musical" launched in Japan in 2018 before making its way to the United States the following year.[19]

Commentary

Sailor Moon introduced many American fangirls to Japanese pop culture. Along with shows like *Dragon Ball Z* and *Pokémon*, the show helped cement anime and manga's popularity in the West. Unlike traditional American cartoons aimed at girls, *Sailor Moon* mixed "feminine" topics such as beauty, friendship, and fashion with thrilling adventure and exciting action that was always dangerous, sometimes violent, and occasionally fatal (the Sailor Scouts actually died in the season 1 finale). In addition, each Sailor Scout boasted a unique personality, meaning the show portrayed several different types of women: from sporty Sailor Jupiter to romance-obsessed Sailor Moon. In *Sailor Moon*, the Sailor Scouts demonstrated

Sailor Moon (center, standing) and the rest of the Sailor Scouts defend Earth and the galaxy from the evil forces of the Dark Kingdom. *Cartoon Network/Photofest*

that girls and young women could inhabit any gender identity and any sexual orientation and be as important as anyone else.

Unfortunately, the original American distributors heavily edited the anime to remove content deemed inappropriate such as death and queer representation. Viewers who watched the Toonami version of the show never saw the deaths that occurred during the season 1 finale. Similarly, Sailors Uranus and Neptune shared a lesbian relationship in the Japanese version while the American version turned them into cousins. The fifth season featuring the Sailor Starlights never even aired during the show's initial American run[20] because this series featured boys transforming "into leather-clad girls in times of need."[21] Fortunately, U.S. releases have since restored these rather daring portrayals, allowing more young queer people the chance to discover their inner Sailor Scout.

Sailor Moon served as part of a vanguard of anime and manga that descended on the United States in the 1990s, changing the face of American animation and comic books for years to come. The success of *Sailor Moon* in the United States led to shows like *Avatar: The Last Airbender* on Nickelodeon and the rebooted *Voltron* and *She-Ra* on Netflix. *Sailor Moon* stood at the forefront of great changes to American pop culture, and thus it deserves recognition as a great cult TV show.

See also *My Little Pony: Friendship Is Magic* (2010–2019)

SPOTLIGHT: TOONAMI

In the late 1990s, Sean Aikens and Jason DeMarco created Toonami, an animation block designed to "showcase some of Cartoon Network's newly acquired teen-oriented IPs."[22] Debuting on March 17, 1997, Toonami introduced many American viewers to anime.[23] Toonami's original line-up consisted of *Cartoon Roulette, Thunder-Cats, Voltron,* and *The Real Adventures of Jonny Quest*[24] but ratings exploded following the addition of *Sailor Moon* and *Dragon Ball Z* in 1998.[25] In 2004, Toonami moved from weekday afternoons to Saturday evenings due to the violence of its newly acquired shows.[26] Toonami left the air in 2008 but returned in 2012[27] after fans successfully campaigned to bring it back.[28] In 2012, Toonami expanded to six hours of programming from 12:00 a.m. to 6:00 a.m.[29]

SAVED BY THE BELL (1989–1992)

Creators: Peter Engel, Sam Bobrick
Cast: Mark-Paul Gosselaar (Zack Morris), Mario Lopez (A. C. Slater), Dustin Diamond (Samuel "Screech" Powers), Lark Voorhies (Lisa Turtle), Tiffani Amber Thiessen (Kelly Kapowski), Elizabeth Berkley (Jessie Spano), Dennis Haskins (Principal Richard Belding)
Genre: Comedy, Romance

Synopsis

A group of popular high school students and their nerdy friend learn about life while engaging in contrived hijinks and shenanigans.

Production History

In 1986, Brandon Tartikoff, president of NBC, set out to produce a primetime series inspired by his sixth-grade teacher, Miss Bliss.[30] He asked Peter Engel to develop the series idea, and Engel brought together a team, including Sam Bobrick to write the pilot and Haley Mills for the lead of *Good Morning, Miss Bliss*.[31] Shot in 1987, the pilot also featured up-and-coming child actors Jonathan Brandis, Brian Austin Green, and Jaleel White.[32] NBC opted not to add the show to its primetime lineup, although they did air the pilot on June 11, 1987,[33] and in 1988 Tartikoff finalized a deal for the Disney Channel to air thirteen episodes in primetime after adding Mark Paul-Gosselaar as Zack Morris and Dustin Diamond as "Screech."[34] Disney did not renew the series for a second season,[35] and Tartikoff revamped it for Saturday mornings,[36] retitling it *Saved by the Bell*.[37] The retooled series debuted on August 20, 1989,[38] airing on Saturday mornings at 11:00 a.m.[39]

At the height of its popularity, *Saved by the Bell* aired in eighty-five countries.[40] The show also spawned two spinoff series, *Saved by the Bell: The College Years* and *Saved by the Bell: The New Class*,[41] as well as the made-for-TV movies *Saved by the Bell: Hawaiian Style* and *Saved by the Bell: Wedding in Las Vegas*. NBC executives planned to end the show after the fourth season, and producers even shot a series finale, after which cast members Tiffani Amber Thiessen and Elizabeth Berkley left to pursue other projects. However, NBC ordered eleven more episodes so producers brought in a new character played by Leanna Creel and the network ran those episodes before airing the finale.[42] Between 1990 and 1997, *Saved by the Bell* earned several award nominations while Voorhees, Gosselar, and Mario Lopez all won Young Artists Awards.[43] These days, fans consider *Saved by the Bell* a bona fide classic for its nostalgic appeal.

Commentary

With its vapid sitcom humor and preachy, after-school-special vibe, *Saved by the Bell* turned Saturday mornings into must-see TV for an entire generation of kids and teenagers. Packed with groan-inducing jokes, underdeveloped characters, and an overworked laugh track (which descended into obnoxious hooting whenever two characters kissed), the show brought live-action comedies back to Saturday mornings following a decade of cartoon dominance. Of course, one could easily label *Saved by the Bell* a live-action cartoon, especially considering the over-the-top antics perpetrated by "comic relief" character Screech (Dustin Diamond, in a performance that effectively tanked his acting career). The show featured hammy acting, strained situations, and daft humor (when brainy Jessie suggests her meathead boyfriend Slater share household chores, he replies, "Sure! You cook, and I'll eat"). Yet *Saved by the Bell* remains beloved by 1990s kids the world over. The young cast likely contributed to the show's popularity as it boasted a bevy of teenage heartthrobs and attractive young actors who set adolescent viewers' hearts aflame.

During its run, *Saved by the Bell* produced several memorable moments, with the most famous (or infamous depending on your point of view) occurring in "Jessie's Song" (S2E9). Jessie develops an addiction to caffeine pills and when Zack attempts to intervene, she freaks out and exclaims, "I'm so excited! I'm so excited! I'm so . . . scared!" before breaking down in histrionic tears. In "Student Teacher Week" (S4E2), the students and teachers of Bayside High swap places, causing inveterate schemer Zack to learn some harsh lessons about responsibility. "Snow White and the Seven Dorks" (S4E20) sees Kelly and Jessie compete for the lead role in the school play, and their rivalry leads to romantic complications that threaten to tear the gang apart. Meanwhile, "Pipe Dreams" (S3E11) tackles the issue of environmentalism as the folks at Bayside discover that the football field sits atop a massive oil reserve that threatens the local wildlife, including the school's mascot, Becky the duck. These episodes perfectly illustrate the absurd comedy and silly situations found in each installment of *Saved by the Bell*, which stands as a cultural touchstone for an entire generation by offering attractive people, life lessons, and memorable moments (both good and bad).

SCRUBS (2001–2010)

Creator: Bill Lawrence
Cast: Zach Braff (Dr. John "J. D." Dorian), Donald Faison (Dr. Christopher Turk), John C. McGinley (Dr. Perry Cox), Sarah Chalke (Dr. Elliot Reid), Judy Reyes (Nurse Carla Espinosa), Ken Jenkins (Dr. Bob Kelso), Neil Flynn (Janitor)
Genre: Comedy, Drama

Synopsis

A medical student joins the wacky staff at Sacred Heart Hospital and learns all about medicine, friendship, and life.

Production History

In 2000, after co-creating *Spin City* for ABC, writer Bill Lawrence hatched an idea for a series about a group of medical students completing their residencies while still in school.[44] Drawing on the real-life experiences of his friends (and even naming some of the characters after them), Lawrence wrote the series with the intention of showing the doctors as goofy people just trying to get through their shifts.[45] Titled *Scrubs*, the show premiered on NBC on October 2, 2001. The series, which earned critical praise and numerous award nominations during its run,[46] originally aired on Tuesday nights[47] but the network shuffled *Scrubs* around the schedule, moving the show seventeen times in seven years.[48] When NBC hesitated to renew *Scrubs* beyond the seventh season, ABC president Steve McPherson stepped in and offered to pick up the show.[49]

Despite the move, the series' future remained uncertain after the eighth season[50] so Lawrence produced the eighth season's finale as a series finale.[51] However, ABC wanted *Scrubs* to continue despite the departure of its highest-paid stars, and the network tried to keep the show alive by hiring unknown actors and younger writers.[52] At that point, Lawrence convinced ABC to let him change the show's title to *Scrubs: Med School*, while lead actor Zach Braff agreed to appear in six episodes and thereby help the show transition to a new lead.[53] Like NBC before it, ABC shuffled the series around the schedule, moving its timeslot three times.[54] The ninth season premiere drew the lowest ratings in the series' history, prompting ABC to finally cancel *Scrubs* for good in May 2010.[55]

Commentary

During its nine seasons, *Scrubs* offered viewers a whimsical peek inside the world of medicine, mainly via the perspective of Zach Braff's goofy intern, John "J. D." Dorian. The show routinely dealt with heavy issues common in medical dramas like depression, suicide, and medical malpractice. At the same time, though, *Scrubs* often felt like a live-action cartoon as it featured madcap cutaways à la *Family Guy* (when asked how people contract mono, J. D. flashes back to his teen years when a girl sneezed on him at a party), weird supporting characters straight out of *The Simpsons* (staff lawyer Ted Buckland resembles put-upon salesman Gil Gunderson), and sidesplitting zingers (while looking at an X-ray, Dr. Cox quips, "Either this kid has a lightbulb up his butt or his colon has a great idea"). *Scrubs* often disrupted the traditional sitcom format to address serious issues as in "My Screwup" (S3E14), which sees Dr. Cox's brother lose his battle with cancer but also features hilarious one-liners like "Shower shorts: for the man that has nothing to hide, but still wants to." Similarly, "My Way Home" (S5E7) references *The Wizard of Oz* as the characters try to make it through a tough shift while still cracking wise ("You never went to assface school but you seem to be an expert at that"). *Scrubs* shifted tones at a breakneck pace but managed to strike the perfect balance between comedy and drama, eliciting big laughs without downplaying the characters' emotional struggles.

Scrubs benefited greatly from the chemistry of its talented ensemble, all of whom displayed some serious comedic chops during the show's run. Long before he turned his attention to making mawkish and overly earnest films about quirky outsiders, Braff charmed viewers with his performance as J. D., the heart of Sacred Heart Hospital. Braff played the character as a sort of sad clown, mugging his way through the humorous bits while bringing an appropriate amount of gravitas to the more somber moments. Meanwhile, Donald Faison turned Dr. Christopher Turk into a screwball ladies' man, veering from silly to sexy at the drop of a hat. Sarah Chalke portrayed Elliot Reid as a neurotic yet competent physician, while John C. McGinley delivered a towering performance as the sardonic Dr. Cox, who routinely belittles others with acidic putdowns like "The only way you could be less productive is if you were the wall on which you were leaning, but then you'd be providing some jackass with a wall on which to lean and reflect on what a jackass he is." From the first episode to the last, the cast expertly played off one another, wringing lots of laughs and plenty of tears from the audience. Over time, the comedy grew much broader and the characters became far more cartoonish, but *Scrubs* still managed to tug on viewers' heartstrings while making their sides ache with laughter, which explains why fans cherish the show to this day.

See also *Police Squad!* (1982)

SCTV (1976–1984)

Creators: Bernard Sahlins, Andrew Alexander
Cast: Joe Flaherty, Eugene Levy, Andrea Martin, Dave Thomas, John Candy, Catherine O'Hara, Harold Ramis, Rick Moranis, Martin Short
Genre: Comedy

Synopsis

Toronto's Second City improv group presents their own variety show filled with wacky recurring characters and bizarre storylines.

Production History

In the spring of 1976, a group of performers and writers (including Joe Flaherty, Eugene Levy, Harold Ramis, and Dave Thomas) gathered in Toronto at the old converted fire station that served as the Canadian home of the famed improv comedy group Second City, originally founded in Chicago in 1959.[56] Driven by envy and pride over their fellow alums' success with *Saturday Night Live*, the group developed the concept for a show called *Second City Television* (commonly known as *SCTV*) based on advice from Bernard Sahlins, Second City stage director Del Close, and Shelton Patinkin (who later served as associate producer on *SCTV*).[57] The show's writers and performers sought to parody not just *Saturday Night Live* but other TV genres as well, with each episode taking a multilayered approach to parodies while also innovating "behind-the-scenes" segments that pulled the curtain back on the entertainment industry.[58]

The first iteration of *SCTV* debuted on Toronto's Global Television Network on September 21, 1976, and it ran for a total of fifty-two half-hour episodes that aired over three years.[59] Although executive producer Sahlins left the show after thirty episodes, the series ended in 1979 due to lack of sponsors.[60] It then migrated to the Canadian Broadcasting Corporation in 1980, which aired an additional twenty-six half-hour episodes.[61] In 1981, NBC picked up *SCTV* and produced thirty-nine 90-minute shows.[62] *SCTV* emerged as a hit on Canadian TV but problems plagued the show during the two years that it aired on NBC, including low ratings, high budget costs, and departing talent (Rick Moranis, Dave Thomas, and Catherine O'Hara all jumped ship around the same time).[63] While fans petitioned and protested to save the series, NBC canceled it in 1983.[64]

SCTV then jumped to Cinemax, becoming the fledgling cable network's first original series, where it ran for one season of eighteen 45-minute installments.[65] Cinemax aired the show from November 1983 to July 1984 though by that point only four of the original cast members remained. The network wanted to bring in additional performers like Jim Carrey, Jim Belushi, and Billy Crystal but the original *SCTV* players rejected this idea.[66] Because Cinemax's pay model prevented many fans from watching the show, it earned low ratings and the cable network pulled the plug after just one season, airing the last episode on July 17, 1984.[67] Even so, *SCTV* remains highly influential and has inspired generations of funny fans including Conan O'Brien,[68] Matt Groening,[69] and Joel Hodgson.[70]

Commentary

SCTV always lived in the long shadow cast by *Saturday Night Live* (which also boasted a cast of Second City alumni who went on to great fame), but it still earned a well-deserved reputation as one of the funniest sketch comedy series ever produced thanks to the involvement of some brilliantly funny comedic writers and performers. The series showcased talented comics like Eugene Levy, John Candy, and Catherine O'Hara (among others), who displayed their comedic chops in wildly humorous skits that featured hilariously memorable characters like Earl Camembert (Levy), Johnny LaRue (Candy), and Lola Heatherton (O'Hara). Meanwhile, *SCTV* had a profound impact on popular culture that extended far beyond the borders of Canada via internationally beloved characters like Bob and Doug McKenzie (Rick Moranis and Dave Thomas), who spawned comedy albums, animated series, action figures, and even a hit film. The show appealed to comedy nerds and pop culture fanatics who loved the smart humor and winking parodies such as "Play It Again, Bob," a riff on Woody Allen's *Play It Again, Sam* which sees Allen (Moranis) turn to Bob Hope (Thomas) for filmmaking advice. *SCTV* offered viewers irreverent comedy and whip-smart homages to all sorts of popular institutions from music to film to television.

Of course, many sketch comedy shows also boast keen wit and shrewd satire, but *SCTV* still managed to stand out from the crowd because of its format, which often bucked the conventional structure of other skit shows. More than just a traditional sketch series, *SCTV* presented itself as a behind-the-scenes peek at the inner workings of a cut-rate TV station owned by tightfisted Guy Caballero (Joe Flaherty), an able-bodied conman who routinely makes use of a wheelchair to earn sympathy and command respect from his disgruntled employees. The station featured a rotating staff of screwy characters including Moe Green (Harold Ramis), Edith Prickley (Andrea Martin), Bobby Bittman (Levy), Count Floyd (Flaherty), and many others. The skits, meanwhile, served as the programming offered by the SCTV Network, which included such recurring bits as "Farm Film Report" (Candy and Flaherty play two redneck film critics who praise movies that feature people or things getting "blowed up real good") and "The Gerry Todd Show" (Moranis plays a bespectacled, smooth-talking veejay who hosts a public access music video show). This conceit allowed *SCTV* to dabble in longform storytelling and establish a solid continuity while also offering up sidesplitting sketches, thereby setting it apart from other sketch comedy shows of the time. While it lacked the longevity and widespread appeal of *Saturday Night Live*, *SCTV* nevertheless established itself as one of the most influential and adored sketch comedy series of all time thanks to its talented performers, unforgettable characters, and uproarious humor.

See also *The Kids in the Hall* (1988–1994), *The State* (1993–1995)

SENSE8 (2015–2018)

Creators: J. Michael Straczynski, Lana Wachowski, Lily Wachowski
Cast: Doona Bae (Sun Bak), Jamie Clayton (Nomi Marks), Tina Desai (Kala Dandekar), Tuppence Middleton (Riley Blue), Max Riemelt (Wolfgang Bogdanow), Miquel Ángel Silvestre (Lito Rodriguez), Aml Ameen (Capheus Onyango, 2015), Toby Onwumere (Capheus Onyango, 2016–2018), Brian J. Smith (Will Gorski), Freema Agyeman (Amanita Caplan), Naveen Andrews (Jonas Maliki), Angelica Turing (Daryl Hannah), Whispers (Terrence Mann)
Genre: Drama, Mystery, Science Fiction, Thriller

Synopsis

After discovering they share a telepathic link, diverse strangers from around the world band together to battle a shadowy group intent on wiping them out.

Production History

In 2003, sisters Lana and Lily Wachowski invited *Babylon 5* creator J. Michael Straczynski to a private screening of *Matrix Revolutions*.[71] Years later, the trio reconvened to develop a television show about connectivity and empathy.[72] During a single weekend in San Francisco, they created the show's structure and started writing scripts while Lana coined the title *Sense8* after deciding on a cast of eight core characters.[73] In 2012, the trio wrote three spec scripts that they shopped around,[74] but the scripts failed to drum up interest in the project.[75] After a few years, they sensed a shift in the television landscape so they tried again and landed a deal with the streaming service innovator Netflix.[76] During production on the first season, the Wachowski sisters directed all twelve episodes with help of James McTeague, Tom Tykwer, and Dan Glass.[77] Straczynski and the Wachowskis remained hands-on with all aspects of production during season 1 but in season 2 Lily left to undergo her transition while Straczynski limited his involvement to the writing phase.[78]

In *Sense8*, eight strangers from around the world, including Sun Bak (Doona Bae, right) and Capheus Onyango (Aml Ameen), find that they share a psychic connection with one another. *Netflix/Photofest*

Netflix announced *Sense8* in March 2013, aiming to make it available to stream in late 2014.[79] Production on the first season ran from June 2013 to December 2013 as the creators took great care "to shoot the show from a subjective perspective," never cutting away from the perspective of the eight central characters, known as "sensates."[80] Season 1 of *Sense8* debuted on June 5, 2015,[81] and it immediately developed a rabid cult following and garnered heaps of critical praise. The show even received a GLAAD award for Outstanding Drama Series in 2016.[82] Unfortunately, none of this prevented Netflix from canceling *Sense8* in June 2017 due to the show's steep budget of $9 million per episode.[83] The cancellation prompted immediate backlash as fans launched hashtag campaigns on social media and bombarded Netflix with calls and emails. In response, the streaming giant approved a two-hour finale episode that debuted on December 23, 2016.[84] *Sense8* remains dormant, but fans hold out hope for a revival.

Commentary

Over the course of its brief life, *Sense8* offered viewers an exhilarating sci-fi story that doubles as a frank and nuanced representation of queer identities. As such, the show built a transnational fanbase drawn in by a heady mixture of progressive storylines, complex characters, engrossing mystery, exotic locales, and thrilling action. *Sense8* served up an exciting adventure narrative wrapped in a fanciful conceit, all while tackling complicated issues such as religion, feminism, queerness, freedom, and violence. Throughout its short run, the show also dealt directly with LGBTQIA+ themes and storylines in a delicate and honest fashion, placing queer characters and performers in central roles (for instance, transgender actress Jamie Clayton plays Nomi, one of the core characters). Daring risks such as these helped *Sense8* carve out its own unique identity and endeared it to fans desperate for something different from the countless other TV shows that centered on more typical characters and topics.

From the start, *Sense8* established itself as a bold new series intent on experimenting with traditional narrative formats that pushed the boundaries of conventional TV storytelling. In addition, with its globe-hopping scenario and kinetic action sequences, the show served up a heaping helping of breathtaking visuals and heart-stopping thrills in each episode. Consider, for instance, "What's Going On?" (S1E4), which sees Sun telepathically draw on Will's police training to infiltrate a sex club, and culminates in a joyous psychic sing-along to the 4 Non Blondes song "What's Up?" Later, in "Jail Break" (S2E3), Sun mounts a daring prison escape filled with the sort of innovative and electrifying action that put the Wachowskis on the map. At the same time, *Sense8* often proved meandering and incoherent, with season 1 taking a long time to cohere, and it routinely suffered from stilted dialogue and a glacial pace that alienated many viewers. Yet hardcore fans considered such weaknesses as virtues because they challenged mainstream modes of storytelling. Film scholar Cáel M. Keegan offers the perfect summation of the show: "A progressive vision of an opening empathetic horizon across race, gender, nation, and sexuality, *Sense8* is the optimistic queer/trans science fiction that in 2015 we didn't yet sense we would need."[85] If the fanbase is any indication, *Sense8* will continue to grow and connect people around the world seeking something new.

SMALLVILLE (2001–2011)

Creators: Alfred Gough, Miles Millar
Cast: Tom Welling (Clark Kent), Allison Mack (Chloe Sullivan), Michael Rosenbaum (Lex Luthor), Kristin Kreuk (Lana Lang), John Glover (Lionel Luthor), Erica Durance (Lois Lane)
Genre: Science Fiction, Drama, Romance

Synopsis

Hunky super-powered teenager Clark Kent navigates high school and young adulthood in a small Kansas town on his way to becoming Superman.

Production History

The success of *Superman: The Animated Series* "showed Warner Bros. that there was still some life left in the Man of Steel."[86] After learning that *Buffy the*

Superpowered teenager Clark Kent (Tom Welling) protects the town of Smallville, Kansas, from supervillains and other nefarious evil-doers. *The WB/Photofest*

Vampire Slayer was moving to UPN in 1999, Peter Roth, president of Warner Bros. Television, set about developing a replacement series.[87] Meanwhile, Alfred Gough and Miles Millar brought an idea for a series about a young Bruce Wayne to Roth, only to learn the company already planned to reboot the Batman film franchise.[88] In June 2000, Tollin/Robbins Productions suggested a young Superman show, and Gough and Millar agreed but only if they could offer a fresh take on Superman,[89] one that allowed them to do more than simply recreate the *Superboy* TV series that ran from 1988 to 1992.[90] The duo then developed the motto "No Flights, No Tights" and decided to focus on Clark Kent's journey to become Superman.[91]

Both the Fox Network and the WB Network wanted the series so Roth pitched it to both. Fox offered more money for the pilot, but the WB made a thirteen-episode commitment with a high per episode license fee, the highest ever paid for a dramatic series' first year.[92] After completing the deal with the WB and getting greenlit in the fall of 2000, Gough and Miller hired David Nutter to direct the pilot.[93] In February 2001 they cast Kristen Kreuk for the female lead but finding Clark Kent took longer, with casting directors auditioning hundreds of actors across the United States. They offered the role to Tom Welling, who initially turned them down due to concerns about the show's nature,[94] but Nutter convinced him to do the series. The last main actor, Michael Rosenbaum, landed the role of Lex Luthor just two weeks before shooting commenced.[95] While the network considered shooting in Australia, Gough and Millar found Vancouver a better fit for a "Middle America landscape" and filming launched in March 2001.[96]

Titled *Smallville*, the series premiered on October 16, 2001, and drew the best ratings for any pilot in the network's seven-year history with over 8 million viewers.[97] The following week, the network ordered another nine installments, increasing the season from thirteen to twenty-two episodes.[98] *Smallville* continued to generate high ratings for the WB, becoming "one of the biggest hits the subsidiary had produced for the parent company."[99] At the start of its sixth season, *Smallville* moved to the newly created CW Network,[100] where it ran until Friday, May 13, 2011, after Welling decided it was time to move on.[101]

Commentary

On debuting in 2001, *Smallville* helped DC Comics succeed where Marvel Comics failed. At that time, Marvel continued to struggle after declaring bankruptcy in 1996, and its live-action and animated offerings failed to compete with those produced by DC, especially given the latter's connection with Warner Bros. *Iron Man* and Walt Disney Studio's acquisition of Marvel changed all that, but DC still dominates the small screen to this day, thanks in part to *Smallville*'s trailblazing take on Superman's origin story.

Throughout the show's ten-season run, producers maintained a strict "No Tights, No Flights" policy, and they simply hinted at Clark Kent's ability to fly, with his costume only glimpsed in the series finale. While *Smallville* lacked Superman, it nevertheless set the stage for the various superhero series that emerged in its wake, mixing teenage angst and drama with fantastical action and adventure. Focusing on a teenage Clark Kent learning about his identity and his powers allowed producers to tell compelling stories that explored teenage life in a metaphorical fashion, much like *Buffy the Vampire Slayer* before it. This approach allowed the writers of *Smallville* to craft original Superman stories featuring original villains, provided Clark stayed in high school. The moment Clark left Smallville and stepped foot in Metropolis, the canonical DC universe seeped in, incorporating heroes (including Martian Manhunter and Aquaman) and villains (such as Brainiac and Doomsday) from Superman's comic book past.

Smallville remains noteworthy in the way it used guest stars to pay homage to the character's long legacy in film and television, most notably Christopher Reeves in his last onscreen role. At the same time, the show introduced new characters and improved pre-existing ones (Michael Rosenbaum remains the best Lex Luthor seen in live-action). The show also enjoys a reputation as the longest running superhero series to date, which suggests that fans appreciated its inventive approach to the character. In fact, Superman fans loved the show so much that they wanted Tom Welling to reprise his role in the CW's "Arrowverse" (Welling ultimately declined to don the costume again after ten years.)[102] In the end, *Smallville* reinvigorated a somewhat tired franchise, which explains why its cult of devoted fans still love it.

See also *Arrow* (2012–2020)

SOUTH PARK (1997–PRESENT)

Creators: Trey Parker, Matt Stone
Cast: Trey Parker (Various), Matt Stone (Various), April Stewart (Various), Mary Kay Bergman (Various), Eliza Schneider (Various), Mona Marshall (Various), Bill Hader (Various), Isaac Hayes (Chef)
Genre: Comedy

Synopsis

Four foul-mouthed children embark on wild adventures in their hometown of South Park, Colorado, and around the world.

Production History

In 1992, University of Colorado students Trey Parker and Matt Stone produced the animated short film *The Spirit of Christmas*,[103] in which Jesus Christ battles a murderous Frosty the Snowman.[104] Four years later, Fox junior executive Brian Graden offered the duo $2,000 to turn the short into a video Christmas card that went viral after he sent it to several of his friends—including George Clooney—who made copies for their friends.[105] The video landed Parker and Stone a deal to produce an animated series for Comedy Central,[106] and they came up with *South Park*. The duo shot the pilot episode, which used cutouts made from construction paper, in roughly seventy days at Celluloid Studios in Denver.[107] Test audiences hated the pilot, which reportedly caused some of the participants to break down in tears.[108]

Regardless, Comedy Central decided to go ahead with the show. The gambit paid off: the first episode of *South Park* premiered on August 13, 1997, and earned big ratings, attracting an audience of approximately 65,000 households.[109] Despite the network's lackluster marketing efforts, nearly 900,000 viewers tuned in to watch the first episode, with college students making up a large percentage of the audience.[110] By the following year, *South Park* had emerged as the highest-rated basic cable program of all time,[111] and in 1999 the show spawned a theatrical film that grossed $83 million worldwide. *South Park* has won numerous Emmy Awards and generated millions of dollars in merchandising during its more than twenty years on the air, and it shows no signs of ending any time soon.[112]

Commentary

For over twenty years now, *South Park* has pushed boundaries while remaining socially, politically, and culturally relevant. Given the show's quick production schedule (most episodes are written, recorded, and animated in just six hectic days[113]), creators Trey Parker and Matt Stone (along with their small crew)

The residents of South Park, Colorado, come face-to-face with yet another wacky scenario. *Comedy Central/Photofest*

can poke fun at sociopolitical events soon after they happen. As such, *South Park* persists and thrives in a world defined by a fast-paced 24-hour news cycle and always-on social media. As Jason Jacobs notes in *The Essential Cult TV Reader*, the "range of setting, character, and reference to the contemporary world of current affairs and popular culture provides *South Park* with a very flexible research for its storytelling."[114] Indeed, during its impressive run, the show has parodied everything from religion ("All about Mormons," S7E12) to politics ("Douche and Turd," S8E8), and from video gamers ("Make Love, Not Warcraft," S10E8) to new technologies ("HumancentiPad," S15E1). With each new episode, *South Park* dishes out timely and hilarious social and cultural commentary sure to offend someone.

At the same time, *South Park* features provocative toilet humor and rude dialogue, both of which have endeared the show to stoners and fans of edgy comedy. By placing crude-but-quotable lines in the mouths of innocent kids, *South Park* not only pushed the envelope but shoved it off a cliff and then laughed uproariously as the envelope pooped itself while screaming in agony. The show, which catered mainly to disaffected young men (which makes sense considering who created it), featured memorably offensive lines like "I haven't seen an Englishman take a blow like that since Hugh Grant" (S1E4, "Big Gay Al's Big Gay Boat Ride") and

"I've lost almost ten pounds now. You see what I mean? I totally know what it's like to be a Jew in the Holocaust now" (S10E7, "Tsst!"). As such, *South Park* helped pave the way for other adult cartoons such as *Aqua Teen Hunger Force*, *Drawn Together*, *Rick and Morty*, and *Big Mouth*. Yet the show also contributed to the rise of the sort of meanspirited humor favored by edgelords and Internet trolls. For better or worse, *South Park* remains a cult classic with a long and complicated legacy.

See also *Aqua Teen Hunger Force* (2000–2015), *Family Guy* (1999–Present), *The Ren & Stimpy Show* (1991–1996)

SPOTLIGHT: TREY PARKER AND MATT STONE

Stone and Parker met while attending the University of Colorado–Boulder.[115] While there, they shot the no-budget film *Cannibal! The Musical*,[116] which eventually earned a cult following after Lloyd Kaufman, head of Troma Entertainment, released it to home video.[117] Not long after, they developed the hit Comedy Central series *South Park*. In the years after the show turned them into household names, Parker and Stone produced or starred in cult films like *Orgazmo*, *BASEketball*, and *Team America: World Police*; short-lived but beloved TV shows like *That's My Bush*; and the Tony Award–winning Broadway smash *The Book of Mormon* (which they developed with the help of *Avenue Q* creator Robert Lopez).

SPACE GHOST COAST TO COAST (1994–2008)

Creator: Mike Lazzo
Cast: George Lowe (Space Ghost), C. Martin Croker (Zorak/Moltar), Andy Merrill (Brak), Dave Willis (Master Shake/Meatwad)
Genre: Comedy, Science Fiction, Talk

Synopsis

A former superhero hosts his own surreal late-night talk show in outer space.

Production History

In 1991, Ted Turner bought the Hanna-Barbera library,[118] which included *Space Ghost*, a show about an intergalactic superhero created by legendary comic book artist Alex Toth.[119] The following year, Turner launched Cartoon Network to rerun the old cartoons he now owned, but he eventually decided that the new channel needed cheap original programming.[120] Unfortunately, Turner had failed to purchase the rights to any of the characters, meaning he could only make new properties out of "the forgettable ones."[121] He tasked Mike Lazzo with developing new concepts using 1960s Hanna-Barbera characters.[122] In 1993, Lazzo met with Khaki Jones and Andy Merrill, and together they hatched an idea to turn Space Ghost into a talk show host.[123] Merrill put together a two-minute pilot using clips from *Space Ghost and Dino Boy* and a press interview with Denzel Washington, which helped the team secure a five-episode order from Cartoon Network.[124]

Production on the series took place mainly at Williams Street Studios in Atlanta, Georgia,[125] while interviews were conducted at CNN bureaus.[126] Crawford Communications, a production company that shared a close relationship with Turner Broadcasting,[127] created new animation to fill gaps in episodes, which required "as many as 1,000 footage edits."[128] *Space Ghost Coast to Coast*, the first adult-oriented animated show produced by Cartoon Network, premiered on April 15, 1994, at 11:15 p.m.[129] The series attained a great deal of popularity and ran until 2004, at which point the "AOL/Time Warner merger marked the end of the freewheeling days at Cartoon Network, and the crew went their separate ways."[130] The show produced two spinoff series, *The Brak Show* and *Harvey Birdman, Attorney at Law*, and it continues to influence animated comedies to this day.

Commentary

With *Space Ghost Coast to Coast* (*SGCC*), the mad geniuses at Williams Street Productions introduced unsuspecting audiences to the warped humor they would later turn into a cottage industry with massively popular cult shows like *Aqua Teen Hunger Force*, *The Brak Show*, and *Sealab 2021*. By repurposing old Hanna-Barbera characters as the cast of a surreal talk show aimed at grownup viewers, series creators Mike Lazzo and Khaki Jones inadvertently laid the groundwork for Cartoon Network's late-night Adult Swim block of programming. Airing in the wee hours of the morning for much of its run, *SGCC* seemed tailor-made for a cult audience of night owls and stoners as it featured shoddy, recycled imagery and nonsensical situations alongside bizarre interviews with celebrities such as Björk, Judy Tenuta, Thom Yorke, and "Weird Al" Yankovic. The show tapped into a very specific vein of Generation X irony, turning 1960s intergalactic superhero Space Ghost into a washed-up loser who hangs out with his former villains and winds up involved in all sorts of wacky escapades. As such, *SGCC* appealed to a wide audience of slackers who identified with the characters even as they laughed at the outrageous circumstances and uproarious dialogue. The show captured the zeitgeist of the 1990s and tickled the funny bone of insomniacs and inebriates everywhere with its unhinged mix of edgy humor and recognizable characters.

Every episode of *SGCC* unleashed new weirdness upon viewers as Space Ghost and his former-villains-turned-captive-stage-crew Zorak, Moltar, and Brak involved themselves in various madcap shenanigans. Consider "Banjo" (S1E7), in which Space Ghost purchases a container of sea monkeys, only for one of them to grow into a giant monster that terrorizes the studio while Space Ghost struggles to interview rapper Schooly D (who would later provide the theme song for *Aqua Teen Hunger Force*) and Yankovic. A few seasons later, in "Piledriver" (S4E18),

Space Ghost's irascible old grandfather (voiced by larger-than-life professional wrestler Randy "Macho Man" Savage) hijacks the show, leading to a full-blown wrestling brawl between the cast in between interviews with rocker Rob Zombie and child star Raven-Symoné. And in "Fire Ant" (S7E1), Space Ghost is bitten by the titular insect and vows revenge, abandoning his interview with guest Conan O'Brien to slowly follow his attacker back to its anthill (the entire episode from the point of the abandoned interview on consists of the leisurely chase). Each episode also contains sidesplitting non-sequiturs like "Oh boy, the Shatner has really hit the fan now. I'm up Dawson's Creek without a paddle!" and "Bears are crazy. They'll bite your head if you're wearing a steak on it." Such nonsensical silliness and wild monkey-business helped turned *SGCC* into a pop cultural phenomenon as well as a bona fide cult classic.

See also *Aqua Teen Hunger Force* (2000–2015), *Frisky Dingo* (2006–2008)

SPACED (1999–2001)

Creators: Simon Pegg, Jessica Hynes
Cast: Jessica Hynes (Daisy Steiner), Simon Pegg (Tim Bisley), Julia Deakin (Marsha Klein), Nick Frost (Mike Watt), Mark Heap (Brian Topp), Katy Carmichael (Twist Morgan)
Genre: Comedy

Synopsis

When two strangers need to find new living arrangements after being dumped, they trick a landlady into believing they are married.

Production History

After meeting on the set of Channel 4's *Six Pairs of Pants* in 1995, young stand-up comedians Simon Pegg and Jessica Hynes developed a close collaborative relationship.[131] Crispin Laser, producer for the Paramount Comedy Channel, approached the duo after they appeared in the 1996 television series *Asylum* and asked them to develop a series in which they would star.[132] Naive and confident, Pegg and Hynes only accepted the offer after Laser agreed to let them write it themselves.[133] They initially wanted to update "the old flat-share sitcom model and create a show that was part *Northern Exposure*, part *X-Files*, a sort of live-action *Simpsons* by way of *The Young Ones*."[134] While developing the idea, Pegg set out to counter British shows that copied the *Friends* formula as they failed to represent his life, his friends, or geek culture in general.[135]

Originally called *Lunched Out*,[136] the idea revolved around Pegg's real-life experience of sleeping on Nick Frost's floor after a break-up and then teaming up with another recently dumped friend to house hunt. This experience shaped the idea at the core of *Spaced* as two people hatch a plan to stay off the streets after their respective relationships come to an end.[137] Hynes, who shared a similar experience, wanted to portray lead characters Tim and Daisy as equals, with neither seeming "lesser or more interesting or more dynamic or more funny than the other."[138] The duo based the show's characters on their friends,[139] with Pegg writing the role of Mike Watt specifically for Nick Frost.[140] Edgar Wright joined the project after impressing Pegg with his interpretation and storyboards of their pilot script.[141]

The series premiered on Channel 4 on September 24, 1999,[142] with the second series debuting nearly two years later on February 23, 2001.[143] The low budget meant that the show faced little network interference throughout.[144] Pegg and Hynes originally planned to produce a third season in which Tim and Daisy would become romantically involved,[145] but *Spaced* wrapped after the second series and the principal players moved on to other projects, finding cult success with *Shaun of the Dead*. That movie helped *Spaced* build a following in the United States.[146] The complete series finally arrived on DVD in North America in July 2008, with BBC America airing episodes to market the set.[147] That same year, Fox ordered a remake of the series from producer McG without the involvement of Pegg or Hynes. However, fans pushed back against the idea[148] so the network dropped the series before airing a single episode.[149]

Commentary

With its winning mixture of sarcastic-but-sweet humor and numerous references to beloved genre fare like *Star Wars*, *Doctor Who*, and *Resident Evil* (to name just a few), *Spaced* attracted a wide audience of aging slackers and pop culture nerds who deeply identified with the characters. More importantly, the show launched the careers of Edgar Wright, Simon Pegg, Nick Frost, and Jessica Hynes, who would all go on to change the face of popular culture in various ways in the years after. *Shaun of the Dead* turned Wright into one of the hottest directors around, but he established his signature kinetic style on *Spaced*, proving adept at directing laidback scenes of characters sitting around talking and exciting action sequences that paid homage to everything from John Woo to *The Matrix*. The show was infused with Wright's unique visual panache (defined by quick cuts and zoom-ins) and distinct comedic sensibilities, both of which helped *Spaced* stand out from other sitcoms of the time. Pegg and Frost, meanwhile, honed their chemistry and comic timing, which they put to good use in films like *Hot Fuzz*, *The World's End*, and *Paul*, all helping to establish them as one of the funniest comedy duos of the twenty-first century. Co-creator Hynes proved every bit as hilarious as her co-stars, pivoting from deadpan wit to over-the-top hysterics on a dime. Her immense talent allowed her to transition into a prolific career both in front of and behind the camera following her stint on the show. In addition to being one of the funniest and most dynamic sitcoms ever made, *Spaced* remains notable for the talent involved in its creation.

Of course, the series proved popular mainly due to its humor, which melds wry Generation X irony with abundant references to nerd culture. As aspiring comic book artist Tim Bisley, Pegg routinely offered up sardonic, pop culture-infused observations such as "You think I'm unemotional, don't you? I can be emotional. Jesus, I cried like child at the end of *Terminator 2*." Later, when Daisy suggests they adopt a dog, Tim objects by paraphrasing a line from *Jurassic Park*: "Yeah, that's how it all starts, with oohs and ahs, but later there's barking and biting." Other episodes offer viewers spot-on parodies of pop culture landmarks such as *The Shining* (S1E1), as the lead characters encounter a pair of creepy twins while exploring their new flat; *Pulp Fiction* (S2E1), with Daisy confronting Mike in a manner that recalls the fateful final meeting between Bruce Willis's Butch and John Travolta's Vincent; and *The Matrix* (S2E1), which sees Daisy battle two smartly attired government agents in a pub. Ultimately, though, *Spaced* was funny, thrilling, and touching in equal measure, presenting charmingly flawed characters who loved one another almost as much as they loved movies, TV shows, and comic books. This allowed viewers to connect to the show on a variety of levels, thus making it a treasured cult phenomenon.

See also *Community* (2009–2015)

SPORTS NIGHT (1998–2000)

Creator: Aaron Sorkin
Cast: Josh Charles (Dan Rydell), Peter Krause (Casey McCall), Felicity Huffman (Dana Whitaker), Joshua Malina (Jeremy Goodwin), Sabrina Lloyd (Natalie Hurley), Robert Guillaume (Isaac Jaffe), Kayla Blake (Kim), Greg Baker (Elliot), Timothy Davis-Reed (Chris)
Genre: Comedy, Drama

Synopsis

The cast and crew of a cable sports program deal with intra-office relationships and hijinks.

Production History

In 1995, writer Aaron Sorkin developed an idea for a movie that he described as "sort of *Broadcast News* at an ESPN-type network."[150] He mentioned his idea to his agent, who suggested turning it into a television series.[151] Twenty-four hours later, Sorkin pitched the show to Jamie Tarses of ABC, who gave it a greenlight.[152] Sorkin then assembled his cast, and production on the series, titled *Sports Night*, began in the summer of 1998.[153] Problems arose almost immediately as Sorkin clashed with executives at ABC who insisted on adding a live audience and laugh track to make the half-hour drama seem more like a traditional sitcom.[154] Despite the tensions occurring behind the scenes, *Sports Night* premiered on September 22, 1998, at 9:30 p.m.[155]

The show's troubles continued throughout production. For instance, Robert Guillaume suffered a stroke on January 14, 1999, forcing producers to write his character out for several episodes,[156] only to later incorporate the actor's recovery into the story.[157] Critics praised *Sports Night*, which nevertheless averaged just 11.2 million viewers per episode.[158] In May 1999, ABC renewed the series for a second season but canceled it once it dropped to fifty-third place in the ratings.[159] The final episode aired on May 16, 2000.[160] Showtime picked up the series for two additional seasons in a deal worth $37 million but those plans quickly fell apart because Sorkin wanted less involvement as he and his wife were expecting their first child and Showtime refused to produce the show without him.[161] In the years after its cancelation, *Sports Night* ran briefly on Comedy Central and streamed on Netflix, which helped the series develop a cult following.[162]

Commentary

While it failed to catch on with a wide audience, *Sports Night* nevertheless would alter the landscape of both television and comedy for years to come. The show established creator Aaron Sorkin's unique approach to creating television shows as he focused mainly on distinctive dialogue and genre-bending narratives that took viewers behind the scenes of various industries and institutions. It also represented one of the first attempts by a comedy series to discard the live audience and laugh track that had defined sitcoms throughout much of the medium's history to that point. In addition, *Sports Night* pioneered Sorkin's trademark "walk and talk" storytelling technique, which popped up in dozens (if not hundreds) of other shows in the years afterward. It helped that *Sports Night* boasted an eclectic cast of talented actors capable of making Sorkin's somewhat peculiar prose sound completely natural. Most importantly, *Sports Night* also laid the groundwork for Sorkin's later acclaimed series such as *The West Wing*, which he co-created with director Thomas Schlamme, and *The Newsroom*. Though short-lived, *Sports Night* introduced TV audiences to Sorkin's ability to craft brilliant stories and dialogue.

The show tickled viewers' ribs with hilarious episodes like "The Hungry and the Hunted" (S1E3), which sees Dan Rydell excuse himself from a conversation by declaring, "I gotta tell you, at this point, the length of this conversation is way out of proportion to my interest in it." Later, in "Thespis" (S1E8), Dana Whitaker announces, "I've named this Thanksgiving. I'm calling it 'The Thanksgiving of Mom's Disapproval.' Included on the two-record set are the hit songs 'Why Aren't You Married?' and 'Sports Is No Place for an Educated Woman,' and 'Didn't Anyone Ever Tell You How to Cook a Turkey?'" *Sports Night* expertly balanced such wry comedy with touching drama in a thought-provoking way, demonstrating that multi-character dramas can entertain even as they challenge viewers. The show also established the template for subsequent series that pull the curtain back on everything from entertainment to politics, including *House of Cards*, *The Good Wife*, and *Veep*. Viewers failed to appreciate *Sports Night* when it aired, but these days fans rightly consider it one of the all-time great cult TV shows.

SPOTLIGHT: AARON SORKIN

Born in Manhattan on June 9, 1961, Aaron Sorkin watched primetime sitcoms growing up, sparking a desire to become a writer.[163] After college, he wrote plays such as *A Few Good Men*, which appeared on Broadway in 1989 and led to a hit movie adaptation in 1992. He followed this success by writing the screenplay for *The American President* before creating television shows like *Sports Night*, *The West Wing*, *Studio 60 on the Sunset Strip*, and *The Newsroom*,[164] all of which earned him numerous awards. When creating his shows, Sorkin strove to keep the writing real, drawing inspiration from Larry Gelbart, who developed *M*A*S*H* for TV.[165] In addition to his TV work, Sorkin also wrote Oscar-worthy films like *The Social Network*, *Moneyball*, and *Steve Jobs*.

STAR TREK (1966–1969)

Creator: Gene Roddenberry
Cast: William Shatner (Capt. James T. Kirk), Leonard Nimoy (Mr. Spock), DeForest Kelly (Dr. Leonard H. "Bones" McCoy), Nichelle Nichols (Cdr. Nyota Uhura), James Doohan (Lt. Cdr. Montgomery "Scotty" Scott), George Takei (Lt. Hikaru Sulu), Walter Koenig (Ensign Pavel Chekov)
Genre: Drama, Science Fiction

Synopsis

The intrepid crew of the starship *Enterprise* explores the galaxy on their mission to seek out new life and new civilizations.

Production History

In the early 1960s, former airline pilot and policeman Gene Roddenberry set out to create a thoughtful science fiction series that tackled social and political topics other shows of the era refused to touch.[166] Drawing inspiration from the Western series *Wagon Train*,[167] Roddenberry developed an idea that he pitched to various studios. MGM rejected the show as too different and too difficult to produce as a weekly series[168] but Desilu showed interest because they wanted to develop a drama and could afford to invest in an ambitious weekly science fiction show.[169] In April 1964, Mort Werner, vice president in charge of programming at NBC, paid Roddenberry $20,000 to further develop the idea and write a pilot script.[170] Roddenberry sent the completed pilot script to NBC in September 1964, and the network approved it with minor revisions.[171] NBC invested $435,000 in the pilot episode, though that amount quickly ballooned to $600,000 with the network's board of directors opting to deficit finance the difference.[172]

Production on *Star Trek* began on November 27, 1964, at Desilu's Culver City studios,[173] but NBC disliked the first episode and ordered a second pilot shot.[174] Upon approving Roddenberry's new script in May 1965,[175] network executives

In the series *Star Trek*, Mr. Spock (Leonard Nimoy) frequently offered up the traditional Vulcan greeting "Live long and prosper." *CBS/Photofest*

gave the production crew just nine days to shoot the new pilot.[176] NBC added *Star Trek* to its 1966–1967 schedule, leaving the crew only six months to prepare.[177] *Star Trek* premiered on September 8, 1966, to solid ratings, prompting the network to order a full season.[178] The show left critics underwhelmed, but it nevertheless won a devoted audience that included scientists, astronauts, and respected authors like Isaac Asimov.[179] Ratings declined during the third season, at which point the network cut the show's already small budget. At the same time, the relationship between Roddenberry and NBC soured even though network executives continued to support *Star Trek*.[180] NBC moved the show to Friday nights at 10:00 p.m., leaving Roddenberry feeling betrayed.[181] The network opted not to renew *Star Trek* for a fourth season, and production wrapped on January 9, 1969.[182] Since then, *Star Trek* has spawned numerous movies, spinoff series, tie-in products, and fan conventions to become one of the fundamental cult television series of all time.

Commentary

Star Trek launched a whole new era of smart, adventurous science fiction shows while cultivating one of the most devoted fanbases in television history (known as "Trekkies" or "Trekkers"). The original series boasted multilayered characters, captivating storylines, and charmingly shoddy special effects, thus appealing to both science fiction fanatics and casual television viewers. During its three-year mission, the show introduced audiences to a diverse cast of characters and spun fantastic yarns that tackled a variety of contemporary sociocultural issues, including racism, sexism, and militarism. *Star Trek* not only featured men and women of color in prominent roles—most notably Nichelle Nichols as Lt. Uhura and George Takei as Lt. Sulu—but portrayed them as competent, valuable members of the crew. The show also took daring risks, including showing what is widely considered TV's first interracial kiss (though one that occurred while the characters involved were under duress) and critiquing the United States' involvement in the Vietnam War (in episodes such as "City on the Edge of Forever" and "A Private Little War"). While such episodes often proved controversial, *Star Trek* nevertheless resonated with viewers because it offered a hopeful vision of a future in which humanity finally puts aside their differences and sets off to explore the stars together.

The show's talented cast brought the characters to vibrant life through their performances. As Capt. Kirk, William Shatner balanced fiery emotion and dashing heroism with touching warmth and amiable humor. DeForest Kelly, meanwhile, played Dr. McCoy as an irascible country physician whose gruff exterior belied a big heart. Leonard Nimoy delivered an instantly iconic performance as Spock, effectively conveying the character's inner turmoil as he sought to reconcile his logic and his emotions. This trio formed the heart of the show but the rest of the cast imbued stereotypical characters like Montgomery Scott and Pavel Chekov with complex personalities, turning them into cherished fan favorites. In addition, *Star Trek* featured exciting stories that offered an intoxicating mix of action, drama, comedy, and heady concepts. Each week viewers watched as the crew traveled to distant worlds and met strange new lifeforms, including sexy extraterrestrial women. Episodes like "Amok Time" (S2E1) and "The Doomsday Machine" (S2E6) saw the crew of the starship *Enterprise* traverse time and space, while installments such as "I, Mudd" (S2E8) and "The Trouble with Tribbles" (S2E15) serve up more amusing escapades. *Star Trek* features something for everyone, which may explain why the original series remains so beloved long after wrapping up its final mission.

See also *Babylon 5* (1994–1998), *Farscape* (1999–2003), *Lost in Space* (1965–1968)

SPOTLIGHT: GENE RODDENBERRY

Born August 19, 1921, in El Paso, Texas, Gene Roddenberry developed an interest in science fiction at a young age.[183] Despite his interest in writing, Roddenberry decided to follow in his father's footsteps and pursue police studies at Los Angeles City College.[184] He also trained as a pilot, and after serving in World War II he flew for Pan Am.[185] He soon abandoned both professions to try his hand at writing television, landing a gig as a technical advisor for the show *Mr. District Attorney* in 1951.[186] Three years later he sold his first script.[187] In 1963, NBC picked up Roddenberry's show *The Lieutenant* but canceled it after just one season. Two years later, Roddenberry launched the science fiction series *Star Trek*,[188] a pop culture phenomenon that continues to this day. Roddenberry died in 1991.[189]

THE STATE (1993–1995)

Creators: Kevin Allison, Jonathan K. Bendis, Michael Ian Black, Robert Ben Garant,
    Todd Holoubek, Michael Patrick Jann, Kerri Kenney, Thomas Lennon, Joe Lo Trug-
    lio, Ken Marino, Michael Showalter, Steven Starr, David Wain
Cast: Kevin Allison, Michael Ian Black, Robert Ben Garant, Todd Holoubek, Michael
    Patrick Jann, Kerri Kenney, Thomas Lennon, Joe Lo Truglio, Ken Marino, Michael
    Showalter, David Wain
Genre: Comedy

Synopsis

In this subversive sketch comedy show, an American comedy troupe presents
bizarre skits.

Production History

In October 1988,[190] New York University students David Wain and Michael
Showalter teamed with nine other friends to form a comedy troupe called the
New Group, which they later renamed the State.[191] Over the next few years, the
group performed live and made videos that eventually caught the attention of
executives at MTV, who in 1992 hired the group to perform on *You Wrote It, You
Watch It*,[192] hosted by comedian (and future host of *The Daily Show*) Jon Stewart.[193]
During that time, the entire troupe received $100 for each short video they pro-
duced.[194] Two years later, the network asked Wain and his cohorts to create a pilot
for their own self-titled sketch comedy series,[195] looking for a show similar to their
stage performances.[196] Inspired by early *Saturday Night Live* episodes,[197] the group
developed a surreal skit show that mixed live, in-studio performances with short
films shot on video. Wain directed and edited the small-scale films while State
member Michael Patrick Jann directed the large-scale films. Meanwhile, Wain and
Jann produced the sketches along with Jim Sharp and Mark Perez, but the entire
group "supervised all creative aspects of the production."[198]

While the pilot they shot never made it to air, it finalized MTV's decision to
pick up the series at thirteen episodes with a $1.9 million budget.[199] *The State*
premiered at 10:00 p.m. on Friday, January 21, 1994. In quick succession, the
second season started on July 10, 1994, and the third season began on December
2, 1994.[200] Throughout production, the network made cuts to offensive sketches
during the scripting and shooting stages[201] yet overall gave the troupe freedom
to be themselves,[202] although tensions arose during the third season over what
type of content to feature in the sketches.[203] Though the show only attracted a
small audience and initially received negative reviews from critics (*Entertainment Weekly* gave the series a C-minus[204] while *The Daily News* proclaimed it "so
terrible it deserves to be studied"[205]), MTV never officially canceled *The State*.[206]
Instead, the actors left for various reasons[207] and informed MTV of their decision

to finish the last seven episodes in 1995.[208] That year, CBS aired *The State's 43rd Annual All-Star Halloween Special*, which received great reviews but low ratings so the network decided not to pursue a series.[209] In 2008, *The State* finally landed on DVD after years of legal wrangling over music licensing issues.[210] In the years after the show went off the air, every member of the State went on to great success with various film and TV projects. In 2014, the group reunited for Tenacious D's second annual Festival Supreme.[211]

Commentary

When it debuted, *The State* announced the arrival of a new generation of comics who brought with them a new style of edgy humor that captured the unruly spirit of the MTV generation. The show looked and sounded like no other sketch comedy series of the time such as the long-running *Saturday Night Live* or even the raucously madcap upstart *The Kids in the Hall* (which was also produced by *Saturday Night Live* creator and showrunner Lorne Michaels). Instead, *The State* tapped into the quick-cut rock-and-roll style of music videos, which still comprised the bulk of MTV's programming during the early to mid-1990s. The troupe of rebellious twentysomethings tapped into the zeitgeist of the 1990s to expertly lampoon everything from slacker culture to alternative rock to advertising. They also poked fun at other sketch comedy traditions via catch-phrase-spouting characters like Doug ("I'm outta here!") and Louie ("I wanna dip my balls in it!"), all while offering up outrageously surreal sketches (including "The Restaurant Sketch," a sober meditation on the nature of comedy, and the fan-favorite skit "Porcupine Racetrack," a lavish musical about a . . . porcupine racetrack). As such, *The State* struck a powerful chord with disillusioned young people looking for a good laugh.

Despite low ratings and poor reviews, *The State* emerged as a highly influential sketch comedy show thanks to the talent involved. The short-lived series showcased the bizarre comedic sensibilities of people like Michael Ian Black, Michael Showalter, and David Wain, all of whom went on to long careers in film and television, producing popular TV shows like *Viva Variety* and *Reno 911!* as well as beloved films like *Wet Hot American Summer* and *They Came Together*. Meanwhile, folks like Thomas Lennon and Robert Ben Garant found mainstream success writing screenplays for popular films like *Night at the Museum* and its two sequels while Joe Lo Truglio joined the cast of beloved sitcom *Brooklyn Nine-Nine* and Kerri Kenny voiced numerous characters in the hit animated series *Bob's Burgers*. In the years after the show's premature end, the cast of *The State* left a profound imprint on the entertainment landscape thanks to their anarchic brand of humor, which continues to inspire generations of young comics, showrunners, and filmmakers to this day. *The State* may have lacked widespread appeal, but it nevertheless launched the careers of several funny people and continues to shape the comedy scene even now.

See also *The Kids in the Hall* (1988–1994), *Mr. Show with Bob and David* (1995–1998)

STEVEN UNIVERSE (2013–PRESENT)

Creator: Rebecca Sugar
Cast: Zach Callison (Steven Universe), Deedee Magno (Pearl), Michaela Dietz (Amethyst), Estelle (Garnet), Tom Scharpling (Greg Universe), Matthew Moy (Lars Barriga), Grace Rolek (Connie Maheswaran), Kate Micucci (Sadie Miller), Shelly Rabara (Peridot), Jennifer Paz (Lapis Lazuli)
Genre: Action, Comedy, Drama, Musical, Science Fiction

Synopsis

A young boy teams with a group of intergalactic warriors to protect the Earth.

Production History

While a teenager, Rebecca Sugar wrote and self-published a comic called *The Ballad of Margo and Dread*, which featured art by her brother Steven (who helped her come up with the story).[212] A few years later, Sugar entered college to study animation, and while there she met School of Visual Arts alum Phil Rynda, who at that time served as lead character designer on Cartoon Network's cult smash *Adventure Time*.[213] Rynda helped Sugar secure a job on the show as a storyboard revisionist, though she soon worked her way up to a position as storyboard artist and later writer on the show.[214] In 2011, she approached Cartoon Network executives and successfully pitched a series featuring her brother as the main character.[215] While developing the new show, Sugar drew on a variety of influences, including Babylonian Ishtar mythology (which she discovered via *Hellboy* creator Mike Mignola), Hayao Miyazaki's *Future Boy Cohan*, and the beaches where she and her brother spent their childhood.[216]

Production moved quickly due to a combination of limited time and resources as well as the fact that the network gave a go-ahead for full production before South Korean animation studio Rough Draft completed all the finished animation.[217] After a last art presentation to the network, the series received an official greenlight.[218] Titled *Steven Universe*, the show officially premiered on November 4, 2013, at 8:00 p.m.,[219] making Sugar "the first solo female series creator in Cartoon Network's twenty-one-year history."[220] The network originally ordered thirteen episodes but asked for an additional thirteen after the premiere earned strong ratings.[221] The first season averaged 5 million viewers per episode, and in July 2014 during a panel at San Diego Comic Con, Cartoon Network announced that they were renewing *Steven Universe* for a second season.[222] Following the fifth season, Cartoon Network aired the musical made-for-TV movie *Steven Universe: The Movie* in September 2019.[223] The show continues to draw strong ratings and remains a fan favorite.

Commentary

Filled with lovable characters and breathtaking action, *Steven Universe* dazzles viewers of all ages with an intoxicating mix of smart sci-fi and jubilant stories, all rendered via vibrant animation. Ostensibly a send-up of magical girl shows (such as *Sailor Moon* and *Princess Tutu*), the show nevertheless subverts this trope by placing a young boy (though one possessed of a decidedly nontraditional masculinity) in the central role. This main character allows *Steven Universe* to play around with the tropes of the genre while also serving up progressive portrayals of gender, relationships, body positivity, queer characters, and more. Since debuting on Cartoon Network in 2013, the series has built a large following among the LGBTQIA+ community thanks to its deft handling of "queer relationships and characters, its interpretation of gender, and its feminist conceptualization."[224] It presents these issues in a way understandable to both kids and adults. More importantly, it avoids preachiness, opting instead to portray difference as perfectly normal. As such, *Steven Universe* resonates with a wide audience while also establishing itself as one of the most groundbreaking kids' shows of the early twenty-first century.

Each episode of *Steven Universe* takes viewers on exciting and heartfelt adventures through colorful worlds populated by unforgettable characters. For instance, in "Mirror Gem" (S1E25), Steven befriends a magical mirror that harbors a dark secret. The following episode, "Ocean Gem" (S1E26), sees rogue gem warrior Lapis Lazuli steal Earth's oceans, thus leading Steven and his comrades on a merry chase. The two-part season 1 finale, consisting of "The Return" (S1E51) and "Jail Break" (S1E53), serves up epic action and powerful drama as Steven and his allies, the Crystal Gems, try to stay one step ahead of series villain Jasper and his hordes of henchmen. At the same time, *Steven Universe* tugs on viewers' heartstrings thanks to touching stories that explore the characters and their relationships. Consider "Lion 3: Straight to Video" (S1E35), in which Steven finds a videotape that contains a poignant message from his dead mother, Rose Quartz. Later, in "Rose's Scabbard" (S1E45), Pearl reveals that she once harbored romantic feelings for Stephen's mother but must now come to terms with the discovery that Rose kept secrets from her. Yet the show also featured humorous dialogue and amusing situations, such as Garnet throwing herself from a moving vehicle rather than listen to a grating rock song. An adventurous spirit, cheeky attitude, and trailblazing stories all made *Steven Universe* a cult favorite.

See also *Adventure Time* (2010–2018), *Avatar: The Last Airbender* (2005–2008), *Sailor Moon* (1992–1997)

STRANGERS WITH CANDY (1999–2000)

Creators: Amy Sedaris, Stephen Colbert, Paul Dinello, Mitch Rouse
Cast: Amy Sedaris (Jerri Blank), Paul Dinello (Geoffrey Jellineck), Stephen Colbert (Chuck Noblet), Deborah Rush (Sara Blank), Greg Hollimon (Onyx Blackman)
Genre: Comedy

Synopsis

A forty-six-year-old ex-drug addict returns to high school and tries to fit in with her much younger classmates while learning important life lessons.

Production History

In 1988,[225] Amy Sedaris, Paul Dinello, and Stephen Colbert met while performing at Second City in Chicago,[226] and when they began touring for Second City, they started performing their own original material.[227] Dinello and Sedaris convinced Colbert to join them in New York,[228] where they created the sketch comedy show *Exit 57* for Comedy Central.[229] That show only ran for twelve episodes in 1995–1996,[230] but the trio wanted to continue working together.[231] Sedaris pitched a series to Comedy Central based on after-school specials.[232] She drew inspiration from the story of Florrie Fisher,[233] a "former prostitute, junkie, jailbird turned public speaker" featured in the 1970 video PSA *The Trip Back*.[234] Comedy Central liked the idea and picked it up.[235]

While trying to think of a title for the new series, Sedaris and pals remembered an after-school special about refusing to take candy from strangers.[236] The trio used their improv skills to sketch out the scenes and dialogue.[237] They created an unaired pilot but made changes to the concept, like a removing a subplot of the lead character, Jerri Blank, working at a hospital because it seemed too cartoonish and they worried it might limit the series' lifespan.[238] The first episode of *Strangers with Candy* premiered on April 7, 1999.[239] Over the course of three seasons and thirty episodes, the showrunners only occasionally clashed with Comedy Central's Standards and Practices as the network usually let them get away with a lot.[240]

Comedy Central never officially notified the trio of the show's cancelation.[241] Nevertheless, Sedaris, Colbert, and Dinello knew that the network commonly only ran a series for three seasons so they created the last episode as a series finale.[242] The final episode of *Strangers with Candy* aired on October 2, 2000.[243] After ironing out distribution issues, the trio reunited for a prequel film that hit movie theaters on July 21, 2006.[244]

Commentary

Strangers with Candy brilliantly sends up after-school specials of the 1970s and 1980s while mining lots of laughs from the foibles of lead character Jerri Blank, a middle-aged high school dropout and former drug-addicted prostitute looking to get her life back on track. Amy Sedaris portrays Jerri as an oblivious loser who longs to do the right thing but rarely succeeds. From killing her many pets (for instance, she accidentally boils her beloved lobster Clawson and allows partygoers to toss Shelley the turtle out a window) to her hilariously doomed efforts to relate to her teenaged classmates (in S3E5, "Blank Relay," Jerri tries out for the school track team only to develop an addiction to steroids), the character seems destined to fail. She also remains completely self-absorbed and callous throughout the series, seemingly unaware of (or merely indifferent to) how her actions affect those around her. Jerri's harebrained schemes often left the audience howling with laughter even as they cringed with discomfort (as in S1E3, "Dreams on the Rocks," which sees Jerri land the lead role in the school play, driving her stepmother, a former actress, to alcoholism). With its unlikeable characters and uncomfortable humor, *Strangers with Candy* seems tailor-made for fans of awkward comedy.

Every episode of the show served up outrageously wacky situations and uproarious dialogue. For instance, in "Behind Blank Eyes" (S2E2), Jerri falls for a blind boy named Alan and convinces him to try out for the football team—to hilariously mortifying results. When the team expresses reluctance to add Alan to the roster, Jerri responds with an impassioned speech: "I hope you're all happy, keeping Alan off the team. Couldn't you, for once, open your minds and hearts and hear something that he couldn't see? I, for one, am glad that Alan is blind, so he can't see what, I am so sad to say, you can't hear." Later, in "Trail of Tears" (S3E3), Jerri believes that she has discovered her Native American heritage and attends a camp run by a counselor who teaches adopted native kids about things like alcoholism and gambling. Upon learning that she is in fact neither Native American nor adopted, Jerri declares, "It's just a coincidence that I have a love of gambling and booze and a knack for catching syphilis." In addition, *Strangers with Candy* launched the careers of Sedaris, Colbert, and Paul Dinello, who all changed the face of comedy in the years after. Despite its short lifespan, the show cast a long shadow, making it one of the greatest cult TV shows ever made.

See also *Family Guy* (1999–Present), *South Park* (1997–Present)

SUPERNATURAL (2005–2020)

Creator: Eric Kripke
Cast: Jared Padalecki (Sam Winchester), Jensen Ackles (Dean Winchester), Misha Collins (Castiel), Jim Beaver (Bobby Singer), Jeffrey Dean Morgan (John Winchester), Felicia Day (Charlie Bradbury)
Genre: Drama, Fantasy, Horror, Mystery, Thriller

Synopsis

Two estranged brothers reunite to continue their father's work of protecting the world from supernatural forces.

Production History

Eric Kripke originally intended *Supernatural* as an anthology focused on urban legends but his idea evolved to focus on a pair of central characters who encounter paranormal phenomena.[245] Kripke pitched the concept to all the major

In *Supernatural*, brothers Sam (Jared Padalecki, left) and Dean Winchester (Jensen Ackles) face off against monsters and other metaphysical threats. *The CW Television Network/Photofest*

networks before landing a deal with the WB Network in 2004.[246] The network rejected Kripke's first script so the writer teamed with co-executive producer Peter Johnson to reduce the backstory and exposition.[247] Kripke canceled his holiday plans and locked himself in his office to focus on completing a rewrite of the pilot script by Christmas.[248] Despite all that effort, WB executives refused to greenlight the script until director David Nutter joined the project and declared that he liked the relationships between the characters at the center of the supernatural stories.[249] When casting the show, the network wanted a young Harrison Ford type, and they found him in Jensen Ackles, the first actor hired[250]—although Peter Roth, president of Warner Bros. Television, suggested he would make a better Dean.[251] Meanwhile, Kripke's wife suggested *Gilmore Girls* actor Jared Padalecki, who read opposite Ackles as Sam.[252] Luckily, the actors displayed great chemistry from the start in the roles they ended up in.[253]

The pilot of *Supernatural* aired on September 13, 2005, drawing nearly 6 million viewers despite mixed reviews. The network ordered a full series pick-up following Nutter's suggestion to bring aboard John Shiban (who previously wrote for *The X-Files*) to help build the show's mythology.[254] While the stories initially focused on urban legends, the actors' chemistry led their characters and relationships to become the focus.[255] Producers strove to balance humor, family drama, and monster-of-the-week narratives, with these elements finally gelling about midway through the first season.[256] Though the network shot the pilot episode in Los Angeles, the series quickly moved to Vancouver to save money and to evoke its spiritual ancestor, *The X-Files*.[257]

At the start of season 2, *Supernatural* moved to the CW Network due to the 2006 merger between the WB and UPN.[258] Despite the move, the show continued to attract the desired demographic of women 18–34, thereby ensuring its longevity.[259] Kripke stepped down as showrunner following the fifth season due to exhaustion, handing the reins to producer Sera Gamble.[260] Gamble left after the seventh season, and Jeremy Carver stepped up until the twelfth season when Andrew Dabb became co-showrunner.[261] In 2019, producers announced the end of *Supernatural* following season 15, thus concluding the long-running adventures of the Winchester brothers.[262]

Commentary

Supernatural owes its longevity to two main factors: the devotion of fangirls and the cultivation of a positive relationship between producers and viewers. The show's structure, themes, and narratives harken back to other shows like *Kung Fu*, *The Incredible Hulk*, *Kolchak: The Night Stalker*, and *The X-Files* because it merged the journey genre with the supernatural genre and created a rich mythology along the way. Additionally, *Supernatural* combined horror, drama, comedy, and romance in a way that recalled other genre mashups like *Dark Shadows*, *Buffy the Vampire Slayer*, and *Charmed*. More importantly, though, *Supernatural* inspired intense devotion from viewers (especially among teenage girls and young women), and in that regard it resembled cult classics such as *Star Trek* and *Doctor Who*. Fangirls loved Sam and Dean Winchester, the handsome and hunky brothers at the heart of *Supernatural*, and their commitment to these characters kept the series alive for fifteen seasons.

Over the years, the show included several Easter Eggs that demonstrated how much everyone involved appreciated the devotion.[263] For instance, in "The Monster at the End of This Book" (S4E18), Sam and Dean learn that a prophet named Chuck wrote a series of books based on their adventures with a fanbase clearly modeled on *Supernatural*'s most dedicated viewers. Meanwhile, "The French Mistake" (S6E15) sees the boys travel to an alternate dimension in which they are actors named Jared Padalecki and Jensen Ackles starring in a show called *Supernatural*. The episode even pokes gentle fun at the fans, with the brothers openly wondering who would watch such a show. Such blatant fan service helped *Supernatural* build a fervent cult audience on a global scale. Starting in 2006, the show spawned conventions in which fans could mingle with the cast and crew, and the stars would routinely take to social media, speaking directly to their admirers about producing the series and sharing insights into their personal lives. Rather than view their fans as losers or fanatics, the cast and crew of *Supernatural* embraced their fans, and this ensured the show a long life and well-deserved reputation as one of the greatest cult TV shows ever made.

See also *Buffy the Vampire Slayer* (1997–2003), *Charmed* (1998–2006), *The X-Files* (1993–2018)

T

TENACIOUS D (1997–2000)

Creators: Jack Black, David Cross, Kyle Gass, Bob Odenkirk
Cast: Jack Black (Jack "JB" Black), Kyle Gass (Kyle "KG" Gass), Paul F. Tompkins (Paul)
Genre: Comedy, Musical

Synopsis

Two talented-but-dimwitted musicians navigate a series of surreal hijinks in their quest to become the greatest band in the world.

Production History

Jack Black and Kyle Gass met in 1985 while performing with the Los Angeles–based theater troupe the Actors' Gang but their friendship took a while to develop, as did their professional partnership.[1] They eventually teamed up as the musical comedy duo Tenacious D, taking their name from a comment made by sportscaster Marv Albert.[2] In 1994, they made their live musical debut at Al's Bar, and soon after comedian David Cross invited them to join other performers in alternative comedy shows around Los Angeles.[3] In 1997, Black and Gass teamed with Cross and Bob Odenkirk to create a series of Tenacious D short films that aired on HBO between 1997 and 2000,[4] with the first premiering on March 24, 1999, at 11:00 p.m.[5]

In 1999, HBO considered ordering ten more episodes of the show but only if Black and Gass relinquished their role as executive producers.[6] Network executives wanted more creative control over the show and wanted to turn Black and Gass into a modern-day version of the Monkees.[7] Unwilling to accept this stipulation, the duo decided to abandon the show and pursue a Tenacious D feature film instead.[8] Black and Gass spent the next few years touring as Tenacious D, and Black also embarked on a successful movie career, appearing in films such as *Shallow Hal*, *School of Rock*, and *King Kong*. In 2006, *Tenacious D in the Pick of Destiny* finally hit theaters,[9] opening to middling reviews and a paltry box office. Nevertheless, Tenacious D remains popular, and in 2018, Black and Gass produced a six-episode, animated YouTube series to accompany the release of their album *Post-Apocalypto*.[10]

Commentary

Though preceded by other fictional bands such as the Monkees, the Partridge Family, and Spinal Tap, comedy rockers Tenacious D nevertheless kick-started an entire genre with their hilariously absurd self-titled HBO series, which inspired a wave of mock musical groups that included Flight of the Conchords, the Lonely Island, and Garfunkel and Oates. Filled with surreal humor and awkwardly hilarious situations, *Tenacious D* launched the careers of several funny people, starting with Jack Black who played a not-so-heightened version of himself as a cherubic agent of chaos with a powerful voice and a rockin' soul trapped in the body of a schlubby loser. The series also showcased the immense talents of Black's longtime pal and bandmate Kyle Gass, who embarked on a lengthy career as a character actor, and Paul F. Tompkins, who emerged as one of the funniest and most beloved comics of the twenty-first century. Black and Gass wrote all six episodes of the series with David Cross, Bob Odenkirk, Tom Gianas, and Bill Odenkirk, the demented minds behind *Mr. Show with Bob and David* and *Human Giant*. As such, *Tenacious D* features the same sort of ridiculous gags ("Sometimes you follow your heart. Sometimes your heart cuts a fart. That's the cosmic shame") and weird circumstances (Black and Gass engage in a ludicrous karate fight to win the heart of a clog-dancing Satanist named Flarna).

Tenacious D also features great songs that rock hard and elicit huge laughs, all written and performed by Black and Gass. The show revolves around the portly pals' efforts to establish themselves as the world's greatest band, which often involves performing at a bar that hosts frequent open mic nights hosted by Paul, who exasperatedly reads exaggerated introductions written by the musicians themselves ("Caution: The surgeon general of rock warns that viewing this band is equal to twenty-nine orgasms"). Each episode affords Black and Gass multiple opportunities to launch into original songs that balance outrageous humor with face-melting guitar licks. For instance, "Jesus Ranch," a trippy tune about cults and oversized vegetables, features the nonsensical lyric, "I fell in love with a baked potato / That's when I started to dance / Yeah, in France." Meanwhile, "Sasquatch" describes the boys' encounter with the elusive cryptid (played by John C. Reilly!) and drops a reference to the old TV series *In Search Of . . .* hosted by Leonard Nimoy. Black and Gass eventually performed their sidesplitting songs for legions of fans in sold-out concerts around the world, but *Tenacious D* reveals the humble and preposterous (not to mention entirely fictional) origin of the greatest band in the world by portraying the hysterically farcical stories that exist behind the music.

See also *Mr. Show with Bob and David* (1995–1998)

> ## *THE TICK* (1994–1997)
>
> *Creator*: Ben Edlund
> *Cast*: Townsend Coleman (the Tick), Rob Paulsen (Arthur), Cam Clarke (Die Fledermaus), Kay Lenz (American Maid), Jess Harnell (Sewer Urchin), Pat Fraley (Mayor Blank)
> *Genre*: Action, Comedy, Fantasy, Science Fiction

Synopsis

Powerful but dim superhero the Tick protects the City alongside his hapless sidekick Arthur and daring pals American Maid and Die Fledermaus.

Production History

While still in high school, Ben Edlund created the Tick as a gag character for his role-playing-game group.[11] In 1986, Edlund's local comic book store, New England Comics, asked to use the character as their "superhero mascot."[12] The store's owners then published a comic book series starring the character, which ran for ten years.[13] The black-and-white series proved "so successful that the initial Tick stories were reprinted nine times in the decade following the character's debut, each time with new material added to the story."[14] A few years later, New Jersey toy company Kiscom approached Edlund about licensing the property.[15] However, they failed to drum up any interest among television studios or networks, so Edlund focused on college until Sunbow Entertainment made an offer to produce a Tick cartoon.[16]

Sunbow asked Edlund and writer Richard Liebmann-Smith to develop a pilot script that Fox promptly rejected. The duo spent five days rewriting the pilot, which Fox accepted.[17] During the first season Townsend Coleman played the Tick while Mickey Dolenz of the Monkees voiced sidekick Arthur.[18] Edlund and his writers removed some of the darker characters and sexual undertones from the source material, but the series maintained the comic's overall spirit.[19] Wanting to learn about the television business, the neophyte Edlund involved himself in all aspects of production.[20]

The Tick debuted on September 24, 1994, and ran for three seasons and thirty-six episodes[21] but the series seemed destined to live in the shadow of the more successful *Teenage Mutant Ninja Turtles*.[22] In 1997 Sunbow negotiated with Fox for a prime-time special, another season, and a feature film[23] but none materialized. Comedy Central picked up the series for syndication, which helped it grow an adult audience.[24] In 2001, Fox launched a short-lived, live-action reboot,[25] while in 2016 Amazon produced their own live-action *Tick* series that lasted two seasons.[26]

Commentary

The Tick offered viewers a hilariously smart deconstruction of the superhero genre long before costumed crimefighters became ubiquitous in both film and television. Featuring a colorful cast of wonderfully weird characters, the show served up big laughs and thrilling action in every episode, delighting comic book fanatics, comedy nerds, and animation aficionados all at once. *The Tick* introduced audiences to ludicrous caped crusaders like Bi-Polar Bear, Baby Boomerangutan, Human Bullet, and Éclair, who all help the title character and his teammates defend the City from nefarious villains such as Chairface Chippendale, Baron Violent, and Dinosaur Neil. The show benefitted from a talented troupe of voice actors starting with Townsend Coleman as the eponymous hero. Meanwhile, as luckless sidekick Arthur, veteran performer Rob Paulsen (taking over from Mickey Dolenz, who left after the first season) displays amazing range, veering from exhausted acceptance to stunned disbelief to explosive anger—often in the same scene. *The Tick* also boasted an impressive array of guest stars, including Roddy McDowall, Mark Hamill, Paul Williams, Bobcat Goldthwait, and Laraine Newman, all hamming it up as outlandish villains or absurd heroes.

The Tick remains one of the most quotable animated comedies ever produced, turning the title character's catchphrase "Spoon!" into a rallying cry for geeks throughout the 1990s. The series perfectly translated Edlund's humorous sensibilities to the screen thanks to hilarious dialogue and uproarious superhero satire. The title character routinely spouted lines like "Isn't sanity really just a one-trick pony anyway? I mean all you get is one trick, rational thinking, but when you're good and crazy, oooh, oooh, oooh, the sky is the limit" and "Deadly Bulb! I'm about to write you a reality check. Or would you prefer the cold, hard cash of truth?" Other characters also delivered amusingly bizarre zingers, such as evil alien warlord Thrakkorzog's declaration "Nature is one call you can't put on

Hapless hero the Tick (left) and his bumbling sidekick Arthur once again leap into battle against the forces of evil. *Fox/Photofest*

hold" or the Evil Midnight Bomber's outburst "So she says to me, do you wanna be a *bad* boy? And I say *yeah* baby *yeah*! Surf's up space ponies! I'm makin' gravy . . . without the lumps." In addition, the show featured outrageously silly situations, including Leonardo da Vinci kidnapping history's greatest inventors (S2E4) and an estranged Tick and Arthur reuniting to battle the villainous Blow-Hole, a giant whale wearing overalls (S2E1). With its wacky humor and super satire, *The Tick* was truly ahead of its time, and it endures thanks to a combination of madcap comedy, flamboyant characters, and over-the-top stories.

TRUE BLOOD (2008–2014)

Creator: Alan Ball
Cast: Anna Paquin (Sookie Stackhouse), Stephen Moyer (Bill Compton), Sam Trammell (Sam Merlotte), Ryan Kwanten (Jason Stackhouse), Chris Bauer (Andy Belle-fleur), Nathan Ellis (Lafayette Reynolds), Carrie Preston (Arlene Fowler), Rutina Wesley (Tara Thornton)
Genre: Drama, Fantasy, Mystery, Romance, Thriller

Synopsis

In a modern-day Louisiana where humans coexist with vampires, a telepathic waitress falls for a suave bloodsucker and together they set off on a series of sexy adventures.

Production History

Despite his indifference toward tales of the living dead, *Six Feet Under* creator Alan Ball read and enjoyed Charlaine Harris's vampire novel *Dead Until Dark*.[27] Midway through the second book in the series, he decided the story would make a good television series.[28] Ball contacted Harris, who informed him that a movie studio owned the rights to produce a film adaptation of the property.[29] Ball waited for the studio's option to run out, at which point he contacted Harris and convinced her to let him adapt *The Southern Vampire Mysteries* as a TV series.[30] Production began in 2005.[31] Initially producers considered Jessica Chastain and Benedict Cumberbatch for the lead roles of Sookie Stackhouse and Bill Compton[32] but the parts ultimately went to Anna Paquin and Stephen Moyer in 2007.[33] Ball wrote and directed the pilot episode,[34] which shot in Los Angeles during the summer of 2007.[35] Soon after, HBO picked up the series, which debuted on September 7, 2008.[36]

During the second season, *True Blood* averaged over 5 million viewers per episode,[37] making it HBO's "most popular series since 'The Sopranos' and 'Sex and the City.'"[38] At that point, the budget increased to $5 million per episode.[39]

HBO executives considered canceling the series, but a vocal fanbase helped keep *True Blood* alive despite the high costs.[40] Ball stepped down as showrunner before the start of the sixth season,[41] which saw a steep drop in the ratings. As such, HBO decided to end *True Blood* after the seventh season,[42] which consisted of just ten episodes. The series finale aired on August 24, 2014, but that same year Ball announced plans to produce a musical version of the show.[43] Later seasons offered diminishing returns, but *True Blood* nevertheless helped fuel the vampire craze that gave rise to *The Twilight Saga*, *The Vampire Diaries*, the *Dark Shadows* reboot, and more.[44]

Commentary

Over the course of seven steamy seasons, *True Blood* served up a heaping helping of sex and violence that delighted viewers who loved following the wild, lurid, and often melodramatic exploits of telepathic Southern waitress Sookie Stackhouse and her bloodsucking beau Bill Compton. Mixing Southern Gothic style with explicit nudity and gore, the show offered fans a complex exploration of female sexuality and desire as well as third-wave feminism and female agency.[45] As portrayed by Oscar-winning actress Anna Paquin, Sookie often stood up for herself and fought for her beliefs, whether confronting a dear friend or an angry vampire. In later seasons, a series of sensational plotlines and an increased focus on minor characters relegated Sookie to the sidelines,[46] leading some fans to express disappointment

Psychic waitress Sookie Stackhouse (Anna Paquin, right) embarks on sexy adventures in a Louisiana populated by vampires and other supernatural beings. *HBO/Photofest*

over her characterization,[47] but *True Blood* devotees (known affectionately as "Truebies") still revere the character and the show to this day.

The show also boasted a wealth of talent behind the scenes, with folks like Alexander Woo, Raelle Tucker, series creator Alan Ball, and author Charlaine Harris contributing scripts. Meanwhile, Michael Lehman, Scott Winant, Daniel Minahan, and other veteran directors all helmed multiple episodes of *True Blood*. As such, *True Blood* featured a mix of gripping stories, stylish visuals, wry humor, torrid sex scenes, and stomach-churning violence. Consider, for instance, the show's first episode, "Strange Love," in which Sookie meets Bill while various supernatural creatures struggle with their primal desires. In addition, while the series focused on a traditional heterosexual relationship—albeit one between a psychic and a vampire—it also featured a dozen queer characters, earning *True Blood* a GLAAD Media Award for Outstanding Drama Series in 2011.[48] The series regularly featured gay, lesbian, and bisexual characters like Sophie-Anne Leclerq (Evan Rachel Wood) and Eddie Gauthier (Stephen Root). Indeed, many critics observed that the series' portrayal of vampires served as an allegory for gay rights, as Ball originally conceived the vampires' struggle with announcing their presence as akin to LGBTQ individuals "coming out of the closet."[49] Though far from a perfect one-to-one comparison,[50] the blood, sex, and allegory all turned *True Blood* into an enduring cult hit that is sure to live on long after its demise.

See also *Buffy the Vampire Slayer* (1997–2003), *Charmed* (1998–2006), *Supernatural* (2005–2020)

THE TWILIGHT ZONE (1959–1964)

Creator: Rod Serling
Cast: Rod Serling (Narrator)
Genre: Science Fiction, Fantasy, Horror, Mystery, Thriller

Synopsis

Rod Serling hosts this anthology series known for its fantastical premises and twist endings.

Production History

After serving in World War II, Rod Serling embarked on a career in television as a writer. In the late 1950s, Serling regularly clashed with network bosses and advertisers over his scripts, which tackled socially relevant issues like civil rights, the Cold War, the Holocaust, and the nuclear arms race.[51] Corporate advertisers pressured networks to censor or change the scripts, and such interference frustrated Serling, who eventually decided to wrap his realistic themes in fantastic storylines.[52] He dusted off an old script called "The Time Element" and showed

During its run, *The Twilight Zone* served up fantastic tales that often featured twist endings as in the classic episode "To Serve Man" (S3E24). *CBS/Photofest*

it to executives at CBS, who purchased the script but left it on the shelf until Bert Granet, producer of *Westinghouse Desilu Playhouse*, picked it up for $10,000.[53] "The Time Element" aired on November 24, 1958, and proved so popular that CBS commissioned an anthology series under the title *The Twilight Zone*. In December 1958, the network spent $75,000 on the pilot episode "Where Is Everybody?"[54] CBS CEO William Paley greenlit the series, provided Serling wrote 80 percent of the scripts during the first season.[55]

The first episode of *The Twilight Zone* premiered on October 2, 1959.[56] Serling ultimately penned 92 of the 156 installments.[57] Critics loved the show, which earned low ratings throughout its run,[58] leaving it perpetually on the verge of cancelation.[59] While CBS executives kept *The Twilight Zone* alive because it brought them critical prestige, they also tried to make the show more cost-effective, first by switching from film to videotape and then by expanding the runtime from thirty minutes to an hour.[60] Unfortunately, these changes only eroded the show's quality and shrank its audience further.[61] For the final season, CBS returned *The Twilight Zone* to its original format[62] though network president Thomas Moore demanded more focus on science fiction and horror. He also tried to change the title to *Witches, Warlocks and Werewolves*, but Serling refused.[63] *The Twilight Zone* ended soon after and Serling moved on to other projects,[64] but his most famous creation lives on thanks to numerous adaptations and reboots.

Commentary

With the original version of *The Twilight Zone*, series creator and host Rod Serling brought what Mark Phillips and Frank Garcia call the "first adult, prime-time fantasy series"[65] to television, the most dominant medium of the twentieth century. The show marked the true emergence of science fiction as allegory on TV, offering stories that commented on all sorts of contemporary political, social, and cultural issues. As such, *The Twilight Zone* set the stage for all the thoughtful sci-fi shows that followed in its wake, laying the groundwork for speculative series like *The Outer Limits*, *Star Trek*, *The X-Files*, and *Black Mirror*. During its five-year run, *The Twilight Zone* tackled heavy topics like McCarthyism ("The Monsters Are Due on Maple Street," S1E22), religion ("The Obsolete Man," S2E29), war ("Deaths-Head Revisited," S3E9), death ("Nothing in the Dark," S3E16), and racism ("I Am the Night—Color Me Black," S5E26). While often censored by the network, *The Twilight Zone* served up plenty of provocative stories and shocking twists.

Yet *The Twilight Zone* also resonated with audiences of the time because Serling clearly conveyed his faith in humanity and created a strictly moral universe with clear distinctions between good and evil. Throughout the show, Serling expressed empathy for his characters, even those who landed in frightening situations due to their own immoral actions. He infused episodes like "The Night of the Meek" (S2E11) and "The Changing of the Guard" (S3E37) with a great deal of heart, and while critics sometimes dismiss such stories as preachy or maudlin, they still helped establish *The Twilight Zone* as one of the most compassionate sci-fi shows of all time. Of course the series is most remembered for its surprise endings, which often left viewers flabbergasted. From classic episodes like "Time Enough at Last" (S1E8) to "Eye of the Beholder" (S2E6), and from "The Midnight Sun" (S3E10) to the oft-parodied "To Serve Man" (S3E24), *The Twilight Zone* served up dozens of astonishing twists that helped earn the show a well-deserved spot in the pantheon of cult TV series. The thought-provoking subtext, big heart, and often bewildering finales all made *The Twilight Zone* a

SPOTLIGHT: ROD SERLING

Upon graduating from Antioch College in 1950, World War II veteran Rod Serling set out to make a living as a television writer. Over the next five years, Serling's scripts netted him critical praise and an Emmy Award.[66] In 1959, Serling created *The Twilight Zone*, a critically acclaimed anthology series that married social commentary with fantastic stories. That show ran until 1964, leaving Serling free to appear in commercials, game shows, and more. In 1968, Serling wrote the screenplay for 20th Century Fox's big-budget science fiction film *Planet of the Apes* though the studio hired blacklisted screenwriter Michael Wilson to rewrite Serling's script. Soon after, Serling developed *Night Gallery*, another anthology series that ran on NBC from 1970 to 1973.[67] Serling spent his final years believing he had failed to change the television industry.[68] He died in June 1975 while undergoing open-heart surgery.[69]

beloved cult series that left behind a long legacy of reboots and that continues to inspire storytellers even today.

See also *Are You Afraid of the Dark?* (1990–2000)

TWIN PEAKS (1990–1991)

Creators: David Lynch, Mark Frost
Cast: Kyle MacLachlan (Special Agent Dale Cooper), Richard Beymer (Benjamin Horne), Lara Flynn Boyle (Donna Hayward), Joan Chen (Josie Packard), Sherilyn Fenn (Audrey Horne), Piper Laurie (Catherine Martell), Peggy Lipton (Norma Jennings)
Genre: Drama, Mystery, Thriller

Synopsis

An FBI special agent arrives in Twin Peaks, Washington, to investigate the death of popular high school girl Laura Palmer.

Production History

In late 1988, David Lynch and Mark Frost met with ABC executives to pitch an idea for a new TV series titled *Northwest Passage*.[70] ABC snatched up the series and partnered with Propaganda Films to produce the pilot but allowed Lynch and Frost to retain ownership of the show.[71] Filming kicked off in February 1989 in the Snoqualmie Valley, thirty miles east of Seattle.[72] However, series composer Angelo Badalamenti pointed out that *Northwest Passage* was the title of a 1937 novel written by Kenneth Roberts, leading Lynch and Frost to change the show's name to *Twin Peaks*.[73] The two-hour pilot episode premiered on April 8, 1990, and drew nearly 35 million viewers, making it the highest-rated TV movie at that time.[74] Throughout the rest of the season, *Twin Peaks* gripped its audience with dream logic, horror, irony, and other elements never before seen within the same show.[75] However, viewership soon decreased to just the most loyal of fans.[76] The first season ended on a cliffhanger that left the central murder mystery unsolved, generating much discussion among critics and fans about "whodunnit."[77]

One month after the start of the show's first season, ABC commissioned a second season of twenty-two episodes.[78] At the same time the network moved the show to Saturday nights to "lure audiences back to Saturday night TV" but that strategy backfired.[79] ABC pulled the show on February 15, 1991, triggering a fan campaign to revive *Twin Peaks*.[80] The network briefly brought the series back in March but pulled the plug for good in June after airing a final two-hour special stitched together from the last two episodes.[81] Nevertheless, *Twin Peaks* lived on. In 1992, fans launched a magazine that ran for thirteen years.[82] The series also became a huge hit in Japan, prompting the Japan Travel Bureau to organize tours to

Dogged FBI agents Dale Cooper (Kyle MacLachlan, left) and Al Rosenfield (Miguel Ferrer) investigate the murder of popular teen Laura Palmer. *ABC/Photofest*

Snoqualmine Valley.[83] Lynch later directed the prequel film *Twin Peaks: Fire Walk with Me* (1992),[84] and in 2017 he produced a third season that aired on Showtime and featured an open ending.[85]

Commentary

With *Twin Peaks*, David Lynch, director of classic cult films like *Eraserhead* and *Blue Velvet*, brought his signature brand of weirdness to the small screen for the first time. In the process, he helped pioneer the sort of ambitious weekly storytelling that defines the so-called Golden Age of TV. He also confused and alienated most viewers while simultaneously inspiring intense devotion in a handful of others. With its twisty storylines, quirky characters, and ominous atmosphere, *Twin Peaks* served up an engrossing mystery that felt like nothing else on television at the time. The show mixed well-worn cop show clichés with a surreal weirdness that delighted fans even as it left other viewers scratching their heads. Each week *Twin Peaks* transported viewers to a picturesque Pacific Northwest town populated by an assortment of unforgettable oddballs including Special Agent Dale Cooper, Dr. Lawrence Jacoby (Russ Tamblyn), Bob (Frank Silva), and Margaret Lanterman (Catherine Coulson). The show also featured eerie dream sequences (such as when Agent Cooper visits the Red Room) and a sly sense of humor (consider MacLachlan's delivery of the line "This is, excuse me, a damn fine cup of coffee"). These elements made *Twin Peaks* a hit with fans of the unconventional.

Over the course of thirty episodes, *Twin Peaks* crafted an absorbing and totally unpredictable mystery narrative, making it essential viewing for folks seeking something a little bit different from everything else on TV at the time. The labyrinthine twists begin with the first episode as Agent Cooper arrives in the titular town and kicks off his investigation into the murder of popular high schooler Laura Palmer by interviewing the suspects, all eccentric, thereby establishing the series' tone. *Twin Peaks* remained grounded in more conventional storytelling until the eighth episode, at which point the show veered deeper into supernatural territory. This new direction culminated in the show's twenty-ninth episode (widely considered by fans as one of the best), which ratchets up the strangeness as Cooper travels to the infamous Black Lodge and meets the Man from Another Place in perhaps the most famous sequence of the series. Episodes like this helped establish *Twin Peaks* as one of the most daring shows to ever air on TV. Though short-lived, the series ushered in a new era of quirky primetime dramas and paved the way for other cinematic auteurs to dabble in broadcast television.[86] All this explains why *Twin Peaks* still resonates with fans decades after its cancelation.

See also *The X-Files* (1993–2018)

U

UPRIGHT CITIZENS BRIGADE (1998–2000)

Creators: Matt Besser, Amy Poehler, Ian Robert, Matt Walsh
Cast: Matt Besser (Agent Adair/Various), Amy Poehler (Agent Colby/Various), Ian
  Roberts (Agent Antoine/Various), Matt Walsh (Agent Trotter/Various), Del Close
  (Narrator)
Genre: Comedy

Synopsis

In this wacky sketch series, a group of oddball agents sow chaos throughout
the universe.

Production History

In the early 1990s, Matt Besser, Ian Roberts, Matt Walsh, and Amy Poehler
met while performing improv at Chicago's ImprovOlympics.[1] Together they
founded the Upright Citizens Brigade, developing an approach to sketches that
involved "getting the audience out of their chairs and out of their comfort zone."[2]
The troupe's name originated with the group seeking to counter a "fake big bad
corporation" they mentioned during an early stage show in Chicago.[3] In 1996,
the Upright Citizens Brigade relocated to New York City to perform improv and
develop a sketch show for television.[4] Thanks to their manager Dave Becky and
development executive Kent Alterman, the troupe secured a deal with Comedy
Central in 1998.[5] Alterman served as executive producer of the series through all
three seasons.[6]

Comedy Central scheduled the new series to air on Wednesday nights after their
successful new show *South Park*.[7] Mixing real-life pranks with filmed sketches,[8]
Upright Citizens Brigade drew on a form of improv, the "Harold," invented by the
group's mentor Del Close.[9] A long-form version of improv, the Harold presents
scenes in an episode as connected to each other. Each episode has a central theme,
the end of each episode circling back to the beginning,[10] and there is a scene bringing the episode's characters together in a location from one sketch in that episode.[11] Given the show's low budget, they often filmed on location around New
York City without permission and had to rely on rip-offs of famous songs because

they could not afford to pay for any real song's license.[12] The four core performers wrote most of the aired sketches and wrote the "Inner Sanctum" scenes for each episode last to capture the improv content of the sketches.[13]

The first episode premiered on August 19, 1998, and the show ran until April 3, 2000. During that time, the troupe experienced little censorship from Comedy Central[14] as the network gave them a great deal of creative freedom.[15] When *Upright Citizens Brigade* ended, fans pressured Comedy Central to release the series on DVD.[16] In 2015, the troupe launched a follow-up series, *The UCB Show*, on NBC Universal's short-lived comedy streaming service Seeso.[17]

Commentary

Filled with surreal skits, bizarre characters, and a completely over-the-top sense of humor, *Upright Citizens Brigade* irrevocably changed the comedy landscape despite lasting only three seasons of just thirty episodes. The series kick-started the careers of Matt Besser, Amy Poehler, Ian Roberts, and Matt Walsh, who went on to create or appear in other much-loved projects such as *Comedy Bang! Bang!* as well as *Parks and Recreation* and *Veep*. Spinning out of the group's live shows, *Upright Citizens Brigade* set itself apart from other sketch shows of the time thanks to its framing device in which a group of secretive agents monitor and create chaos throughout the universe. In each episode, the skits all connect to one another, featuring characters that appear and reappear throughout only to come together at the end. As such, *Upright Citizens Brigade* feels more cohesive than the average sketch comedy series even as it serves up dozens of wacky characters and outrageous situations in each installment (including a sex-obsessed psychic, a businessman with a hand shaped like a baby's head, and Mogomra the Giant Country Lobster). With its penchant for quirky comedy, the show cultivated a devoted audience of weirdos.

Upright Citizens Brigade delighted viewers with its nonsensical skits, weird storylines, and uproarious dialogue based on a credo of upsetting the way of things and the powers that be. In "Children's Revolution" (S1E5), the agents agree to help a child take revenge on a school bully and along the way they encounter a kid with an infuriating verbal condition. Meanwhile, "Master Dialection" (S2E1) follows the group as they introduce the concept of baby fighting to the suburbs and force a boxer to go ten rounds with a horse. The following episode, "Bomb Squad" (S2E2), sees two lazy bomb squad officers seize an illegal dildo bong from a laidback man who explains, "I made this bong out of a dildo I found. Its name is bonga-longa-dingdong." A few episodes later, in "Infested with Friars" (S2E6), the agents unleash a hoard of mutated comedians on a theme restaurant while a teenager fakes his own kidnapping to avoid curfew. "Virtual Reality" (S3E9) features one of the show's most hilariously disturbing moments as four NASA employees find themselves trapped in a lodge due to a snowstorm and admit shocking secrets to one another. Every episode of *Upright Citizens Brigade* featured such boundary-pushing humor, which explains why the show now enjoys a reputation as a cult classic sketch comedy series.

See also *Key & Peele* (2012–2015), *The Kids in the Hall* (1988–1994), *Mr. Show with Bob and David* (1995–1998), *The State* (1993–1995)

V

VERONICA MARS (2004–PRESENT)

Creator: Rob Thomas
Cast: Kristen Bell (Veronica Mars), Enrico Colantoni (Keith Mars), Percy Daggs III
  (Wallace Fennel), Jason Dohring (Logan Echolls), Francis Capra (Eli Navarro)
Genre: Drama, Mystery, Thriller

Synopsis

A teenage girl investigates mysteries in her home town.

Production History

Developed by young-adult author (and former high school teacher) Rob Thomas,[1] *Veronica Mars* started out as an untitled teen novel about a boy detective named Keith Mars.[2] Thomas had written for shows like the teen drama *Dawson's Creek* and *Cupid* (on which he also served as executive producer), and he decided to retool his idea into a spec script for a television series.[3] Thomas wanted to tell a longform story that combined teen issues, detective cases, melodrama, high concepts, and affable characters.[4] He took his idea to executives at UPN, who picked up the show despite initial uncertainty about some of the show's darker themes (for instance, the pilot episode deals with Veronica's rape).[5] The first episode of *Veronica Mars* premiered on September 22, 2004, earning critical praise and a legion of fans, including horror icon Stephen King and *Buffy the Vampire Slayer* creator Joss Whedon.[6] The show aired on UPN for two years before moving to the newly formed CW Network, where it ran for an additional year.[7]

Veronica Mars remained on the verge of cancelation throughout its run, prompting fans to mount campaigns to keep the show alive, including flying a plane towing a banner with the message "RENEW VERONICA MARS! CW 2006!" between UPN offices in Los Angeles and CW headquarters in Burbank.[8] Meanwhile, the announcement of the show's cancelation at the end of the third season inspired a "Bars for Mars" fan group to send more than two thousand Mars chocolate-bar wrappers to CW executives.[9] Despite these efforts, *Veronica Mars* ended its initial run on May 22, 2007. Thomas tried to revive the series by pitching an updated version with Mars joining the FBI but the CW was not interested.[10] In 2013, Thomas launched a highly successful Kickstarter campaign to fund a *Veronica Mars* movie that hit theaters in 2014,[11] and streaming giant Hulu released a fourth season of the show on July 19, 2019,[12] with a fifth season currently being considered by Hulu.[13]

Commentary

Noir and detective genres traditionally feature male leads: tough, no-nonsense gumshoes possessed of a quick wit, an itchy trigger finger, and an eye for the ladies. Such stories tend to relegate women to the sidelines, positioning them as femme fatales, mobster molls, or chaste victims. *Veronica Mars* upended these genre conventions by drawing on tales of women detectives like Nancy Drew, Miss Marple, and Jessica Fletcher. Yet those characters rarely led any sort of personal life outside their investigative work. In contrast, *Veronica Mars* portrayed the title character as a fully formed person whose relationships proved every bit as important as the mysteries she investigated.

Equal parts "noirish case-driven mystery show" and "teen coming-of-age melodrama set against a background of haves and have-nots,"[14] *Veronica Mars* revolved around a character identifiable to both teenagers and young adults alike. Each week, fans watched as Veronica tried to solve various mysteries, all while navigating her life at home and at school. Many fans developed a powerful emotional attachment to the character as evidenced by their numerous attempts to save the series from cancelation. After the series was canceled, fans remained active online through dedicated sites such as marsinvestigations.net and VeronicaMarsCW on MySpace

Plucky teen Veronica Mars (Kristen Bell, center) investigates mysteries in the fictional suburban neighborhood of Neptune, California. *The CW/Photofest*

as well as podcasts like Veronica Mars Fan on LastFM.[15] Their actions helped bring the series back for both a theatrical movie and a continuation.

The fans' attachment makes sense given that *Veronica Mars* started with a high school girl falling from grace and earning a reputation as a social outcast. While their exact experiences may differ, many teenagers deal with a similar social awkwardness. Although the main stories focused primarily on the mysteries, the show also featured an ordinary teenager dealing with the same issues and making the same snarky remarks as viewers of that age. Additionally, *Veronica Mars* dealt with complex issues like date rape, violence, and domestic abuse in a realistic fashion that respected the victims and their experiences. It is no wonder then that *Veronica Mars* developed such a devoted fanbase: the series never talked down to its young viewers, recognizing the struggles faced by teenagers while also celebrating their strengths. It remains to be seen if that fanbase will persist after the shocking end of season 4 and the desire by Rob Thomas to focus more on mystery and less on romance in any future episodes. But given the emotionally intense reaction to that cliffhanger, the series will undoubtedly be around for the foreseeable future.[16]

See also *Buffy the Vampire Slayer* (1997–2003), *Crazy Ex-Girlfriend* (2015–2019), *Gilmore Girls* (2000–2007)

W

THE WALKING DEAD (2010–PRESENT)

Creators: Frant Darabont, Angela Kang
Cast: Andrew Lincoln (Rick Grimes), Melissa McBridge (Carol Peletier), Norman Reedus (Daryl Dixon), Lauren Cohan (Maggie Greene), Danai Gurira (Michonne), Chandler Riggs (Carl Grimes)
Genre: Drama, Horror, Thriller

Synopsis

After the zombie apocalypse leaves the world in ruins, a ragtag group of survivors band together to face dangers posed by both the living and the living dead.

Production History

In October 2003, Image Comics launched writer Robert Kirkman's monthly zombie comic book *The Walking Dead* despite fears that the extreme gore might not appeal to readers.[1] The company's anxieties proved unfounded because comic fans turned the book—which appeared right at the start of an emergent zombie craze—into a massive hit.[2] Hollywood soon expressed interest in adapting the comic but Kirkman decided to wait for a better offer.[3] Three years later, writer and director Frank Darabont visited his local comic book store and picked up the first trade paperback collection of *The Walking Dead*. After reading it, Darabont approached Kirkman about adapting the property for television, and Kirkman agreed.[4] Darabont pitched the idea to various networks and NBC ordered a pilot script but network executives wanted the zombies removed from the story so Darabont took the project elsewhere.[5] Five years later, Darabont teamed with Gale Ann Hurd to produce *The Walking Dead*, and she brought it to executives at AMC.[6] The network snatched up the project, ordering six episodes based on the pilot script.[7]

AMC president Charlie Collier fully committed to *The Walking Dead* and gave the show time to tell its character-driven story. The network ran the ninety-minute pilot episode with limited commercials on October 31, 2010.[8] The episode drew 5.3 million viewers,[9] making it the highest-rated cable network debut of 2010.[10] Now nearly ten years after its premiere, *The Walking Dead* remains the highest-rated

Sheriff Rick Grimes (Andrew Lincoln, center) leads a group of desperate survivors through a post-apocalyptic landscape infested by flesh-hungry zombies. *AMC/Photofest*

show on cable despite a steep decline in viewers during the show's ninth season.[11] The series continues to dominate popular culture, spawning numerous ancillary products (including toys, T-shirts, board games, and cookbooks),[12] inspiring academic scholarship,[13] and generating two spinoff series.[14] In 2019, AMC announced a *Walking Dead* feature film.[15]

Commentary

Before *The Walking Dead*, zombies rarely appeared on television. After *The Walking Dead* emerged as one of the highest-rated cable series of all time, other networks sought to capitalize on the zombie craze with shows like *Z Nation*, *iZombie*, and *Kingdom*. The series not only capitalized on the zombie frenzy of the early twenty-first century, it also helped showrunners finally crack how to translate the living dead from the big screen to the boob tube. In the process, it additionally reinvigorated genre shows—especially horror series—by embracing the blood and gore of zombie movies like *Dawn of the Dead* and melding it with the smart, atmospheric horror needed to sustain regular viewership. Realism is required to produce the terrors normally associated with zombies, and *The Walking Dead* carefully constructed such realism in its zombies, characters, and situations.

Beyond crafting a well-done zombie story, the show's producers creatively used the different technologies of the period to maintain a loyal fanbase. For instance, in 2011 AMC debuted the innovative *Talking Dead*, a recap show that allowed fans to potentially interact with the show's cast and crew, thus giving them a reason to stay tuned to the network after the end credits rolled. At the same time AMC launched a web series to expand on the stories featured on the TV show. Meanwhile, the spinoff series *Fear the Walking Dead* premiered in 2015, fleshing out the zombie apocalypse with stories depicting events that happen concurrently in Los Angeles. Most recently, AMC announced a *Walking Dead* theatrical feature, at last bringing the series to the medium that started the zombie craze. *The Walking Dead* allowed the network to develop a transmedia story, one told across multiple formats and platforms. Creating such a story gave fans a chance to experience more of what they loved and allowed producers to more fully capitalize on and profit from that fandom. The success of *The Walking Dead* prompted numerous other television shows to experiment with such transmedia productions but few achieved the popularity of Kirkman's epic, terrifying tale of the living dead.

See also *Supernatural* (2005–2020)

THE WIRE (2002–2008)

Creators: David Simon, Ed Burns
Cast: Dominic West (James McNulty), Wendell Pierce (William "Bunk" Moreland), Lance Reddick (Cedric Daniels), John Doman (William Rawls), Deirdre Lovejoy (Rhonda Pearlman), Sonja Sohn (Shakima Greggs), Seth Gilliam (Ellis Carver), Domenick Lombardozzi (Thomas "Herc" Hauk), Clarke Peters (Lester Freamon), Andre Royo (Reginald "Bubbles" Cousins), Michael Kenneth Williams (Omar Little), Idris Elba (Russell "Stringer" Bell)
Genre: Drama; Thriller

Synopsis

Intersecting stories of drug dealers and law enforcement officers reveal a struggle to maintain law and order in Baltimore and the slow decay of the city's social institutions.

Production History

In the mid-1990s, David Simon, a former crime reporter for the *Baltimore Sun* who contributed scripts to the fast-paced cop drama *Homicide: Life on the Streets*,[16] teamed with Baltimore police detective Ed Burns to write a script about the gritty reality of the drug trade.[17] They spent the next three years developing *The Corner*, a powerful miniseries that aired on HBO in 1997 and won a handful of Emmy Awards the next year.[18] Following the cancellation of *Homicide* in 1999, Simon and Burns decided to tackle the cop genre with *The Wire*, a realistic police procedural based on their own experiences.[19] Thanks to the success of *The Corner*, HBO

Detectives James McNulty (Dominic West, left) and William "Bunk" Moreland (Wendell Pierce) navigate government bureaucracy while trying to clean up the streets of Baltimore. *HBO/Photofest*

wanted to work with the duo again,[20] but network executives remained skeptical about a new cop show designed specifically to challenge the genre.[21] After spending a year revising their pilot script, Simon and Burns finally convinced HBO's programming executives to take a chance on *The Wire*.[22]

The network ordered a thirteen-episode season, with production beginning in November 2001.[23] Simon and Burns opted to shoot the series in Baltimore for the purposes of authenticity.[24] Meanwhile, casting director Alexa Fogel assembled a cast of stage actors, musicians, and novice performers, including some of the cops, gangsters, and politicians who inspired certain characters. *The Wire* also broke ground because it featured more African Americans in central roles than any other show on TV at the time.[25] Given the complexity of the narrative, HBO executives remained apprehensive about the show and refused to screen the first five episodes for TV critics ahead of the series premiere on June 2, 2002.[26] Their fears proved unfounded as the show received rave reviews.[27] *The Wire* earned solid ratings, enough for HBO to order a second season that drew more viewers and additional critical appraise.[28] Ratings dropped during the show's third season, though season 4 did well enough to justify a fifth and final season.[29] These days, many critics consider *The Wire* the best TV show ever made.[30]

Commentary

Throughout its acclaimed run, *The Wire* told gripping stories about the devastating effects of things like institutional bias and systemic power structures and did so with hard-hitting, unflinching realism. The show served up some of the most profound social, cultural, and political commentary in the history of television, taking viewers deep inside Baltimore's social system to expose the failures of cultural institutions such as government, the media, education, capitalism, labor, and the criminal justice system. *The Wire* deconstructed the police procedural genre, turning it completely on its head to offer viewers a fresh look at inner-city life that provided unprecedented insight into the experiences of both cops and criminals. The show went far beyond the stories covered on the evening news to explore the various ways that criminals avoid the police and manipulate the rule of law for their own ends, and how the cops in turn circumvent both legal and budgetary restraints. In addition, *The Wire* struck the perfect balance between cheeky humor and gritty drama thanks to powerful teleplays written by the likes of Dennis Lehane, George Pelecanos, Richard Price, and series co-creators David Simon and Ed Burns. The show also boasted captivating performances from an incredible ensemble cast that included Dominic West, Wendell Pierce, Lance Reddick, and slam-poet-turned-actress Sonja Sohn. *The Wire* had all the elements of a classic cop drama but used them in such a way that it emerged as one of the medium's true modern masterpieces.

Throughout its sixty episodes, *The Wire* proved extremely transgressive as it routinely challenged the tropes of a well-worn genre and pushed the envelope in terms of storytelling and how it treated its nearly sixty main or minor characters. Critics Allan Sepinwall and Matt Zoller Seitz note that "*The Wire* grants abundant humanity to all but the most minor characters, insisting that they were all connected, and that the only thing stopping them from walking in one another's shoes is a simple twist of fate."[31] They go on to explain that "both sides of the conflict [between cops and criminals] are shown to be prisoners of a system interested only in perpetuating itself, a grim farce in which idiocy becomes policy because that's how life works."[32] Indeed, while many viewers consider James McNulty the show's central protagonist, the show is actually about Baltimore itself. The city becomes the central character in each of the show's five seasons, which all explore different aspects of the crumbling metropolis and reveal how it is changing for better and for worse. Regardless of its focus, *The Wire* served up riveting tales about cops, criminals, and the demise of American public institutions, earning it a devoted cult audience and a richly deserved reputation as perhaps the greatest TV show of all time.

X

THE X-FILES (1993–2018)

Creator: Chris Carter
Cast: David Duchovny (Fox Mulder), Gillian Anderson (Dana Scully), William B.
Davis (Smoking Man), Mitch Pileggi (Walter Skinner, 1994–2008), Tom Braidwood
(Melvin Frohike, 1994–2018), Bruce Harwood (John Fitzgerald Byers, 1994–2018),
Dean Haglund (Richard Langly, 1994–2018), Nicholas Lea (Alex Krycek, 1994–
2002), Robert Patrick (John Doggett 2000–2002), Annabeth Gish (Monica Reyes,
2001–2018)
Genre: Drama, Mystery, Science Fiction, Thriller

Synopsis

Two intrepid FBI agents investigate paranormal events and government conspiracies while shadowy figures seek to keep them in the dark or put them in the grave.

Production History

When Peter Roth became president of Fox television production in 1992, he hired Chris Carter, along with other writers and producers, to develop new material for the network.[1] However, Robert Greenblatt, then Fox executive vice-president for primetime programming, was reluctant to develop Carter's new pitch for *The X-Files*. Carter persisted, further developing the initial idea with a twenty-page outline that changed Greenblatt's mind.[2] Once the series was greenlit, production began in Vancouver. Wanting to make the show as scary and upsetting as he could within the limits of broadcast television,[3] Carter drew inspiration from shows like *Kolchak: The Night Stalker*, *The Twilight Zone*, and *The Avengers*.[4] David Duchovny and Gillian Anderson were cast without reading together, but luckily their chemistry emerged in the network reading for the pilot.[5] Fox ordered thirteen episodes after seeing a rough cut of the pilot,[6] and *The X-Files* premiered on Friday, September 10, 1993.

Despite being given a dead-zone slot on Friday nights, *The X-Files* found viewers, who in turn became highly devoted and motivated fans. The emergence of the World Wide Web helped these fans (known as "X-Philes") find one another and share information about the series. Once Fox saw this loyal fandom grow, they ordered more episodes. In 1996, Fox moved the series to a more favorable Sunday-night slot, and ratings improved to about 20 million viewers each week, placing the show in the top 20 for all broadcast series airing at the time.[7] In the summer of 1998, a movie was released to bridge seasons 5 and 6, and its success prompted Fox to bring the production to Los Angeles.[8]

Unfortunately, this move to Los Angeles changed the look of the series, and the hectic pace of creating feature-quality episodes began to wear on both cast and crew. Citing creative fatigue because filming one season required ten months, Duchovny left after season 8.[9] At the same time, he filed a lawsuit over the syndication profits of the series, claiming that Fox undervalued *The X-Files* when selling the syndication rights to FX, a 20th Century Fox cable network.[10] Anderson remained on the series for the ninth season, joined by Robert Patrick and Annabeth Gish as new FBI agents. However, without the chemistry of Mulder and Scully, the show suffered, and Fox canceled it after that season. Mulder and Scully reunited in the final episode and then returned in the subsequent 2008 film and rebooted limited series of 2016 and 2018.

Commentary

A lot has been written about *The X-Files* since it debuted in 1993. The show's serial nature and focus on mythology and world-building paved the way for similar shows like *Buffy the Vampire Slayer* and *Lost*. The portrayal of Dana Scully as an equal

Courageous FBI agents Fox Mulder (David Duchovny, left) and Dana Scully (Gillian Anderson) investigate yet another creepy, paranormal mystery. *Fox Broadcasting/Photofest*

partner, medical doctor, and FBI agent to Fox Mulder helped develop the television model of a strong female character that reflected and shaped 1990s third-wave feminism. The series' popularity also cemented Fox Network as the fourth commercial broadcast channel in the United States (the network had been on the air eight years before *The X-Files* helped distinguish it from ABC, CBS, and NBC). Many television creators emerged from the show, including Howard Gordon and Alex Gansa (*24, Homeland*), Vince Gilligan (*Breaking Bad*), Tim Minear and James Wong (*American Horror Story*), and Frank Spotnitz (*The Man in the High Castle*).

The X-Files worked because it was different from everything else on broadcast television. The seriality, characters, and feature-film-quality production and tone all distinguished it from its competition. The series also tapped into the cultural and social zeitgeist of the time by making the government the enemy and embracing, even encouraging, conspiracy theories. The American public grew increasingly wary of the federal government after Watergate, and they were willing to believe that the government could hide even the most significant information, such as the existence of extraterrestrials. Indeed, the 1998 film illustrated this unease because it directly referenced the 1995 Oklahoma City bombing by anti-government, right-wing terrorists Timothy McVeigh and Terry Nichols. The show tapped into and exploited this unease up until the terror attacks of September 11, 2001, which (for a time) rekindled people's trust in the government.[11]

The emergence of the World Wide Web helped foment this unease as people increasingly shared fake news and conspiracy theories (which continued through social media). The Web, however, played another big role in the series' impact by contributing to the development of Internet fandom and fan practices that have only intensified since the series' release. Across the burgeoning Web, fans gathered in chatrooms, discussion boards, and forums to discuss and dissect episodes, share information or spoilers about upcoming episodes, and engage in fan theories about the show. Journalists and scholars alike studied *X-Files* fan communities like the David Duchovny Estrogen Brigade to understand audiences, and even the show's producers engaged with the groups to understand how well they were doing. Thus *The X-Files* is arguably the first series to develop a large, highly devout online fan-

SPOTLIGHT: CHRIS CARTER

Born October 13, 1957, in California, Chris Carter decided to make movies after watching *Raiders of the Lost Ark* six times in six days.[12] He graduated from California State University at Long Beach with a degree in journalism and then wrote and edited for *Surfing* magazine before landing a gig at Walt Disney Studios in 1985. While with Disney, Carter wrote for *The Disney Sunday Movie* but decided he wanted to produce instead. After working for NBC, Carter approached executives at Fox about producing a TV show, which eventually became *The X-Files*. That series became a cult hit, allowing Carter to create the thematically similar shows *Millennium* (1996–1999), *Harsh Realm* (1999–2000), and *The X-Files* spin-off *The Lone Gunmen* (2001). Carter also directed the feature film *The X-Files: I Want to Believe* (2008) before reviving the show for two limited series in 2016 and 2018. Carter has produced other series but none performed as well as those he created for Fox.

base that served to define the nature of fandom, thereby shaping perceptions about fans and the relationship between Hollywood and fans for decades to come.

See also *Lost* (2004–2010), *Supernatural* (2005–2020)

XENA: WARRIOR PRINCESS (1995–2001)

Creators: Sam Raimi, John Schulian, R. J. Stewart
Cast: Lucy Lawless (Xena), Renée O'Connor (Gabrielle), Ted Raimi (Joxer), Kevin Smith (Ares)
Genre: Action, Comedy, Drama, Fantasy

Synopsis

A warrior princess with a tortured past seeks to redeem herself by fighting corrupt warlords and evil gods in the ancient world.

Production History

After scoring a hit with the syndicated action series *Hercules: The Legendary Journeys*, producers Sam Raimi and Robert Tapert turned their attention to developing the spinoff show *Xena: Warrior Princess*. Like its predecessor, *Xena* would be shot in New Zealand, helping build that country's film industry.[13] For the title role, Raimi and Tapert originally cast British actress Vanessa Angel, star of the television adaptation of the John Hughes cult classic *Weird Science*.[14] However, Angel fell ill right before she was scheduled to arrive on set[15] so Tapert considered four other actresses before settling on the then-unknown actress Lucy Lawless, who had appeared in *Hercules* as two different characters.[16] Similarly, Raimi and Tapert wanted Sunny Doench as Gabrielle but she refused to leave her partner in the United States, so the role went to Renee O'Connor.[17] In 1994, Xena debuted on *Hercules* because Tapert wanted a dark figure to counter the more lighthearted title character,[18] and this first appearance served as Lawless's breakthrough role.[19] Tapert originally wanted to kill Xena after three episodes but producers liked the character enough to remodel the planned spinoff series for her,[20] turning her into a former villain seeking redemption.[21]

Xena debuted as part of Universal Television's syndicated Action Pack block of programming on September 4, 1995.[22] Critics dismissed the show as either campy nonsense aimed at children or a lesbian fantasy romp,[23] but viewers turned it into an instant hit.[24] *Xena* developed one of the earliest online fandoms as cast and crew sometimes participated in online *Xena* discussion boards,[25] and producers even hired fanfic writer Melissa Good to write two episodes.[26] *Xena* also resonated with queer viewers, who turned the title character into an LGBT icon[27] even as the show's queer subtext vexed Universal executives.[28] *Xena* ended in 2001 after six seasons, coinciding with the apparent demise of syndicated original programming as networks discovered it was cheaper to produce their own content.[29]

Xena (Lucy Lawless) prepares to once again jump into battle against the forces of evil. *Universal TV/Photofest*

In 2009, Tapert quashed rumors about a *Xena* film, explaining that legal issues prevented such a project.[30] Six years later, NBC tapped Javier Grillo-Marxuach to helm a reboot without Lawless,[31] but Grillo-Marxuach left the project in April 2017 due to creative differences (he wanted to fully explore the lesbian subtext).[32]

Commentary

Xena: Warrior Princess offered viewers progressive messages of female empowerment wrapped in a goofy, sexy, low-budget action series that also served up heaping helpings of drama and pathos. The show, which *Buffy the Vampire Slayer* creator Joss Whedon called a trailblazer,[33] revolved around a smart, charismatic, and altogether capable woman, which explains why it resonated with girls and young women. Throughout *Xena*'s six seasons, the title character repeatedly demonstrated her fierce independence while appearing strong and feminine, sexy and mighty, dirty and beautiful, vulnerable and tough all at once, thereby sending a powerful message to viewers of all sexes. *Xena* also featured numerous other strong female characters, starting with Xena's sidekick Gabrielle, and the series never once questioned their abilities or their gender. The series thereby normalized such inspiring portrayals and helped pave the way for other "girl power" series like *Buffy*, *Charmed*, and *Dark Angel*.

Xena featured the sort of silly-but-thrilling action that defined producer Sam Raimi's early movies, with Xena and Gabrielle engaging in exciting action scenes marked by kinetic camera work (which also helped hide the fact that famed New Zealand stuntwoman Zoë Bell doubled for Lucy Lawless during the more rigorous stunts). The duo battled hordes of bad guys while tossing off groan-inducing one-liners, often alongside frequent guest stars like Ted Raimi (as Xena's other sidekick, the hapless Joxer) and Bruce Campbell (playing the dashing but cowardly King of Thieves, Autolycus).

Yet the show also often exploited the leads' beauty and chemistry. As Xena, Lawless swaggered across the screen with a tough sexiness that contrasted nicely with the sweet girl-next-door attractiveness of Gabrielle. As such, the two lead actresses frequently found themselves in sexually charged situations, usually while scantily clad. In addition, the show frequently capitalized on the sexual tension between Xena and Gabrielle and used it to fuel viewers' more salacious fantasies. Nonetheless, Xena never undermined the lead characters' competence, thus striking the perfect balance between exploitation and empowerment. Though initially dismissed as silly nonsense by many critics, *Xena* is now considered a pioneering show about strong women navigating a male-dominated society.

SPOTLIGHT: SAM RAIMI AND ROB TAPERT

Robert Gerard Tapert was born on May 14, 1955, in Royal Oak, Michigan, and four years later, on October 23, so was Samuel Marshall Raimi. Raimi grew up with an 8 mm movie camera and a desire to make movies,[34] but it was not until Tapert attended Michigan State University that he met Raimi and Bruce Campbell through Ivan Raimi, Tapert's roommate and Samuel Raimi's older brother.[35] Since then, Tapert and Raimi have been partners in television and film production, beginning with *The Evil Dead* in 1983, which Raimi also directed. While they often worked together on movies like *Darkman*, *A Simple Plan*, *The Gift*, and *Drag Me to Hell*, they also have worked individually on various projects such as Raimi directing three Spider-Man movies and Tapert producing television series *American Gothic*. In 2002, Tapert and Raimi founded Ghost House Pictures to produce horror movies like *The Grudge*, *The Possession*, and *Crawl*.[36]

Y

THE YOUNG ONES (1982–1984)

Creators: Ben Elton, Rik Mayall, Lise Mayer
Cast: Adrian Edmondson (Vyvyan), Rik Mayall (Rick), Nigel Planer (Neil), Christopher Ryan (Mike), Alexei Sayle (The Balowski Family)
Genre: Comedy

Synopsis

Four very different college students living in a ramshackle London flat embark on a series of surreal adventures.

Production History

Upon graduating from Manchester University,[1] Rik Mayall and Adrian Edmondson landed jobs at the Comedy Store, the center of London's alternative comedy scene, where they performed as a double act under the name 20th Century Coyote.[2] While there, they met Alexei Sayle, the club's leftist MC,[3] and Nigel Planer and Peter Richardson, another double-act known as the Outer Limits.[4] Soon after, they all set out and founded a rival club, the Comic Strip, and established a reputation as some of the funniest comics in England.[5] They soon caught the attention of executives at Channel 4, who gave the upstart comics their own six-episode series called *The Comic Strip Presents . . .*, which debuted on November 2, 1982.[6] Meanwhile, the BBC also approached the group about starring in a more traditional sitcom.[7] That show, based on a concept created by Mayall, his then-girlfriend Lise Mayer, and Ben Elton, a former college friend embarking on a standup career, premiered on November 16, 1982, under the title *The Young Ones* but without the involvement of Richardson, who clashed with BBC producer Paul Jackson and exited the series before filming.[8] Stage actor Christopher Ryan stepped in to fill Richardson's role.

Most of the performers played characters developed for their stage acts:[9] Mayall as Rick, an unhinged poet and political agitator who inexplicably loves Cliff Richard; Planer as Neil, a down-on-his-luck pacifist hippie; Edmonson as violent punk rocker Vyvyan; and Sayle as various supporting characters including every member of the Balowski family, a clan of Russian hucksters and eccentrics. Ryan, meanwhile, landed the role of Mike, the resident straight man and the only character created

234

exclusively for the show.[10] Originally the BBC wanted a more conventional sitcom,[11] but the performers included live musical performances to change the program's classification from "comedy" to "variety" and therefore secure a bigger budget.[12] *The Young Ones* left most critics confused, with some calling it the worst show on TV. Young viewers, however, loved it, and many used the newly released VCR technology to record episodes and re-watch them.[13] The show ran on BBC2 for two seasons, airing a total of twelve episodes between 1982 and 1984.[14] In 1985, struggling music video network MTV aired *The Young Ones* in the United States, earning huge ratings that prompted executives to acquire the rights to *The Comic Strip Presents . . .*[15] The core cast created or starred in other beloved shows in the years after, but *The Young Ones* remains their biggest hit around the world.

Commentary

The Young Ones offered absurdism with a dark edge, balancing outrageous toilet humor and reactionary left-wing politics. The show successfully married the anarchic spirit of punk rock with the nonsensical humor of *Monty Python's Flying Circus*, thereby appealing to disenfranchised viewers living through the Reagan and Thatcher administrations. The series offered a radical alternative to the stale sitcoms of the era, presenting audiences on both sides of the Atlantic with a wildly different type of chaotic humor. Indeed, *The Young Ones* often veered off on weird and unexpected tangents, such as Mike discovering Buddy Holly, alive and subsisting on English beetles, dangling upside-down from his bedroom ceiling, or Neil getting so high that he floats to the moon and meets a pair of snarky aliens. Even more bizarre, a mysterious figure lurks in the background of every single episode, and fans now consider him the boys' unofficial fifth roommate.[16] Needless to say, *The Young Ones* is a weird show.

The series succeeds largely on the strength of its cast, who deliver completely unhinged performances throughout. Rik Mayall plays Rick with wide-eyed, madcap abandon, screeching out lines like "Vyvyan's baby will be a pauper. Oliver Twist! Jeffrey Dickens! Back to Victorian values! I hope you're satisfied, Thatcher!" at the top of his lungs (S2E2, "Cash"). Meanwhile, Adrian Edmondson delivers a balls-to-the-wall performance as Vyvyan, a punk rocker who sports a wild orange fauxhawk and often uses his own body as a battering ram. As hippie peacenik Neil, Nigel Planer delivers his lines in a morose drawl, muttering things like "I won't say anything 'cause no one ever listens to me, anyway. I might as well be a Leonard Cohen album" (S1E5, "Interesting"). Rounding out the regular cast, Christopher Ryan imbues Mike with oily charm as he tries to bed every woman on the show, while Alexei Sayle delights as the Balowski family, a clan of oddball communists who enjoy tormenting the boys. The show also featured numerous guest stars and musical acts, including Stephen Fry, Hugh Laurie, Dawn French, Jennifer Saunders, Robbie Coltrane, Emma Thompson, Madness, Dexy's Midnight Runners, the Damned, and Motörhead. More than a typical sitcom, *The Young Ones* set a new standard for surreal, gross-out humor that remains unmatched to this day.

See also *Absolutely Fabulous* (1992–2012), *The Black Adder* (1982–1983)

Notes

INTRODUCTION

1. Sara Gwenllian-Jones and Roberta E. Pearson, "Introduction," in *Cult Television*, ed. Sara Gwenllian-Jones and Roberta A. Pearson, xii (Minneapolis: University of Minnesota Press, 2004).

2. Mark Jancovich and Nathan Hunt, "The Mainstream, Distinction, and Cult TV," in Gwenllian-Jones and Pearson, *Cult Television*, 28; David Lavery, "Introduction: How Cult TV Became Mainstream," in *The Essential Cult TV Reader*, ed. David Lavery, 2 (Lexington: University Press of Kentucky, 2010).

3. Stacey Abbott, "Introduction: 'Never Give Up—Never Surrender!' The Resilience of Cult Television," in *The Cult TV Book: From* Star Trek *to* Dexter, *New Approaches to TV Outside the Box*, ed. Stacey Abbot, 2 (New York: Soft Skull Press, 2010).

4. Ibid., 1.

5. Jancovich and Hunt, "The Mainstream, Distinction, and Cult TV," 27; Roberta Pearson, "Observations on Cult Television," in Abbott, *The Cult TV Book*, 8.

6. Abbott, "Introduction: 'Never Give Up—Never Surrender!'" 3.

7. Ibid., xii.

8. Ibid., xvi.

9. Gwenllian-Jones and Pearson, "Introduction," ix.

10. Sergio Angelini and Miles Booy, "Members Only: Cult TV from Margins to Mainstream," in Abbott, *The Cult TV Book*, 21.

11. Gwenllian-Jones and Pearson, "Introduction," xiii.

12. Ibid., xiii.

13. Ibid., ix.

14. Abbott, "Introduction: 'Never Give Up—Never Surrender!'" 2.

15. Angelini and Booy, "Members Only," 19.

16. Stacy Abbot, "Innovative TV," in Abbott, *The Cult TV Book*, 91.

17. Matt Hills, "Mainstream Cult," in Abbott, *The Cult TV Book*, 67.

18. Abbot, "Innovative TV," 98.

A

1. Emine Saner, "'Being Silly Is What They Do Best': The Return of French and Saunders," *Guardian*, December 23, 2017, www.theguardian.com/tv-and-radio/2017/dec/23/being-silly-is-what-they-do-best-the-return-of-french-and-saunders.

2. Ibid.

3. Angelina I. Karpovich, "Absolutely Fabulous," in *The Essential Cult TV Reader*, ed. David Lavery, 7–14 (Lexington: University Press of Kentucky, 2010).

4. Rebecca Hawkes, "Dawn French on Her Jealousy towards Jennifer Saunders after *Ab Fab*—And Why She Said No to Kissing Harry Styles," *Telegraph*, March 7, 2017, www .telegraph.co.uk/comedy/what-to-see/dawn-french-jealousy-towards-jennifer-saunders -ab-fab-said.

5. Clare Thorp, "Seven Facts You Never Knew about *Absolutely Fabulous*," *Telegraph*, June 8, 2016, www.telegraph.co.uk/films/absolutely-fabulous/seven-facts-only-super fans-know.

6. Jenna Sauers, "Meet the Real-Life Edina Monsoon from *Absolutely Fabulous*," Jeze-bel, December 21, 2011, https://jezebel.com/meet-the-real-life-edina-monsoon-from-abso lutely-fabulo-5870062.

7. Joanna Hunkin, "The Real-Life Inspiration behind *Absolutely Fabulous*' Patsy Stone," *NZ Herald*, January 1, 2017, www.nzherald.co.nz/entertainment/news/article.cfm.

8. Jeff Kaye, "'Absolutely Fabulous': Absolute Fright for the States?" *Los Angeles Times*, July 23, 1994, www.latimes.com/archives/la-xpm-1994-07-23-ca-19004-story.html.

9. Ibid.

10. Garry Berman, *Best of the Britcoms: From* Fawlty Towers *to* The Office (New York: Taylor Trade, 2011), 104.

11. Kaye, "'Absolutely Fabulous.'"

12. Beth Kleid, "Cheers, Sweeties," *Los Angeles Times*, June 11, 1995, www.latimes.com/ archives/la-xpm-1995-06-11-tv-11764-story.html.

13. Tanner Stransky, "Kristen Johnston: The Scoop on Her 'Absolutely Fabulous' Return to TV," *Entertainment Weekly*, January 31, 2009, https://ew.com/article/2009/01/31/ absolutley-fabu.

14. Berman, *Best of the Britcoms*, 105.

15. Ibid.

16. Guy Lodge, "Film Review: 'Absolutely Fabulous: The Movie,'" *Variety*, June 29, 2016, https://variety.com/2016/film/reviews/absolutely-fabulous-the-movie-re view-1201805735.

17. Huw Fullerton, "Jennifer Saunders Says There'll Be No More *Absolutely Fabulous*: 'That. Is. It.'" *Radio Times*, November 29, 2016, www.radiotimes.com/news/2016-11-29/ jennifer-saunders-says-therell-be-no-more-absolutely-fabulous-that-is-it.

18. Paul Flynn, "Why *Absolutely Fabulous* Now Looks Absolutely Prescient," *Guard-ian*, August 29, 2011, www.theguardian.com/commentisfree/2011/aug/29/absolutely -fabulous-prescient-ab-fab.

19. Lodge, "Film Review: 'Absolutely Fabulous: The Movie.'"

20. James Welsh, "'Ab Fab' Stars Receive GLBT Pride Award," Digital Spy, June 27, 2002, www.digitalspy.com/tv/ustv/a7694/ab-fab-stars-receive-glbt-pride-award.

21. Hannah Hamad, "Saunders, Jennifer (1958)," BFI Screenonline, 2014, www.screen online.org.uk/people/id/499531/index.html.

22. Angelina Karpovich, "Absolutely Fabulous," in Lavery, *The Essential Cult TV Reader*, 7.

23. Berman, *Best of the Britcoms*, 103.

24. Jason Krell, "How Pendleton Ward and His Friends Created a New Era of Cartoons," Gizmodo, April 18, 2014, https://gizmodo.com/how-pendleton-ward-and-his-friends -created-a-new-era-of-1564883809.

25. Ibid.

26. Ibid.

27. Chris McDonnell, *Adventure Time: The Art of Ooo* (New York: Abrams Books, 2014), 24.

28. Ibid., 25.

29. Ibid., 32.

30. Eric Kohn, "'Adventure Time' Is Slowly Going Off the Air, and Everyone's Moving On," IndieWire, February 24, 2017, www.indiewire.com/2017/02/adventure-time-ending -cartoon-network-1201785332.

31. Ibid.

32. Ibid.

33. Bill Bradley, "8 Facts You Didn't Know about 'Adventure Time,' Even If You Were Born in Ooo," HuffPost, October 27, 2017, www.huffingtonpost.com/2014/10/27/adven ture-time-facts_n_6030432.html.

34. Ibid.

35. Kohn, "'Adventure Time' Is Slowly Going Off the Air."

36. Mathew Klickstein, "The Adventures of *The Adventures of Pete & Pete*," Vulture, February 20, 2012, https://www.vulture.com/2012/02/the-adventures-of-the-adventures-of -pete-pete.html.

37. Marah Eakin, "Exploring *The Adventures of Pete & Pete*'s Genesis and Highlights (Part 1 of 4)," AV Club, July 3, 2012, https://tv.avclub.com/exploring-the-adventures-of-pete -and-pete-s-genesis-and-1798232246.

38. Ibid.

39. Seb Patrick, "Why *The Adventures of Pete & Pete* Is a '90s Nickelodeon Classic," Den of Geek! August 23, 2016, www.denofgeek.com/us/257987/the-adventures-of-pete-and -pete-a-90s-nickelodeon-classic.

40. Ibid.

41. Marah Eakin, "Inside *The Adventures of Pete & Pete* Reunion," AV Club, March 2, 2012, https://tv.avclub.com/inside-the-adventures-of-pete-and-pete-reunion-1798230198.

42. Patrick, "Why *The Adventures of Pete & Pete*."

43. Klickstein, "The Adventures of *The Adventures of Pete & Pete*."

44. Ibid.

45. Ibid.

46. Eakin, "Inside *The Adventures of Pete & Pete*.

47. Steve Weintraub, "Aqua Teen Hunger Force Interviews," Collider, April 11, 2007, http://collider.com/aqua-teen-hunger-force-interviews.

48. Blake Butler, "'Aqua Teen Hunger Force Forever' Is the End of an Era, but Its Creators Didn't Want It to End," Vice, June 24, 2015, www.vice.com/en_us/article/zngnja/ aqua-teen-hunger-force-forever-is-the-end-of-an-era-111.

49. Philip Stamato, "Saying Goodbye to 'Aqua Teen Hunger Force' with Co-creator Dave Willis," Vulture, July 22, 2015, www.vulture.com/2015/07/saying-goodbye-to-aqua -teen-hunger-force-with-co-creator-dave-willis.html.

50. Tegan O'Neil, "The End of *Aqua Teen Hunger Force* Marks the End of an Era for TV Animation," AV Club, September 1, 2015, https://tv.avclub.com/the-end-of-aqua-teen -hunger-force-marks-the-end-of-an-e-1798283745.

51. Garrett Martin, "The Life and Death of *Aqua Teen Hunger Force*," *Paste Magazine*, July 17, 2015, www.pastemagazine.com/articles/2015/06/aqua-teen-hunger-force-forever.html.

52. Ibid.

53. O'Neil, "The End of *Aqua Teen Hunger Force*."

54. Martin, "The Life and Death of *Aqua Teen Hunger Force*."

55. Ibid.

56. O'Neil, "The End of *Aqua Teen Hunger Force*."

57. Ashley Burns and Chloe Schildhause, "The Creators of 'Aqua Teen Hunger Force' Reflect on the Show's 13-Season Run," Uproxx, August 26, 2015, https://uproxx.com/tv/ aqua-teen-hunger-force-series-finale-creators-interview/2.

58. O'Neil, "The End of *Aqua Teen Hunger Force*."

59. Kevin Slane, "Looking Back at the Boston Mooninite Panic, 10 Years Later," Boston.com, January 31, 2017, www.boston.com/news/local-news/2017/01/31/looking-back-at-the-boston-mooninite-panic-10-years-later.

60. Stamato, "Saying Goodbye to 'Aqua Teen Hunger Force.'"

61. Martin, "The Life and Death of *Aqua Teen Hunger Force.*"

62. Butler, "'Aqua Teen Hunger Force Forever.'"

63. O'Neil, "The End of *Aqua Teen Hunger Force.*"

64. Alex Wilgus, "The Satirical Vision of Aqua Teen Hunger Force," The Common Vision, August 1, 2014, http://thecommonvision.org/features/satirical-vision-aqua-teen-hunger-force.

65. Butler, "'Aqua Teen Hunger Force Forever.'"

66. Joseph Langdon, "The History of Cartoon Network's Adult Swim," Ranker, 2019, www.ranker.com/list/history-of-adult-swim-cartoon-network/joesph-langdon; and Bryan Menegus, "The History of Adult Swim's Rise to Greatness," Gizmodo, April 11, 2016, https://gizmodo.com/an-oral-history-of-adult-swim-1770248730.

67. Josef Adalian, "Stoner Week: How Adult Swim Conquered Late-Night TV," Vulture, July 2, 2015, www.vulture.com/2015/07/stoner-week-how-adult-swim-conquered-late-night.html.

68. Langdon, "The History of Cartoon Network's Adult Swim."

69. Ibid.

70. Adalian, "Stoner Week"; Langdon, "The History of Cartoon Network's Adult Swim."

71. Matt Barone, "Rejection, Scares, and Ryan Gosling: Looking Back at Nickelodeon's 'Are You Afraid of the Dark?'" Complex, October 30, 2014, www.complex.com/pop-culture/2014/10/interview-are-you-afraid-of-the-dark-dj-machale.

72. Ibid.

73. Ibid.

74. Ibid.

75. Julia Bianco, "15 TV Shows You Didn't Know Were Canadian," ScreenRant, June 8, 2016, https://screenrant.com/tv-shows-did-not-know-were-canadian.

76. Erin McCarthy, "25 Future Stars Who Appeared on *Are You Afraid of the Dark?*" Mental Floss, August 15, 2017, http://mentalfloss.com/article/58475/25-future-stars-who-appeared-are-you-afraid-dark.

77. Jess Joho, "How We Faced Much More Than the Dark in 'Are You Afraid of the Dark?'" Mashable, May 17, 2018, https://mashable.com/2018/05/17/are-you-afraid-of-the-dark-horror-nostalgia-week/#6gvcVrNSRaqR.

78. Barone, "Rejection, Scares, and Ryan Gosling."

79. Ibid.

80. Matthew Klickstein, *Slimed: An Oral History of Nickelodeon's Golden Age* (New York: Penguin, 2013), 192–93.

81. Barone, "Rejection, Scares, and Ryan Gosling."

82. Ibid.

83. Roger Cormier, "15 Frightening Facts about Are You Afraid of the Dark?" Mental Floss, October 28, 2016, http://mentalfloss.com/article/87757/15-frightening-facts-about-are-you-afraid-dark.

84. Barone, "Rejection, Scares, and Ryan Gosling."

85. Chris Evangelista, "'Are You Afraid of the Dark?' Reboot Cast and Story Revealed," SlashFilm, June 10, 2019, www.slashfilm.com/are-you-afraid-of-the-dark-reboot-cast.

86. Mike Sprague, "Just How Scary Will *Are You Afraid of the Dark* Be?" Dread Central, September 10, 2018, www.dreadcentral.com/news/282335/282335/.

87. Sprague, "Just How Scary."

88. Kristen Lopez, "Decades Later, Nothing Has Topped 'Are You Afraid of the Dark?' for Kid-Friendly Horror," SlashFilm, August 21, 2018, www.slashfilm.com/are-you-afraid -of-the-dark-revisited.

89. Marlow Stern, "Why 'Arrested Development's' 4th Season Is a Bust: Contracts and More," Daily Beast, July 11, 2017, www.thedailybeast.com/why-arrested-develop ments-4th-season-is-a-bust-contracts-and-more.

90. *Balboa Observer-Picayune*, "Interview: Katie O'Connell," November 24, 2005, https://web.archive.org/web/20110604010723/http://the-op.com/view/article.php.

91. Ibid.

92. Ibid.

93. Jennifer Maas, "Rejoice, 'Arrested Development' Fans! Ron Howard's Season 5 Narration Is Underway," *The Wrap*, March 2, 2018, www.thewrap.com/ron-howard-arrested -development-season-5-narration-script.

94. Jaime Weinman, "Five Opinionated Facts about *Arrested Development*," *Mac-Lean's*, May 23, 2013, www.macleans.ca/culture/television/five-opinionated-facts-about -arrested-development.

95. Rob Owen, "Time May Be Running Out for 'Arrested Development,'" *Post-Gazette* (Pittsburgh), February 11, 2005.

96. Ian Crouch, "'Arrested Development' Is Back Where It Started," *New Yorker*, June 15, 2018, www.newyorker.com/culture/on-television/arrested-development-is-back -where-it-started.

97. Josef Adalian, "Hurwitz Takes a Hike," *Variety*, March 27, 2006, https://variety .com/2006/scene/markets-festivals/hurwitz-takes-a-hike-1117940467.

98. Crouch, "'Arrested Development' Is Back."

99. Tim Goodman, "R.I.P., 'Arrested Development': Critics' Fave Not Given Room to Grow," *SF Gate*, March 28, 2006, www.sfgate.com/entertainment/article/R-I-P-Arrested -Development-critics-fave-2500890.php.

100. Owen, "Time May Be Running Out."

101. Goodman, "R.I.P., 'Arrested Development.'"

102. Weinman, "Five Opinionated Facts."

103. Colin Mahan, "Three Times the *Arrested Development*," TV.com, July 26, 2006, www .tv.com/news/three-times-the-arrested-development-5534.

104. Gem Wheeler, "Arrested Development: The Story So Far," Den of Geek, May 26, 2013, www.denofgeek.com/tv/arrested-development/25771/arrested-development-the -story-so-far.

105. Dusty Stowe, "What to Expect from *Arrested Development* Season 6," Screen Rant, March 16, 2019, https://screenrant.com/arrested-development-season-6-renewal-release -date-story.

106. Weinman, "Five Opinionated Facts."

107. Crouch, "'Arrested Development' Is Back."

108. Joe Rhodes, "A Fanboy Shows Superheroes the Way," *New York Times*, December 6, 2013, www.nytimes.com/2013/12/08/arts/television/with-arrow-greg-berlanti-finds -a-formula-for-success.html.

109. Jarett Wieselman, "Behind the Scenes Casting Secrets from 'Gossip Girl,' 'Arrow,' and More," Buzzfeed, October 6, 2015, www.buzzfeed.com/jarettwieselman/the-man -who-helped-build-the-cw.

110. Alex Strachan, "Stephen Amell Brings Arrow to Small Screen," Canada.com, October 11, 2012, https://o.canada.com/entertainment/television/stephen-amell-brings -arrow-to-small-screen.

111. Allison Jasper, "Exclusive: 'Arrow' Archery Expert Talks Season 3," Archery 360, October 9, 2014, www.archery360.com/2014/10/09/exclusive-arrow-archery-expert-talks -season-3.

112. Strachan, "Stephen Amell."

113. Laura Prudom, "How *Arrow* Became the Best Superhero Show on Television," The Week, December 12, 2013, https://theweek.com/articles/454437/how-arrow-became -best-superhero-show-television.

114. Maureen Ryan, "'Arrow': How Did Stephen Amell Do That Ladder Stunt?" Huff-Post, October 11, 2012, www.huffpost.com/entry/arrow-stephen-amell-ladder_n_1936348.

115. Allison Keene, "The CW Announces Fall Premiere Dates with Major Lineup Changes," Collider, June 28, 2012, http://collider.com/the-cw-fall-2012–Premiere-dates.

116. Julian Cardillo, "The CW Universe Still Needs 'Arrow,' Even If the Viewers Don't," Gotham Sports Network, December 5, 2016, https://gothamsn.com/the-cw-universe-still -needs-arrow-even-if-the-viewers-dont-64b1e83e25e0.

117. Nellie Andreeva, "'Arrow' to End with 10-Episode Eighth Season on the CW," *Deadline*, March 6, 2019, https://deadline.com/2019/03/arrowend-with-10-episode-sesaon -8-final-season-canceled-1202570893.

118. Ibid.

119. Ibid.

120. Alex Warner, "30 Surprising Things about the Making of 'Arrow,'" *Marie Claire*, December 13, 2017, www.marieclaire.com/culture/g14415578/arrow-tv-show-surprising -facts.

121. Eduardo Vasconcellos, "Interview: Avatar's Bryan Konietzko and Michael Dante DiMartino," IGN, May 13, 2012, www.ign.com/articles/2007/09/06/interview-avatars -bryan-konietzko-and-michael-dante-dimartino.

122. Andrew Whalen, "On Its 10-Year Anniversary 'Avatar: The Last Airbender' Cre-ators Give an Oral History of the Finale," *Newsweek*, July 19, 2018, www.newsweek.com/ avatar-last-airbender-finale-anniversary-sozins-comet-season-3-last-episode-1033919.

123. Lisa Granshaw, "An Oral History of *Avatar: The Last Airbender*, Cast Looks Back as Show Celebrates 10th Anniversary of Finale," Syfy Wire, July 30, 2018, www.syfy .com/syfywire/an-oral-history-of-avatar-the-last-airbender-cast-looks-back-as-show -celebrates-10th.

124. Nicole Clark, "'Avatar: The Last Airbender' Is Still One of the Greatest Shows of All Time," Vice, July 20, 2018, www.vice.com/en_us/article/5943jz/avatar-the-last -airbender-is-still-one-of-the-greatest-shows-of-all-time.

125. Ibid.

126. Joanna Robinson, "How a Nickelodeon Cartoon Became One of the Most Powerful, Subversive Shows of 2014," *Vanity Fair*, December 19, 2014, www.vanityfair.com/holly wood/2014/12/korra-series-finale-recap-gay-asami.

127. Whalen, "On Its 10-Year Anniversary 'Avatar.'"

128. Clark, "'Avatar: The Last Airbender.'"

129. Ibid.

130. Whalen, "On Its 10-Year Anniversary 'Avatar.'"

131. Mark Harrison, "The Last Airbender: What Went Wrong?" Den of Geek, July 2, 2019, www.denofgeek.com/us/movies/the-last-airbender/246802/the-last-airbender -what-went-wrong.

132. Michelle Jaworski, "'Legend of Korra' Goes Digital after Nickelodeon Takes It Off the Air," Daily Dot, July 24, 2014, www.dailydot.com/parsec/legend-of-korra-goes-digital.

133. Anton Olsen, "*Avatar: The Last Airbender* from Dark Horse and Nickelodeon," *Wired*, February 8, 2011, www.wired.com/2011/02/avatar-the-last-airbender-from-dark-horse -and-nickelodeon.

134. Brandon Katz, "What's Happening with Netflix's Live-Action 'Avatar: The Last Airbender' Remake?" *Observer*, May 30, 2019, https://observer.com/2019/05/avatar-the -last-airbender-netflix-details-release-date-plot.

135. Dave Rogers, *The Complete Avengers: The Full Story of Britain's Smash Crime-Fighting Team!* (New York: St. Martin's Press, 1989), 12.

136. Ibid.

137. Ibid.

138. Andrew Roberts, "First-Rate Man of Mystery: Brian Clemens, the Screenwriter Who Made *The Avengers* Iconic," *Independent*, January 16, 2015, www.independent.co.uk/arts -entertainment/tv/features/first-rate-man-of-mystery-brian-clemens-the-screenwriter -who-made-the-avengers-iconic-9981638.html.

139. Rogers, *The Complete Avengers*, 12.

140. Vincent Cosgrove, "On 'The Avengers,' Catherine Gale Was a Proto-Emma Peel," *New York Times*, July 9, 2006, www.nytimes.com/2006/07/09/arts/television/09cosg.html.

141. Ibid.

142. Angelina I. Karpovich, "The Avengers," in *The Essential Cult TV Reader*, ed. David Lavery, 37 (Lexington: University Press of Kentucky, 2010).

143. Noel Murray, "The Appeal of *The Avengers*' Stylish, Lascivious Vision of British-ness," AV Club, January 31, 2013, https://tv.avclub.com/the-appeal-of-the-avengers -stylish-lascivious-vision-1798236339.

144. Ibid.

145. Ibid.

146. Simon Heffer, "How *The Avengers* Transformed Sixties Television," *Telegraph*, August 10, 2015, www.telegraph.co.uk/culture/tvandradio/11794141/How-The-Avengers -transformed-Sixties-television.html.

147. Ibid.

148. Ibid.

149. Paul Sutton, "The Avengers/New Avengers (ITV, 1961–1969)/(ITV, 1976–1977)," in *The Cult TV Book: From Star Trek to Dexter, New Approaches to TV Outside the Box*, ed. Stacey Abbott, 64–65 (New York: Soft Skull Press, 2010).

150. MI6, "The Avengers (1961–1969)," 2019, www.mi6-hq.com/sections/beyond_ bond/the_avengers.php3.

151. Heffer, "How *The Avengers* Transformed Sixties Television."

152. MI6, "The Avengers (1961–1969)."

153. Anthony Clark, "Avengers, The (1961–69)," BFI Screen Online, 2014, www.screenon line.org.uk/tv/id/473728/index.html.

154. Karpovich, "The Avengers," 37–38.

155. Ibid., 41.

B

1. David Bassom, *Creating Babylon 5* (New York: Del Rey Ballantine Books, 1997), 25.

2. Ibid., 5.

3. Lisa Granshaw, "An Oral History of Babylon 5: The Beloved TV Novel That Showed a Different Way to Tell Sci-fi," SyFy Wire, June 27, 2018, www.syfy.com/syfywire/an-oral -history-of-babylon-5-the-beloved-tv-novel-that-showed-a-different-way-to-tell-sci.

4. Bassom, *Creating Babylon 5*, 25.

5. Granshaw, "An Oral History of Babylon 5."

6. Bassom, *Creating Babylon 5*, 26.

7. Ibid., 26.

8. Bassom, *Creating Babylon 5*, 6; Granshaw, "An Oral History of Babylon 5."

9. Bassom, *Creating Babylon 5*, 26.

10. Ibid., 25.

11. Johnny Brayson, "Why 'Babylon 5' Is Peak '90s Sci-fi TV," CometTV.com, August 20, 2018, www.comettv.com/2018/08/babylon-5–Peak-90s-sci-fi-tv.

12. Bassom, *Creating Babylon 5*, 27.

13. Ibid., 58.

14. Ibid., 46.

15. Ibid., 59.

16. Granshaw, "An Oral History of Babylon 5."

17. Robin Parrish, "J. Michael Straczynski Planning to Reboot 'Babylon 5' on the Big Screen," Tech Times, August 9, 2014, www.techtimes.com/articles/12575/20140809/j-michael-straczynski-planning-reboot-babylon-5-big-screen.htm.

18. Joe Anderton, "Babylon 5 Revival Won't Ever Happen, Insists Series Creator," Digital Spy, April 23, 2018, www.digitalspy.com/tv/ustv/a855453/babylon-5-revival-wont-ever-happen-j-michael-straczynski.

19. Bassom, *Creating Babylon 5*, 34.

20. Mark Phillips and Frank Garcia, *Science Fiction Television Series: Episode Guides, Histories, and Casts and Credits for 62 Prime Time Shows, 1959–1989* (Jefferson, NC: McFarland & Company, 1996), 29.

21. Ibid., 29–30.

22. Ibid.

23. Annette Porter, David Lavery, and Hillary Robson, *Finding Battlestar Galactica: An Unauthorized Guide* (Naperville, IL: Sourcebooks, 2008), 5.

24. Ibid., 6.

25. Phillips and Garcia, *Science Fiction Television Series*, 30.

26. Ibid., 31.

27. Ibid.

28. Porter, Lavery, and Robson, *Finding Battlestar Galactica*, 5.

29. Phillips and Garcia, *Science Fiction Television Series*, 35.

30. Ibid.

31. Ibid.

32. Porter, Lavery, and Robson, *Finding Battlestar Galactica*, 7.

33. Ibid., 8–9.

34. Ibid., 9.

35. Ibid., 14.

36. Liz Shannon Miller, "'Battlestar Galactica' Is Now a Classic—15 Years Ago, Fans Thought It Was a Mistake," IndieWire, December 14, 2018, www.indiewire.com/2018/12/battlestar-galactica-scifi-series-game-changing-1202027949.

37. Porter, Lavery, and Robson, *Finding Battlestar Galactica*, 4.

38. Gregory J. Bonann, *Baywatch: Rescued from Prime Time* (Beverly Hills, CA: New Millennium Press, 2000), 12–13.

39. Ibid., 36.

40. Ibid., 38.

41. Ibid., 45.

42. Ibid., 40.

43. Ibid., 48.

44. Ibid., 52.

45. Ibid.

46. Ibid., 54, 57.

47. Ibid., 61.

48. Ibid.

49. Ibid., 67.

50. Ibid., 77.

51. Bonann, *Baywatch*, 78; Bill Carter, "Stand Aside, CNN, America's No. 1 TV Export Is—No Scoffing, Please—'Baywatch,'" *New York Times*, July 3, 1995, www.nytimes .com/1995/07/03/business/media-television-stand-aside-cnn-america-s-no-1-tv-export -no-scoffing-please.html; Chris Lee, "How 'Baywatch' Went from an Early Belly Flop to the Big Screen," *New York Times*, May 4, 2017, www.nytimes.com/2017/05/04/movies/ how-baywatch-went-from-an-early-belly-flop-to-the-big-screen.html.

52. Bonann, *Baywatch*, 81; Lee, "How 'Baywatch.'"

53. Bonann, *Baywatch*, 82.

54. Carter, "Stand Aside, CNN."

55. Bonann, *Baywatch*, 83.

56. Ibid., 85.

57. Ibid., 97, 101, 110.

58. Bonann, *Baywatch*, 114; Lee, "How 'Baywatch.'"

59. Bonann, *Baywatch*, 136.

60. BBC, "Wave of Protest over Baywatch Movie," BBC News, February 26, 1999, http://news.bbc.co.uk/2/hi/entertainment/286274.stm.

61. Tim Ryan, "'Baywatch' May Relocate to Hawaii," *Star Bulletin*, March 4, 1999, http://archives.starbulletin.com/1999/03/04/news/story1.html.

62. Erika Engle, "'Baywatch' Calls It Quits in Hawaii," *Pacific Business News*, February 11, 2001, www.bizjournals.com/pacific/stories/2001/02/12/story2.html.

63. Lee, "How 'Baywatch.'"

64. John J. O'Connor, "'Beauty and the Beast' on CBS," *New York Times*, September 25, 1987, www.nytimes.com/1987/09/25/arts/tv-weekend-beauty-and-the-beast-on-cbs .html.

65. Seth Abramovitch, "George R. R. Martin on Writing TB's 'Beauty and the Beast': 'It was such a smart show,'" *Hollywood Reporter*, March 16, 2018, www.hollywoodreporter .com/live-feed/george-r-r-martin-writing-tvs-beauty-beast-was-a-smart-show-986786.

66. Caroline Preece, "Looking Back at *Beauty and the Beast*," Den of Geek! September 11, 2012, www.denofgeek.com/tv/beauty-and-the-beast/22629/looking-back-at-beauty-and -the-beast.

67. Seth Abramovitch, "Hollywood Flashback: In 1987, Linda Hamilton and Ron Perlman Brought 'Beauty and the Beast' to TV," *Hollywood Reporter*, March 16, 2017, www .hollywoodreporter.com/news/hollywood-flashback-1987-linda-hamilton-ron-perlman -brought-beauty-beast-tv-985531.

68. Ron Perlman, "Ron Perlman on Starring in TV's 'Beauty and the Beast': 'That was the feeling I had growing up,'" *Hollywood Reporter*, March 17, 2017, www.hollywood reporter.com/heat-vision/ron-perlman-starring-tvs-beauty-beast-was-feeling-i-had-grow ing-up-987002.

69. O'Connor, "'Beauty and the Beast' on CBS."

70. Jeremy Gerard, "The Success of 'Beauty and the Beast,'" *New York Times*, November 24, 1988, www.nytimes.com/1988/11/24/arts/the-success-of-beauty-and-the-beast.html.

71. Rebecca Hawkes, "Inside George R. R. Martin's Battle to Make a More 'Sexual' Beauty and the Beast," *Telegraph*, March 3, 2017, www.telegraph.co.uk/tv/0/inside -george-rr-martins-battle-make-sexual-beauty-beast.

72. Gerard, "The Success of 'Beauty and the Beast.'"

73. John O'Connor, "Beast Tries to Survive Loss of the Other Half of the Title," *New York Times*, December 20, 1989, www.nytimes.com/1989/12/20/arts/review-television-beast -tries-to-survive-loss-of-the-other-half-of-the-title.html.

74. Abramovitch, "George R. R. Martin on Writing."

75. Jeremy Gerard, "TV Notes," *New York Times,* June 1, 1989, www.nytimes.com/1989/06/01/theater/tv-notes.html.

76. O'Connor, "Beast Tries to Survive Loss."

77. Gerard, "TV Notes."

78. Preece, "Looking Back at *Beauty and the Beast.*"

79. O'Connor, "Beast Tries to Survive Loss."

80. Hawkes, "Inside George R. R. Martin's Battle"; Preece, "Looking Back at *Beauty and the Beast.*"

81. Preece, "Looking Back at *Beauty and the Beast.*"

82. Hawkes, "Inside George R. R. Martin's Battle."

83. Abramovitch, "Hollywood Flashback."

84. J. F. Roberts, *The True History of* The Black Adder (London: Preface Publishing, 2012), 17–18.

85. Garry Berman, *Best of the Britcoms: From* Fawlty Towers *to* The Office (New York: Taylor Trade, 2011), 56.

86. Ibid.

87. Ibid.

88. Ibid.

89. Roberts, *The True History of* The Black Adder, 89.

90. Ibid., 90.

91. Ibid., 92.

92. Ibid., 93.

93. Ibid., 104.

94. Berman, *Best of the Britcoms*, 56.

95. Ibid.

96. Ibid.

97. Ibid.

98. Don Shirley, "TV Reviews: 'Blackadder' Back, 'Third and Oak' on A&E," *Los Angeles Times,* November 2, 1989, www.latimes.com/archives/la-xpm-1989-11-02-ca-49-story.html.

99. Berman, *Best of the Britcoms*, 58.

100. Paul Jones, "We Have Some Cunning Plans for a New Series of Blackadder That Might Just Work," *Radio Times,* July 1, 2019, www.radiotimes.com/news/tv/2019-07-01/blackadder-new-series.

101. Edward Gross and Mark A. Altman, *Slayers and Vampires: The Complete Uncensored, Unauthorized Oral History of Buffy and Angel* (New York: Tor, 2017), 20.

102. Ibid., 52.

103. Ibid., 59.

104. Ibid., 65.

105. Ibid., 94.

106. Ibid., 99.

107. Ibid., 118.

108. John Kenneth Muir, *Terror Television: American Series, 1970–1999* (Jefferson, NC: McFarland & Company, 2000), 502–3.

109. Gross and Altman, *Slayers and Vampires*, 114.

110. Ibid., 214.

111. Gross and Altman, *Slayers and Vampires*, 214–15.

112. Ibid., 258.

113. Jesse Schedeen, "Why BOOM! Studios Decided to Reboot Buffy the Vampire Slayer," IGN, January 23, 2019, www.ign.com/articles/2019/01/23/why-boom-studios-decided-to-reboot-buffy-the-vampire-slayer.

114. Lesley Goldberg, "'Buffy the Vampire Slayer' Inclusive Reboot in the Works with Joss Whedon," *Hollywood Reporter*, July 20, 2018, www.hollywoodreporter.com/live-feed/ buffy-vampire-slayer-reboot-inclusive-take-joss-whedon-works-1128888.

115. Milly Williamson, *The Lure of the Vampire: Gender, Fiction and Fandom from Bram Stoker to Buffy* (New York: Columbia University Press, 2005), 62.

116. Gross and Altman, *Slayers and Vampires*, 28.

117. Emma John, "Joss Whedon: 'I Kept Telling My Mum Reading Comics Would Pay Off," *Guardian*, June 1, 2013, www.theguardian.com/culture/2013/jun/02/joss-whedon -reading-comics-pay-off.

118. Alison Eldridge, "Joss Whedon," *Encyclopedia Britannica*, June 19, 2019, www.bri tannica.com/biography/Joss-Whedon.

119. Ibid.

C

1. Caroline Preece, "Why *Charmed* Deserves to Be Celebrated," Den of Geek! January 13, 2017, www.denofgeek.com/uk/tv/charmed/46479/why-charmed-deserves-to-be -celebrated.

2. David A. Keeps, "When Aaron Spelling Ruled Television: An Oral History of Entertainment's Prolific, Populist Producer," *Hollywood Reporter*, September 18, 2015, www .hollywoodreporter.com/features/aaron-spelling-ruled-television-an-823391.

3. Edward Gross, "Constance Burge: The Charmed One," TV Zone, www.visimag .com/tvzone/t126_feature.htm.

4. Ibid.

5. Keeps, "When Aaron Spelling Ruled Television."

6. John Kenneth Muir, *Terror Television: American Series, 1970–1999* (Jefferson, NC: Mc-Farland & Company, 2000), 532.

7. Tierney Bricker, "The Wicked behind-the-Scenes Drama of the Original *Charmed*: The Feuds, Firings and Feminist Fury," ENews, October 12, 2018, www.eonline.com/ news/976593/the-wicked-behind-the-scenes-drama-of-the-original-charmed-the-feuds -firings-and-feminist-fury.

8. Keeps, "When Aaron Spelling Ruled Television."

9. Muir, *Terror Television*, 532.

10. Keeps, "When Aaron Spelling Ruled Television."

11. Bricker, "The Wicked behind-the-Scenes Drama."

12. Ibid.

13. Andy Swift, "*Charmed* 10 Years Later: Showrunner Talks Prue's Death, Phoebe's Tragic Love, Billie's Rumored Spinoff and More," Yahoo! Entertainment, May 20, 2016, www.yahoo.com/entertainment/charmed-10-years-later-showrunner-180005033.html.

14. TV Line, "*Charmed*: An Oral History," May 20, 2016, https://tvline.com/gallery/ charmed-anniversary-photos-biggest-moments-prue-death-phoebe-cole/charmed-season -1-beginning.

15. Ibid.

16. Ibid.

17. Bricker, "The Wicked behind-the-Scenes Drama"; TV Line, "*Charmed*."

18. Bricker, "The Wicked behind-the-Scenes Drama."

19. Bricker, "The Wicked behind-the-Scenes Drama"; TV Line, "*Charmed*."

20. TV Line, "*Charmed*."

21. Swift, "*Charmed* 10 Years Later."

22. Bricker, "The Wicked behind-the-Scenes Drama."

23. Josef Adalian, "A Reboot for *Charmed* Is in the Works at CBS," Vulture, October 25, 2013, www.vulture.com/2013/10/reboot-of-charmed-is-in-the-works-at-cbs.html.

24. Bricker, "The Wicked behind-the-Scenes Drama."

25. Muir, *Terror Television*, 531.

26. Princess Weekes, "Was *Charmed* Ever Really a *Feminist* Show?" The Mary Sue, January 29, 2018, www.themarysue.com/charmed-feminist-show.

27. K. C. Ifeyani, "The 40th Anniversary of 'Charlie's Angels' . . . And the Uneasy History of 'Jiggle TV,'" Fast Company, October 7, 2016, www.fastcompany.com/3064009/the-40th-anniversary-of-charlies-angelsand-the-uneasy-history-of-jiggle-tv.

28. David Crow, "*Community*: Series Review and Appreciation," Den of Geek, February 7, 2013, www.denofgeek.com/us/tv/community/56932/community-series-review-and-appreciation; Steven Hyden, "How Dan Harmon Went from Doing ComedySportz in Milwaukee to Creating NBC's *Community*," AV Club, October 19, 2009, https://web.archive.org/web/20091023172513/http://www.avclub.com/milwaukee/articles/how-dan-harmon-went-from-doing-comedysportz-in-mil,34126.

29. Hyden, "How Dan Harmon Went from Doing ComedySportz."

30. The Week, "*Community* Pulled from NBC's Schedule: The Backlash," November 16, 2011, https://theweek.com/articles/480168/community-pulled-from-nbcs-schedule-backlash.

31. Josef Adalian, "Dan Harmon Is No Longer Showrunner on *Community*," Vulture, May 18, 2012, www.vulture.com/2012/05/dan-harmon-community-future-nbc-sony.html.

32. Ibid.

33. Lacey Rose, "'Community's' Dan Harmon Reveals the Wild Story behind His Firing and Rehiring," *Hollywood Reporter*, July 17, 2013, https://web.archive.org/web/20140426055322/http://www.hollywoodreporter.com/news/communitys-dan-harmon-reveals-wild-586084?page=show.

34. Crow, "*Community*."

35. Ibid.

36. Adalian, "Dan Harmon Is No Longer Showrunner."

37. Rose, "'Community's' Dan Harmon."

38. Allan Sepinwall and Matt Zoller Seitz, *TV (The Book): Two Experts Pick the Greatest American Shows of All Time* (New York: Grand Central Publishing, 2016), 215.

39. Ryan Gajewski, "'Rick and Morty' Creators on 'More Chaotic' Season 2, 'Community' Movie's Status, *Hollywood Reporter*, July 24, 2015, www.hollywoodreporter.com/live-feed/rick-morty-season-2-dan-810874.

40. Andrew Wallenstein, "Yahoo Shutters Video Service Yahoo Screen (Exclusive)," *Variety*, January 4, 2016, https://web.archive.org/web/20160104215616/http://variety.com/2016/digital/news/yahoo-shutters-video-service-yahoo-screen-exclusive-1201671374.

41. Gajewski, "'Rick and Morty' Creators."

42. Hyden, "How Dan Harmon Went from Doing ComedySportz."

43. *TV Guide*, "Dan Harmon," 2019, www.tvguide.com/celebrities/dan-harmon/bio/286815.

44. Hyden, "How Dan Harmon Went from Doing ComedySportz."

45. Brian Raftery, "How Dan Harmon Drives Himself Crazy Making *Community*," *Wired*, September 22, 2011, www.wired.com/2011/09/mf_harmon.

46. Hyden, "How Dan Harmon Went from Doing ComedySportz."

47. Ibid.

48. Raftery, "How Dan Harmon Drives Himself Crazy."

49. Eric Goldman, "Dan Harmon and Justin Roiland on the Inspiration behind *Rick and Morty*, the New Adult Swim Animated Series," IGN, December 2, 2013, www.ign.com/

articles/2013/12/02/dan-harmon-and-justin-roiland-on-the-inspiration-behind-rick-and
-morty-the-new-adult-swim-animated-series.

50. Joe Matar, "Dan Harmon Talks *Anomalisa, Community* Movie, *Rick and Morty*," Den of
Geek, December 7, 2015, www.denofgeek.com/us/tv/dan-harmon/251143/dan-harmon
-talks-anomalisa-community-movie-rick-and-morty.

51. Fred Patten, "'Cowboy Bebop: The Movie' . . . At Last," Animation World Network,
March 31, 2003, https://web.archive.org/web/20151004201534/http:/www.awn.com/
animationworld/cowboy-bebop-movie-last.

52. Justin Sevakis, "Otakon 2013: Shinichiro Watanabe Focus Panel," Anime News Network, August 14, 2013, www.animenewsnetwork.com/convention/2013/otakon/7; Julian
Rizzo-Smith, "The Many Inspirations of Cowboy Bebop Director Shinichiro Watanabe,"
IGN, November 23, 2017, www.ign.com/articles/2017/11/24/the-many-inspirations-of
-cowboy-bebop-director-shinichiro-watanabe.

53. Rizzo-Smith, "The Many Inspirations."

54. Rizzo-Smith, "The Many Inspirations"; Sevakis, "Otakon 2013."

55. Patten, "'Cowboy Bebop'"; Rizzo-Smith, "The Many Inspirations."

56. H. D. Russell, "*Cowboy Bebop*—Whatever Happens, Happens," *Escapist*, March
14, 2016, http://v1.escapistmagazine.com/articles/view/moviesandtv/reviews/
goanimereviews/16872-Cowboy-Bebop-Anime-Review#&gid=gallery_5966&pid=1.

57. Todd DuBois, "Otakon 2013: Press Conference and Public Q &A with Director
Shinichiro Watanabe," Anime Superhero, August 21, 2013, https://animesuperhero.com/
otakon-2013-with-shinichiro-watanabe.

58. Jonathan Clements and Helen McCarthy, *The Anime Encyclopedia: A Guide to Japanese
Animation since 1917* (Berkeley, CA: Stonebridge Press, 2001), 70.

59. DuBois, "Otakon 2013."

60. Monica Kim, "Can *Cowboy Bebop*'s Creator Make More People Take Anime Seriously?" *Atlantic*, January 3, 2014, www.theatlantic.com/entertainment/archive/2014/01/
can-em-cowboy-bebop-em-s-creator-make-more-people-take-anime-seriously/282806.

61. Patten, "'Cowboy Bebop.'"

62. Joe Otterson, "'Cowboy Bebop': John Cho, Mustafa Shakir Among Four Cast in
Netflix Live-Action Series," *Variety*, April 4, 2019, https://variety.com/2019/tv/news/
cowboy-bebop-netflix-live-action-series-cast-1203180399.

63. Anime News Network, "Shinichiro Watanabe," 2019, www.animenewsnetwork
.com/encyclopedia/people.php?id=774.

64. DuBois, "Otakon 2013."

65. Ibid.

66. Ibid.

67. Sevakis, "Otakon 2013."

68. Joe Otterson, "'Blade Runner' Anime Series Set at Adult Swim, Crunchyroll," *Variety*, November 29, 2019, https://variety.com/2018/tv/news/blade-runner-anime-series
-adult-swim-crunchyroll-1203047083.

69. Ibid.

70. Eric Thurm, "How *Crazy Ex-Girlfriend* Is Reinventing the TV Musical," MTV, March
21, 2016, www.mtv.com/news/2796929/how-my-crazy-ex-girlfriend-is-reinventing-the
-tv-musical.

71. E. Alex Jung, "The Hardest-Working Show in Show Business," Vulture, February
2018, www.vulture.com/2018/02/crazy-ex-girlfriend-season-3-finale.html.

72. Lorne Manly, "The Great American Musical, Side B, in 'Crazy Ex-Girlfriend,'" *New
York Times*, October 7, 2015, www.nytimes.com/2015/10/11/arts/television/the-great
-american-musical-side-b-in-my-crazy-ex-girlfriend.html.

73. Ibid.

74. Jung, "The Hardest-Working Show."

75. Manly, "The Great American Musical."

76. Jung, "The Hardest-Working Show."

77. Nellie Andreeva, "'Crazy Ex-Girlfriend' Pilot Now Going Forward," *Deadline*, February 9, 2015, https://deadline.com/2015/02/crazy-ex-girlfriend-pilot-dead-showtime-roadies-billions-good-1201369490.

78. Manly, "The Great American Musical."

79. Ibid.

80. Thurm, "How *Crazy Ex-Girlfriend* Is Reinventing."

81. Ibid.

82. TV by the Numbers, "The CW Announces Fall 2015 Premiere Dates," June 24, 2015, https://tvbythenumbers.zap2it.com/1/the-cw-announces-fall-2015-premiere-dates-october-launches-for-all-scripted-series/422230.

83. Kaitlin Thomas, "The CW Orders More *iZombie* and *Crazy Ex-Girlfriend*, But Doesn't Give Them Full Seasons," TV.com, November 23, 2015, www.tv.com/news/the-cw-orders-more-izombie-and-crazy-ex-girlfriend-but-doesnt-give-them-full-seasons-144831277446.

84. Rick Kissell, "The CW Renews Fall Series Slate, Including 'The 100,' Season 12 of 'Supernatural,'" *Variety*, March 11, 2016, https://variety.com/2016/tv/news/the-cw-renews-11-series-slate-including-the-100-supernatural-1201728203.

85. Lake Schatz, "*Crazy Ex-Girlfriend* to End After Next Season," Consequence of Sound, April 2, 2018, https://consequenceofsound.net/2018/04/crazy-ex-girlfriend-to-end-after-next-season.

86. Samantha Highfill, "*Crazy Ex-Girlfriend*'s Final Season Will Have 18 Episodes, *Entertainment Weekly*, July 13, 2018, https://ew.com/tv/2018/07/13/crazy-ex-girlfriend-final-season-18-episodes.

87. Ashley Burns, "From Near 'Simpsons' Spinoff to a Check against Hollywood Ridiculousness: Why 'The Critic' Still Matters," Uproxx, November 29, 2016, https://uproxx.com/hitfix/the-critic-mike-reiss-al-jean.

88. Burns, "From Near 'Simpsons' Spinoff"; Jesse Hassenger, "*The Critic*: The Complete Series," PopMatters, February 22, 2004, www.popmatters.com/critic-complete-series-2496227916.html.

89. Burns, "From Near 'Simpsons' Spinoff."

90. Burns, "From Near 'Simpsons' Spinoff"; Hassenger, "*The Critic*."

91. Burns, "From Near 'Simpsons' Spinoff"; Hassenger, "*The Critic*."

92. Nathan Rabin, "The Critic: *The Critic*," AV Club, November 6, 2011, https://tv.avclub.com/the-critic-the-critic-1798170322.

93. Burns, "From Near 'Simpsons' Spinoff."

94. Ibid.

95. Burns, "From Near 'Simpsons' Spinoff"; Libby Cudmore, "It Didn't Stink, So Why Did *The Critic* Fail to Become a Hit Show?" Consequence of Sound, January 22, 2019, https://consequenceofsound.net/2019/01/the-critic-25th-anniversary.

96. Cudmore, "It Didn't Stink."

97. Burns, "From Near 'Simpsons' Spinoff."

98. Ibid.

99. Ibid.

100. Chris Turner, *Planet Simpson: How a Cartoon Masterpiece Documented an Era and Defined a Generation* (London: Ebury Press, 2005), 133.

101. Cudmore, "It Didn't Stink."

102. Ibid.

103. Burns, "From Near 'Simpsons' Spinoff."

D

1. Allie Conti, "The Oral History of 'Daria,'" Vice, March 2, 2017, www.vice.com/en_us/article/qkxbvb/the-oral-history-of-daria; Kathy M. Newman, "'Misery Chick': Irony, Alienation and Animation in MTV's *Daria*," in *Prime Time Animation: Television Animation and American Culture*, ed. Carol A. Stabile and Mark Harrison, 186 (New York: Routledge, 2003).

2. Conti, "The Oral History of 'Daria.'"

3. Ibid.; Newman, "'Misery Chick,'" 188.

4. Conti, "The Oral History of 'Daria.'"

5. Howard Rosenberg, "Brainy 'Beavis' pal 'Daria' Spins Off," *Los Angeles Times*, March 3, 1997, www.latimes.com/archives/la-xpm-1997-03-03-ca-34294-story.html.

6. Ibid.

7. Conti, "The Oral History of 'Daria.'"

8. Newman, "'Misery Chick,'" 186.

9. Conti, "The Oral History of 'Daria.'"

10. Newman, "'Misery Chick,'" 202.

11. Ibid., 200–202.

12. Joy Press, "Tracee Ellis Ross on Bringing MTV's *Daria* Universe Back to Life with *Jodie*," *Vanity Fair*, June 13, 2019, www.vanityfair.com/hollywood/2019/06/daria-mtv-reboot-spinoff-jodie-tracee-ellis-ross.

13. Jonathan Malcolm Lampley, "Dark Shadows," in *The Essential Cult TV Reader*, ed. David Lavery, 84 (Lexington: University Press of Kentucky, 2010).

14. Ibid., 84–85.

15. Craig Hamrick and R. J. Jamison, *Barnabas & Company: The Cast of the TV Classic* Dark Shadows (Bloomington, IN: iUniverse, 2012), 3.

16. Joyce Millman, "Dark Shadows," *Salon*, May 21, 2002, www.salon.com/2002/05/20/dark_shadows.

17. Lampley, "Dark Shadows," 85.

18. Donald Liebenson, "Fangs for the Memories: *Dark Shadows* Celebrates 50 Years," *Vanity Fair*, October 28, 2016, www.vanityfair.com/hollywood/2016/10/dark-shadows-celebrates-50-years.

19. Lampley, "Dark Shadows," 88.

20. Ibid., 85.

21. Ibid., 86.

22. Ibid., 85.

23. Ibid., 86.

24. Ibid.

25. Ibid., 87.

26. Ibid., 88.

27. Kate Bowles, "Soap Opera: 'No End of Story, Ever,'" in *The Australian TV Book*, ed. Graeme Turner and Stuart Cunningham, 119 (St. Leonards, Australia: Allen & Unwin, 2000).

28. Lampley, "Dark Shadows," 84.

29. Joe Garner and Michael Ashley, *It's Saturday Morning: Celebrating the Golden Era of Cartoons, 1960s–1990s* (Bellevue, WA: Quarto Publishing Group, 2018), 195.

30. Ibid.

31. Ibid.

32. *Oh My Disney*, "Darkwing Duck: 25 Years Later," September 9, 2016, https://ohmy.disney.com/insider/2016/09/09/darkwing-duck-25-years-later.

33. *Oh My Disney*, "Darkwing Duck."

34. Joe Strike, "The Tad Stones Interview—Part 2," Animation World Network, July 12, 2004, www.awn.com/animationworld/tad-stones-interview-part-2.

35. Shaun Manning, "25 Years Later, Darkwing Duck Is Still a Little Dangerous," Comic Book Resources, September 3, 2016, www.cbr.com/25-years-later-darkwing-duck-is-still-a-little-dangerous.

36. *Oh My Disney*, "Darkwing Duck."

37. Garner and Ashley, *It's Saturday Morning*, 196.

38. Ibid.

39. Ibid., 197.

40. Trent Moore, "It's Been 25 Years, But the Time Is Finally Right for a *Darkwing Duck* Revival," SyFy Wire, September 12, 2106, www.syfy.com/syfywire/its-been-25-years-time-finally-right-darkwing-duck-revival.

41. *Oh My Disney*, "Darkwing Duck."

42. Trent Moore, "Cult Hit Superhero Cartoon *Darkwing Duck* to Be Revived as New Comic Series," SyFy Wire, January 22, 2016, www.syfy.com/syfywire/cult-hit-superhero-cartoon-darkwing-duck-be-revived-new-comic-series.

43. Christian Holub, "*DuckTales* in Exclusive Clip," *Entertainment Weekly*, May 14, 2019, https://ew.com/tv/2019/05/14/darkwing-duck-ducktales-clip.

44. Garner and Ashley, *It's Saturday Morning*, 195.

45. Jordan Zakarin, "Life Is Like a Hurricane: An Oral History of the Disney Afternoon," SyFy Wire, November 1, 2018, www.syfy.com/syfywire/disney-afternoon-oral-history-ducktales-darkwing-rescue-rangers.

46. *Oh My Disney*, "Life Is Like a Hurricane: A Brief History of the Disney Afternoon," April 24, 2016, https://ohmy.disney.com/insider/2016/04/24/life-is-like-a-hurricane-a-brief-history-of-the-disney-afternoon.

47. Zakarin, "Life Is Like a Hurricane."

48. *Oh My Disney*, "Life Is Like a Hurricane."

49. Ibid.

50. Zakarin, "Life Is Like a Hurricane."

51. Allan Sepinwall and Matt Zoller Seitz, *TV (The Book): Two Experts Pick the Greatest American Shows of All Time* (New York: Grand Central Publishing, 2016), 70.

52. Horace Newcomb, "Deadwood," in *The Essential HBO Reader*, ed. Gary R. Edgerton and Jeffrey P. Jones, 94 (Lexington: University Press of Kentucky, 2008).

53. Ibid., 95.

54. Ibid., 94.

55. Ibid., 101.

56. Ibid.

57. Sepinwall and Seitz, *TV (The Book)*, 73–74.

58. Ibid.

59. Matt Zoller Seitz, "Sundown on *Deadwood*," Vulture, April 23, 2019, www.vulture.com/2019/04/david-milch-deadwood-movie.html.

60. Newcomb, "Deadwood," 96.

61. Kathryn Ellis, *Degrassi Generations: The Official 411* (New York: Pocket Books, 2005), 9.

62. Ibid., 154.

63. Ben Neihart, "DGrassi Is Tha Best Teen TV N Da WRLD!" *New York Times Magazine*, March 20, 2005, www.nytimes.com/2005/03/20/magazine/dgrassi-is-tha-best-teen-tv-n-da-wrld.html.

64. Ellis, *Degrassi Generations*, 10.

65. Keith Henderson, "They Want Kids to Want to Turn This On: PBS's 'Degrassi Junior High' Treats Teen Themes Honestly," *Christian Science Monitor*, September 14, 1987, www.csmonitor.com/1987/0914/hgrass-f.html.

66. Ellis, *Degrassi Generations*, 14.

67. Ibid.

68. Ibid.

69. Ibid., 10–11.

70. Ibid., 11.

71. Neihart, "DGrassi Is Tha Best."

72. Ibid.

73. Ibid.

74. Ellis, *Degrassi Generations*, 11.

75. Allison Bowsher, "Degrassi's Most Famous Celebrity Fans," Much.com, July 17, 2015, www.much.com/degrassis-most-famous-celebrity-fans.

76. Dan Harrison, "Warren Littlefield," Television Academy, December 12, 2011, https://interviews.televisionacademy.com/interviews/warren-littlefield.

77. Karen Herman, "Jay Sandrich," Television Academy, December 4, 2001, https://interviews.televisionacademy.com/interviews/jay-sandrich.

78. Dino-Day Ramos, "Binge-Watching 'A Different World': 17 Things You Totally Forgot about This Guilt-Free 'Cosby Show' Spin-Off," *Entertainment Tonight*, April 30, 2015, www.etonline.com/news/163731_17_things_you_forgot_about_a_different_world.

79. Mark Harris, "The Evolution of *A Different World*," *Entertainment Weekly*, April 12, 1991, https://ew.com/article/1991/04/12/evolution-different-world.

80. Diane Haithman, "Different Touch to 'Different World,'" *Los Angeles Times*, October 6, 1988, www.latimes.com/archives/la-xpm-1988-10-06-ca-4490-story.html; Harris, "Evolution."

81. Darnell Hunt, "Different World, A," Television Academy, 2017, https://interviews.televisionacademy.com/shows/different-world-a#about.

82. Robin R. Means Coleman and Andre M. Cavalcante, "Two *Different Worlds*: Television as a Producer's Medium," in *Watching While Black: Centering the Television of Black Audiences*, ed. Beretta E. Smith-Shomade, 34–35 (New Brunswick, NJ: Rutgers University Press, 2012).

83. Ibid., 36.

84. John Stark and Mike Alexander, "Dancer and Choreographer Debbie Allen: She's Moved to Prime-Time Directing," *People*, November 14, 1988, https://people.com/archive/its-a-different-world-for-dancer-and-choreographer-debbie-allen-shes-moved-to-prime-time-directing-vol-30-no-20.

85. Ibid.

86. Ibid., 37.

87. Haithman, "Different Touch to 'Different World.'"

88. *JET*, "Debbie Allen Tells Why 'A Different World' Is Rated Tops among Black TV Viewers" (1992), 82:58–59.

89. Coleman and Cavalcante, "Two *Different Worlds*," 40.

90. Ramos, "Binge-Watching 'A Different World.'"

91. Stephen J. Abramson, "Debbie Allen," Television Academy, April 15, 2011, https://interviews.televisionacademy.com/interviews/debbie-allen?clip=58726#highlight-clips.

92. Ibid.

93. Ramos, "Binge-Watching 'A Different World.'"

94. Alan Kistler, *Doctor Who: Celebrating Fifty Years* (Guilford, UK: Globe Pequot Press, 2013), 2; Jim Leach, *Doctor Who* (Detroit, MI: Wayne State University Press, 2009), 4.

95. Kistler, *Doctor Who*, 3.

96. Ibid.

97. Ibid., 4.

98. Ibid., 5.

99. Ibid.

100. Ibid.

101. Ibid., 9.

102. Ibid., 10.

103. Ibid.

104. Ibid., 14.

105. Ibid.

106. Ibid., 15–16.

107. Ibid.

108. Ibid., 17.

109. Leach, *Doctor Who*, 1.

110. Ibid.

111. Ibid., 2.

112. Ibid., 85–86.

113. Ibid., 2.

114. John Tulloch and Manuel Alvarado, *Doctor Who: The Unfolding Text* (London: Macmillan Press, 1983), 5.

115. Juliette Harrisson, "*Doctor Who*'s History Political & Social Consciousness," Den of Geek! November 28, 2018, www.denofgeek.com/us/tv/doctor-who/277876/doctor-whos-history-of-political-social-consciousness.

116. Lois Gresh and Danny Gresh, *Dragon Ball Z: An Unauthorized Guide* (New York: St. Martin's Press, 2000), 25–26

117. Ibid., 34–35.

118. Ibid., 24–25.

119. Ollie Barder, "Kazuhiko Torishima on Shaping the Success of 'Dragon Ball' and the Origins of 'Dragon Quest,'" *Forbes*, October 15, 2016, www.forbes.com/sites/olliebarder/2016/10/15/kazuhiko-torishima-on-shaping-the-success-of-dragon-ball-and-the-origins-of-dragon-quest/#c1c77d625e55.

120. Ibid.

121. Ibid.

122. Jonathan Clements and Helen McCarthy, *The Anime Encyclopedia: A Guide to Japanese Animation since 1917* (Berkeley, CA: Stone Bridge Press, 2001), 101–2.

123. Gresh and Gresh, *Dragon Ball Z*, 24–25.

124. Hal Erickson, *Television Cartoon Shows: An Illustrated Encyclopedia, 1949 through 2003* (Jefferson, NC: McFarland & Company, 2005), 283–85.

125. Brigid Alverson, "20 Years Ago, *Dragon Ball Z* Came to America to Stay," Comic Book Resources, September 18, 2016, www.cbr.com/20-years-ago-dragon-ball-z-came-to-america-to-stay.

126. Andrew Rivera, "How *Dragon Ball Z* Won the West," Now This Nerd, January 26, 2018, www.nowthisnerd.co/how-dragon-ball-z-won-the-west-nowthis-nerd.

127. Steve Harmon, "Reprinted Interview: 30-Something Questions with Gen Fukunaga," Dragonball Z Otaku Alliance, September 9, 1999, https://web.archive.org/web/20030819181750/http://www.dbzoa.net/features/gen_int.php.

128. Tom Usher, "'Dragon Ball Z' Superfans Tell Us Why the Franchise Is Still So Popular," Vice, January 31, 2019, www.vice.com/en_us/article/a3bgx8/dragon-ball-z-super-fans-tell-us-why-the-franchise-is-still-so-popular.

129. Erickson, *Television Cartoon Shows*, 284.

F

1. Josh Dean, "Seth MacFarlane's $2 Billion *Family Guy* Empire," Fast Company, November 1, 2008, www.fastcompany.com/1042476/seth-macfarlanes-2-billion-family-guy

-empire; Wendy Hilton-Morrow and David T. McMahon, "*The Flintstones* to *Futurama*: Networks and Prime Time Animation," in *Prime Time Animation: Television Animation and American Culture*, ed. Carol A. Stabile and Mark Harrison, 86 (New York: Routledge, 2003); Lacey Rose, "Seth MacFarlane: The Restless Mind of a Complicated Cartoonist," *Hollywood Reporter*, October 12, 2011, www.hollywoodreporter.com/news/seth-macfarlane-cartoonist-246805.

2. Dean, "Seth MacFarlane's $2 Billion"; Hilton-Morrow and McMahon, "*The Flintstones* to *Futurama*," 86; Rose, "Seth MacFarlane."

3. Dean, "Seth MacFarlane's $2 Billion"; Rose, "Seth MacFarlane."

4. Dean, "Seth MacFarlane's $2 Billion"; Rose, "Seth MacFarlane."

5. Dean, "Seth MacFarlane's $2 Billion"; Rose, "Seth MacFarlane"; Tim Stack, "A Brief History of the 'Family Guy,'" *Entertainment Weekly*, April 18, 2005, https://ew.com/article/2005/04/18/brief-history-family-guy.

6. Stack, "A Brief History of the 'Family Guy.'"

7. Dean, "Seth MacFarlane's $2 Billion"; Hilton-Morrow and McMahon, "*The Flintstones* to *Futurama*"; Rose, "Seth MacFarlane."

8. M. Keith Booker, *Drawn to Television: Prime-Time Animation from* The Flintstones *to* Family Guy (Westport, CT: Praeger, 2006), 82.

9. Hilton-Morrow and McMahon, "*The Flintstones* to *Futurama*," 86.

10. Booker, *Drawn to Television*, 82.

11. Stack, "A Brief History of the 'Family Guy.'"

12. Ibid.

13. Booker, *Drawn to Television*, 82.

14. Ibid.

15. Ibid.

16. Dean, "Seth MacFarlane's $2 Billion."

17. Paul Simpson and David Hughes, *Farscape: The Illustrated Companion* (New York: Tor, 2000), 8.

18. Brian Henson, Ben Browder, and Rockne O'Bannon, "Audio Commentary for 'Premiere,'" in Farscape: *Complete Series* (New York: Cinedigm, 2013), Blu-Ray.

19. Simpson and Hughes, *Farscape*, 11–12.

20. Ibid., 12.

21. Lisa Granshaw, "The Bad Timing of 'Bad Timing': An Oral History of *Farscape*'s Surprise Series Finale," SyFy Wire, March 27, 2018, www.syfy.com/syfywire/the-bad-timing-of-bad-timing-an-oral-history-of-farscapes-surprise-series-finale.

22. Simpson and Hughes, *Farscape*, 13.

23. Trent Moore, "15 Years Later: Why *Farscape* Still Matters," SyFy Wire, March 19, 2014, www.syfy.com/syfywire/15-years-later-why-farscape-still-matters.

24. Simpson and Hughes, *Farscape*, 13.

25. Ibid., 14.

26. Ibid., 15.

27. Ibid., 10.

28. Moore, "15 Years Later."

29. Jes Battis, "Farscape," in *The Essential Cult TV Reader*, ed. David Lavery, 104–55 (Lexington: University Press of Kentucky, 2010).

30. Granshaw, "The Bad Timing of 'Bad Timing.'"

31. Ibid.

32. Battis, "Farscape," 110.

33. Garry Berman, *Best of the Britcoms: From* Fawlty Towers *to* The Office (New York: Taylor Trade, 2011), 17.

34. Ibid.

35. David Bianculli, *The Platinum Age of Television: From* I Love Lucy *to* The Walking Dead, *How TV Became Terrific* (New York: Anchor Books, 2016), 292.

36. Douglas McCall, *Monty Python: A Chronology 1969–2012* (Jefferson, NC: McFarland & Company, 2014), 35.

37. "*Fawlty Towers* at 40: Seven Surprising Facts about the Perfect Sitcom," *The Week*, September 25, 2015, www.theweek.co.uk/65445/fawlty-towers-at-40-seven-surprising -facts-about-the-perfect-sitcom.

38. Ibid.

39. Ibid.

40. Ibid.

41. Berman, *Best of the Britcoms*, 18.

42. McCall, *Monty Python*, 44.

43. Ibid., 54.

44. Bianculli, *The Platinum Age of Television*, 292.

45. *Glasgow Herald*, "Divorce for Cleese," September 9, 1978.

46. McCall, *Monty Python*, 65.

47. Anna Green, "13 High-Strung Facts about *Fawlty Towers*," Mental Floss, June 7, 2016, http://mentalfloss.com/article/80111/13-high-strung-facts-about-fawlty-towers.

48. Ibid.

49. Brian Jay Jones, *Jim Henson: The Biography* (New York: Ballantine Books, 2013), 324–25.

50. Ibid., 324–25; Henson.com, "Jim Henson's Red Book, 7/3–11/1981," July 11, 2011, www.henson.com/jimsredbook/2011/07/73-111981; Christopher Finch, *Jim Henson: The Works, the Art, the Magic, the Imagination* (New York: Random House, 1993), 202–3.

51. Lily Rothman, "10 Things You Didn't Know about *Fraggle Rock*," *Time*, May 14, 2013, http://entertainment.time.com/2013/05/14/10-things-you-didnt-know-about-fraggle -rock.

52. Finch, *Jim Henson*, 203; Jones, *Jim Henson*, 326–27.

53. Jones, *Jim Henson*, 341.

54. Ibid., 337.

55. Ibid., 338–39.

56. Robin Levinson King. "Inside Toronto's Shared History with *Fraggle Rock*," *The Star*, March 20, 2015, www.thestar.com/entertainment/television/2015/03/20/inside-torontos -shared-history-with-fraggle-rock.html.

57. Jones, *Jim Henson*, 340.

58. Ibid., 341.

59. Ibid., 342.

60. Ibid., 387.

61. Ibid., 11.

62. Ibid., 12.

63. Ibid., 19.

64. Ibid., 20–22, 25.

65. Ibid., 33–37.

66. Ibid., 41.

67. Ibid., 44–45.

68. Ibid., 138.

69. Robert Lloyd, "2 Good 2 Be 4gotten: An Oral History of *Freaks and Geeks*," *Vanity Fair*, December 6, 2012, www.vanityfair.com/hollywood/2013/01/freaks-and-geeks-oral -history.

70. Brent Hodge, "Freaks and Geeks: The Documentary," *Cultureshock*, July 16, 2018, A&E TV; Genevieve Koski, "Paul Feig Walks Us through *Freaks and Geeks* (Part 1 or 5),"

AV Club, April 9, 2012, https://tv.avclub.com/paul-feig-walks-us-through-freaks-and-geeks-part-1-of-1798230923.

71. Lloyd, "2 Good 2 Be 4gotten"; Jennifer Vineyard, "An Oral History of the Nerdier Half of *Freaks and Geeks*," Vulture, November 11, 2015, www.vulture.com/2015/10/freaks-and-geeks-oral-history-of-the-nerdier-half.html.

72. Lloyd, "2 Good 2 Be 4gotten."

73. Ibid.

74. Lloyd, "2 Good 2 Be 4gotten"; Vineyard, "An Oral History of the Nerdier Half."

75. Lloyd, "2 Good 2 Be 4gotten."

76. Ibid.

77. Ibid.

78. Hodge, "Freaks and Geeks"; Michael Schneider, "Former NBC Exec Garth Ancier Responds to Seth Rogen about *Freaks and Geeks*' Cancellation," *TV Guide*, October 14, 2014, www.tvguide.com/news/freaks-geeks-seth-rogen-cancellation-nbc-garth-ancier-1088062; Allan Sepinwall and Matt Zoller Seitz, *TV (The Book): Two Experts Pick the Greatest American Shows of All Time* (New York: Grand Central Publishing, 2016), 137.

79. Hodge, "Freaks and Geeks"; Lloyd, "2 Good 2 Be 4gotten."

80. Sepinwall and Seitz, *TV (The Book)*, 134.

81. Lloyd, "2 Good 2 Be 4gotten"; Robert Lloyd, "Too Good and Weird," *L.A. Weekly*, May 10, 2000, www.laweekly.com/too-good-and-weird.

82. Lloyd, "2 Good 2 Be 4gotten"; Jonathan Gray, "Freaks and Geeks," *The Essential Cult TV Reader*, ed. David Lavery, 120–21 (Lexington: University Press of Kentucky, 2010).

83. Gray, "Freaks and Geeks," 120–21.

84. Jonathan Bernstein, "'Life Is Messy': Judd Apatow on *Freaks and Geeks*, Lena Dunham and His Return to Standup," *Guardian*, July 8, 2017, www.theguardian.com/film/2017/jul/08/judd-apatow-freaks-and-geeks-big-sick-lena-dunham.

85. Amanda Green, "20 Things You Might Not Know about Freaks and Geeks," Mental Floss, February 5, 2016, http://mentalfloss.com/article/56049/20-things-you-might-not-have-known-about-freaks-and-geeks.

86. Justin Heckert, "The Making of *Frisky Dingo*," *Atlanta Magazine*, October 2005, 115.

87. Ibid.

88. Ibid., 136.

89. Ibid., 146.

90. Ibid.

91. Emma Loggins, "Exclusive: Adam Reed on the Origins of FX's 'Archer,'" FanBolt, November 21, 2015, www.fanbolt.com/6121/exclusive-adam-reed-on-the-origins-of-fxs-archer.

92. Brooke Hatfield, "Frisky Business: Adult Swim behind the Scenes," *Paste Magazine*, March 1, 2008, www.pastemagazine.com/articles/2008/03/frisky-business-adult-swim-behind-the-scenes.html.

93. Ibid.

94. Susan Stewart, "Look! Past the Cubicles and the Copy Machine! A Superhero!" *New York Times*, October 14, 2006, www.nytimes.com/2006/10/14/arts/television/14stew.html.

95. Dan Iverson, "August TV Preview," IGN, June 14, 2012, www.ign.com/articles/2007/08/02/august-tv-preview?

96. Joe Reid, "Today in TV History: 'Frisky Dingo' Ended Its Two-Season Run with a Bonanza of Weirdness," Decider, https://decider.com/2016/03/23/today-in-tv-history-frisky-dingo-ended-its-two-season-run-with-a-bonanza-of-weirdness.

97. David McCutcheon, "*Frisky Dingo* S1 Due," IGN, www.ign.com/articles/2008/02/22/frisky-dingo-s1-due.

98. David McCutcheon, *"Frisky Dingo* S2 Due," IGN, www.ign.com/articles/ 2008/10/28/frisky-dingo-s2-due.

99. Reid, "Today in TV History."

100. Brian Doherty, "Matt Groening," *Mother Jones*, March 1999, www.motherjones .com/media/1999/03/matt-groening; Dan Snierson, *"Futurama* Returns—But There's a Twist," *Entertainment Weekly*, September 8, 2017, https://ew.com/tv/2017/09/08/futurama -returns-twist.

101. Wendy Hilton-Morrow and David T. McMahon, *"The Flintstones* to *Futurama*: Networks and Prime Time Animation," in *Prime Time Animation: Television Animation and American Culture*, ed. Carol A. Stabile and Mark Harrison, 85 (New York: Routledge, 2003).

102. Doherty, "Matt Groening"; Snierson, *"Futurama* Returns."

103. Doherty, "Matt Groening."

104. Ibid.

105. Ibid.

106. Hilton-Morrow and McMahon, *"The Flintstones* to *Futurama*," 86.

107. Snierson, *"Futurama* Returns.

108. Nick Shaerf, "Long Live *Futurama*," Paley Matters, June 7, 2019, https://paley matters.org/long-live-futurama-a9d0aff7da8a; Allan Sepinwall and Matt Zoller Seitz, *TV (The Book): Two Experts Pick the Greatest American Shows of All Time* (New York: Grand Central Publishing, 2016), 255.

109. Shaerf, "Long Live *Futurama*."

110. Henry Hanks, "Good News, Everyone: 'Futurama' is back!" CNN, June 24, 2010, www.cnn.com/2010/SHOWBIZ/TV/06/23/futurama.return.

111. Shaerf, "Long Live *Futurama*."

112. Ibid.

113. Ibid.

114. Snierson, *"Futurama* Returns.

115. Matthew Hart, "How *Futurama* Nailed the Science of Comedy," Nerdist, July 26, 2016, https://nerdist.com/article/how-futurama-nailed-the-science-of-comedy.

116. Alicja Zelazko, "Matt Groening," *Encyclopaedia Britannica*, 2019, www.britannica .com/topic/The-Simpsons.

117. Andrew Duncan, "Matt Groening Interview," *Radio Times*, September 24, 1999, https://web.archive.org/web/20000824042839/http://www.frcr.com/library/radio_ times1.html.

118. Zelazko, "Matt Groening."

119. Duncan, "Matt Groening Interview."

120. Zelazko, "Matt Groening."

121. Snierson, *"Futurama* Returns; Zelazko, "Matt Groening Interview."

122. Duncan, "Matt Groening Interview."

123. Zelazko, "Matt Groening."

124. Ibid.

G

1. Jamie Greene, "An Oral History of *Gargoyles*, Disney's Groundbreaking Animated Series," SyFy Wire, November 7, 2018, www.syfy.com/syfywire/an-oral-history-of-gar goyles-disneys-groundbreaking-animated-series.

2. Ibid.

3. Ibid.

4. Ibid.

5. Ibid.

6. Ibid.

7. Ibid.

8. *Oh My Disney*, "What Made Gargoyles So Groundbreaking," 2015, https://ohmy.disney.com/insider/2015/09/17/what-made-gargoyles-so-groundbreaking.

9. Ibid.

10. Jordan Calhoun, "'I Knew It Was Something Special': An Exclusive Interview with *Gargoyles* creator Greg Weisman," Black Nerd Problems, 2017, https://blacknerdproblems.com/i-knew-it-was-something-special-an-exclusive-interview-with-gargoyles-creator-greg-weisman.

11. Greene, "An Oral History of *Gargoyles*."

12. Ibid.

13. Ibid.

14. Ibid.

15. Calhoun, "'I Knew It Was Something Special.'"

16. Bill Graham, "Disney Taps G.I. Joe: The Rise of Cobra Scribes to Pen *Gargoyles* Film," Collider, July 19, 2011, http://collider.com/david-elliot-disney-gargoyle-film-paul-lovett; Ben Pearson, "Jordan Peele Reportedly Wants to Direct a 'Gargoyles' Movie at Disney," SlashFilm, June 12, 2018, www.slashfilm.com/jordan-peele-gargoyles-movie.

17. Danijel Striga, "15 Things You Forgot about *Gargoyles*," ScreenRant, December 23, 2016, https://screenrant.com/disney-gargoyles-facts-trivia-secrets.

18. Sherwood Schwartz, *Inside Gilligan's Island: From Creation to Syndication* (Jefferson, NC: McFarland & Company, 1988), 25.

19. Schwartz, *Inside Gilligan's Island*, 1–2.

20. Allan Sepinwall and Matt Zoller Seitz, *TV (The Book): Two Experts Pick the Greatest American Shows of All Time* (New York: Grand Central Publishing, 2016), 321.

21. Schwartz, *Inside Gilligan's Island*, 27–29; Russell Johnson and Steve Cox, *Here on Gilligan's Isle* (New York: HarperCollins, 1992), 16.

22. Schwartz, *Inside Gilligan's Island*, 47.

23. Ibid.

24. Ibid., 54.

25. Ibid., 51.

26. Schwartz, *Inside Gilligan's Island*, 54; Johnson and Cox, *Here on Gilligan's Isle*, 18–19.

27. Schwartz, *Inside Gilligan's Island*, 70, 79.

28. Ibid., 86.

29. Ibid., 90.

30. Schwartz, *Inside Gilligan's Island*, 106–7; Johnson and Cox, *Here on Gilligan's Isle*, 17–18.

31. Schwartz, *Inside Gilligan's Island*, 164.

32. Schwartz, *Inside Gilligan's Island*, 201–3; Sylvia Stoddard, *TV Treasures: A Companion Guide to Gilligan's Island* (New York: St. Martin's Paperbacks, 1996), 306.

33. Schwartz, *Inside Gilligan's Island*, 207–10.

34. Ibid., 216, 223.

35. Ibid., 234.

36. Ibid., 240.

37. Ibid., 243.

38. Sepinwall and Seitz, *TV (The Book)*, 321.

39. A. S. Berman, *The Gilmore Girls Companion* (Albany, NY: BearManor Media, 2010), 20–21.

40. Ibid., 25.

41. Ibid., 26.

42. Ibid., 29.

43. Ibid., 30.

44. Ibid., 32.

45. Ibid., 33.

46. Ibid.

47. Ibid., 36.

48. Ibid., 44.

49. Ibid., 46.

50. Samantha Highfill, "*Gilmore Girls*: An Oral History," *Entertainment Weekly*, November 25, 2016, https://ew.com/article/2016/11/25/gilmore-girls-oral-history.

51. Highfill, "*Gilmore Girls*"; Berman, *The Gilmore Girls Companion*, 393.

52. Berman, *The Gilmore Girls Companion*, 397.

53. Ibid., 453.

54. Ibid., 455.

55. Highfill, "*Gilmore Girls*"; Tony Sokol and Kayti Burt, "*Gilmore Girls* Revival Cast, Release Date, Trailer, and Posters," Den of Geek! October 25, 2016, www.denofgeek.com/us/tv/gilmore-girls/252610/gilmore-girls-revival-cast-release-date-trailer-and-posters.

56. Kaitlyn Tiffany, "The New *Gilmore Girls* Is Weirdly Hostile toward Fans, Women, and Storytelling in General," The Verge, November 28, 2016, www.theverge.com/2016/11/28/13765088/gilmore-girls-year-in-the-life-review-netflix; Patricia Garcia, "11 Things in *Gilmore Girls: A Year in the Life* That Made Absolutely No Sense," *Vogue*, November 28, 2016, www.vogue.com/article/gilmore-girls-a-year-in-the-life-nonsense.

57. Stephanie Topacio Long, "12 Facts about 'The Golden Girls' That Give Fans a Look Behind the Lanai," Bustle, April 5, 2016, www.bustle.com/articles/152068-12-facts-about-the-golden-girls-that-give-fans-a-look-behind-the-lanai.

58. James Colucci, *Golden Girls Forever: An Unauthorized Look behind the Lanai* (New York: HarperCollins, 2016), 6.

59. Ibid., 7–8.

60. Ibid.

61. Ibid.

62. Ibid., 11–12.

63. Ibid., 14.

64. Ibid., 15.

65. Kara Kovalchik, "20 Fun Facts about *The Golden Girls*," Mental Floss, September 14, 2017, http://mentalfloss.com/article/56215/20-fun-facts-about-golden-girls.

66. Ibid.

67. Ibid.

68. Collucci, *Golden Girls Forever*, 17.

69. Ibid., 21.

70. Ibid., 22–23.

71. Vincent Terrace, *Television Series of the 1980s: Essential Facts and Quirky Details* (Lanham, MD: Rowman & Littlefield, 2017), 89.

72. Ibid., 363.

73. Ibid., 364–65.

74. Ibid., 354.

75. Ibid., 49–51.

76. Chris Pastrick, "'Golden Girls'—As Puppets—Coming to Pittsburgh's Byham Theater," *TribLive*, August 20, 2019, https://triblive.com/aande/theater-arts/golden-girls-as-puppets-coming-to-pittsburghs-byahm-theater.

H

1. Jesse McLean, *The Art and Making of* Hannibal: *The Television Series* (London: Titan Books, 2015), 8.

2. Ibid.

3. Abbie Bernstein, "*Hannibal* News on Season 1, Season 2 and Beyond from Showrunner Bryan Fuller," AssignmentX, June 13, 2013, www.assignmentx.com/2013/exclusive-interview-hannibal-news-on-season-1-season-2-and-beyond-from-showrunner-bryan-fuller.

4. Ibid.

5. Ibid.

6. McLean, *The Art and Making of* Hannibal, 10.

7. Ibid.

8. Nellie Andreeva, "'NBC Gives Straight-to-Series Order to 'Hannibal,' Picks Up 'Notorious' Drama Pilot," *Deadline*, February 14, 2012, https://deadline.com/2012/02/nbc-gives-series-order-to-hannibal-picks-up-notorious-drama-pilot-231085.

9. McLean, *The Art and Making of* Hannibal, 10–11.

10. Clark Collis, "David Tennant almost Starred in NBC's *Hannibal*," *Entertainment Weekly*, April 21, 2018, https://ew.com/tv/2018/04/21/david-tennant-hannibal.

11. Bernstein, "*Hannibal* News."

12. Eric Goldman, "*Hannibal*: How Bryan Fuller Approached the Iconic Character," IGN, April 3, 2012, www.ign.com/articles/2013/04/04/hannibal-how-bryan-fuller-approached-the-iconic-character-and-why-clarice-starling-cant-appear-red-dragon-the-silence-of-the-lambs?page=1.

13. Kristin Acuna, "There Is a Simple Reason No One Is Watching NBC's Excellent 'Hannibal,'" *Business Insider*, July 17, 2014, www.businessinsider.com/why-no-one-is-watching-hannibal-2014-7.

14. Zack Sharf, "'Hannibal': Bryan Fuller Explains the One Murder Too Bloody and Disgusting for Broadcast Television," IndieWire, October 13, 2017, www.indiewire.com/2017/10/hannibal-bryan-fuller-murder-cut-scene-graphic-1201887137.

15. AJ Marechal, "NBC Pulls 'Hannibal' Episode in Wake of Violent Tragedies," *Variety*, April 19, 2013, https://variety.com/2013/tv/news/nbc-pulls-episode-4-of-hannibal-in-wake-of-newtown-boston-bombings-1200390579.

16. Michael Ausiello, "*Hannibal* Cancelled at NBC," TV Line, June 22, 2015, https://tvline.com/2015/06/22/hannibal-cancelled-nbc-season-4.

17. *TV Guide*, "Bryan Fuller," 2019, www.tvguide.com/celebrities/bryan-fuller/bio/286341.

18. LivingDeadGuy.com, "Bryan Fuller Bio," 2013, http://livingdeadguy.com/bryan-fuller-bio.

19. Ibid.

20. Ibid.

21. Ibid.

22. Daniel Holloway, "'American Gods' Showrunners Bryan Fuller, Michael Green Exit," *Variety*, November 29, 2017, https://variety.com/2017/tv/news/american-gods-1202626402.

23. Brian C. Baer, *How He-Man Mastered the Universe: Toy to Television to the Big Screen* (Jefferson, NC: McFarland & Company, 2017), 24.

24. Ibid.

25. Ibid., 25.

26. Ibid., 27.

27. Jamie Greene, "A Thorough Oral History of *He-Man and the Masters of the Universe*, the Game-Changing '80s Toon," SyFy Wire, February 1, 2019, www.syfy .com/syfywire/a-thorough-oral-history-of-he-man-and-the-masters-of-the-universe-the -game-changing-80s.

28. Baer, *How He-Man Mastered the Universe*, 30.

29. Ibid., 40.

30. Ibid., 46–47.

31. Baer, *How He-Man Mastered the Universe*, 46–47; Greene, "A Thorough Oral History of *He-Man*."

32. Baer, *How He-Man Mastered the Universe*, 48–49.

33. Ibid., 49.

34. Ibid., 51.

35. Ibid.

36. Ibid., 52.

37. Joe Garner and Michael Ashley, *It's Saturday Morning: Celebrating the Golden Era of Cartoons, 1960s–1990s* (Bellevue, WA: Quarto Publishing Group, 2018), 127.

38. Baer, *How He-Man Mastered the Universe*, 38–39.

39. Ibid., 53.

40. Baer, *How He-Man Mastered the Universe*, 51.

41. Ibid., 50.

42. Ibid., 50, 53.

43. Greene, "A Thorough Oral History of *He-Man*."

44. Loren Bouchard, "Interview with Lauren Bouchard," Home Movies*: Season One* (Los Angeles: Shout Factory, 2004), DVD, Disc 1; Cynthia Werthamer, "Poundstone Heads Talented Cast of 'Home Movies,'" *Ocala Star-Banner*, April 24, 1999, https://news.google .com/newspapers?nid=1356&dat=19990424&id=_uFPAAAAIBAJ&sjid=rQgEAAAAIBAJ &pg=3788,5353392&hl=en.

45. Werthamer, "Poundstone Heads Talented Cast."

46. Ibid.

47. G4 TV, Home Movies *Creator Brendon Small Video*, YouTube, February 13, 2006, www.youtube.com/watch?v=Iamh5tOdEKk.

48. Dennis Tracy, "'Home Movies' and Its Sublime Weirdness," *Marquette Wire*, May 7, 2016, https://marquettewire.org/3950209/ae/tracy-home-movies-and-its-sublime -weirdness.

49. Werthamer, "Poundstone Heads Talented Cast."

50. Erik Adams, "Before TV Revivals Happened Every Day, Adult Swim Turned *Home Movies*' Camera Back On," AV Club, May 17, 2018, www.avclub.com/before-tv-revivals -happened-every-day-adult-swim-turne-1826075574.

51. Brendon Small, "I Am a Comedy Person Who Makes *Metalocalypse*, the Dethklok Records, *Home Movies* and the Galaktikon Record," BestofAMA.com, April 26, 2012, https:// bestofama.com/amas/stth5.

52. Bouchard, "Interview with Lauren Bouchard."

53. Laura Fries, "Home Movies," *Variety*, April 26, 1999, https://variety.com/1999/tv/ reviews/home-movies-2-1200457163.

54. M. Keith Booker, *Drawn to Television: Prime-Time Animation from* The Flintstones *to* Family Guy (Westport, CT: Praeger, 2006), 181.

55. Ibid.

56. G4 TV, Home Movies *Creator Brendon Small*; Tracy, "'Home Movies.'"

57. Tracy, "'Home Movies.'"

58. Timothy Burke and Kevin Burke, *Saturday Morning Fever: Growing Up with Cartoon Culture* (New York: St. Martin's Griffin, 1999), 127.

59. Andy Lewis, "Inside Sid & Marty Krofft's Trippy World: 'We Screwed with Every Kid's Mind,'" *Hollywood Reporter*, January 15, 2016, www.hollywoodreporter.com/news/inside-sid-marty-kroffts-trippy-856067.

60. Karen Herman, "Sid and Marty Krofft," Academy of Television Arts and Sciences, July 27, 2000, https://interviews.televisionacademy.com/interviews/marty-krofft.

61. Lewis, "Inside Sid & Marty Krofft's Trippy World."

62. Herman, "Sid and Marty Krofft."

63. Ibid.

64. Ibid.

65. Ibid.

66. Ibid.

67. Ibid.

68. Burke and Burke, *Saturday Morning Fever*, 128; Herman, "Sid and Marty Krofft"; Fred Russell, "Passing Show," *Bridgeport Post*, January 22, 1970, 21.

69. Mark McCray, *The Best Saturdays of Our Lives* (Bloomington, IN: iUniverse, 2015), 48.

70. Herman, "Sid and Marty Krofft."

71. Lewis, "Inside Sid & Marty Krofft's Trippy World"; Maggie Wang, "*H.R. Pufnstuf* Returns to Kids TV for the First Time in over 45 Years in Sid & Marty Krofft's Preschool Hit *Mutt & Stuff* on Nickelodeon," October 13, 2015, www.nickpress.com/press-releases/2015/10/13/h-r-pufnstuf-returns-to-kids-tv-for-first-time-in-over-45-years-in-sid-marty-kroffts-preschool-hit-mutt-stuff-on-nickelodeon.

72. Burke and Burke, *Saturday Morning Fever*, 130.

I

1. Staff of *Iron Chef, Iron Chef: The Official Book*, tr. Kaoru Hoketsu (New York: Berkeley Books, 2000), 69.

2. Ibid., 131.

3. Ibid., 133.

4. Staff of *Iron Chef, Iron Chef*, 93; Jake Vigliotti, "The Untold Truth of *Iron Chef*," Mashed, February 22, 2018, www.mashed.com/38874/untold-truth-iron-chef/.

5. Staff of *Iron Chef, Iron Chef*, 94; Fuji TV, "The Iron Man of Cooking," October 16, 2012, https://web.archive.org/web/20121018002313/http:/www.fujitv.co.jp/fujitv/news/pub_2012/121016-371.html.

6. Staff of *Iron Chef, Iron Chef*, 54–55.

7. Ibid., 81.

8. Ibid., 102.

9. Staff of *Iron Chef, Iron Chef*; Fuji TV, "The Iron Man of Cooking."

10. Staff of *Iron Chef, Iron Chef*, 95.

11. Ibid., 29.

12. Ibid., 65–66.

13. Ibid., 1.

14. Staff of *Iron Chef, Iron Chef*, 2–6; Vigliotti, "The Untold Truth of *Iron Chef*."

15. Elizabeth Sherman, "Your Guide to Every 'Iron Chef' Spin-Off," *Food & Wine*, July 26, 2017, www.foodandwine.com/news/iron-chef-spin-offs.

16. Fuji TV, "The Iron Man of Cooking."

17. Sonali Kohli, "When Cooking Became Competition," *Atlantic*, October 2, 2014, www.theatlantic.com/entertainment/archive/2014/10/the-year-when-cooking-became-a-competition/381037.

18. Ron Rosenbaum, "Anthony Bourdain's Theory on the Foodie Revolution," *Smithsonian Magazine*, July 2014, www.smithsonianmag.com/arts-culture/anthony-bourdains -theory-foodie-revolution-180951848.

19. Jordan Reid, "The (Real) 'It's Always Sunny in Philadelphia' Origin Story," *Observer*, July 29, 2016, https://observer.com/2016/07/the-real-its-always-sunny-in-philadelphia -origin-story.

20. Ibid.

21. Indigo Productions, "The $85 TV Pilot: The Origins of *It's Always Sunny in Philadelphia*, June 3, 2014, www.indigoprod.com/nyc-video-production-blog/2014/06/the-85-tv -pilot-the-origins-of-its-always-sunny-in-philadelphia.

22. Ibid.

23. Ibid.

24. Ibid.

25. Eric Goldman, "*It's Always Sunny in Philadelphia* Premiere," IGN, June 28, 2006, www.ign.com/articles/2006/06/28/its-always-sunny-in-philadelphia-premiere.

26. Reid, "The (Real) 'It's Always Sunny in Philadelphia.'"

27. Ibid.

28. Ibid.

29. Indigo Productions, "The $85 TV Pilot."

30. Ibid.

31. Edward Wyatt, "The Writers Are the Actors Are the Producers," *New York Times*, September 9, 2007, www.nytimes.com/2007/09/09/arts/television/09wyat.html.

32. Scott Davis, "Here's How Danny DeVito Saved 'It's Always Sunny in Philadelphia' from Getting Canceled," *Business Insider*, March 11, 2015, www.businessinsider.com/how -danny-devito-joined-its-always-sunny-in-philadelphia-2015-3.

33. Wyatt, "The Writers Are the Actors."

34. Jennifer M. Wood, "The Nightman Cometh: An Oral History of *It's Always Sunny in Philadelphia*'s Musical Episode-Turned-Live Show Phenomenon," *GQ*, October 3, 2018, www.gq.com/story/the-nightman-cometh-oral-history.

35. Whitney Matheson, "The 'Nightman Cometh' to a City Near You," *USA Today*, August 6, 2009, http://content.usatoday.com/communities/popcandy/post/2009/08/ the-nightman-cometh-to-a-city-near-you/1#.XUyfqehKhPY.

36. Kimberly Roots, "*American Horror Story, Mayans M.C., It's Always Sunny* Set Fall Premieres," TV Line, June 24, 2019, https://tvline.com/2019/06/24/ahs-1984-premiere -date-american-horror-story-season-9-fx.

37. Nellie Andreeva, "FX Boss on 'It's Always Sunny': "There Is a Good Chance It May Go Past Season 14," *Deadline*, February 4, 2019, https://deadline.com/2019/02/fx-boss-its -always-sunny-there-is-season-15-renewal-past-14-1202549259.

J

1. Sherry Spradlin, dir., *Bob Ross: The Happy Painter* (Roanoke, VA: Blue Ridge PBS, 2011), DVD.

2. Danny Hajek, "The Real Bob Ross: Meet the Meticulous Artist behind Those Happy Trees," NPR, August 29, 2016, www.npr.org/2016/08/29/490923502/the-real-bob-ross -meet-the-meticulous-artist-behind-those-happy-trees.

3. Linda Shrieves, "Bob Ross Uses His Brush to Spread Paint and Joy," *Orlando Sentinel*, July 7, 1990, www.orlandosentinel.com/news/os-xpm-1990-07-07-9007060122-story.html.

4. Spradlin, *Bob Ross*.

5. Ibid.

6. Ibid.

7. Shrieves, "Bob Ross Uses His Brush."

8. Spradlin, *Bob Ross*.

9. Ibid.

10. Ibid.

11. Ibid.

12. Hajek, "The Real Bob Ross"; Joe Kloc, "The Soothing Sounds of Bob Ross," *Newsweek*, October 1, 2014, www.newsweek.com/2014/10/10/soothing-sounds-bob-ross-274466.html.

13. Shrieves, "Bob Ross Uses His Brush."

14. Spradlin, *Bob Ross*.

15. Spradlin, *Bob Ross*; Kloc, "The Soothing Sounds of Bob Ross."

16. Kloc, "The Soothing Sounds of Bob Ross."

17. Spradlin, *Bob Ross*.

18. Hajek, "The Real Bob Ross."

19. Bob Ross, "World Map with Links," 2019, www.bobross.com/Articles.asp?ID=253.

20. Bob Ross, "Update from Comic-Con San Diego," July 21, 2019, https://experience .bobross.com/2019/07/21/update-from-comic-con-san-diego.

21. Matt Porter, "5.6 Million People Watched Bob Ross' Twitch Marathon," IGN, May 2, 2017, hwww.ign.com/articles/2015/11/09/56-million-people-watched-bob-ross-twitch -marathon.

22. The Biography.com, "Bob Ross Biography," April 12, 2019, www.biography.com/ artist/bob-ross.

K

1. Zadie Smith, "Brother from Another Mother," *New Yorker*, February 23, 2015, www .newyorker.com/magazine/2015/02/23/brother-another-mother.

2. Ibid.

3. Michael Schneider, "Keegan-Michael Key on Why *Key & Peele* Has to End, What's Next and the Comedy Central Series' Legacy," *TV Insider*, September 9, 2015, www.tvin sider.com/38401/keegan-michael-key-on-why-key-and-peele-has-to-end.

4. Ibid.

5. Ibid.

6. Jenni Runyan, "Comedy Central Greenlights Two New Series for the 2012 Season," Comedy Central Press Release, June 28, 2011, https://web.archive.org/web/2012022218 0100/http:/www.comedycentral.com/press/press_releases/2011/062911_nick-kroll-and -keyandpeele-pickup.jhtml.

7. Smith, "Brother from Another Mother."

8. Joe Berkowitz, "Innovation through Improvisation: How 'Key & Peele' Busted the Formula and Created Something New," Fast Company, December 9, 2013, www.fast company.com/1682938/innovation-through-improvisation-how-key-peele-busted-the -formula-and-created-something-new.

9. B. Alan Orange, "Key & Peele Launch Obama Anger Translator," MovieWeb, January 12, 2012, https://movieweb.com/key-peele-launch-obama-anger-translator.

10. Comedy Central, "Keegan-Michael Key and Jordan Peele Come to Comedy Central with New Series 'Key & Peele,'" TV by the Numbers, January 4, 2012, https://tvbythenum bers.zap2it.com/press-releases/keegan-michael-key-and-jordan-peele-come-to-comedy -central-with-new-series-key-peele/115317.

11. Philiana Ng, "Comedy Central Renews 'Key & Peele' for Season 2," *Hollywood Reporter*, February 14, 2012, www.hollywoodreporter.com/news/key-and-peele-renewed -comedy-central-290530.

12. Berkowitz, "Innovation through Improvisation."

13. Steve Pond, "'Key & Peele' to End Its Comedy Central Run after This Season (Exclusive)," *The Wrap*, July 25, 2015, www.thewrap.com/key-peele-to-end-its-comedy-central -run-after-this-season-exclusive.

14. Lesley Goldberg, "Comedy Central Expands 'Key & Peele,' Develops Animated Spinoff," *Hollywood Reporter*, March 12, 2014, www.hollywoodreporter.com/live-feed/ comedy-central-expands-key-peele-687906.

15. Pond, "'Key & Peele.'"

16. Elizabeth Blair, "For 'Black Nerds Everywhere,' Two Comedy Heroes," NPR, January 27, 2012, www.npr.org/2012/01/27/145838407/for-black-nerds-everywhere-two -comedy-heroes.

17. Marisa Guthrie, "Key and Peele: 'Lorne Michaels Has a History of Relating to White Men' (Q&A)," *Hollywood Reporter*, December 18, 2013, www.hollywoodreporter.com/ news/key-peele-obama-judd-apatow-666399; Wesley Morris, "Jordan Peele's X-ray Vision," *New York Times*, December 20, 2017, www.nytimes.com/2017/12/20/magazine/ jordan-peeles-x-ray-vision.html.

18. Guthrie, "Key and Peele"; Morris, "Jordan Peele's X-ray Vision."

19. Guthrie, "Key and Peele."

20. Maritza Fernandez, "Jordan Peele (1979–)," Blackpast, December 18, 2018, www .blackpast.org/african-american-history/peele-jordan-1979.

21. Paul Myers, *The Kids in the Hall: One Dumb Guy* (Toronto: Anansi Press, 2018), 23–24; Alex Yablon, "The Strange and Lasting Comedy Genius of *The Kids in the Hall*," Vulture, May 1, 2015, www.vulture.com/2015/05/weird-comedy-genius-of-the-kids-in-the-hall .html; John Semley, *This Is a Book about The Kids in the Hall* (Toronto: ECW Press, 2016), 34.

22. Myers, *The Kids in the Hall*, 43; John Semley, "Hall Pass: An Oral History of *The Kids in the Hall*," *Now Magazine*, December 5, 2013, https://nowtoronto.com/culture/stage/ hall-pass.

23. Myers, *The Kids in the Hall*, 49–51.

24. Ibid., 54.

25. Ibid., 56–57.

26. Ibid., 78.

27. Ibid., 98–99.

28. Semley, "Hall Pass"; Yablon, "The Strange and Lasting Comedy Genius."

29. Myers, *The Kids in the Hall*, 101.

30. Ibid., 103.

31. Ibid., 104–5.

32. Ibid., 112.

33. Ibid., 133.

34. Myers, *The Kids in the Hall*, 113–14; Semley *This Is a Book*, 109.

35. Semley, *This Is a Book*, 108.

36. Myers, *The Kids in the Hall*, 117.

37. Ibid., 135.

38. Semley, *This Is a Book*, 112.

39. Ibid., 135.

40. Ibid., 194–95.

41. Ibid., 205.

42. Ibid., 205–6.

43. Semley, "Hall Pass."

44. Ibid.

45. Amanda Wicks, *The Kids in the Hall*: Better Together," *Paste Magazine*, May 27, 2015, www.pastemagazine.com/articles/2015/05/kids-in-the-hall-better-together.html.

46. John Kenneth Muir, *Terror Television: American Series, 1970–1999* (Jefferson, NC: McFarland & Company, 2000), 65–66.

47. Ibid.

48. Ibid.

49. Allan Sepinwall and Matt Zoller Seitz, *TV (The Book): Two Experts Pick the Greatest American Shows of All Time* (New York: Grand Central Publishing, 2016), 329.

50. Muir, *Terror Television*, 66.

51. Ibid., 66–67.

52. Ibid., 67.

53. Ibid., 66.

54. Sepinwall and Seitz, *TV (The Book)*, 329.

55. Muir, *Terror Television*, 68.

56. Michael O'Connell, "When 'The X-Files' Became A-List: An Oral History of Fox's Out-There Success Story," *Hollywood Reporter*, January 7, 2016, www.hollywoodreporter .com/features/x-files-became-a-list-852398.

57. Muir, *Terror Television*, 67.

58. Ibid., 69.

59. Ibid., 70–71.

L

1. Blake J. Harris, "An Oral History of 'The League,'" ESPN, December 9, 2015, www .espn.com/nfl/story/_/id/14320491/an-oral-history-league.

2. Ibid.

3. Ibid.

4. Ibid.

5. Ibid.

6. The Futon Critic, "FX Ups Ante in Comedy: Places Series Orders for 'The League' and 'Louie,'" August 20, 2009, www.thefutoncritic.com/news/2009/08/20/fx-ups-ante -in-comedy-places-series-orders-for-the-league-and-louie-32443/20090820fx01.

7. Harris, "An Oral History of 'The League.'"

8. Nellie Andreeva, "Duplass in 'League' with FX," *Backstage*, July 15, 2009, www.back stage.com/magazine/article/duplass-league-fx-57915.

9. Harris, "An Oral History of 'The League.'"

10. Scott Porch, "'The League' Creators Jeff and Jackie Schaffer on Their Show's Final Season," *New York Times*, September 9, 2015, https://artsbeat.blogs.nytimes .com/2015/09/09/the-league-interview-jeff-schaffer-jackie-fx.

11. Ben Travers, "'The League' Reunion: Cast and Creators Open to Revival, Share One Regret about Airing on Cable," IndieWire, June 8, 2019, www.indiewire.com/2019/06/ the-league-reunion-cast-revival-fx-1202148419.

12. Steve Heisler, "*The League*'s Jeff Schaffer and Jackie Marcus Schaffer," AV Club, October 13, 2010, https://tv.avclub.com/the-league-s-jeff-schaffer-and-jackie-marcus -schaffer-1798222044.

13. Nellie Andreeva, "FX Renews 'The League' for Fourth Season," *Deadline*, December 13, 2011, https://deadline.com/2011/12/fx-renews-the-league-for-fourth-season-204708.

14. Katey Rich, "FX Ships Off *It's Always Sunny* and *The League* to Anchor New Network FXX," Cinema Blend, 2013, www.cinemablend.com/television/FX-Ships-Off-It-Always -Sunny-League-Anchor-Network-FXX-54098.html.

15. Harris, "An Oral History of 'The League.'"

16. Nick de Semlyen, "The Making of the *Lost* Pilot: An Oral History," *Empire*, September 22, 2014, www.empireonline.com/movies/features/making-lost-pilot.

17. Ibid.

18. Ibid.

19. Ibid.

20. Ibid.

21. Emily Zemler, "The *Lost* Creators Come Clean," *Esquire*, May 7, 2014, www.esquire .com/entertainment/tv/interviews/a26345/lost-creators-interview.

22. Olga Craig, "The Man Who Discovered 'Lost'—And Found Himself Out of a Job," *Telegraph*, August 14, 2005, www.telegraph.co.uk/news/worldnews/northamerica/ usa/1496199/The-man-who-discovered-Lost-and-found-himself-out-of-a-job.html.

23. Ibid.

24. Zemler, "The *Lost* Creators Come Clean."

25. Tim Molloy, "Damon Lindelof's History of 'Lost' (A Show He Longed to Quit)," *The Wrap*, September 23, 2011, www.thewrap.com/damon-lindelofs-history-lost-show-he -longed-quit-31281.

26. Zemler, "The *Lost* Creators Come Clean."

27. Cindy McLennan, "*Lost*: Showrunners Had to Fight to End the ABC TV Show," TV Series Finale, June 12, 2017, https://tvseriesfinale.com/tv-show/lost-showrunners-fight -end-abc-tv-show.

28. Ibid.

29. Tim Ryan, "'Lost' Opportunity," *Honolulu Star-Bulletin*, January 26, 2005, http:// archives.starbulletin.com/2005/01/26/news/story2.html.

30. Ibid.

31. McLennan, "*Lost*."

32. Molloy, "Damon Lindelof's History."

33. Marc Dolan, "Lost," in *The Essential Cult TV Reader*, ed. David Lavery, 155 (Lexington: University of Kentucky Press, 2010).

34. Adam Augustyn, "J. J. Abrams," *Encyclopedia Britannica*, August 21, 2019, www .britannica.com/biography/J-J-Abrams.

35. Ibid.

36. Ibid.

37. Ibid.

38. Ibid.

39. Ibid.

40. Ed Shifres, Lost in Space: *The True Story* (Austin, TX: Windsor Group Publishing House, 1998), 39.

41. Ibid., 12.

42. Ibid., 43.

43. Ibid., 65.

44. Ibid., 162–63.

45. Ibid., 68.

46. James Van Hise, "*Lost in Space*: A Retrospective of the Original Sci-fi TV Show," *Cinefantastique* 29, no. 12 (1998): 26.

47. Ibid., 5.

48. Shifres, Lost in Space, 68.

49. Ibid., 77.

50. Ibid., 164.

51. Ibid., 89.

52. Ibid., 169.

53. Ibid., 170.

54. Ibid., 169.

55. Van Hise, "*Lost in Space*," 26.

56. Van Hise, "*Lost in Space*," 28; Joel Eisner and Barry Magen, Lost in Space *Forever* (Staunton, VA: Windsong Publishing, 1992), 9.

57. Van Hise, "*Lost in Space*," 27.

58. Ibid.

59. Eisner and Magen, Lost in Space *Forever*, 17.

60. Shifres, Lost in Space, xx.

61. Ibid., xxiv.

62. Ibid., xxi.

63. Ibid., xxiv.

64. Shifres, Lost in Space, 31; Eisner and Magen, Lost in Space *Forever*, 280.

65. Ibid., 21.

66. Ibid., 31.

67. Christopher Inoa, "What Went Wrong on the 1998 *Lost in Space* Movie," SyFy Wire, April 13, 2018, www.syfy.com/syfywire/what-went-wrong-on-the-1998-lost-in-space-movie.

68. Tony Sokol and Joseph Baxter, "*Lost in Space* Netflix Reboot Trailer, Release Date, Cast and Story Details," Den of Geek! April 6, 2018, www.denofgeek.com/us/tv/lost-in-space/250778/lost-in-space-netflix-reboot-trailer-release-date-cast-and-story-details.

69. Van Hise, "*Lost in Space*," 28.

70. Shifres, Lost in Space, xx.

71. James Caldwell, "AAA News: El Rey Announces AAA Lucha Libre Show for U.S. TV: Timeslot, Show Title, More Details," *Pro Wrestling Torch*, July 10, 2014, www.pwtorch.com/artman2/publish/Other_News_4/article_79511.shtml#.XU9BS-hKhPZ.

72. Denise Petski, "Mark Burnett's 'Lucha Underground' Wrestling Series Renewed for Season 2," *Deadline*, September 21, 2015, https://deadline.com/2015/09/mark-burnett-lucha-underground-wrestling-series-renewed-season-2-1201542051.

73. Shelli Weinstein, "El Rey Network, Mark Burnett Announce Production of 'Lucha Underground,'" *Variety*, August 27, 2014, https://variety.com/2014/tv/news/el-rey-network-mark-burnett-announce-production-of-lucha-underground-1201291953.

74. Spencer Hall, "The 25 Secrets of *Lucha Underground*," SB Nation, July 19, 2016, www.sbnation.com/2016/7/19/12215628/lucha-underground.

75. Brian Steinberg, "Univision to Use El Rey Wrestling Show to Bolster UniMás," *Variety*, October 27, 2014, https://variety.com/2014/tv/news/univision-to-use-el-rey-wrestling-show-to-bolster-unimas-1201340092/.

76. Ibid.

77. Mike Johnson, "More on Issues with Konnan, AAA and Others in Recent Weeks," *PW Insider*, February 7, 2016, www.pwinsider.com/article/99604/more-on-issues-with-konnan-aaa-and-others-in-recent-weeks.html?p=1.

78. Scott Fried, "*Lucha Underground* in Financial Trouble," What Culture, February 18, 2016, http://whatculture.com/wwe/lucha-underground-in-financial-trouble.

79. Ibid.

80. Felix Upton, "*Lucha Underground* Might Be Cancelled before Season 5 Due to Change at El Rey Network," *Ringside News*, November 8, 2018, www.ringsidenews.com/2018/11/08/lucha-underground-might-cancelled-season-5-due-change-el-rey-network.

81. Brandon Stroud, "Your First Look at the Ice Cold New 'Temple' for *Lucha Underground* Season 4," Uproxx, February 12, 2018, https://uproxx.com/prowrestling/lucha-underground-season-4-new-temple-pics-tickets.

82. Ryan Satin, "*Lucha Underground* Star Files Dispute against El Rey Network," *Pro Wrestling Sheet*, February 6, 2019, www.prowrestlingsheet.com/lucha-underground-king-cuerno-dispute/#.XU9E4ehKhPY.

83. Shawn S. Lealos, "*Lucha Underground* Update: PJ Black Explains Why Season 5 Is Delayed," Monsters and Critics, June 4, 2019, www.monstersandcritics.com/wrestling/lucha-underground-update-pj-black-explains-why-season-5-is-delayed.

M

1. Bryan Bishop, "Live and Direct: The Definitive Oral History of 1980s Digital Icon Max Headroom," The Verge, April 2, 2015, www.theverge.com/2015/4/2/8285139/max-headroom-oral-history-80s-cyberpunk-interview.

2. Mark Phillips and Frank Garcia, *Science Fiction Television Series: Episode Guides, Histories, and Casts and Credits for 62 Prime Time Shows, 1959–1989* (Jefferson, NC: McFarland & Company, 1996), 203.

3. Bishop, "Live and Direct."

4. Phillips and Garcia, *Science Fiction Television Series*, 203.

5. Ibid., 203–4.

6. Ibid., 204.

7. Ibid.

8. Ibid.

9. Ibid.

10. Ibid., 204–5.

11. Ibid., 206–7.

12. Bishop, "Live and Direct."

13. Philips and Garcia, *Science Fiction Television Series*, 206–7.

14. Douglas McCall, *Monty Python: A Chronology 1969–2012* (Jefferson, NC: McFarland & Company, 2014), 4.

15. Ibid., 5.

16. Ibid.

17. Ibid.

18. Ibid.

19. Marcia Landy, "Monty Python's Flying Circus," in *The Essential Cult TV Reader*, ed. David Lavery, 167 (Lexington: University Press of Kentucky, 2010).

20. McCall, *Monty Python*, 6.

21. Ibid., 8.

22. Ibid., 10–11.

23. Ibid., 14.

24. Ibid., 18.

25. Ibid., 23.

26. McCall, *Monty Python*, 36; Landy, "Monty Python's Flying Circus," 26.

27. McCall, *Monty Python*, 27.

28. Ibid., 36.

29. Ibid., 46; Landy, "Monty Python's Flying Circus," 1–2.

30. McCall, *Monty Python*, 46; Landy, "Monty Python's Flying Circus," 1–2.

31. McCall, *Monty Python*, 142.

32. Ibid., 144.

33. Ibid., 189.

34. Naomi Odenkirk, *Mr. Show: What Happened?* (Winnipeg, Canada: Westcan Printing Group, 2002), 13; Marc Spitz, "*Mr. Show*: The Oral History," Spin, March 13, 2011, www .spin.com/2011/03/mr-show-oral-history.

35. Odenkirk, *Mr. Show*, 13.

36. Odenkirk, *Mr. Show*, 16–17; Spitz, "*Mr. Show*"; Erik Adams, "God Dammit! Here Are the 10 *Mr. Show* Episodes You Need to See before *With Bob and David*," AV Club, November 12, 2015, https://tv.avclub.com/god-dammit-here-are-the-10-mr-show-episodes-you -need-1798286979.

37. Odenkirk, *Mr. Show*, 17.

38. Ibid., 18.

39. Ibid., 19.

40. Ibid.

41. Ibid., 20.

42. Ibid., 21.

43. Ibid.

44. Ibid.

45. Ibid., 67.

46. Ibid., 40.

47. Ibid., 41.

48. Ibid., 43.

49. Ibid., 47–48.

50. Ibid., 67.

51. Ibid.

52. Ibid., 84.

53. Ibid., 79–80.

54. Spitz, "*Mr. Show*."

55. Odenkirk, *Mr. Show*, 92.

56. Ibid., 11.

57. Onion A.V. Club, *The Tenacity of the Cockroach: Conversations with Entertainment's Most Enduring Outsiders* (New York: Three Rivers Press, 2002), 281–82.

58. Spitz, "*Mr. Show*."

59. Tekaramity, "Exclusive Season 1 Retrospective Interview of Lauren Faust," Equestria Daily, September 16, 2011, www.equestriadaily.com/2011/09/exclusive-season-1-retro spective.html.

60. Tekaramity, "Exclusive Season 1 Retrospective"; Joe Strike, "Of Ponies and Bronies," Animation World Network, July 5, 2011, www.awn.com/blog/ponies-and-bronies.

61. Tekaramity, "Exclusive Season 1 Retrospective."

62. Lisa Miller, "How *My Little Pony* Became a Cult for Grown Men and Preteen Girls Alike," The Cut, November 6, 2014, www.thecut.com/2014/11/understanding-the-cult-of -my-little-pony.html.

63. Miller, "How *My Little Pony*"; Tekaramity, "Exclusive Season 1 Retrospective"; *CBC News*, "*My Little Pony: Friendship Is Magic* TV Show to End after 9 Seasons," May 1, 2019, www.cbc.ca/news/canada/british-columbia/my-little-pony-friendship-is-magic-tv -show-to-end-after-9-seasons-1.5119096.

64. Sherilyn Connelly, *Ponyville Confidential: The History and Culture of* My Little Pony, *1981–2016* (Jefferson, NC: McFarland & Company, 2017), 67, 69, 73.

65. Ibid., 74.

66. Tekaramity, "Exclusive Season 1 Retrospective."

67. Miller, "How *My Little Pony*."

68. Michael O'Connell, "'My Little Pony: Friendship is Magic' Renewed for Fifth Season," *Hollywood Reporter*, May 7, 2014, www.hollywoodreporter.com/live-feed/my-little-pony-friendship-is-magic-renewed-fifth-season-702056.

69. Miller, "How *My Little Pony*."

70. Kimberly Nordyke, "'My Little Pony' Sets Ninth and Final Season on Discovery Family (Exclusive)," *Hollywood Reporter*, March 8, 2019, www.hollywoodreporter.com/live-feed/my-little-pony-sets-final-season-discovery-family-1193235.

71. Madeleine Fernando, "'My Little Pony Live' Musical Slated for 2020 North American Tour," *Billboard*, June 3, 2019, www.billboard.com/articles/business/touring/8514281/my-little-pony-live-musical-north-american-tour-2020.

72. Miller, "How *My Little Pony*."

73. Ibid.

74. "Unofficial" Cats Don't Dance, "Sawyer Animator Lauren Faust," 2009, www.cdd4ever.com/CATCHAT/CatChat.html.

75. Strike, "Of Ponies and Bronies."

76. Michele Byers, "My So-Called Life," in *The Essential Cult TV Reader*, ed. David Lavery, 174–75 (Lexington: University Press of Kentucky, 2010).

77. Gwynne Watkins, "The Agony and the Angst: An Oral History of *My So-Called Life*," *Elle*, November 16, 2016, www.elle.com/culture/movies-tv/a40594/my-so-called-life-cast-interviews.

78. Byers, "My So-Called Life," 175.

79. Jeff Jensen, "From the EW Archives: Looking Back at *My So-Called Life*," *Entertainment Weekly*, September 10, 2004, https://ew.com/article/2004/09/10/looking-back-my-so-called-life.

80. Watkins, "The Agony and the Angst."

81. Ibid.

82. Jensen, "From the EW Archives."

83. Ibid.

84. Ibid.

85. Watkins, "The Agony and the Angst."

86. Byers, "My So-Called Life," 176.

87. Ibid.

88. Ibid.

89. Brian Rafferty, "*Mystery Science Theater 3000*: The Definitive Oral History of a TV Masterpiece," *Wired*, April 22, 2014, www.wired.com/2014/04/mst3k-oral-history.

90. Ibid.

91. David Ray Carter, "Cinemasochism: Bad Movies and the People Who Love Them," in *In the Peanut Gallery with* Mystery Science Theater 3000*: Essays on Film, Fandom, Technology and the Culture of Riffing*, ed. Robert G. Weiner and Shelley E. Barbra, 103–4 (Jefferson, NC: McFarland & Company, 2011).

92. Rafferty, "*Mystery Science Theater 3000*."

93. Jim Vorel, "The 25-Episode History of *Mystery Science Theater 3000*," Paste, August 10, 2015, www.pastemagazine.com/articles/2015/08/the-25-episode-history-of-mystery-science-theater.html.

94. Rafferty, "*Mystery Science Theater 3000*."

95. Vorel, "The 25-Episode History."

96. Rafferty, "*Mystery Science Theater 3000*."

97. Eirik Gumeny, "20 Things You Didn't Know about *Mystery Science Theater 3000*," ScreenRant, April 13, 2017, https://screenrant.com/mst3k-mystery-science-theatre-3000-trivia.

98. Ibid.

99. Rafferty, *"Mystery Science Theater 3000."*

100. Ibid.

101. Ibid.

102. Jennifer M. Wood, "15 Things You Might Not Know about *Mystery Science Theater 3000*," MentalFloss, November 23, 2017, http://mentalfloss.com/article/53849/16-things-you-might-not-know-about-mystery-science-theater-3000.

103. Kinsey Lowe, "'Mystery Science Theater 3000' Raises $6.3M for 14-Episode Revival," *Deadline*, December 12, 2015, http://deadline.com/2015/12/mystery-science-theater-3000-raises-funds-for-reboot-1201665886.

104. William Hughes, "Robot Roll-Call: The New *MST3K* Gets a Release Date and a Full Cast Photo," AV Club, February 22, 2017, https://news.avclub.com/robot-roll-call-the-new-mst3k-gets-a-release-date-and-1798258113.

105. Clint Worthington, "TV Review: *Mystery Science Theater 3000* Returns Yet Again for 'The Gauntlet,'" Consequence of Sound, November 25, 2018, https://consequenceofsound.net/2018/11/tv-review-mystery-science-theater-3000-the-gauntlet.

106. Sarah Sloboda, "Joel Hodgson Biography," Fandango, 2019, www.fandango.com/people/joel-hodgson-296790/biography.

107. Joshua Miller, "Our Q&A with Joel Hodgson, Creator of 'Mystery Science Theater 3000,'" *Milwaukee Magazine*, July 13, 2017, www.milwaukeemag.com/qa-joel-hodgson-creator-mystery-science-theater-3000.

108. Keith Phipps, "Joel Hodgson," AV Club, April 21, 1999, www.avclub.com/joel-hodgson-1798207993.

109. Ibid.

O

1. Alexander Larman, "Gervais, Ricky (1961–)," BFI Screen Online, 2014, www.screenonline.org.uk/people/id/513105.

2. Ibid.

3. Garry Berman, *Best of the Britcoms: From* Fawlty Towers *to* The Office (New York: Taylor Trade, 2011), 138–39.

4. BBC, "Ricky and Steve on Production," September 24, 2014, www.bbc.co.uk/comedy/theoffice/defguide/defguide13.shtml.

5. Michael R. Farkash, "'The Office' (U.K.): THR's 2003 review," *Hollywood Reporter*, January 23, 2019, www.hollywoodreporter.com/review/office-uk-review-tv-show-1177681.

6. Larman, "Gervais, Ricky."

7. Berman, *Best of the Britcoms*, 139.

8. Ibid.

9. BBC, "Ricky and Steve."

10. Berman, *Best of the Britcoms*, 139.

11. HuffPost, "Ricky Gervais Explains Why the British 'Office' Had Such a Brief Run," September 6, 2016, www.huffpost.com/entry/ricky-gervais-the-office_n_1421772.

12. Berman, *Best of the Britcoms*, 140.

13. Ibid.

14. Farkash, "'The Office.'"

15. Robert Mitchell, "BBC Worldwide Sets Up 'The Office' in India," *Variety*, February 20, 2018, https://variety.com/2018/tv/news/bbc-worldwide-sets-up-the-office-india-1202704700.

16. Laura Turner Garrison, "Exploring the International Franchises of *The Office*," Vulture, May 4, 2011, www.vulture.com/2011/05/exploring-the-international-franchises-of-the-office.html.

17. Mitchell, "BBC Worldwide Sets Up 'The Office.'"

18. Nellie Andreeva, "'Outlander' Novels from Ron Moore & Sony," *Deadline*, November 6, 2012, https://deadline.com/2012/11/outlander-tv-series-starz-ron-moore-sony-366615.

19. Lynette Rice, "'Outlander': How Author Diana Gabaldon Really Feels about Sam Heughan and Caitriona Balfe," *Entertainment Weekly*, March 1, 2016, https://ew.com/article/2016/03/01/outlander-diana-gabaldon-sam-heughan-caitriona-balfe.

20. Dominic Patten, "Starz's 'Outlander' Officially Names Sam Heughan as Lead," *Deadline*, July 29, 2013, https://deadline.com/2013/07/outlander-series-star-starz-533220.

21. Jethro Nededog, "'Super 8's' Caitriona Balfe to Play Claire on Starz's 'Outlander,'" *The Wrap*, July 16, 2014, www.thewrap.com/super-8s-caitriona-balfe-to-play-claire-on-starzs-outlander.

22. Brian Ferguson, "*Outlander* Could Run for Five Years Says Moore," *Scotsman*, August 23, 2014, www.scotsman.com/lifestyle-2-15039/outlander-could-run-for-five-years-says-moore-1-3518732.

23. McKenzie Jean-Philippe, "Yes, *Outlander* Is Based on Books: Here's Everything to Know about the Epic Series," *Oprah Magazine*, May 15, 2019, www.oprahmag.com/entertainment/books/a27395417/outlander-books.

24. Rice, "'Outlander.'"

25. *Scotland Now*, "*Outlander*'s Gaelic Expert Àdhamh Ó Broin Teaches Sayings in the Celtic Language," February 17, 2016, www.scotlandnow.dailyrecord.co.uk/lifestyle/outlanders-gaelic-expert-dhamh—7449039.

26. Philiana Ng, "Starz's 'Outlander' Gets First Poster, Premiere Date," *Hollywood Reporter*, May 8, 2014, www.hollywoodreporter.com/live-feed/outlander-premiere-date-poster-revealed-702417.

27. James Hibberd, "'Outlander' Renewed for Second Season," *Entertainment Weekly*, August 15, 2014, https://ew.com/article/2014/08/15/outlander-renewed-second-season.

28. Meredith Carey, "*Outlander* Filming Locations around the World," *Condé Nast Traveler*, January 27, 2019, www.cntraveler.com/gallery/outlander-filming-locations-around-the-world.

29. Caroline Hallemann, "Everything We Know So Far about *Outlander* Season 5," *Town & Country*, August 29, 2019, www.townandcountrymag.com/leisure/arts-and-culture/a20648462/outlander-season-5.

30. Joe Bish, "Twenty Years of 'Oz': The Show That Changed TV Forever," Vice, June 6, 2017, www.vice.com/en_us/article/3kzzaj/20-years-of-oz-the-show-that-changed-tv-forever.

31. Ethan Alter, "Return to 'Oz': An Oral History of the Pioneering Prison Drama," Yahoo! July 12, 2017, www.yahoo.com/entertainment/hbo-oz-20th-anniversary-oral-history-153416770.html.

32. Ibid.

33. Ibid.

34. Ibid.

35. Adam Dunn, "The End of 'Oz,'" CNN, February 21, 2003, www.cnn.com/2003/SHOWBIZ/TV/02/21/oz.end/index.html.

36. Levinson.com, "Oz Production Notes," 2008, www.levinson.com/lf/oz/prod.htm.

37. Bish, "Twenty Years of 'Oz.'"

38. Alter, "Return to 'Oz.'"

39. Ibid.

40. levinson.com, "Oz Production Notes."

41. Alter, "Return to 'Oz.'"

42. TomFontana.com, "Archive," 2019, www.tomfontana.com/archive/archive_1.html.

43. Noel Murray, Tim Grierson, David Fear, and Sean T. Collins, "End Game: TV's Best and Worst Series Finales," *Rolling Stone*, May 12, 2015, www.rollingstone.com/tv/tv-lists/ end-game-tvs-best-and-worst-series-finales-170942/best-mash-172617.

44. Dunn, "The End of 'Oz.'"

45. Allan Sepinwall and Matt Zoller Seitz, *TV (The Book): Two Experts Pick the Greatest American Shows of All Time* (New York: Grand Central Publishing, 2016), 141.

46. Michele Malach, "Oz," in *The Essential HBO Reader*, eds. Gary R. Edgerton and Jeffrey P. Jones, 58 (Lexington: University of Kentucky Press, 2008).

P

1. Ashley Burns and Chloe Schildhause, "You Go Big or You Go Home: An Oral History of the Creation and Evolution of 'Parks and Recreation,'" Uproxx, February 23, 2015, https://uproxx.com/feature/parks-and-recreation-evolution-oral-history.

2. Ibid.

3. Amy Poehler, *Yes Please* (New York: Harper Collins, 2014), 246–47.

4. Ibid.

5. Ibid., 247.

6. Ibid., 251.

7. Ibid., 246–47.

8. Ibid., 250.

9. Ibid.

10. Allan Sepinwall and Matt Zoller Seitz, *TV (The Book): Two Experts Pick the Greatest American Shows of All Time* (New York: Grand Central Publishing, 2016), 194.

11. Poehler, *Yes Please*, 252.

12. Ibid., 253.

13. Emily Nussbaum, "We'll Always Have Pawnee," *New Yorker*, February 25, 2015, www.newyorker.com/culture/cultural-comment/well-always-have-pawnee.

14. Dan Snierson, "'Parks and Recreation': Michael Schur on the Decision to End the Show," *Entertainment Weekly*, May 21, 2014, https://ew.com/article/2014/05/21/parks -and-recreation-season-7-final-michael-schur.

15. Josef Adalian, "How *Parks and Recreation* Managed to Survive for 7 Seasons," Vulture, February 23, 2015, www.vulture.com/2015/02/parks-and-recreation-ratings.html.

16. Snierson, "'Parks and Recreation.'"

17. Nussbaum, "We'll Always Have Pawnee."

18. Justin Wm. Moyer, "Remembering When 'Parks and Recreation' Was Terrible," *Washington Post*, February 25, 2015, www.washingtonpost.com/news/morning-mix/ wp/2015/02/25/remembering-when-parks-and-recreation-was-terrible.

19. David Bianculli, *The Platinum Age of Television: From* I Love Lucy *to* The Walking Dead, *How TV Became Terrific* (New York: Anchor Books, 2016), 32; Joe Garner and Michael Ashley, *It's Saturday Morning: Celebrating the Golden Era of Cartoons, 1960s–1990s* (Bellevue: Quarto Publishing Group, 2018), 159.

20. Garner and Ashley, *It's Saturday Morning*, 160; Caseen Gaines, *Inside Pee-wee's Playhouse: The Untold, Unauthorized, and Unpredictable Story of a Pop Phenomenon* (Toronto, Canada: ECW Press, 2011), 7, 12.

21. Gaines, *Inside Pee-wee's Playhouse*, 25.

22. Ibid., 26.

23. Ibid., 30–31.

24. Ibid., 35–36.

25. Ibid., 38.

26. Ibid.

27. Ibid., 39.

28. Ibid., 41–42.

29. Bianculli, *The Platinum Age of Television*, 32–33.

30. Gaines, *Inside Pee-wee's Playhouse*, 42.

31. Ibid., 56–57.

32. Ibid., 58.

33. Mike Ayers, "10 Tales from Paul Reubens's Time Making 'Pee-wee's Playhouse,'" *Wall Street Journal*, November 4, 2014, https://blogs.wsj.com/speakeasy/2014/11/04/paul-reubens-pee-wee-playhouse-interview.

34. Gaines, *Inside Pee-wee's Playhouse*, 53.

35. Ibid., 48.

36. Ibid., 65.

37. Ibid., 66.

38. Ibid., 115–16.

39. Ibid., 118.

40. Ibid.

41. Joe Garner and Michael Ashley, *It's Saturday Morning: Celebrating the Golden Era of Cartoons, 1960s–1990s* (Bellevue: Quarto Publishing Group, 2018), 208.

42. Ashley Burns and Chloe Schildhause, "The Behind-the-Scenes Story of the Rise and Fall of 'Pinky and the Brain,'" Uproxx, January 10, 2016, https://uproxx.com/tv/pinky-and-the-brain-anniversary-interview.

43. Garner and Ashley, *It's Saturday Morning*, 211.

44. Roger Cormier, "13 Fun Facts about *Pinky and the Brain*," Mental Floss, April 27, 2016, http://mentalfloss.com/article/68259/13-fun-facts-about-pinky-and-brain.

45. Garner and Ashley, *It's Saturday Morning*, 210.

46. Burns and Schildhause, "The Behind-the-Scenes Story."

47. Takineko, "The Silver Age of Animation," RetroJunk, 2007, www.retrojunk.com/article/show/456/the-silver-age.

48. Burns and Schildhause, "The Behind-the-Scenes Story."

49. Ibid.

50. Garner and Ashley, *It's Saturday Morning*, 213.

51. Burns and Schildhause, "The Behind-the-Scenes Story."

52. Ibid.

53. Takineko, "The Silver Age of Animation."

54. Gordon Jackson, "Every Single *Pinky and the Brain* Plan to Take Over the World, Ranked," Gizmodo, May 30, 2016, https://io9.gizmodo.com/every-single-pinky-and-the-brain-plan-to-take-over-the-1778890186.

55. Iain Blair, "Raising the Spoof," *Chicago Tribune*, November 27, 1988, https://finance.yahoo.com/news/naked-gun-reboot-still-happening-says-co-creator-david-zucker-155016946.html.

56. Diane Werts "Badge of Humor—Short-Lived 1982 Series That Spoofed Cop Shows Comes with Some Great Extras," *Herald-Leader*, November 10, 2006.

57. David Misch, "Police Squad!" davidmisch.com, 2019, https://davidmisch.com/television/police-squad.

58. Jerry Zucker, Jim Abrahams, David Zucker, and Robert K. Weiss, "Audio Commentary for 'A Substantial Gift (A Bird in the Hand),'" *Police Squad: The Complete Series* (Los Angeles: CBS Paramount, 2006), DVD.

59. J. Zucker, Abrahams, D. Zucker, and Weiss, "Audio Commentary"; Jay Carr, "Exposing a Trio of Film Makers Who Take Spoofs Quite Seriously," *Globe*, December 12, 1988.

60. Misch, "Police Squad!"

61. J. Zucker, Abrahams, D. Zucker, and Weiss, "Audio Commentary"; Pacific Pioneer Broadcasters, "'Naked Gun' & 'Police Squad!' Ed Williams—Pacific Pioneer Broadcasters Oral History Interview," YouTube, September 21, 2018, www.youtube.com/watch?v=DlCDAyK8rhw.

62. J. Zucker, Abrahams, D. Zucker, and Weiss, "Audio Commentary."

63. Tom Shales, "Okay, Hands Up! 'Police Squad!' Back and Copping Laughs," *Washington Post*, July 1, 1982, www.washingtonpost.com/archive/lifestyle/1982/07/01/okay-hands-up-police-squad-back-and-copping-laughs/e98470d6-a30c-4f94-a095-01624c6c32c6/?utm_term=.65a7c62ec751.

64. Allan Sepinwall and Matt Zoller Seitz, *TV (The Book): Two Experts Pick the Greatest American Shows of All Time* (New York: Grand Central Publishing, 2016), 218.

65. Blair, "Raising the Spoof"; J. Zucker, Abrahams, D. Zucker, and Weiss, "Audio Commentary."

66. Tom Butler, "'Naked Gun' Reboot Still Happening, Says Co-creator David Zucker," Yahoo Movies UK, October 22, 2018, https://finance.yahoo.com/news/naked-gun-reboot-still-happening-says-co-creator-david-zucker-155016946.html.

67. Douglas L. Howard, "The Prisoner," in *The Essential Cult TV Reader*, ed. David Lavery, 190 (Lexington: University Press of Kentucky, 2010).

68. Mark Phillips and Frank Garcia, *Science Fiction Television Series: Episode Guides, Histories, and Casts and Credits for 62 Prime Time Shows, 1959–1989* (Jefferson, NC: McFarland & Company, 1996), 265.

69. Ibid.

70. Ibid., 263.

71. Howard, "The Prisoner," 190.

72. Phillips and Garcia, *Science Fiction Television Series*, 264.

73. Ibid., 265.

74. Sergio Angelini, "The Prisoner (ITV, 1967–1968)," in *The Cult TV Book: From Star Trek to Dexter, New Approaches to TV Outside the Box*, ed. Stacey Abbott, 103 (New York: Soft Skull Press, 2010).

75. Phillips and Garcia, *Science Fiction Television Series*, 266.

76. Howard, "The Prisoner," 197–98.

77. Ibid.

78. Andrew Pixley, *The Prisoner: A Complete Production Guide* (London: Network Distributing, 2007), 7.

79. Ibid., 195.

80. Ibid.

81. Phillips and Garcia, *Science Fiction Television Series*, 269.

82. Ibid.

83. Scott Thill, "Review: 'The Prisoner' Reboot Takes Sci-Fi Out of Spy-Fi," *Wired*, November 13, 2009, www.wired.com/2009/11/review-the-prisoner-2009.

84. Angie Han, "Ridley Scott Looking to Remake '60s Cult Hit Series 'The Prisoner' as a Movie," SlashFilm, January 11, 2016, www.slashfilm.com/ridley-scott-the-prisoner.

85. Howard, "The Prisoner," 194.

86. Matthew Sweet, "How Did *The Prisoner* Ever Get Made?" *Telegraph*, September 29, 2017, www.telegraph.co.uk/tv/2017/08/20/did-prisoner-ever-get-made.

87. Ibid.

88. Ibid.

89. Howard, "The Prisoner," 196–97.

Q

1. Mark Phillips and Frank Garcia, *Science Fiction Television Series: Episode Guides, Histories, and Casts and Credits for 62 Prime Time Shows, 1959–1989*, 279 (Jefferson, NC: McFarland & Company, 1996).

2. Ibid.

3. Ibid.

4. Television Academy Foundation, "Donald P. Bellisario Interview, Part 3 of 3," The Interviews, April 28, 2008, https://interviews.televisionacademy.com/interviews/donald-bellisario.

5. Ibid.

6. Phillips and Garcia, *Science Fiction Television Series*, 280.

7. Ibid., 281.

8. Kathryn VanArendonk, "Talking with Scott Bakula about *Quantum Leap*'s 30th Anniversary," Vulture, March 29, 2019, www.vulture.com/2019/03/scott-bakula-quantum-leap-30th-anniversary.html.

9. Lynnette Porter, "Quantum Leap," in *The Essential Cult TV Reader*, ed. David Lavery, 202 (Lexington: University Press of Kentucky, 2010).

10. Ibid.

11. Phillips and Garcia, *Science Fiction Television Series*, 283.

12. Television Academy Foundation, "Donald P. Bellisario Interview."

13. Phillips and Garcia, *Science Fiction Television Series*, 283.

14. Porter, "Quantum Leap," 202.

15. Steven Weinstein, "'Quantum Leap' Ratings Jump on Final Telecast," *Los Angeles Times*, May 7, 1993, www.latimes.com/archives/la-xpm-1993-05-07-ca-32482-story.html.

16. Garin Pirnia, "15 Facts about *Quantum Leap*," Mental Floss, March 27, 2019, http://mentalfloss.com/article/79397/16-accelerated-facts-about-quantum-leap.

17. Porter, "Quantum Leap," 204–5.

18. Ibid., 201.

19. Pirnia, "15 Facts about *Quantum Leap*."

20. Mark Aldridge and Andy Murray, *T Is for Television: The Small Screen Adventures of Russell T. Davies* (Surrey, UK: Reynolds & Hearn, 2008), 97–99.

21. Ibid.

22. Bernard Weinraub, "A Controversial British Series Seduces Showtime," *New York Times*, May 14, 2000, www.nytimes.com/2000/05/14/arts/television-radio-a-controversial-british-series-seduces-showtime.html.

23. Russell T. Davies, "'Transmission Was Madness. Honestly,'" *Guardian*, September 15, 2003, www.theguardian.com/media/2003/sep/15/channel4.gayrights.

24. Aldridge and Murray, *T Is for Television*, 100–101.

25. Ibid.

26. Ibid., 102.

27. Davies, "'Transmission Was Madness.'"

28. Aldridge and Murray, *T Is for Television*, 109; Louis Staples, "Twenty Years On, *Queer as Folk* Remains a More Radical and Fearless Tribute to Gay Life Than Many LGBT+ Shows Today," *Independent*, February 23, 2019, www.independent.co.uk/voices/queer-as-folk-stuart-vince-nathan-russell-t-davies-lgbtq-discrimination-tv-culture-20th-anniversary-a8793316.html.

29. Davies, "'Transmission Was Madness.'"

30. Ibid.

31. Charles Kaiser, "The Queerest Show on Earth," *New York*, September 18, 2000, http://nymag.com/nymetro/arts/features/3788.

32. Ibid.

33. Weinraub, "A Controversial British Series."

34. Joe Otterson, "'Queer as Folk' Reboot in Development at Bravo," *Variety*, December 18, 2018, https://variety.com/2018/tv/news/queer-as-folk-reboot-bravo-1203092157.

35. Joe Otterson, "'One of Us Is Lying' Series, 'Queer as Folk' Reboot Move to NBCUniversal Streaming Service," *Variety*, August 15, 2019, https://variety.com/2019/tv/news/one-of-us-is-lying-series-nbcuniversal-streaming-service-1203303483.

36. Kaiser, "The Queerest Show on Earth."

37. Staples, "Twenty Years On."

38. Ibid.

39. Ibid.

40. Kaiser, "The Queerest Show on Earth."

41. Ibid.

42. Aldridge and Murray, *T Is for Television*, 12.

43. Mark Aldridge, "Davies, Russell T. (1963–)," BFI Screen Online, 2014, www.screenonline.org.uk/people/id/1256045/index.html.

44. Ibid.

45. BBC, "Russell T. Davies," August 11, 2009, www.bbc.co.uk/wales/arts/sites/russell-t-davies/pages/biography.shtml.

46. Ibid.

47. Ibid.

48. Ibid.

R

1. Garry Berman, *Best of the Britcoms: From* Fawlty Towers *to* The Office (New York: Taylor Trade Publishing, 2011), 73.

2. Dee Amy-Chinn, "Red Dwarf," in *The Essential Cult TV Reader*, ed. David Lavery, 208 (Lexington: University Press of Kentucky, 2010).

3. Berman, *Best of the Britcoms*, 73.

4. Amy-Chinn, "Red Dwarf," 212.

5. Ibid., 210.

6. Ibid., 208.

7. Berman, *Best of the Britcoms*, 74.

8. Andrew Ellard, "Flibble Tuning In," Red Dwarf: The Official Site, December 22, 2000, www.reddwarf.co.uk/features/interviews/bill-young/index.cfm.

9. Ibid., 75.

10. Ibid.

11. Ibid., 75–76.

12. Ibid., 76.

13. Ellard, "Flibble Tuning In"; Amy-Chinn, "Red Dwarf," 212.

14. Sam Ashurst, "The *Red Dwarf* Cast and Creator Talk Us through the Upcoming Season 12 Episode by Episode," Digital Spy, December 10, 2017, www.digitalspy.com/tv/a840451/red-dwarf-season-12-episodes.

15. Sam Warner, "*Red Dwarf* Star Danny John-Jules Gives Update on the Series' Return," Digital Spy, June 27, 2019, www.digitalspy.com/tv/a28204565/red-dwarf-danny-john-jules-update-series-13-return.

16. Thad Komorowski, *Sick Little Monkeys: The Unauthorized* Ren & Stimpy *Story* (Albany, NY: Bear Manor Media, 2013), 46.

17. Komorowski, *Sick Little Monkeys*, 48–49; Marc Snetiker, "Nicktoons 25th Anniversary Oral History of *Rugrats, Doug, Ren & Stimpy*," *Entertainment Weekly*, August 11, 2016, https://ew.com/article/2016/08/11/nicktoons-25th-anniversary-oral-history-doug-rugrats-ren-stimpy.

18. Komorowski, *Sick Little Monkeys*, 51.

19. Ibid., 56.

20. Snetiker, "Nicktoons 25th Anniversary."

21. Komorowski, *Sick Little Monkeys*, 61.

22. Snetiker, "Nicktoons 25th Anniversary."

23. Komorowski, *Sick Little Monkeys*, 125.

24. Matthew Klickstein, *Slimed: An Oral History of Nickelodeon's Golden Age* (New York: Penguin, 2013), 171–72.

25. Komoroski, *Sick Little Monkeys*, 102.

26. Ibid., 176.

27. Klickstein, *Slimed*, 167–69.

28. Ibid.

29. Ibid.

30. Ibid., 178.

31. Ibid., 180–81.

32. Komoroski, *Sick Little Monkeys*, 266.

33. Matt Schimkowitz, "No, Sir, I Don't Like It: The Misfire That Was 'Ren and Stimpy's Adult Party Cartoon,'" Vulture, Jun 3, 2013, www.vulture.com/2013/06/no-sir-i-dont-like-it-the-misfire-that-was-ren-and-stimpys-adult-party-cartoon.html. Fifteen years later, two women alleged that Kricfalusi sexually exploited them when they were teenagers, a revelation that derailed his animation career. See Ariane Lang, "The Disturbing Secret behind an Iconic Cartoon: Underage Sexual Abuse," Buzzfeed, March 29, 2018, www.buzzfeednews.com/article/arianelange/john-kricfalusi-ren-stimpy-underage-sexual-abuse#.liPDDDx1j; and Sam Barsanti, "*Ren & Stimpy* Creator John Kricfalusi Accused of Sexually Exploiting Teenage Girls," AV Club, March 29, 2018, https://news.avclub.com/ren-stimpy-creator-john-kricfalusi-accused-of-sexuall-1824193943.

34. Klickstein, *Slimed*, 168.

35. Darryn King, "*Rocko's Modern Life*: Inside the Barely Contained Chaos of a Nickelodeon Classic," *Vanity Fair*, November 29, 2018, www.vanityfair.com/hollywood/2018/11/inside-rockos-modern-life-nickelodeon-cartoon.

36. Lisa Kiczuk, "The *Rocko's Modern Life* FAQ," Rocko's Modern Life FAQ, September 17, 1997, www.title14.com/rocko/contributors/murray.html.

37. Kiczuk, "The *Rocko's Modern Life* FAQ"; King, "*Rocko's Modern Life*."

38. Kiczuk, "The *Rocko's Modern Life* FAQ."

39. King, "*Rocko's Modern Life*."

40. Kiczuk, "The *Rocko's Modern Life* FAQ."

41. Ibid.

42. Ibid.

43. Ibid.

44. King, "*Rocko's Modern Life*."

45. Ibid.

46. Kiczuk, "The Rocko's Modern Life FAQ."

47. Allen Neuwirth, *Makin' Toons: Inside the Most Popular Animated TV Shows and Movies* (New York: Allworth Press, 2003), 252.

48. Rosie Knight, "*Rocko's Modern Life* Stars Talk Creating the Iconic Nicktoon in the Early '90s," Nerdist, July 25, 2017, https://nerdist.com/article/an-oral-history-of-making-cartoons-at-nicktoons-in-the-90s.

49. King, *"Rocko's Modern Life."*

50. Kiczuk, "The *Rocko's Modern Life* FAQ."

51. Allegra Frank, "Nickelodeon's Early Days Were 'Loose and Crazy,' Says *Rocko's Modern Life* Creator," Polygon, November 21, 2018, www.polygon.com/interviews/2018/11/21/18104961/rockos-modern-life-creator-joe-murray-interview.

52. Kiczuk, "The *Rocko's Modern Life* FAQ"; King, *"Rocko's Modern Life."*

53. King, *"Rocko's Modern Life."*

54. Kiczuk, "The *Rocko's Modern Life* FAQ."

55. Jamie Lovett, *"Rocko's Modern Life* Netflix Special Poster and Release Date Revealed," Comic Book, July 16, 2019, https://comicbook.com/tv-shows/2019/07/16/rockos-modern-life-netflix-special-release-date.

56. Jenny Atkins, "Teen Alienation from Novel to Screen," Hackwriters, 2005, www.hackwriters.com/roswell.htm; Stan Beeler, "Roswell," in *The Essential Cult TV Reader*, ed. David Lavery, 219 (Lexington: University Press of Kentucky, 2010).

57. Patrick Lee, "Laura J. Burns and Melinda Metz Graduate from *Roswell High* to TV, SciFi.com, April 5, 2002, https://web.archive.org/web/20050207003845/http://www.scifi.com/sfw/issue254/interview.html.

58. Beeler, "Roswell," 214.

59. Atkins, "Teen Alienation from Novel to Screen."

60. Ibid.

61. Roger Cormier, "16 Out-Of-This-World Facts about *Roswell*," Mental Floss, May 14, 2017, https://mentalfloss.com/article/69524/16-out-world-facts-about-roswell.

62. Ibid.

63. Ibid.

64. Laurin Sydney, "Viewer Alienation Not a Problem for Teen Drama 'Roswell,'" CNN, October 14, 1999, www.cnn.com/SHOWBIZ/TV/9910/14/roswell.

65. Cormier, "16 Out-Of-This-World Facts"; SciFi.com, "News of the Week," June 26, 2001, https://web.archive.org/web/20080514042620/http://www.scifi.com/sfw/issue213/news.html.

66. Beeler, "Roswell," 214–15.

67. Ibid., 219.

68. SciFi.com, "News of the Week."

69. Atkins, "Teen Alienation from Novel to Screen."

70. Beeler, "Roswell," 214.

71. Mehera Bonner, "Everything You Need to Know about the CW's 'Roswell' Reboot, 'Roswell, New Mexico,'" *Cosmopolitan*, December 11, 2018, www.cosmopolitan.com/entertainment/tv/a25456027/roswell-new-mexico-reboot-news-date-cast-spoilers.

72. Beeler, "Roswell," 216.

73. Ibid., 217.

74. Ibid., 214

75. Ibid.

76. Amy Amatangelo, "The CW's Lazy *Roswell, New Mexico* Is the Remake Craze at Its Worst," *Paste Magazine*, January 14, 2019, www.pastemagazine.com/articles/2019/01/roswell-new-mexico-the-cw-remake-review.html.

S

1. Jay Navok and Sushil K. Rudranath, *Warriors of Legend: Reflections of Japan in Sailor Moon (Unauthorized)* (North Charleston, SC: BookSurge, 2006), 19.

2. Ibid.

3. Ibid., 7.

4. Victoria McNally, "A Ridiculously Comprehensive History of *Sailor Moon*—Part 1: Made in Japan," The Mary Sue, June 18, 2014, www.themarysue.com/sailor-moon-history -part-1.

5. Navok and Rudranath, *Warriors of Legend*, 19.

6. Ibid.

7. Ibid.

8. Jenny Reese, *Popular TV Shows of the '90s: Frasier, Friends, Seinfeld, ER, Baywatch and Other Television Landmarks* (Self-Published: Six Degrees Books, 2011), 123.

9. Ibid.

10. Navok and Rudranath, *Warriors of Legend*, 20.

11. Fred Ladd, Astro Boy *and Anime Come to the Americas: An Insider's View of the Birth of a Pop Culture Phenomenon* (Jefferson, NC: McFarland & Company, 2009), 99.

12. Ibid., 100.

13. Ibid., 101.

14. Victoria McNally, "A Ridiculously Comprehensive History of *Sailor Moon*, Part 2: Coming to America," The Mary Sue, June 25, 2014, www.themarysue.com/sailor-moon -history-part-2.

15. Jonathan Clements and Helen McCarthy, *The Anime Encyclopedia: A Guide to Japanese Animation since 1917* (Berkeley, CA: Stonebridge Press, 2001), 338.

16. Navok and Rudranath, *Warriors of Legend*, 21.

17. McNally, "A Ridiculously Comprehensive History of *Sailor Moon*, Part 2."

18. Navok and Rudranath, *Warriors of Legend*, 21–22.

19. Taimur Dar, "*Sailor Moon* Musical Fights for Love and Justice on Broadway This March," The Beat, December 7, 2018, www.comicsbeat.com/sailor-moon-musical-fights -for-love-and-justice-on-broadway-this-march.

20. Kristy Ambrose, "10 Times *Sailor Moon* Was Way Ahead of Its Time," ScreenRant, August 17, 2019, https://screenrant.com/sailor-moon-best-forward-thinking-scenes.

21. Clements and McCarthy, *The Anime Encyclopedia*, 338.

22. Cecilia D'Anastasio, "What Made Toonami So Good," Kotaku, January 20, 2017, https://kotaku.com/what-made-toonami-so-good-1791425114.

23. Ibid.

24. Ibid.

25. Elijah Watson, "The Oral History of Cartoon Network's Toonami," Complex, March 21, 2017, www.complex.com/pop-culture/2017/03/oral-history-of-toonami.

26. Ibid.

27. D'Anastasio, "What Made Toonami So Good."

28. Ibid.

29. Scott Green, "Toonami Expands to Six Hours," Crunchyroll, September 26, 2012, www.crunchyroll.com/anime-news/2012/09/26-1/toonami-expands-to-six-hours.

30. Peter Engel, *I Was Saved by the Bell: Stories of Life, Love, and Dreams That Do Come True* (Los Angeles: Top Hat Words, 2016), 157–58; Anna Pratt, "'Saved by the Bell' Executive Producer Talks about the Show, Life, Book," PRI, February 27, 2017, www.pri.org/sto ries/2017-02-27/saved-bell-executive-producer-talks-about-show-life-book.

31. Ibid.

32. Engel, *I Was Saved by the Bell*, 158.

33. Ibid.

34. Ibid., 159.

35. Ibid., 164.

36. Pratt, "'Saved by the Bell.'"

37. Vincent Terrace, *Television Series of the 1980s: Essential Facts and Quirky Details* (Lanham, MD: Rowman & Littlefield, 2017), 194.

38. Michael Rothman and Lesley Messer, "25 Things You Never Knew about 'Saved by the Bell,'" ABC News, August 20, 2014, https://abcnews.go.com/Entertainment/25-things-knew-saved-bell/story?id=25027830.

39. Dustin Diamond, *Behind the Bell* (Montreal, Canada: Transit Publishing, 2009), 9.

40. Pratt, "'Saved by the Bell.'"

41. Natalie Finn, "Inside the Secrets of *Saved by the Bell*: Why That Saturday Morning Magic Would Be So Hard to Reboot," E! News, August 20, 2018, www.eonline.com/news/960842/inside-the-secrets-of-saved-by-the-bell-why-that-saturday-morning-magic-would-be-so-hard-to-reboot.

42. Ibid.

43. Diamond, *Behind the Bell*, 22.

44. NPR, "'Scrubs' and 'Garden State' Star Zach Braff," Fresh Air, October 4, 2004, www.npr.org/templates/story/story.php?storyId=4060240.

45. Ibid.

46. Ibid.

47. Michael Schneider, "'Scrubs' Skirmish," *Variety*, February 28, 2008, https://web.archive.org/web/20121107181618/http://www.variety.com/article/VR1117981634?refCatId=14.

48. Ibid.

49. Eric Goldman, "*Scrubs* Season 7 Confirmed," IGN, April 23, 2007, www.ign.com/articles/2007/04/23/scrubs-season-7-confirmed.

50. Will Harris, "A Chat with Bill Lawrence: The 'Scrubs' Exit Interview," Premium Hollywood, May 6, 2009, www.premiumhollywood.com/2009/05/06/a-chat-with-bill-lawrence-the-scrubs-exit-interview.

51. Edward Wyatt, "Goodbye, Hello: Resuscitating a Sitcom," *New York Times*, November 25, 2009, www.nytimes.com/2009/11/29/arts/television/29scrubs.html.

52. Ibid.

53. Ibid.

54. Ibid.

55. Kate Stanhope, "ABC Cancels *Scrubs*, *FlashForward*, *Romantically Challenged* and *Better Off Ted*," *TV Guide*, May 14, 2010, www.tvguide.com/news/scrubs-flashforward-canceled-1018433.

56. Jeff Robbins, *Second City Television: A History and Episode Guide* (Jefferson, NC: McFarland & Company, 2008), 5.

57. Robbins, *Second City Television*, 6; Mike Thomas, *The Second City Unscripted: Revolution and Revelation at the World-famous Comedy Theater* (New York: Villard Books, 2009), 91–93.

58. Robbins, *Second City Television*, 5.

59. Ibid.

60. Thomas, *The Second City*, 100–101.

61. Robbins, *Second City Television*, 5.

62. Ibid.

63. Ibid.

64. Dave Thomas, *SCTV: Behind the Scenes* (Toronto, Canada: McClelland & Stewart, 1996), 196.

65. Ibid.

66. Ibid., 200.

67. Ibid., 6–7.

68. Alan Bisbort, "When SCTV Ruled the World," Please Kill Me, April 26, 2018, https://pleasekillme.com/when-sctv-ruled-the-world.

69. Ramsey Ess, "Harold Ramis's 'SCTV' Legacy," Vulture, February 25, 2014, www
.vulture.com/2014/02/harold-ramis-sctv-legacy.html.

70. Ibid.

71. Jazz Tangeay, "Straczynski Talks 'Sense8' and the Outrageous Show's Diversity,"
Awards Daily TV, June 9, 2016, www.awardsdaily.com/tv/interview-sense8-straczynski.

72. Ibid.

73. Abbie Bernstein, "*Sense8*: J. Michael Straczynski Talks Season 1—Exclusive
Interview," Assignment X, August 17, 2015, www.assignmentx.com/2015/j-michael
-straczynski-on-sense8-exclusive-interview.

74. Cynthia Littleton, "Wachowskis Shopping Their First TV series," *Variety*, October 2, 2012, https://variety.com/2012/tv/news/wachowskis-shopping-their-first-tv
-series-1118060175.

75. Tangeay, "Straczynski Talks 'Sense8.'"

76. Ibid.

77. Davis Schneiderman, "Making *Sense8*: A Conversation with Aleksandar Hemon,"
Entropy, August 1, 2018, https://entropymag.org/making-sense8-a-conversation-with
-aleksandar-hemon.

78. Tangeay, "Straczynski Talks 'Sense8.'"

79. PR Newswire, "Sci-Fi Giants the Wachowskis and J. Michael Straczynski Team-
Up to Create 'Sense8,'" March 27, 2013, www.prnewswire.com/news-releases/only
-on-netflix-sci-fi-giants-the-wachowskis-and-j-michael-straczynski-team-up-to-create
-sense8-200215501.html.

80. Tangeay, "Straczynski Talks 'Sense8.'"

81. Robert Lloyd, "Review: Wachowskis' 'Sense8' on Netflix Is a Stylish If Still Murky
Vision," *Los Angeles Times*, June 5, 2015, www.latimes.com/entertainment/la-et-st-sense8
-review-20150605-column.html.

82. Cáel M. Keegan, *Lana and Lily Wachowski* (Chicago: University of Illinois Press,
2018), 106–7.

83. Dana Getz, "Netflix's *Sense8* Special Starts Production," ScreenRant, September 26,
2017, https://screenrant.com/sense8-special-production-netflix.

84. Keegan, *Lana and Lily Wachowski*, 106–7.

85. Ibid., 108.

86. Bruce Scivally, *Superman on Film, Television, Radio and Broadway* (Jefferson, NC: Mc-
Farland & Company, 2008), 141.

87. Lincoln Geraghty, "Introduction: Investigating *Smallville*," in *The* Smallville *Chronicles: Critical Essays on the Television Series*, ed. Lincoln Geraghty, xiv (Lanham, MD: Scare-
crow Press, 2011).

88. Paul Simpson, Smallville *Season 1: The Official Companion* (London: Titan Books,
2004), 11.

89. Ibid.

90. Geraghty, "Introduction: Investigating *Smallville*," xiv.

91. Simpson, Smallville *Season 1*, 12.

92. Scivally, *Superman on Film*, 143.

93. Simpson, Smallville *Season 1*, 16.

94. Scivally, *Superman on Film*, 143.

95. Ibid., 144.

96. Simpson, Smallville *Season 1*, 17.

97. Scivally, *Superman on Film*, 149–50.

98. Ibid.

99. Ibid., 155.

100. Ibid., 157.

101. Jay Bobbin, "After 10 Years, 'Smallville' Flies Out of the CW's lineup," *Chicago Tribune*, May 4, 2011, www.chicagotribune.com/zap-smallville-finale-story-story.html.

102. Molly Freeman, "Tom Welling Turned Down Superman Return on CW Supergirl," ScreenRant, April 15, 2019, https://screenrant.com/supergirl-superman-tom-welling -return.

103. Allan Sepinwall and Matt Zoller Seitz, *TV (The Book): Two Experts Pick the Greatest American Shows of All Time* (New York: Grand Central Publishing, 2016), 160.

104. Jason Jacobs, "South Park," in *The Essential Cult TV Reader*, ed. David Lavery, 229 (Lexington: University Press of Kentucky, 2010).

105. James Hibberd, "The Wild, Profane, Unlikely Story of 'South Park,'" *Entertainment Weekly*, March 18, 2015, https://ew.com/article/2015/03/18/wild-profane-unlikely -story-south-park; David Bianculli, *The Platinum Age of Television: From* I Love Lucy *to* The Walking Dead, *How TV Became Terrific* (New York: Anchor Books, 2016), 56.

106. Sepinwall and Seitz, *TV (The Book)*, 160.

107. Hibberd, "The Wild, Profane, Unlikely Story."

108. Ibid.

109. David Simmons, "South Park (Comedy Central 1997–)" in *The Cult TV Book: From* Star Trek *to* Dexter, *New Approaches to TV Outside the Box*, ed. Stacey Abbott, 1 (New York: Soft Skull Press, 2010).

110. Hibberd, "The Wild, Profane, Unlikely Story."

111. Simmons, "South Park," 1.

112. Ryan Parker, "Holy Shit, 'South Park' Is 20! Trey Parker, Matt Stone on Censors, Tom Cruise and Scientology's Role in Isaac Hayes Quitting," *Hollywood Reporter*, September 14, 2016, www.hollywoodreporter.com/features/south-park-20-years-history-trey -parker-matt-stone-928212.

113. Amid Amidi, "'6 Days to Air' Reveals *South Park*'s Insane Production Schedule," Cartoon Brew, August 6, 2012, www.cartoonbrew.com/ideas-commentary/6-days-to-air -reveals-south-parks-insane-production-schedule-67657.html.

114. Jacobs, "South Park," 231.

115. Allison Levine, "This Week in Colorado History: *South Park* Debuts 22 Years Ago," 9News, August 19, 2019, www.9news.com/article/news/this-week-in-colorado-history -south-park-debuts-22-years-ago/73-6ae28eb1-9d1e-4ad3-a6ce-5cd5750cec22.

116. Mark Mancini, "11 Bite-Sized Facts about *Cannibal! The Musical*," Mental Floss, October 31, 2017, http://mentalfloss.com/article/84873/11-bite-sized-facts-about-cannibal -musical.

117. Christopher J. Olson, *100 Greatest Cult Films* (Lanham, MD: Rowman & Littlefield, 2018), 34.

118. K. Thor Jensen, "'Space Ghost Coast to Coast' Is Still Influential and Funny, 25 Years Later," Geek.com, April 12, 2019, www.geek.com/television/space-ghost-coast-to-coast -is-still-influential-and-funny-25-years-later-1782448; K. Thor Jensen, "Transmissions from the Ghost Planet: A Definitive History of *Space Ghost Coast to Coast*," SyFy Wire, June 19, 2014, www.syfy.com/syfywire/transmissions-from-the-ghost-planet-a-definitive-history -of-space-ghost-coast-to-coast.

119. Noel Murray, "*Space Ghost Coast to Coast*, 'Surprise,'" AV Club, June 21, 2012, https://tv.avclub.com/space-ghost-coast-to-coast-surprise-1798232096.

120. Jensen, "'Space Ghost"; Jensen, "Transmissions from the Ghost Planet."

121. Jensen, "Transmissions from the Ghost Planet."

122. Sean T. Collins, "The Phantom Fame: 'Space Ghost Coast to Coast,' Secretly TV's Most Influential Show," Grantland, October 7, 2015, https://grantland.com/hollywood -prospectus/the-phantom-fame-space-ghost-coast-to-coast-secretly-tvs-most-influential -show.

123. Jenson, "Transmissions from the Ghost Planet"; Heather Kenyon, "Late Nite with Space Ghost," *Animation World Magazine*, July 1998, www.awn.com/mag/issue3.4/3.4pages/3.4kenyon.html.

124. Jenson, "Transmissions from the Ghost Planet"; Kenyon, "Late Nite with Space Ghost."

125. Murray, "*Space Ghost Coast to Coast*."

126. Kenyon, "Late Nite with Space Ghost."

127. Ibid.

128. Jensen, "Space Ghost."

129. Tim Sommer, "With 'Space Ghost Coast to Coast' Adult Swim Ushered in Comedy's 'Blank Stare' Era, *Observer*, May 31, 2017, https://observer.com/2017/05/space-ghost-coast-to-coast-adult-swim.

130. Jensen, "Space Ghost."

131. Patricio Chile, "*Spaced* and the Mechanics of the Perfect Comedy Team," Vulture, January 9, 2012, www.vulture.com/2012/01/spaced-and-the-mechanics-of-the-perfect-comedy-team.html; Lucy Glover, "Interview with Simon Pegg," Spaced Out, January 25, 2000, www.spaced-out.org.uk/about-spaced/interviews/simon/onelist.shtml.

132. Simon Pegg, *Nerd Do Well: A Small Boy's Journey to Becoming a Big Kid* (New York: Gotham Books, 2011), 299.

133. Ibid.

134. Ibid.

135. Erin Biba, "Simon Pegg's Geek Roots Show in *Spaced*," *Wired*, July 21, 2008, www.wired.com/2008/07/simon-peggs-gee.

136. Pegg, *Nerd Do Well*, 299.

137. Ibid., 291.

138. Daniel Dylan Wray, "An Oral History of 'Spaced,'" Vice, November 18, 2016, www.vice.com/en_us/article/kwk3ga/oral-history-of-spaced-simon-pegg-nick-frost-edgar-wright-jessica-hynes-katy-carmichael.

139. Ibid.

140. Pegg, *Nerd Do Well*, 300.

141. Pegg, *Nerd Do Well*; Wray, "An Oral History of 'Spaced.'"

142. Emma Perry, "*Spaced* (1999–2001)," BFI Screen Online, 2014, www.screenonline.org.uk/tv/id/966650.

143. Channel 4, "Nick Frost and Simon Pegg," Spaced Out, February 2, 2001, www.spaced-out.org.uk/about-spaced/interviews/c4020201.shtml.

144. Wray, "An Oral History of 'Spaced.'"

145. Ibid.

146. Biba, "Simon Pegg's Geek Roots."

147. John Scott Lewinski, "*Spaced* Set to Invade U.S. via DVD, Cable," *Wired*, July 18, 2008, www.wired.com/2008/07/spaced-set-to-i?_ga=2.154679743.603041572.1564960933-1457780010.1564960933#previouspost.

148. Ibid.

149. Mayer Nissim, "Simon Pegg: 'No More *Spaced*,'" Digital Spy, September 23, 2009, www.digitalspy.com/tv/a178723/simon-pegg-no-more-spaced.

150. Kate Atkinson, "*Sports Night*: Looking back at Aaron Sorkin's Gone-Too-Soon Series," *Entertainment Weekly*, November 6, 2014, https://ew.com/tv/2014/11/06/sports-night-oral-history.

151. Ibid.

152. Ibid.

153. Ibid.

154. Ibid.

155. Caryn James, "Goings-On behind the Television Anchors' Smiles," *New York Times*, September 21, 1998, www.nytimes.com/1998/09/21/arts/television-review-new-season -goings-on-behind-the-television-anchors-smiles.html.

156. *Orlando Sentinel*, "'Sports Night' Regroups after Star's Stroke," January 26, 1999, www.orlandosentinel.com/news/os-xpm-1999-01-26-9901250297-story.html.

157. Jeff Merron, "Keeping It Real on 'Sports Night,'" ESPN, November 12, 2002, www .espn.com/page2/s/merron/021112.html.

158. *Orlando Sentinel*, "'Sports Night.'"

159. Atkinson, "*Sports Night.*"

160. Merron, "Keeping It Real on 'Sports Night.'"

161. *South Florida Sun-Sentinel*, "Showtime Won't Get *Sports Night*," June 22, 2000, www .sun-sentinel.com/news/fl-xpm-2000-06-22-0006210413-story.html#.

162. Ian Crouch, "The Cult of 'Sports Night,'" *New Yorker*, June 21, 2012, www.new yorker.com/culture/culture-desk/the-cult-of-sports-night.

163. David Bianculli, *The Platinum Age of Television: From* I Love Lucy *to* The Walking Dead, *How TV Became Terrific* (New York: Anchor Books, 2016), 466

164. Ibid., 465–66.

165. Ibid. 466.

166. Mark Phillips and Frank Garcia, *Science Fiction Television Series: Episode Guides, Histories, and Casts and Credits for 62 Prime Time Shows, 1959–1989* (Jefferson, NC: McFarland & Company, 1996), 400.

167. Stephen E. Whitfield, *The Making of* Star Trek (New York: Del Rey Books, 1968), 22.

168. Ibid., 37.

169. Robert Greenberger, Star Trek: *The Complete Unauthorized History* (Minneapolis, MN: Voyageur Press, 2012), 17.

170. Whitfield, *The Making of* Star Trek, 41–42.

171. Greenberger, Star Trek, 21.

172. Ibid., 19.

173. Ibid., 2.

174. Ibid., 22.

175. Ibid., 23.

176. Ibid., 25.

177. Ibid.

178. Ibid., 33.

179. Phillips and Garcia, *Science Fiction Television Series*, 401.

180. Ibid., 405.

181. Greenberger, Star Trek, 45.

182. Ibid., 50.

183. Whitfield, *The Making of* Star Trek, 31.

184. Greenberger, Star Trek, 14.

185. Ibid.

186. Ibid.

187. Ibid., 15.

188. Ibid. 16.

189. Phillips and Garcia, *Science Fiction Television Series*, 406.

190. David Wain, "*The State*: FAQ," DavidWain.com, 2019, http://davidwain.com/ thestatefaq.

191. Patrick Lyons, "How 'The State' Made Comedy Weirder and Better," Vice, May 7, 2016, www.vice.com/en_us/article/7bd58x/why-the-state-is-the-missing-link-of-90s -comedy.

192. Wain, "*The State*: FAQ."

193. Julie Seabaugh, "An Oral History of the Oral History of *The State*," *LA Weekly*, May 3, 2016, www.laweekly.com/an-oral-history-of-the-oral-history-of-the-state.

194. Ibid.

195. Wain, "*The State*: FAQ."

196. Corey Stulce, *The Union of* The State (Self-published, 2016), 176.

197. Seabaugh, "An Oral History of the Oral History."

198. Wain, "*The State*: FAQ."

199. Stulce, *The Union of* The State, 211.

200. Ibid., 229, 271, 302.

201. Wain, "*The State*: FAQ."

202. Stulce, *The Union of* The State, 180.

203. Ibid., 299.

204. Ken Tucker, "The State," *Entertainment Weekly*, June 17, 1994, https://ew.com/article/1994/06/17/state.

205. Wain, "*The State*: FAQ."

206. Ibid.

207. Ibid.

208. Stulce, *The Union of* The State, 336.

209. Wain, "*The State*: FAQ."

210. Nathan Rabin, "*The State*: The Complete Series," AV Club, July 22, 2009, https://film.avclub.com/the-state-the-complete-series-1798206592.

211. Jon Blistein, "Comedy Troupe *The State* Prep Oral History," *Rolling Stone*, March 29, 2016, www.rollingstone.com/culture/culture-news/comedy-troupe-the-state-prep-oral-history-91554.

212. Chris McDonnell, Steven Universe: *Art & Origins* (New York: Abrams, 2017), 14–15.

213. Ibid., 18.

214. Ibid.

215. Ibid., 19.

216. Zack Smith, "Rebecca Sugar Brings *Steven Universe* to Life," Newsarama, November 4, 2013, www.newsarama.com/19471-rebecca-sugar-brings-steven-universe-to-life.html.

217. McDonnell, Steven Universe, 25.

218. Ibid., 60.

219. Smith, "Rebecca Sugar Brings *Steven Universe*."

220. McDonnell, Steven Universe, 25.

221. *Deadline*, "Cartoon Network Orders More Episodes of Rookies 'Uncle Grandpa,' 'Steven Universe,'" November 14, 2013, https://deadline.com/2013/11/paw-patrol-season-two-cartoon-network-634956.

222. Lesley Goldberg, "Comic-Con Exclusive: Cartoon Network Renews 'Adventure Time,' 'Regular Show,' 3 More," *Hollywood Reporter*, July 25, 2014, www.hollywoodreporter.com/live-feed/comic-con-cartoon-network-renews-721092.

223. Alec Mojalad, "*Steven Universe: The Movie* Trailer Released at SDCC 2019," Den of Geek! July 19, 2019, www.denofgeek.com/us/movies/steven-universe/275083/steven-universe-movie-release-date-trailer-cast-news.

224. Patricia Martin, "What *Steven Universe* Can Teach Us about Queerness, Gender Identity, and Feminism," Black Girl Nerds, April 11, 2017, https://blackgirlnerds.com/steven-universe-can-teach-us-queerness-gender-identity-feminism.

225. Paul Schrodt, "*Strangers with Candy*: A Mini-Oral History," *GQ*, June 5, 2018, www.gq.com/story/strangers-with-candy-mini-oral-history.

226. Kara Warner, "*Strangers with Candy*: An Interview with Amy Sedaris and Pinello," Black Film, June 23, 2006, www.blackfilm.com/20060623/features/strangerswithcandy1.shtml.

227. Steve Birmingham, "Blank Generation: Amy Sedaris on 'Strangers with Candy,'" *Austin Chronicle*, July 21, 2006, www.austinchronicle.com/screens/2006-07-21/388486.

228. Schrodt, *"Strangers with Candy."*

229. Warner, *"Strangers with Candy."*

230. Dan Neilan, *"Strangers with Candy* Worked Because of the Unstoppable Trio behind Its Creation," AV Club, June 6, 2018, https://news.avclub.com/strangers-with-candy -worked-because-of-the-unstoppable-1826605471.

231. Ramsey Ess, "Colbert, Sedaris and Dinello Discuss the Life and Death of Jerri Blank," Vulture, September 7, 2012, www.vulture.com/2012/09/colbert-sedaris-and -dinello-discuss-the-life-and-death-of-jerri-blank.html.

232. Neilan, *"Strangers with Candy"*; Schrodt, *"Strangers with Candy."*

233. Warner, *"Strangers with Candy."*

234. Ess, "Colbert, Sedaris and Dinello."

235. Neilan, *"Strangers with Candy."*

236. Warner, *"Strangers with Candy."*

237. Ibid.

238. Birmingham, "Blank Generation."

239. Schrodt, *"Strangers with Candy."*

240. Ibid.

241. Birmingham, "Blank Generation."

242. Ibid.

243. Schrodt, *"Strangers with Candy."*

244. Warner, *"Strangers with Candy."*

245. Nicholas Knight, Supernatural: *The Official Companion Season 1* (London: Titan Books, 2007), 8; Laura Prudom, "'Supernatural' at 200: The Road So Far, An Oral History," *Variety*, November 11, 2014, https://variety.com/2014/tv/spotlight/supernatural-oral -history-200-episodes-ackles-padalecki-kripke-1201352537.

246. Knight, Supernatural, 8; Prudom, "'Supernatural.'"

247. Knight, Supernatural.

248. Ibid., 9.

249. Ibid.

250. Ibid.

251. Prudom, "'Supernatural.'"

252. Knight, Supernatural, 10.

253. Ibid.

254. Ibid., 12.

255. Ibid., 13.

256. Ibid., 14.

257. Ibid.

258. Alison Peirse, "Supernatural," in *The Essential Cult TV Reader*, ed. David Lavery, 263 (Lexington: University Press of Kentucky, 2010).

259. Karen Petruska, "Crossing Over: Network Transition, Critical Reception, and *Supernatural* Longevity," in *TV Goes to Hell: An Unofficial Road Map of* Supernatural, ed. Stacey Abbot and David Lavery, 227 (Toronto, Canada: ECW Press, 2011).

260. Petruska, "Crossing Over," 229; Prudom, "'Supernatural.'"

261. Laura Prudom, "How 'Supernatural' Outlived the WB and Learned the Secret to Immortality," *Variety*, September 21, 2016, www.yahoo.com/entertainment/supernatural -outlived-wb-learned-secret-immortality-170056706.html.

262. Nellie Andreeva and Denise Petski, "'Supernatural' to End after Season 15 on the CW," *Deadline*, https://deadline.com/2019/03/supernatural-to-end-after-season-15-on -the-cw-1202581010.

263. Zoe Thomas, "How 'Supernatural' Became an Ode to Its Fans," Film School Rejects, April 15, 2019, https://filmschoolrejects.com/supernatural-fans.

T

1. Mike Schuster, "Read This, Gently: 10 Things You Didn't Know about Tenacious D," IFC.com, April 9, 2015, www.ifc.com/shows/comedy-bang-bang/blog/2015/04/10 -things-you-didnt-know-about-tenacious-d; Hugh Hart, "'D' Is for Dynamic Duo," *SF Gate*, November 26, 2006, www.sfgate.com/entertainment/article/D-is-for-dynamic -duo-2466349.php.

2. Schuster, "Read This, Gently."

3. Hart, "'D' Is for Dynamic Duo"; Allan Johnson, "Tenacious D Is a Band, and the Humorous Duo Gets Around," *Chicago Tribune*, June 11, 1999, www.chicagotribune.com/ news/ct-xpm-1999-06-11-9906110231-story.html; Heather Phares, "Tenacious D," All Music, 2019, www.allmusic.com/artist/tenacious-d-mn0000017021/biography.

4. Cameron Tung, "Gods of Rock (in Their Own Minds): The Early Days of Tenacious D," Vulture, May 16, 2012, www.vulture.com/2012/05/gods-of-rock-in-their-own-minds -the-early-days-of-tenacious-d.html.

5. Phil Gallo, "Tenacious D," *Variety*, March 23, 1999, https://variety.com/1999/tv/ reviews/tenacious-d-1200456842.

6. Schuster, "Read This, Gently."

7. Paul Fischer, "Exclusive Interview: Jack Black & Kyle Gass," Moviehole, February 23, 2007, https://web.archive.org/web/20070223201835/http://www.moviehole.net/ interviews/20061115_exclusive_interview_jack_black.html.

8. Schuster, "Read This, Gently."

9. Stephen Holden, "The Heavy Journey to Becoming a Rock God," *New York Times*, November 22, 2006, www.nytimes.com/2006/11/22/movies/22dest.html.

10. Alex Young, "Tenacious D Announce New Album and Animated Series, *Post-Apocalypto*," Consequence of Sound, September 4, 2018, https://consequenceofsound .net/2018/09/tenacious-d-post-apocalypto.

11. Kimberly Potts, "'The Tick': How Creator Ben Edlund Rebooted His Vision for the New Amazon Pilot," Yahoo! Entertainment, August 19, 2016, www.yahoo.com/entertain ment/why-amazon-reboot-tick-going-000000874.html.

12. Ibid.

13. Eric Francisco, "A Brief History of America's Best Worst Superhero," Inverse, July 28, 2016, www.inverse.com/article/18891-the-tick-reboot-amazon-peter-serafinowicz -original-show.

14. Ron Hogan, "*The Tick*: The History of a Laugh-Out-Loud Superhero Satire," Den of Geek! April 4, 2019, www.denofgeek.com/us/tv/the-tick/267230/the-tick-the-history-of -a-laugh-out-loud-superhero-satire.

15. Deborah Reber, "Tick Fever Endures: Ben Edlund Talks about the Evolution of Everyone's Favorite Blue Superhero," *Animation World Magazine*, July 1997, www.awn.com/ mag/issue2.4/awm2.4pages/2.4reberedlund.html.

16. Ibid.

17. Hogan, "*The Tick*."

18. John Orquiola, "*The Tick*'s Comic Book & TV History Explained," ScreenRant, August 28, 2017, www.syfy.com/syfywire/why-amazons-the-tick-is-more-relevant-now -than-ever-before.

19. Reber, "Tick Fever Endures."

20. Ibid.

21. Orquiola, *"The Tick's* Comic Book."

22. Hogan, *"The Tick."*

23. Reber, "Tick Fever Endures."

24. Orquiola, *"The Tick's* Comic Book."

25. Jamie Loftus, "Why Amazon's *The Tick* Is More Relevant Now Than Ever Before," SyFy Wire, February 24, 2018, www.syfy.com/syfywire/why-amazons-the-tick-is-more -relevant-now-than-ever-before.

26. Alec Bojalad, *"The Tick* Canceled after Two Seasons," Den of Geek! May 16, 2019, www.denofgeek.com/us/tv/the-tick/281100/will-the-tick-season-3-news.

27. Travis Fickett, *"Six Feet Under Creator* Gets Bloody," IGN, May 12, 2012, www.ign .com/articles/2008/07/12/six-feet-under-creator-gets-bloody.

28. Ibid.

29. Ibid.

30. Ibid.

31. Brigid Cherry, "Before the Night Is Through: *True Blood* as Cult TV," in True Blood: *Investigating Vampires and Southern Gothic,* ed. Brigid Cherry, 4 (New York: I.B. Taurus, 2012).

32. Antonia Blyth, "'True Blood' Creator Alan Ball Gives Details of Musical Version in the Works," *Deadline,* November 18, 2018, https://deadline.com/2018/11/true-blood -alan-ball-musical-version-1202504615.

33. Nellie Andreeva, "Moyer, HBO Make 'Blood' Pact," *Hollywood Reporter,* April 9, 2007, www.hollywoodreporter.com/news/moyer-hbo-make-blood-pact-133609.

34. Ibid.

35. Blyth, "'True Blood' Creator Alan Ball."

36. Cherry, "Before the Night Is Through," 4.

37. Ibid., 7–8.

38. *New York Times,* "'True Blood' Shows Ratings Growth for HBO," November 23, 2008, https://mediadecoder.blogs.nytimes.com//2008/11/23/true-blood-shows-ratings -growth-for-hbo.

39. Seth Kelley, "10 of the Most Expensive TV Shows Ever Made," MarketPlace, December 11, 2014, www.marketplace.org/2014/12/11/business/10-most-expensive-tv-shows -ever-made.

40. Ibid.

41. Matt Fowler, *"True Blood*: Alan Ball Stepping Down as Showrunner," IGN, February 27, 2012, www.ign.com/articles/2012/02/27/true-blood-alan-ball-stepping-down-as -showrunner.

42. Roth Cornet, *"True Blood* to End after Season 7," IGN, September 3, 2013, www.ign .com/articles/2013/09/03/true-blood-to-end-after-season-7.

43. Blyth, "'True Blood' Creator Alan Ball."

44. Scott Neumyer, "How 'True Blood' Lost Its Bite," *Rolling Stone,* June 19, 2014, www .rollingstone.com/tv/tv-news/how-true-blood-lost-its-bite-124901.

45. Cherry, "Before the Night Is Through," 14.

46. Zainab Akande, "'True Blood': How Bill Compton Made Sookie Stackhouse Lose Her Groove," IndieWire, September 6, 2014, www.indiewire.com/2014/09/true-blood -how-bill-compton-made-sookie-stackhouse-lose-her-groove-22502.

47. Shoshana Kessock, *"True Blood* Fan Confession: I'm So Over Sookie," Tor.com, June 15, 2012, www.tor.com/2012/06/15/true-blood-fan-confession-im-so-over-sookie.

48. Daniel Reynolds, "Photos: The LGBT Characters of *True Blood,"* *Advocate,* June 20, 2014, www.advocate.com/arts-entertainment/television/2014/06/20/photos-lgbt -characters-true-blood.

49. J. Bryan Lowder, *"True Blood*'s Queer Legacy," *Slate*, June 25, 2014, https://slate.com/human-interest/2014/06/true-blood-reviewed-why-hbos-vampire-show-is-a-queer-masterpiece.html.

50. Ibid.

51. Allan Sepinwall & Matt Zoller Seitz, *TV (The Book): Two Experts Pick the Greatest American Shows of All Time* (New York: Grand Central Publishing, 2016), 92.

52. Jonathan Malcolm Lampley, "The Twilight Zone," in *The Essential Cult TV Reader*, ed. David Lavery, 292 (Lexington: University Press of Kentucky, 2010).

53. Stewart T. Stanyard, *Dimensions behind the Twilight Zone: A Backstage Tribute to Television's Groundbreaking Series* (Toronto, Canada: ECW Press, 2007), 12.

54. Ibid., 13.

55. Ibid., 14.

56. Lampley, "The Twilight Zone," 293.

57. Ibid.

58. David Bianculli, *The Platinum Age of Television: From* I Love Lucy *to* The Walking Dead*, How TV Became Terrific* (New York: Anchor Books, 2016), 398.

59. Mark Phillips and Frank Garcia, *Science Fiction Television Series: Episode Guides, Histories, and Casts and Credits for 62 Prime Time Shows, 1959–1989* (Jefferson, NC: McFarland & Company, 1996), 469.

60. Lampley, "The Twilight Zone," 296.

61. Ibid.

62. Stan Beeler, *"The Twilight Zone* (CBS, 1959–1964)" in *The Cult TV Book: From* Star Trek *to* Dexter*, New Approaches to TV Outside the Box*, ed. Stacey Abbott, 57 (New York: Soft Skull Press, 2010).

63. Phillips and Garcia, *Science Fiction Television Series*, 472.

64. Beeler, *"The Twilight Zone,"* 58.

65. Phillips and Garcia, *Science Fiction Television Series*, 467.

66. Lampley, "The Twilight Zone," 292.

67. Ibid., 296.

68. Sepinwall and Seitz, *TV (The Book)*, 94.

69. Lampley, "The Twilight Zone," 297.

70. Brad Dukes, *Reflections: An Oral History of* Twin Peaks (Short/Tall Press, 2014), 9–12.

71. Ibid., 15.

72. Ibid., 24.

73. Ibid., 41.

74. History.com, *"Twin Peaks* Premieres on ABC," August 21, 2018, www.history.com/this-day-in-history/twin-peaks-premieres-on-abc.

75. James Parker, "How 'Twin Peaks' Invented Modern Television," *Atlantic*, June 6, 2018, www.theatlantic.com/magazine/archive/2017/06/how-twin-peaks-invented-modern-television/524493.

76. David Bianculli, "Twin Peaks," in *The Essential Cult TV Reader*, ed. David Lavery, 301 (Lexington: University Press of Kentucky, 2010).

77. Ibid., 301–2.

78. Dukes, *Reflections*, 151.

79. Bianculli, "Twin Peaks," 302.

80. Bianculli, "Twin Peaks," 302; Andreas Halskov, *TV Peaks:* Twin Peaks *and Modern Television Drama* (Odense: University Press of Southern Denmark, 2015), 11.

81. Bianculli, "Twin Peaks," 303.

82. Ibid., 306.

83. John Kenneth Muir, *Terror Television: American Series, 1970–1999* (Jefferson, NC: McFarland & Company, 2000), 252.

84. Halskov, *TV Peaks*, 11.

85. HeadStuff, "What Year Is This? Is *Twin Peaks: The Return* the Greatest Achievement in the History of Television?" September 11, 2017, www.headstuff.org/entertainment/film/twin-peaks-the-return.

86. Muir, *Terror Television*, 252.

U

1. Matt Besser, Amy Poehler, Ian Roberts, and Matt Walsh, "Audio Commentary for 'Time Machine,'" *Upright Citizens Brigade: The Complete First Season* (Los Angeles: Paramount, 1998), DVD; Alex Remington, "The Return of America's Best Sketch Comedy Group," HuffPost, September 21, 2007, www.huffpost.com/entry/the-return-of-americas-be_b_65383.

2. Amy Poehler, *Yes Please* (New York: HarperCollins, 2014), 111.

3. Poehler, *Yes Please*, 111–12; Brian Raftery, "And . . . Scene," *New York Magazine*, September 23, 2011, http://nymag.com/arts/comics/features/upright-citizens-brigade-2011-10.

4. Raftery, "And . . . Scene"; Nathan Rabin, "Upright Citizens Brigade," AV Club, September 2, 1998, www.avclub.com/upright-citizens-brigade-1798207964.

5. Poehler, *Yes Please*, 190.

6. Julie Seabaugh, "*Night After Night* to *@midnight*: An Oral History of Comedy Central (Part 1)," AV Club, April 4, 2016, https://tv.avclub.com/night-after-night-to-midnight-an-oral-history-of-come-1798246395.

7. Poehler, *Yes Please*, 190.

8. Remington, "The Return of America's Best Sketch Comedy Group."

9. Poehler, *Yes Please*, 191.

10. Poehler, *Yes Please*, 191; Ramsey Ess, "Looking Back at the Upright Citizen's Brigade TV Show with the UCB4," Vulture, February 22, 2013, www.vulture.com/2013/02/looking-back-at-the-upright-citizens-brigade-tv-show-with-the-ucb-4.html.

11. Matt Besser, Amy Poehler, Ian Roberts, and Matt Walsh, "Audio Commentary for 'Power Marketing,'" *Upright Citizens Brigade: The Complete First Season* (Los Angeles: Paramount, 1998), DVD.

12. Matt Besser, Amy Poehler, Ian Roberts, and Matt Walsh, "Audio Commentary for 'The Bucket of Truth,'" *Upright Citizens Brigade: The Complete First Season* (Los Angeles: Paramount, 1998), DVD.

13. Besser, Poehler, Roberts, and Walsh, "Audio Commentary for 'Power Marketing.'"

14. Rabin, "Upright Citizens Brigade."

15. Megan McKenna, "Upright Citizens Brigade Finds Success with Sketch Comedy," *Daily Collegian*, November 24, 2003, www.collegian.psu.edu/arts_and_entertainment/article_881ca479-1349-5883-b0be-0bc043d0157a.html.

16. Ibid.

17. William Hughes, "The Trailer for Seeso's New *UCB Show* Is a Real Comedy Nerd Treasure Trove," AV Club, December 3, 2015, https://tv.avclub.com/the-trailer-for-seeso-s-new-ucb-show-is-a-real-comedy-n-1798287042.

V

1. Sue Turnbull, "Veronica Mars," in *The Essential Cult TV Reader*, ed. David Lavery, 315 (Lexington: University Press of Kentucky, 2010).

2. Ibid.

3. Ibid.

4. Ibid., 315–16.

5. Ibid., 317.

6. Ibid., 2.

7. Ibid., 316.

8. Ibid., 320.

9. Turnbull, "Veronica Mars," 320; Michael Ausiello, "*Veronica Mars* Is Now 'Officially Dead,'" *TV Guide*, June 11, 2007, www.tvguide.com/news/veronica-mars-officially-8545.

10. Turnbull, "Veronica Mars," 320; Eric Goldman, "*Veronica Mars* Is Dead, But Kristen Bell Is Now CW's *Gossip Girl*," IGN, May 17, 2007, https://web.archive.org/web/20071012222825/http://tv.ign.com/articles/789/789402p1.html.

11. Graeme McMillan, "*Veronica Mars* Kickstarter Breaks Records, Raises Over $2M in 12 Hours," *Wired*, March 14, 2013, www.wired.com/2013/03/veronica-mars-kickstarter-record.

12. Andrew Liptak, "Hulu Has Released *Veronica Mars* Season 4 a Week Early," The Verge, July 19, 2019, www.theverge.com/2019/7/19/20701161/hulu-veronica-mars-kristen-bell-season-4-released-early.

13. Nellie Andreeva, "'Veronica Mars' Creator Thinks There Will Be Another Season, Explains Why That Tragic Twist Was Needed," *Deadline*, July 26, 2019, https://deadline.com/2019/07/veronica-mars-season-5-renewal-details-season-4-tragic-twist-backlash-1202655328.

14. Turnbull, "Veronica Mars," 315.

15. Ibid., 320.

16. Andreeva, "'Veronica Mars.'"

W

1. Paul Ruditis, *The Walking Dead Chronicles: The Official Companion Book* (New York: Abrams, 2011), 23.

2. Ibid.

3. Ibid., 43.

4. Ibid., 44–45.

5. Ibid., 45.

6. Ibid., 46.

7. Ibid., 51.

8. Ibid., 68.

9. Hugh Armitage, "'The Walking Dead' Breaks AMC Records," Digital Spy, February 11, 2010, www.digitalspy.com/tv/ustv/a285475/the-walking-dead-breaks-amc-records.

10. Ibid.

11. John Squires, "Even with the Lowest Rated Finale to Date, 'The Walking Dead' Remains the Highest Rated Series on Cable," Bloody Disgusting, April 2, 2019, https://bloody-disgusting.com/tv/3553772/even-lowest-rated-finale-date-walking-dead-remains-highest-rated-series-cable.

12. Dalvin Brown, "The Best 'Walking Dead' Swag for Superfans," Mashable, February 22, 2018, https://mashable.com/2018/02/22/the-walking-dead-season-8-midseason-premier-merchandise.

13. Erica E. Phillips, "Zombie Studies Gain Ground on College Campuses," *Wall Street Journal*, March 3, 2014, www.wsj.com/articles/zombie-studies-gain-ground-on-college-campuses-1393906046.

14. John Saavedra and Alec Bojalad, "*The Walking Dead*: New Spinoff Series Cast Revealed," Den of Geek! July 19, 2019, www.denofgeek.com/us/tv/the-walking -dead/280366/the-walking-dead-third-series-cast-release-date-trailer-news.

15. Dalton Ross, "Rick Grimes *The Walking Dead* Movie Coming to Theaters," *Entertainment Weekly*, July 19, 2019, https://ew.com/comic-con/2019/07/19/walking-dead-rick -grimes-movie-theaters.

16. Allan Sepinwall and Matt Zoller Seitz, *TV (The Book): Two Experts Pick the Greatest American Shows of All Time* (New York: Grand Central Publishing, 2016), 39.

17. Ibid., 40.

18. Brian G. Rose, "The Wire," in *The Essential HBO Reader*, ed. Gary R. Edgerton and Jeffrey P. Jones, 84 (Lexington: University Press of Kentucky, 2008); Marc Spitz, "*Maxim* Interrogates the Makers and Stars of *The Wire*," *Maxim*, June 4, 2012, www.maxim.com/ entertainment/maxim-interrogates-makers-and-stars-wire.

19. Rose, "The Wire," 84–85.

20. Jonathan Abrams, *All the Pieces Matter: The Inside Story of* The Wire (New York: Crown Archetype, 2018), 8.

21. Rose, "The Wire," 84.

22. Ibid.

23. Ibid.

24. Spitz, "Maxim Interrogates."

25. Dorian Lynskey, "*The Wire*, 10 Years On: 'We Tore the Cover Off a City and Showed the American Dream Was Dead,'" *Guardian*, March 6, 2018, www.theguardian.com/tv -and-radio/2018/mar/06/the-wire-10-years-on-we-tore-the-cover-off-a-city-and-showed -the-american-dream-was-dead.

26. Rose, "The Wire," 89.

27. Ibid.

28. Ibid.

29. Ibid.

30. Emma Jones, "How *The Wire* Became the Greatest TV Show Ever Made," BBC, April 13, 2018, www.bbc.com/culture/story/20180412-how-the-wire-became-the-greatest-tv -show-ever-made.

31. Sepinwall and Seitz, *TV (The Book)*, 38

32. Ibid.

X

1. Brian Lowry, *The Truth Is Out There: The Official Guide to* The X-Files (New York: HarperCollins, 1995), 9.

2. Michael O'Connell, "When 'The X-Files' Became A-list: An Oral History of Fox's Out-There Success Story," *Hollywood Reporter*, January 7, 2016, www.hollywoodreporter.com/ features/x-files-became-a-list-852398.

3. John Nugent, "X-Files Archive: Chris Carter Interview," *Empire*, January 1, 2013, www .empireonline.com/movies/features/x-files-archive-chris-carter-q.

4. Nugent, "X-Files Archive"; Ed Gross, "*The X-Files*: A Complete History," *Empire*, January 28, 2016, www.empireonline.com/movies/features/x-files-history.

5. Gross, "*The X-Files*"; Nick De Semlyen, "X-Files Archive: David Duchovny and Gillian Anderson in Conversation," *Empire*, January 1, 2013, www.empireonline.com/movies/ features/x-files-archive-david-duchovny-gillian-anderson-conversation.

6. O'Connell, "When 'The X-Files' Became A-list."

7. Ibid.

8. Ibid.

9. De Semlyen, "X-Files Archive."

10. O'Connell, "When 'The X-Files' Became A-list."

11. Ibid.

12. *TV Guide*, "Chris Carter," 2018, www.tvguide.com/celebrities/chris-carter/bio/144476.

13. Jessica Mason, "Twenty Years Later, a Look at How *Xena: Warrior Princess* Changed Television," The Mary Sue, October 6, 2015, www.themarysue.com/twenty-years-later-a-look-at-how-xena-warrior-princess-changed-television.

14. Jake Rossen, "11 Fierce Facts about *Xena: Warrior Princess*," Mental Floss, June 18, 2016, http://mentalfloss.com/article/68156/11-fierce-facts-about-xena-warrior-princess.

15. Ibid.

16. Christy Box, "17 Mind-Blowing Secrets Fans Didn't Know about *Xena: Warrior Princess*," ScreenRant, January 5, 2018, https://screenrant.com/xena-warrior-princess-facts-trivia-secrets.

17. Ibid.

18. Rossen, "11 Fierce Facts about *Xena*."

19. Brooke Carter, "What Happened to Lucy Lawless—News & Updates," *Gazette Review*, December 31, 2016, https://gazettereview.com/2017/01/happened-lucy-lawless-news-updates.

20. Rossen, "11 Fierce Facts about *Xena*."

21. Juliette Harrison, "Why *Xena: Warrior Princess* Was Groundbreaking," Den of Geek! July 2, 2018, www.denofgeek.com/us/tv/xena-warrior-princess/274623/why-xena-warrior-princess-was-groundbreaking.

22. Daniel Cerone, "There's Action Off the Beaten Path," *Los Angeles Times*, January 16, 1994, www.latimes.com/archives/la-xpm-1994-01-16-ca-12369-story.html.

23. Cathy Young, "What We Owe Xena," *Salon*, September 16, 2005, www.salon.com/2005/09/15/xena_2.

24. Rossen, "11 Fierce Facts about *Xena*."

25. Young, "What We Owe Xena."

26. Ibid.

27. Kayla Kumari Upadhyaya, "Read This: How *Xena* became an LGBT and Feminist Icon," AV Club, June 17, 2016, https://news.avclub.com/read-this-how-xena-became-an-lgbt-and-feminist-icon-1798248438.

28. Rossen, "11 Fierce Facts about *Xena*."

29. Don Caplan, "'Xena' Slain by Cost Cutting," *New York Post*, October 17, 2000, https://nypost.com/2000/10/17/xena-slain-by-cost-cutting.

30. Box, "17 Mind-Blowing Secrets."

31. Joe Otterson, "'Xena: The Warrior Princess' to Be Rebooted at NBC," *The Wrap*, July 20, 2015, www.thewrap.com/xena-the-warrior-princess-to-be-rebooted-at-nbc.

32. Box, "17 Mind-Blowing Secrets."

33. Young, "What We Owe Xena."

34. Hal Erickson, "Sam Raimi," Fandango, 2019, www.fandango.com/people/sam-raimi-548385/biography.

35. Robert G. Tapert and Mary D. Brooks, "Biography," Robert Tapert, 2019, www.robtapert.com.

36. Erickson, "Sam Raimi."

Y

1. Martyn Palmer, "How We Met: Rik Mayall and Adrian Edmonson," *Independent*, February 20, 1994, www.independent.co.uk/arts-entertainment/how-we-met-rik-mayall -and-adrian-edmonson-1395270.html.

2. Chris Maume, "Rik Mayall: Comedian and Actor Who Helped Revolutionize the British Comedy Scene as the Punk Poet and Cliff Richard Fan, Rick," *Independent*, June 10, 2014, www.independent.co.uk/news/obituaries/rik-mayall-comedian-and-actor-who -helped-revolutionise-the-british-comedy-scene-as-the-punk-poet-and-9517289.html.

3. Marc Edward Heuck, "'The Young Ones': The '80s British Sitcom Helped Define the MTV Generation's Sense of Humor," Night Flight, July 20, 2016, http://nightflight .com/the-young-ones-the-80s-british-sitcom-helped-define-the-mtv-generations-sense -of-humor.

4. Rick Fulton, "*The Young Ones* Never Gets Old as New Documentaries Look at Sitcom That Changed TV Forever," *Daily Record*, May 23, 2018, www.dailyrecord.co.uk/entertain ment/tv-radio/young-ones-never-gets-old-12579171.

5. Heuck, "'The Young Ones'"; BBC, "The Comic Strip Presents . . .," October 28, 2014, www.bbc.co.uk/comedy/thecomicstrip.

6. Heuck, "'The Young Ones.'"

7. Ibid.

8. Hannah Hamad, "Young Ones, The (1982–84)," BFI Screen Online, 2014, www .screenonline.org.uk/tv/id/476396/index.html.

9. Heuck, "'The Young Ones.'"

10. Ibid.

11. Ibid.

12. Robert Ham, "Ranking *The Young Ones*' Musical Performances," *Paste Magazine*, February 9, 2016, www.pastemagazine.com/articles/2016/02/ranking-the-young-ones -musical-performances.html.

13. Justin Quirk, "'Shut Up You Hippy!'" *Guardian*, October 20, 2007, www.theguardian .com/stage/2007/oct/20/comedy.television.

14. Erik Arbriss, "Jessi Klein on the Offbeat, Anarchic Humor of *The Young Ones*," Vulture, October 9, 2018, www.vulture.com/2018/10/jessi-klein-interview-young-ones -british-comedy.html.

15. Heuck, "'The Young Ones.'"

16. Peter Farquhar, "Revealed: There Really Was a Creepy Fifth Housemate Lurking in Cult British TV Show *The Young Ones*," *Business Insider*, June 18, 2016, www.businessinsider .com.au/ben-elton-knew-nothing-about-the-young-ones-creepy-fifth-housemate-2016-6.

Index

ABC, 2, 18, 21, 24–25, 44, 48, 51, 58, 82, 95, 99, 115, 119, 127–28, 130, 136–37, 155–56, 178–79, 193–94, 215, 230

Abrahams, Jim, 155–56

Abrams, J. J., 119, 121, 159

Absolutely Fabulous, 1–2, 235

Adult Swim, 8, 10, 38–41, 64, 75, 78, 97, 190

adventure, 16, 17, 26, 72, 82, 123, 134, 143, 175, 183, 186

Adventure Time, 3–6, 18, 135, 200, 201

The Adventures of Pete & Pete, 6–8, 11, 171

Allen, Debbie, 57–58

Allen, Irwin, 121–23

AMC, 158, 223–25

Amell, Stephen, 14–15

Ancier, Garth, 34, 74

animated, 51, 62, 76, 83, 153, 170, 188; adult-oriented, 38, 77, 168, 190; anime, xiv, 10, 16–17, 39–41, 62, 174–76; cartoon, 51, 76, 77, 94, 135, 152, 153, 169, 175, 177, 208; comedy, 44, 65, 209; feature, 134, 169; series, 4, 8, 16, 38, 41, 44, 46, 52, 64, 75, 79, 80, 96, 98, 123, 167, 169, 174, 181, 185, 187, 199, 206; special, 100, 134

anthology series, 11, 48, 141, 203, 213, 214

Apatow, Judd, 38, 44, 74, 75

Aqua Teen Hunger Force, 8–10, 77, 169, 189, 190, 191

Are You Afraid of the Dark?, 10–12, 215

Arrested Development, 12–14, 39, 118, 140, 150

Arrow, 14–15, 186

Atkinson, Rowan, 29–31

audience: broad, 5, 54, 61, 92; cult, xiii–xiv, 13, 25, 44, 74, 79, 190, 205; female, 15, 46; fragmented, xiv, xv; live, 110, 193, 194;

mainstream, xiv, xv; male, 15; niche, xiv, 10, 38

Avatar: The Last Airbender, 16–17, 176, 201

The Avengers, 18–20, 159, 228

Babylon 5, 21–23, 68, 166, 182, 197

Ball, Alan, 210, 212

Batman: The Animated Series, 16, 51, 80, 82, 95, 210

Battlestar Galactica, 23–26, 143

Baywatch, 26–27

BBC, 30, 55, 59–60, 68–69, 129–30, 141, 165–66, 234–35

BBC America, 142, 192

Beauty and the Beast, 28–29, 36, 82, 212

Beavis and Butt-Head, 46, 47, 169

Bellisario, Donald P., 160

Berlanti, Greg, 14

Besser, Matt, 218, 219

Black, Jack, 132, 206–7

The Black Adder, 29–31, 235

Bloom, Rachel, 41–42

Bonann, Gregory J., 26

Booth, Connie, 68–69

Bouchard, Loren, 96–98

Brillstein, Bernie, 72, 132

broadcast, 27, 145, 217, 228, 229, 230

Brooks, James L., 44, 79

Buffy the Vampire Slayer, 29, 31–33, 34, 35, 36, 56, 87, 116, 137, 173, 185, 186, 205, 212, 220, 222, 229, 232

Burge, Constance, 34

Burns, Ed, 225, 227

cable, xiii, xiv, 6, 27, 78, 88, 90, 113, 124, 138, 144, 145, 163, 181, 187, 223, 224

Camp, Bob, 167–68

Carter, Chris, 116, 228, 230

cartoon. *See* animated

Cartoon Network, xiv, 4–5, 8–9, 10, 39–40, 62, 64, 76, 78, 97, 175, 176, 189–90, 200–201

CBS, 26, 28, 35, 42, 83–84, 112, 114, 115, 122–23, 127, 151, 158, 198, 213, 230

Channel 4, 141, 162, 163, 191, 192, 234

Chapman, Graham, 129, 131

Charmed, 33, 34–36, 205, 212, 232

children's programming, 7, 8, 17, 55, 62, 71, 95, 99, 134, 151, 152, 164, 168, 169

Cleese, John, 68–70, 129–30

Cohen, David X., 77–78

Colbert, Stephen, 201–3

Comedy Central, 1, 3, 44, 78, 97, 110–11, 138–39, 187, 189, 194, 202, 208, 218–19

comic book, 5, 16, 25, 32, 33, 38, 48, 51, 67, 122, 158, 161, 176, 186, 189, 192, 193, 208, 209, 223. *See also* manga

Comic Strip club, 3, 234, 235

Community, 36–38, 84, 85, 150, 193

cop drama, 116, 145, 156, 216, 225, 226, 227. *See also* crime; FBI; police procedural

Cowboy Bebop, 10, 39–41

Crazy Ex-Girlfriend, 41–43, 87, 222

crime, 18, 40, 128, 156, 157. *See also* cop drama; FBI; police procedural

The Critic, 43–45, 65

Cross, David, 12, 131–32, 206, 207

Curtis, Dan, 48, 115

Curtis, Richard, 29–31

CW Network, 14–15, 28, 42, 172, 186, 205, 220

Daniels, Greg, 148

Darabont, Frank, 223

Daria, 46–47, 55, 56, 137

Dark Shadows, 48–50, 116, 205, 211

Darkwing Duck, 50–52, 82

Davies, Russell T., 60, 162–64

DC Comics, 14, 158, 186

Deadwood, 52–54, 147

Degrassi Junior High, 54–56, 137

Dieckmann, Katherine, 6–7

A Different World, 56–58

DiMartino, Michael Dante, 16

Dinello, Paul, 201–3

Disney, 50–52, 80–82, 119, 177, 186, 230

Doctor Who, 59–61, 91, 123, 162, 163, 164, 192, 205

Dragon Ball Z, 17, 61–63, 175, 176

DVD, 11, 13, 64, 74, 76, 78, 192, 199, 219

Edlund, Ben, 208

educational, 96, 103

Eichler, Glenn, 46–47

Eisner, Michael, 52, 80

Elton, Ben, 30, 234

Engel, Peter, 176–77

family-friendly, 123, 134

Family Guy, 10, 45, 64–65, 78, 179, 189, 203

fan activism, xv, 7, 28, 66, 74, 129, 138, 160, 162, 172–73, 176, 181, 183, 192, 219, 220

fandom, xv, 61, 118, 162, 225, 228, 230

fans, xiii–xv, 3, 13, 15, 19, 25, 27, 33, 37, 38, 44, 51, 55, 58, 62, 63, 69, 87, 89, 93, 105, 108, 114, 120, 123, 125, 128, 130, 134, 150, 153, 158, 166, 181, 184, 186, 205, 207, 211, 215–17, 220–22, 223, 224, 228, 230, 235; fangirls, 162, 175, 205; nerds, 30, 38, 40, 42, 98, 118, 133, 181, 192, 209

fantasy, xiii, 15, 16, 28, 29, 43, 61, 80, 82, 94–95, 125, 143–44, 147, 162, 172, 214, 231

Farscape, 23, 66–68, 73, 167, 197

Faust, Lauren, 133–35

Fawlty Towers, 30, 31, 68–70, 131

FBI, 91, 92, 215, 216, 220, 228, 229

Feig, Paul, 13, 74–75, 149

Fontana, Tom, 145–46

Fox, 66, 77–78, 110, 171, 185, 187, 192, 208, 228–30

Fraggle Rock, 70–73

Freaks and Geeks, 73–75, 137, 140

French, Dawn, 1, 3, 131

Frisky Dingo, 10, 75–77, 191

Fuji TV, 62, 101–3

Fuller, Bryan, 91–93

Futurama, 45, 77–79, 166, 167

FX, 38, 104, 117, 229

Gabaldon, Diana, 143–44

Gargoyles, 16, 51, 52, 80–82, 95, 134

Gass, Kyle, 206–7

Generation X, 47, 89, 137, 169, 190, 192

genre, xiii, xv, 14, 15, 17, 19, 23, 40, 48, 53, 103, 116, 123, 128, 134, 155, 156, 159, 166, 173, 192, 194, 201, 205, 207, 208, 221, 224, 225, 226, 227

Gervais, Ricky, 141–42

Gilliam, Terry, 126

Gilligan's Island, 83–85

Gilmore Girls, 85–87, 204, 222

The Golden Girls, 88–90
Gough, Alfred, 184–86
Grade, Lew, 157–58
Grant, Rob, 165–66
Groening, Matt, 77–79, 181

Hannibal, 91–93
Harmon, Dan, 36–38, 84
Harris, Charlaine, 210, 212
Harris, Susan, 88
Hasselhoff, David, 26
HBO, 21, 29, 52–53, 72, 113–14, 117, 126,
    131–32, 138, 145–46, 151, 206–7, 210–11,
    225–26
He-Man and the Masters of the Universe,
    93–96
Henson, Brian, 66
Henson, Jim, 70–73
Herman, Pee-wee. *See* Reubens, Paul
Hodgson, Joel, 75, 138–40, 181
Holzman, Winnie, 135–36
Home Movies, 10, 45, 47, 96–98
horror, 11, 32, 48, 49, 56, 93, 111, 112, 114,
    116, 125, 205, 213, 215, 220, 224, 233
Howerton, Glenn, 104
H.R. Pufnstuf, 98–100, 152
Hulu, 221
Hurwitz, Mitchell, 12–13, 90
Hynes, Jessica, 191–92

Idle, Eric, 129
improv, 3, 38, 97, 110, 112, 113, 117, 141,
    150, 180, 202, 218–19
Iron Chef, 101–3
irony, 169, 190, 192, 215
It's Always Sunny in Philadelphia, 14, 39,
    104–6, 118
ITV, 18, 158

Jankel, Annabel, 126
Jean, Al, 44
Jones, Khaki, 190
Jones, Terry, 129
The Joy of Painting, 107–9

Kanno, Yoko, 39, 41
Katims, Jason, 171
Katzenberg, Jeffrey, 50, 80
Kenny, Tom, 3, 131, 132, 169, 171
Key, Keegan-Michael, 110–11
Key & Peele, 110–12, 219

The Kids in the Hall, 112–15, 131, 133, 182,
    199, 219
Kirkman, Robert, 223
Kolchak: The Night Stalker, 115–16, 205, 228
Konietzko, Bryan, 16
Koslow, Ron, 28
Kricfalusi, Jon, 167–68
Kripke, Eric, 203–5
Krofft, Marty, 98–99
Krofft, Sid, 98–99

LaMarche, Maurice, 43, 44, 77, 153
Larson, Glen A., 23–24
Lawrence, Bill, 178–79
Lazzo, Mike, 8, 10, 189, 190
The League, 106, 117–18, 210
LGBTQ, 137, 184, 201, 212, 231
Lieber, Jeffrey, 119
Lindelof, Damon, 119
Lost, 85, 119–21, 159, 229, 231
Lost in Space, 26, 121–23, 197
Lucha Underground, 124–25
Lumley, Joanna, 1, 3
Lynch, David, 114, 215–16
Lynn, Susie Lewis, 46

MacFarlane, Seth, 64–65
MacNeille, Tress, 43, 44, 77, 153
Maiellaro, Matt, 8
Mallon, Jim, 138
manga, 16, 62, 174, 175, 176. *See also* comic
    book
Markstein, George, 157, 159
Max Headroom, 126–28
Mayall, Rik, 234–35
Mayer, Lise, 234
McElhenney, Rob, 104
McGoohan, Patrick, 157–59
McKenna, Aline Brosh, 41–42
McRobb, Will, 6
Merchant, Stephen, 141–42
Merrill, Andy, 189–90
Michaels, Lorne, 112–13, 114, 199
Milch, David, 52–53
Millar, Miles, 184–86
Millennials, 89, 137
Monty Python, 68, 69, 70, 129–30, 153, 154
Monty Python's Flying Circus, 70, 114, 115,
    129–31, 132, 235
Moore, Ronald D., 25, 143–44, 172
Morton, Rocky, 126

Mr. Show with Bob and David, 112, 115, 131–33, 199, 207, 219
MTV, 46–47, 137, 198–99, 235
Murray, Joe, 169–70
My Little Pony: Friendship Is Magic, 133–35, 176
My So-Called Life, 47, 55, 56, 75, 135–37
mystery, 120, 183, 215, 216, 217, 221, 222
mystery box, 119, 159
Mystery Science Theater 3000, 79, 138–40, 167

Naylor, Doug, 165–66
NBC, 26–27, 36–38, 48, 57, 74, 83, 86, 88, 91–92, 95, 99, 127, 148, 160, 177, 178–79, 180–81, 195–97, 214, 219, 223, 230, 232
Netflix, 13, 14, 16, 38, 40, 41, 44, 74, 79, 87, 109, 123, 139, 170, 176, 182–83, 194
Newman, Sydney, 18, 59
Nickelodeon, 4, 6, 7, 11, 16, 17, 99, 167–68, 169, 170, 176
Nutter, David, 14, 171, 185, 204

O'Bannon, Rockne, 66
O'Brien, Conan, 119, 181, 191.
Odenkirk, Bob, 131–33, 206, 207
The Office, 14, 141–43, 148, 15
Outlander, 29, 143–45, 162
Oz, 145–47

Paley, William, 83, 213
Palin, Michael, 129
paranormal, 116, 203, 228. *See also* supernatural
Parker, Trey, 187–89
Parks and Recreation, 14, 39, 143, 148–50, 219
parody, 51, 76, 79, 89, 112, 114, 155, 180
Paulsen, Rob, 153, 208, 209
PBS, xiv, 30, 55, 107–8, 130, 165
Pee-wee's Playhouse, 100, 150–52
Peele, Jordan, 110–12
Pegg, Simon, 191–92
Pinky and the Brain, 153–54
Poehler, Amy, 148, 218, 219
police procedural, 155, 225, 227. *See also* cop drama; crime; FBI
Police Squad!, 155–57, 180
popular (pop) culture, 8, 20, 23, 33, 37, 38, 40, 44, 47, 51, 62, 65, 75, 84, 87, 98, 111, 112, 116, 119, 131, 133, 134, 139, 140, 172, 175, 176, 181, 188, 192, 193, 197, 224
The Prisoner, 20, 157–59
puppets, 67, 72, 73, 89, 99, 112, 151, 152

Quantum Leap, 160–62
queer, 3, 15, 33, 89, 90, 125, 144, 161, 163, 164, 176, 183, 184, 201, 212, 231
Queer as Folk, 162–64

Raimi, Sam, 231–33
Red Dwarf, 79, 165–67
Reed, Adam, 75–76
Reiss, Mike, 43–44
The Ren & Stimpy Show, 167–69, 171, 189
Reubens, Paul, 150–51
Rice, Jeffrey Grant, 115
Roberts, Ian, 218–19
Rocko's Modern Life, 8, 155, 169–71
Roddenberry, Gene, 23, 195–97
Rodriguez, Robert, 124
romance, 13, 28, 29, 68, 87, 134, 143, 144, 145, 161, 175, 205, 222
Ross, Bob, 107–8
Roswell, 171–73
Roth, Peter, 185, 204, 228
Russo, Anthony, 13, 38
Russo, Joseph, 13, 38

Sailor Moon, 17, 40, 174–76, 201
satire, 79, 128, 181, 209, 210
Saturday Night Live, 44, 113, 114, 133, 140, 148, 151, 180, 181, 182, 198, 199
Saunders, Jennifer, 1–3, 235
Saved by the Bell, 137, 176–78
Schaffer, Jackie Marcus, 117
Schaffer, Jeff, 117
Schrab, Rob, 38, 149
science fiction, xiii, 21, 22, 23, 24, 25, 40, 59, 61, 68, 77, 79, 93, 95, 111, 116, 123, 125, 128, 138, 144, 162, 164, 166, 172, 184, 195, 196, 197, 213, 214
Sci-Fi Channel, 25, 66–68, 115, 139
Scrubs, 178–80
Scheimer, Lou, 95
Schur, Michael, 148
Schuyler, Linda, 55
Schwartz, Sherwood, 83–84
SCTV, 114, 115, 180–82
Second City, 110, 113, 180, 181, 202
Sedaris, Amy, 202–3
Sense8, 182–84
Serling, Rod, 11, 212–14
Sherman-Palladino, Amy, 85–87
Simon, David, 225–27
The Simpsons, 12, 44, 45, 64, 65, 77, 78, 79, 153, 179, 189, 191

sitcom, 1, 7, 12, 14, 30, 36, 45, 58, 65, 68, 69, 85, 88, 89, 108, 165, 177, 179, 191, 192, 193, 194, 195, 199, 234, 235
Small, Brendon, 96, 97, 98
Smallville, 14, 15, 33, 116, 173, 184–86
soap opera, 27, 48, 49, 62, 87
social media, 2, 79, 183, 188, 205, 230
social satire, 83, 112
Sorkin, Aaron, 193–95
South Park, 65, 98, 187–89, 203, 218
space, 21, 23, 24, 25, 39, 40, 59, 60, 66, 67, 94, 123, 138, 165, 166, 186, 197
Space Ghost Coast to Coast, 8, 10, 77, 189–91
Spaced, 191–93
Spelling, Aaron, 34–35
Spielberg, Steven, 153
Sports Night, 193–94, 195
spy, 13, 19, 157, 158, 159
Star Trek, 22, 25, 26, 66, 121, 123, 128, 166, 172, 195–97, 205, 214; *Deep Space Nine*, 21, 22, 23, 93, 197; *Discovery*, 93, 197; *Enterprise*, 197; *The Next Generation*, 82, 197; *Voyager*, 23, 68, 93, 197
The State, 115, 133, 182, 198–99, 219
Steven Universe, 5, 18, 200–201
Stone, George, 126
Stone, Matt, 187–89
Stones, Tad, 50
Straczynski, J. Michael, 21–23, 95, 182–83
Strangers with Candy, 201–3
streaming, xiii, xiv, xv, 13, 87, 108, 139, 163, 182, 183, 219, 221
Sugar, Rebecca, 5, 200
superhero, 7, 14, 15, 50, 51, 75, 76, 174, 186, 189, 190, 208, 209
supernatural, 11, 29, 34, 48, 49, 116, 124, 204, 205, 212, 217
Supernatural, 14, 33, 50, 116, 203–5, 212, 225, 231
Sweet, Roger, 94
syndication, xiv, 27, 44, 62, 72, 95, 99, 142, 208, 229

Tapert, Robert, 231–33
Tartikoff, Brandon, 88, 160, 177
teenagers, 33, 55, 62, 74, 80, 82, 134, 137, 172, 177, 221, 222

Tenacious D, 133, 199, 206–7
Thomas, Rob, 220, 222
Thompson, Matt, 75–76
thriller, 14, 18, 27, 126
The Tick, 51, 82, 208–10
Toonami, 62, 175, 176
Toriyama, Akira, 62
True Blood, 29, 33, 50, 210–12
TV movie, 22, 46, 60, 83, 115, 116, 177, 200, 215
20th Century Fox, 12, 24, 83, 122, 229.
The Twilight Zone, 11, 112, 115, 128, 159, 212–14, 228
Twin Peaks, 7, 51, 93, 121, 159, 215–17

UPN, 26, 32, 96, 97, 172, 185, 205, 220
Upright Citizens Brigade, 115, 218–19

vampires, 12, 31, 49, 115, 116, 210–12
variety show, 38, 113, 131, 180
Veronica Mars, 33, 43, 75, 87, 220–22

Wachowski, Lana, 41, 182, 184
Wachowski, Lily, 41, 182, 184
The Walking Dead, 223–25
Walsh, Matt, 218, 219
Ward, Pendleton, 4, 5
Warner Bros., 19, 21, 22, 48, 50, 93, 151, 153, 185, 186, 204
Watanabe, Shinichirô, 39, 40, 41
WB Network, 32, 34, 35, 48, 86, 153, 171, 172, 185, 186, 204, 205
Weisman, Greg, 80, 82
Westerns, 52, 53, 195
Whedon, Joss, 32, 33, 220, 232
Willis, Dave, 8, 10
The Wire, 147, 225–27
World Wide Web, 10, 128, 162, 228, 230
Wright, Edgar, 192

Xena: Warrior Princess, 231–33
The X-Files, 23, 33, 116, 121, 191, 204, 205, 214, 217, 228–30

The Young Ones, 3, 31, 191, 234–35

Zucker, David, 155–56
Zucker, Jerry, 155–56

About the Authors

Christopher J. Olson is a PhD student in the English Department at the University of Wisconsin, Milwaukee, with a media, cinema, and digital studies concentration. Olson is the author of *100 Greatest Cult Films* (2018) and co-author or co-editor of *Convergent Wrestling: Participatory Culture, Transmedia Storytelling, and Intertextuality in the Squared Circle* (2019); *Heroes, Heroines, and Everything in Between: Challenging Gender and Sexuality Stereotypes in Children's Entertainment Media* (2017); *Possessed Women, Haunted States: Cultural Tensions in Exorcism Cinema* (2016); and *Making Sense of Cinema: Empirical Studies into Film Spectators and Spectatorship* (2016).

CarrieLynn D. Reinhard is an associate professor at Dominican University in River Forest, Illinois. She is author of the monograph *Fractured Fandoms: Contentious Communication in Fan Communities* (2018) and co-author or co-editor of *Convergent Wrestling: Participatory Culture, Transmedia Storytelling, and Intertextuality in the Squared Circle* (2019); *Heroes, Heroines, and Everything in Between: Challenging Gender and Sexuality Stereotypes in Children's Entertainment Media* (2017); *Possessed Women, Haunted States: Cultural Tensions in Exorcism Cinema* (2016); and *Making Sense of Cinema: Empirical Studies into Film Spectators and Spectatorship* (2016).